Advance Praise for *India's Long Road*

"A *tour de force*: a brilliant, lucid and comprehensive analysis of what could be put right in the Indian economy, and especially in government policy. The good news is that many of the proposed changes are surely feasible and have been practised in other countries. They might really lead India to fulfil its potential. For the world, the economic transformation of a nation of more than one billion people would be a huge event." —W. Max Corden, *Emeritus Professor of International Economics, Johns Hopkins University, and Honorary Professorial Fellow, Department of Economics, University of Melbourne*

India's long Road by Vijay Joshi, a leading macroeconomist, deserves to be required reading for anyone interested in India's performance and prospects. While being strongly grounded in economic theory, it succeeds in setting out a superb descriptive and prescriptive analysis of India's political economy in a readable style, without jargon or algebra. Its sensible and firm policy recommendations are based on careful argument and evidence. In consequence, the book will be valuable not only for the general reader but also for policymakers. It would also make an excellent text for students of the Indian economy. —T.N. Srinivasan, *Samuel C. Park Jr. Professor of Economics Emeritus and Professor Emeritus of International and Area Studies, Yale University*

I only wish that this book had been available 20 years earlier, when I was appointed Chief Economist for South Asia in the World Bank. To have had available such a well-argued and reasonable guide to the many problems confronting India in its quest to join the modern world by a leading member of the Indian diaspora would have been invaluable. I would particularly have valued the chapters on political economy. —John Williamson, *Senior Fellow Emeritus at the Peterson Institute for International Economics*

India's Long Road is a *tour de force*: it will be the new standard for those who want to learn about the Indian economy. Joshi provides lucid economic analysis and broad insights into the current and coming global context for India's future development. —Nirvikar Singh, *Distinguished Professor of Economics, University of California, Santa Cruz*

A cogent and sobering analysis of the enormity of the challenges India faces in ensuring inclusive, enduring and sustainable economic growth. Vijay Joshi lays out with rare clarity the necessary reforms that India must undertake – and the obstacles rooted in the country's political economy – if it is to fulfil its historical responsibility to improve the well-being of a sixth of humanity. One of the best – and most accessible – books on a complex and contentious subject. —Devesh Kapur, *Madan Lal Sobti Professor of Contemporary India and Director, Center for Advanced Study of India, University of Pennsylvania*

INDIA'S LONG ROAD

INDIA'S LONG ROAD

The Search for Prosperity

Vijay Joshi

OXFORD
UNIVERSITY PRESS

OXFORD
UNIVERSITY PRESS

Oxford University Press is a department of the University of Oxford. It furthers
the University's objective of excellence in research, scholarship, and education
by publishing worldwide. Oxford is a registered trade mark of Oxford University
Press in the UK and certain other countries.

Published in the United States of America by Oxford University Press
198 Madison Avenue, New York, NY 10016, United States of America.

© Vijay Joshi 2017

CIP data is on file at the Library of Congress
ISBN 978–0–19–061013–5

3 5 7 9 8 6 4

Printed by Sheridan Books, Inc., United States of America

CONTENTS

ACKNOWLEDGEMENTS

This book was initially planned to be a joint work with the distinguished Indian journalist T. N. Ninan. We worked together for a time but later parted, amicably, and decided to write two independent books in our different writing styles, with a minimum of overlap. (Ninan's book has been published separately by Oxford University Press.) By then, he had commented perceptively and extensively on early drafts of well over half of the chapters that appear in this book; and he continued to provide sound advice and encouragement thereafter. One of the great advantages of our partnership, I found, was that doors to Delhi offices opened much faster when I was with him. We did many interviews together. I am deeply grateful to him for his help and kindness.

Many people have lent a hand in making this book a reality. A select band must receive special thanks because I turned to one or more of them for advice whenever I got stuck, and they gave it willingly and generously. Some of them also wrote excellent newspaper columns that I found very helpful. (I could not refer to more than a few of these, else the bibliography would have been several times longer.) In addition to Ninan, this group comprises Shankar Acharya, Montek Ahluwalia, Swaminathan Aiyar, Abhijit Banerjee, Pranab Bardhan, Surjit Bhalla, Paul Collier, Nitin Desai, M. Govinda Rao, Ashok Gulati, Devesh Kapur, Geeta Kingdon, James Manor, Pratap Bhanu Mehta, Rakesh Mohan, Sudipto Mundle, Karthik Muralidharan, Urjit Patel, Indira Rajaraman, and Sandip Sukhtankar.

Others with whom I have had productive and relevant conversations, interviews, or correspondence, whose writings have influenced me, or who have helped in other important ways, are Isher Ahluwalia, Sabina Alkire, Christopher Allsopp, Ritu Anand, Sudhir Anand, Premachandra Athukorala, Richard Baldwin, Sanjaya Baru, Kaushik Basu, Suman Bery, David Bevan, Jagdish Bhagwati, Bharati Bhargava, Aditya Bhattacharjea, Amar Bhide, Christopher Bliss, Andrea Boltho, Barry Bosworth, John Buckels, Wendy Carlin, Avirup Chakraverty, Elizabeth Chatterjee,

Sumanta Chaudhuri, Sonali Chowdhry, Max Corden, Jishnu Das, Monica Das Gupta, Bibek Debroy, Ashok Desai, Meena Deshpande, Sudhir Deshpande, Faisal Devji, Kate Doornik, Navroz Dubash, Anirudha Dutta, Valpy Fitzgerald, Maitreesh Ghatak, Anurabha Ghosh, Subir Gokarn, Nandini Gooptu, Omkar Goswami, Sangeeta Goyal, Poonam Gupta, Salman Haidar, Jeffrey Hammer, John Harriss, Barbara Harriss-White, Geoffrey Haydon, Judith Heyer, Himanshu, Anwarul Hoda, Andrew Hurrell, Bimal Jalan, Beata Javorcik, Sisira Jayasuriya, Mahesh Jethmalani, Vijay Kelkar, Joanna Kenner, Sunil Khilnani, Kenneth King, Kenneth Kletzer, Ananya Kotiya, Paul Krugman, Alok Kshirsagar, Rajiv Kumar, Jawid Laiq, Rajiv Lall, (the late) Sanjaya Lall, Laurence Leaver, (the late) Ian Little, Ajay Mahal, Rohini Malkani, Walter Mattli, Matthew McCartney, Rajnish Mehra, Santosh Mehrotra, Shivshankar Menon, Prachi Mishra, Deepak Mohanty, Dilip Mookherjee, Alan Morrison, Arpita Mukherjee, Partha Mukhopadhyay, Rinku Murgai, David Mutimer, Amrita Narlikar, Peter Neary, Nandan Nilekani, Susham Page, Prakash Page, Arvind Panagariya, Jyoti Parikh, Kirit Parikh, Ila Patnaik, R. D. Pradhan, Lant Pritchett, Niranjan Rajadhyaksha, Lavanya Rajamani, Raghuram Rajan, C. Rangarajan, Bharat Reddy, Y. V. Reddy, Dani Rodrik, Manish Sabharwal, Shyam Saran, Abhijit Sen, Amartya Sen, Anupama Sen, Kunal Sen, Shekhar Shah, Shylashri Shankar, Alok Sheel, Parthasarathi Shome, Rukshad Shroff, Henry Shue, Abhijit Singh, Manmohan Singh, Nirvikar Singh, Devinder Sivia, T. N. Srinivasan, Margaret Stevens, Frances Stewart, Duvvuri Subbarow, Arvind Subramanian, Kate Sullivan, Kamakshya Trivedi, Maya Tudor, Ravi Vaidya, John Vickers, David Vines, Bhaskar Vira, Arvind Virmani, Jessica Wallack, Michael Walton, Andrew Whitehead, John Williamson, Dominic Wilson, Martin Wolf, Ngaire Woods, Simon Wren-Lewis, and Yogendra Yadav. I have also learned a great deal from my participation in the highly stimulating India Policy Forum annual conferences in Delhi, organized by the Brookings Institution and the National Council of Applied Economic Research.

For all the people mentioned above, the usual disclaimer applies with more than the customary force. They are not responsible for the errors in the book or the thoughts expressed therein. Indeed, I am well aware that some of them will disagree vehemently with some or even most of my views.

Thanks are due to my literary agent Catherine Clarke of Felicity Bryan Associates, and David Pervin, Emily Mackenzie, and Sasirekka Gopalakrishnan, my editorial team at Oxford University Press. They are all highly effective professionals, wise in their counsel, patient and tolerant of my failings, and a pleasure to work with. I am grateful to the editor of *India Review* for permission to reproduce the material which appears in the book as Tables 4.1 to 4.4. I also owe a debt of gratitude to the Warden and Fellows of Merton College, Oxford, and the President and Fellows of St. John's College, Oxford, for providing me with research support and a highly congenial work environment.

Three things kept me going through the difficult times when the book seemed an impossible mountain to climb. The first was reading novels and listening to music. The second was the delicious food produced on a regular basis by my son Viru, who is a chef. Last, and most important, was the support of Mary, my wife, who combines in her person exciting companionship and unwavering dependability.

In addition to Mary and Viru, this book is dedicated to my parents. My father, R.C. Joshi, would have preferred to be an academic but joined the Indian Civil Service as a way out of poverty, when he passed the demanding competitive examination. I think he would have liked reading this book, had he been alive. My mother, Shashikala Joshi, now 96 years old, has been the mainstay of our extended family, unstinting in her love and care for all its members. My debt to her is immeasurable.

PART I

Setting the Stage

CHAPTER 1

India at the Cusp

'India is a geographical term. It is no more a united nation than the Equator'. Winston Churchill's jibe was essentially right about India's past. Notwithstanding its cultural unity, India was not, properly speaking, a nation before it came under British rule. But the jibe was also a claim that India would not survive as a cohesive entity if it became independent. On this Churchill proved to be spectacularly wrong. Undivided India reacted to British colonialism by becoming a nation (or two nations). It suffered the wrenching trauma and tragedy of partition, which seemed to lend some credence to Churchill's withering remark (though why partition happened, and to what extent the British Raj was itself responsible for it, is still fiercely disputed). Since then, however, to the amazement of many early doubters, India has maintained national unity in the face of bewildering social contrasts, as well as occasional secessionist movements and external threats. And that has not been the sole achievement of its people and their leaders. Many other substantial tasks have been accomplished, not with complete success but success all the same. Democracy was introduced from the very start of independence and has recognizably been preserved despite some imperfections in its working. The power of caste differences, a fundamental feature of traditional Indian society, has been diluted and tempered though not broken. The same goes for language differences, which have lost their edge as a basis for conflict, and remain an issue only in an attenuated form. Religious pluralism has largely been protected, though it continues to face major challenges and remains vulnerable to attack. All in all, only a very churlish commentator would claim that India has not been reasonably successful in the pursuit of formidably demanding political and social goals.

This book is about another equally important aspect of India's past and future career, the effort to achieve economic prosperity. Jawaharlal Nehru's famous speech at the 'stroke of the midnight hour', when India became independent, spoke of 'ending poverty and ignorance and disease and inequality of opportunity' and building a 'prosperous, democratic and progressive' nation. How has India done? For the first three decades after independence, growth performance was poor (though better than under colonial rule). The poverty ratio did not fall, and the number of people in poverty rose substantially. In those days, India was often compared to a slow-moving snail or tortoise. It was thought of as 'a country of the future that will always remain so', a country that would never get its act together, even sometimes as a 'basket case'. Things have changed. Since around 1980, and especially after the economic reforms in 1991, India has been among a dozen or so of the fastest growing countries of the world. The poverty ratio has more than halved, and the absolute number of poor people has also fallen significantly. As a result, India has ascended rapidly in the animal world of metaphors. There is now a tendency to think of it as an 'uncaged tiger' that will leap ahead to overtake both China and the United States. As will become clear to the reader, I take a darker view. Be that as it may, there is no doubt that India matters. If it attained its economic aims, it would better the lives of hundreds of millions of people. It would also signal the ability of a poor country to do so without sacrificing democracy, the rule of law, and personal freedoms.

THE SEARCH FOR PROSPERITY

Though India's economic advance now attracts hyped-up predictions and exaggerated hopes, I have the sense that the foundations of its success are fragile. I also think, in apparent contradiction, that it is performing below its potential. That India will eventually become a prosperous country is all but certain. The question is how long this will take. This issue has become all the more pertinent because India's growth has slowed in the last few years. Though it is by some measures the third-largest economy in the world, it still has a quarter of its billion-plus people surviving in dire poverty, and more than two-thirds of its people poor enough to have extremely circumscribed opportunities to lead a fulfilling life.[1]

An ambitious goal for India would be to become a prosperous country by, say, 2040. What does prosperity mean? At a first pass, it could be defined as the level of per capita income enjoyed by countries in the lowest quartile of high-income countries today, with the rider that national income should be widely shared and even the poorest people should have decent standards of living. To reach the said goal comfortably, India would require high-quality per capita growth of income of around 7 per cent a year for a period of 24 years, from 2016.[2] By 'high quality' growth I mean, firstly, growth that is inclusive. If per capita growth were 7 per cent a year, then high-quality growth would require that the incomes of poor people also rise by at least 7 per cent a year (or preferably by quite a lot more). Secondly, by high-quality growth, I mean growth that is environmentally friendly.

If India were to maintain 7 per cent a year per capita growth until 2040, India's per capita income at purchasing power parity (PPP) would rise from its current level of about $5600 to five times its current level, i.e. to about $28,000. (All the income figures in this paragraph are in constant 2011 PPP dollars.)[3] This would make India firmly a high-income country by today's standards, with a per capita income comparable to countries such as Greece and Portugal that are at the top of the lowest quartile of high-income countries today.[4] If, in addition, growth was inclusive, the incomes of the poorest Indians would also increase by at least a multiple of five and probably a lot more, a change that would obviously make a huge positive difference to their lives. With 8 per cent a year per capita growth, India's per capita income in 2040 would be $35,000, roughly equal to that of South Korea in 2016.[5] (South Korea is approximately the median country today in a ranking of high-income countries by per capita income.) With 6 per cent a year per capita growth, India's per capita income would quadruple and reach around $22,000, a level at which it would just about slip into the category of high-income countries by today's standards, comparable to countries such as Chile and Hungary.

THE ARGUMENT OF THE BOOK

The argument of this book is that with 'business-as-usual' policies India will be hard put to achieve high-quality and enduring per capita growth of even 6 per cent a year, let alone 8 per cent a year, which would be necessary for it to become a prosperous nation in the next quarter century. However, radical reform, along the lines adumbrated in the chapters that follow, would increase greatly the chances of attaining the said objective.

It is necessary, to begin with, to understand the magnitude of the project. Inter-country experience is very relevant. I refer here to the highly illuminating study by Lant Pritchett and Lawrence Summers, which examines growth from 1950 in all countries for which data exist.[6] It demonstrates that there is very little persistence in the growth rates of countries over medium and long horizons, and that 'regression to the mean [i.e. the mean world growth rate] is perhaps the single most important empirical fact about cross-national growth rates'. Suppose 'super-fast growth' is defined as per capita income growth above 6 per cent a year. The Pritchett-Summers analysis shows that from 1950 to 2010, there have been only three countries that have had super-fast growth for three decades or more on the run, viz. China (1977–2010: 8.1 per cent a year), South Korea (1962–1991: 6.9 per cent a year) and Taiwan (1962–1994: 6.8 per cent a year).[7] Only China has had a per capita growth rate of more than 8 per cent a year for 30 years. Another very striking fact is that, apart from the above three countries, there has been no other country that has had per capita growth of 6 per cent a year for a continuous period *of even two decades*.[8] In most countries, super-fast growth phases are typically quite short and nearly always end in a sharp deceleration (to the world growth rate).[9] India's performance so far has been creditable but not exceptional. There has been only one long-ish period of super-fast growth in India's history: 2003–2011.[10] To resume that pace and maintain or exceed it over a long period, India would have to overcome the headwinds of regression to the mean, and join the very small band of exceptional countries.

The second reason for stressing the enormity of India's future task follows directly from the first. What Pritchett and Summers have documented is not all that surprising when one thinks about it. Growth is a long-distance race. Super-fast growth for a couple of decades or more is like running the distance of a marathon at the speed of a sprint. Most countries cannot make it. Many countries have brief high-growth spurts that fizzle out due to lack of stamina. Fast-growing countries slow down because they have fiscal explosions or fall prey to rent-seeking oligarchies and crony capitalists or simply fail to sustain the pace of productivity improvement.[11] In recent years, India has looked vulnerable to falling at each of these hurdles. I emphasize again that India's aim is not just fast growth but high-quality, fast growth. That sets the bar higher than fast growth pure and simple. (While fast growth makes inclusion easier to achieve, it does not make inclusion inevitable. For example, several Latin American countries, such as Brazil, Ecuador, and Paraguay, grew rapidly in the 1970s but the fruits of growth were not widely shared.)

What are the prospects for India achieving the challenging goal of rapid, high-quality per capita growth of 6 to 8 per cent a year for the next two or three decades? The reforms undertaken in India at the start of the 1990s, and thereafter, were effective, but are now running out of steam, and were in any case partial and incomplete. Moreover, India's rapid growth in the first decade of the present century was propelled by a highly liquid and expanding world economy. Such a benign global environment looks very unlikely to return any time soon. In the domestic arena, progress remains to be made in many areas such as public sector ownership, rules governing bankruptcy and exit, infrastructure provision, labour market reform, and delivery of public services. These involve substantive matters in which 'reform by stealth', which has been the Indian way of doing things, will be unlikely to suffice. There is also increasingly manifest a contrast between the country's dynamic private sector (though the shine has been fading recently) and its weak and ineffective government sector. This disjunction has now reached such a level as to seriously endanger India's ambitions. At the same time, a combination of crony capitalism and excessive ambition has caused leading private companies to trip up on their own greed and zeal. More liberalization is certainly necessary. But it will not be sufficient because the state no longer performs its core functions effectively.

Each country has to work out for itself the right balance between the state and the market to suit its particular circumstances. India has failed to do that. The Indian state has systematically underestimated the prevalence and the cost of 'government failure'. It often intervenes, arbitrarily or to correct supposed market failures, without any clear evidence that the market is failing, and so ends up damaging resource allocation and stifling business drive. That is why India is regarded as one of the worst places in the world to do business. Sometimes the government intervenes justifiably, but in a ham-fisted way, for example in its regulation of land, labour, and capital markets. It quite properly intervenes for redistributive purposes but does so ineptly and ineffectively through price controls, which impair economic efficiency by distorting relative prices, and through administrative delivery mechanisms, which are costly and corrupt. It fails to harness private initiatives in public services such as health care and education because it ignores the distinction between paying for services and producing them. It does not understand the importance of putting the incentive structure right for getting government functionaries to perform. It does not fully appreciate that private sector competition with the public sector is necessary to improve the quality of provision of public services.

At the same time, the Indian state does not deliver in the areas that fall squarely in its province, such as administering law and order, ensuring macroeconomic stability, delivering speedy justice, ensuring that public services are provided, and creating an effective and adequate safety-net for poor people. On macroeconomic stability, India has avoided rampant turmoil but periodic inflation spikes remain a major problem, while the fiscal position remains weak, and vulnerable to growing demands on the state.

There is also plenty of evidence that the culture of public service has deteriorated, and that government incompetence and venality have become pervasive. The popular perception that sleaze and crony capitalism are rife at all levels of government is not far off the mark. (At the same time, the fear of being blamed for honest mistakes has also paralyzed government administration in recent years.)

It follows from this sorry tale that both the state and the state-market relationship need urgent reform, which is no easy task in the context of India's political economy, with its democratic turbulence and powerful vested interests. Without such a reconstruction, however, the project of rapid and high-quality growth is very unlikely to succeed. In the ensuing chapters, I attempt to give substance to these judgements, and to chart the way forward.

SECURITY, POWER, AND GLOBAL AMBITION

I do not address the topic of India's external security and foreign relations (other than economic diplomacy) in this book. A deep analysis would require a volume on its own. But a few observations are called for to supply the backdrop for my argument.

It is obvious that in order to achieve economic development, India will have to manage its regional and international relations skillfully to ensure that they are a source of help, not of hindrance. This is by no means straightforward because India suffers from the handicap of living in a disturbed and dangerous neighbourhood, which contains Pakistan, which has some of the features of a rogue state, and China, which may be on course to becoming a global superpower rivalling the United States.[12]

India's relationship with Pakistan is in a permanently volatile condition. The status of Kashmir remains undecided, though the 'line of control' has held. Nobody will say so publicly but the eventual sensible outcome may well be a division of Kashmir between India and Pakistan along the line of control, though this may take decades of diplomacy to achieve. (Land-locked Kashmir is surely not a viable state: any eventual agreement will have to give considerable autonomy to the two halves of Kashmir, within India and Pakistan.) All-out war between India and Pakistan is fortunately improbable. India has decisive conventional military superiority but Pakistan, like India, has a nuclear arsenal, so there is mutual deterrence. A more troubling possibility is that Pakistan may become a failed state, and a locus for terrorist activity against India on an even bigger scale than is presently the case. A not unrelated possibility is that India will suffer a fall-out from the fundamentalist and sectarian conflicts in the Gulf and West Asia. It is surely incontestable that India should follow open-handed and tolerant policies towards its Muslim population so that it does not become alienated. With Pakistan, it is clearly essential to keep trying to reach an accord, while remaining prepared to repel any attempt at armed aggression.

On balance, China is the bigger problem. Despite protestations of aiming for a 'peaceful rise', it seems determined to establish its dominance not merely in the South China Sea but also over the Indian Ocean. To this end, it has established a network of military and commercial facilities and ports (the so-called 'string of pearls') that, in effect, encircle India's coastline.[13] Furthermore, China has plans to build overland transport routes to India's north and north-west and east: for example, a road linking Sinkiang with Karachi and Gwadar, all the way across disputed mountainous territory that India claims; a railway line from Lhasa, the capital of Tibet, to Kathmandu, the capital of Nepal; and a road linking China and Burma. Over-arching these developments is the vision of a 'Silk Road' through Central Asia and a 'Maritime Silk Road' through the Indian Ocean. China is also actively courting many South Asian, Central Asian, and African countries with trade and investment deals. In addition, it is rapidly expanding its blue water navy that is on course to becoming the most formidable naval force in the world, second only to the United States. It would be prudent to assume that China is trying to establish pre-eminence in the Asia-Pacific, and to be a global power to rival America. With the economic prowess that it has acquired in the past three decades, this is no longer an unrealistic aim.

Thus, the existing and growing power imbalance relative to China is undoubtedly something that India will have to live with and deal with. Fortunately, India has its own advantages. China invites defensive reactions. The prospect of a revanchist China has alarmed many countries, not only in Asia but elsewhere, and not only small countries but also the United States. And correspondingly, the attraction of India as an ally has increased manifold. One instance of this is the remarkable United States–India civil nuclear agreement of 2008, which ended years of 'apartheid' that India had to suffer in its ability to acquire nuclear materials and technology. Another example is the significant warming of relations between India and Japan, Australia and Vietnam. Many countries find India's rise much more acceptable than China's because they perceive it to be a fast-growing country that is also democratic and non-threatening. Of course, India's attraction will last only if it maintains these qualities, its economic momentum as well as its liberal democratic credentials.

How should India conduct its foreign relations in the prospective global environment? America's status as a 'hyper-power' appears to be in decline.

The world is now multipolar but with United States–China rivalry as one of its major axes. As of now, India's best strategy is surely to continue with its delicate balancing act between the two. With China, it should cooperate economically, as it has done in supporting the Brics Bank and the Asian Infrastructure Investment Bank as a junior partner, but at the same time build enough strength, conventional or 'asymmetric', to deter China from military adventurism. With the United States, it should keep the possibility of an alliance open but not enter into a formal pact unless it became absolutely necessary. (This is because India does not see eye to eye with the United States on many issues. There are good reasons to preserve strategic autonomy unless a major conflict with China seems imminent.)

Should India start thinking of itself as a potential 'Great Power'? The term was used by the former US Secretary of State Condoleezza Rice in New Delhi in 2005, and harks back to 19th century Europe. Despite India's growing international significance, deliberate pursuit of Great Power status would surely be unwise, if not foolish. New Delhi has many major domestic challenges to keep it fully occupied for a long time to come. Moreover, the fundamental source of India's power is going to be economic. If India can maintain high growth rates and use that growth to achieve widespread prosperity within a democratic system, its national security, broadly defined, will improve, and with that, its global influence will inevitably grow. The role of foreign policy should be to ensure that the balance of power in the country's neighbourhood, as well as India's diplomatic alliances and footprint, are such as to enable and reinforce India's pursuit of high-quality and rapid economic development. More ambitious foreign policy goals would either obstruct the achievement of this objective or would be attained quite naturally in the course of time by achieving it.

READER'S GUIDE

The book has five parts. Part I is introductory. Chapter 1 (the present chapter) sets the stage and explains briefly what the book is about and what it is not about. Chapter 2 is a broad-brush review of India's post-independence history and economic performance. Chapter 3 defines the aims of economic development, and weighs up the roles of the state and the market in achieving them.

Part II focuses on the challenge of accomplishing rapid growth. Chapter 4 begins with an introduction to the sources of growth in India, and proceeds to examine one of these, viz. capital accumulation, and the 'animal spirits' that drive it. Chapter 5 analyzes India's 'employment problem' and how it should be tackled to speed up growth by harnessing the so-called 'demographic dividend'. Chapter 6 ranges widely over the distortions in the economy that are holding back productivity improvement, and the corrective measures required. Chapter 7 examines productivity growth in relation to public and private ownership, with particular attention to the infrastructure sectors. It also considers the problem of making growth environmentally sustainable.

Part III examines the 'stability' and 'inclusion' aspects of the development objective. Chapter 8 is concerned with how to achieve macroeconomic stability in its various dimensions. It looks closely at why things went wrong on this front after 2008, and how to avoid a replay of that experience in future. Chapter 9 is about the promotion of inclusive development through enhancement of social opportunities, especially the provision of education and health care. It takes a cool and critical look at the role of the state and the private sector in providing these essential services. Chapter 10 is about inclusion via 'social protection' and income redistribution. In India, this takes place primarily through price subsidies. In contrast, the chapter advocates achieving egalitarian aims, including a universal 'basic income', by the use of cash transfers. The existing methods of reaching the poor are shown to be ineffective and costly. There is, in addition, an analysis of how enhanced cash transfers could be financed with relative ease if the existing dysfunctional price subsidies were eliminated.

Part IV moves on to the political economy of Indian development. Chapter 11 is concerned with domestic political economy. It pays close attention to the problem of weak state capacity, which has bedeviled the attempts of the Indian state to intervene beneficially. It also examines the growth of corruption in the country and the remedies to treat it. Chapter 12 investigates India's economic relationship with the rest of the world. It considers India's engagement with the world economy, what it needs to do to advance its interests, and how it should position itself on global economic issues.

Part V concludes the book with a single, long chapter. It brings the threads of the argument together to outline a 'radical reform model' that should guide India's economic policies. In the light of this model, it also assesses the performance of the Modi government, which has been in power for two years, since May 2014. The chapter ends with some reflections on the shape of India's future.

The division between the various parts of the book is for convenience only. There is no suggestion that the topics in the different parts are unconnected. For example, education figures in Part III on 'Stability and Inclusion' but is obviously very relevant for growth. Employment is discussed in Part II on 'The Growth Challenge' but is also crucially important for inclusive development. Institutional quality and change are examined in Part IV on 'Political Economy' but matter greatly for both growth and inclusion. These and other such interconnections are fully recognized in the text.

NOTES FOR THE READER

1. In this book, in any sentence about India with an economic content, 'year' refers to the Indian financial year (April–March). For example, the year 2010 refers to financial year 2010/11, the year 2011 refers to financial year 2011/12, etc. I sometimes refer to financial years explicitly but not always (to avoid cluttering up the text). In sentences without an economic content, 'year' refers to the calendar year. Thus the year 2010 refers to the calendar year 2010 etc.

2. I use the abbreviation 'Rs.' to denote 'Rupees'. Note that 'lakh' means 'hundred thousand' and 'crore' means 'ten million'. Thus, Rs.100 crores = Rs.1 billion, and Rs.1 lakh crores = Rs.1 trillion. The average Rupee-Dollar exchange rate in 2014 and 2015 was $1 = Rs. 61.1 and $1 = Rs. 65.5 respectively.

3. The book was completed in December 2015. However, just before it went to press, some footnotes were added in the last chapter to comment on some relevant events in the first three months of 2016, such as the Central government budget for 2016/17.

NOTES

1. India is the third-largest economy, behind only the United States and China, in terms of 'purchasing power parity' (PPP) dollars, and the ninth largest economy in current dollars. But its per capita income rank is 123rd in PPP dollars and 143rd in current dollars, among 185 countries. These are all World Bank figures. Measurement in PPP dollars provides a rough comparison of standards of living across countries. (PPP rates of exchange are calculated by comparing the prices of similar goods and services across countries.)

2. It would be idle to pretend that rapid improvement in the living standards of poor people could be secured without rapid growth. Growth is not a sufficient condition for widespread prosperity but it is in practice a necessary condition. Only if growth is rapid does it become politically feasible to make it inclusive.

3. The most recent World Bank figures for cross-country incomes at purchasing power parity are in constant 2011 PPP dollars, and relate to the year 2014. I have taken the liberty of adopting these figures as representative of 2016.

4. Though the World Bank provides per capita income data for countries in both current and PPP dollars, it classifies countries into 'low-income', 'lower-middle-income', 'upper-middle-income', and 'high-income' on the basis of per capita income in current dollars, not PPP dollars. There are 80 high-income countries

in the World Bank's classification. Correspondingly, I have assumed that the top 80 countries in the ranking of countries by per capita income in PPP dollars count as 'high-income' countries. On this basis, the average per capita income of high-income countries is around $41,000 (PPP) in 2016. US per capita income is around $56,000 (PPP) and that of Norway around $66,000 (PPP). Needless to say, the assertions and examples in this paragraph should be regarded as very rough approximations.

5. The above calculations are *not* about convergence. With 8 per cent a year per capita growth, India's per capita income in 2040 would reach South Korea's per capita income in 2016, not South Korea's per capita income in 2040, because South Korea would have grown in the interim.

6. Pritchett and Summers (2014).

7. I include South Korea though its super-fast growth period is 29 years (i.e. just short of 30 years).

8. If the window were widened to include countries that have experienced super-fast growth for a decade or more but less than two decades, six more countries, viz., Japan, Singapore, Ireland, Cambodia, Chile, and Sierra Leone, would pass the test. If the window were further widened to include countries that have had continuous super-fast growth episodes of eight years or more, eleven more countries would qualify, including India. (But several of them, e.g. Gabon, Jordan, Morocco, Portugal, Greece, Ecuador, Dominican Republic, Paraguay, and Cyprus, have not exactly distinguished themselves after their high-growth spurts, which took place in the 1960s or 1970s.) A few countries have had fast but not super-fast per capita growth for several decades: Botswana (1960–2010: 5.7 per cent), Singapore (1960–2010: 5.2 per cent), Indonesia (1967–1996: 4.7 per cent), Thailand (1958–1987: 4.9 per cent), Malaysia (1960–2010: 4.5 per cent), and Vietnam (1990 onwards: 5.5 per cent). Singapore stands out. Its rapid growth for 50 years has put its per capita income ahead of the United States.

9. China, South Korea, and Taiwan are exceptions to the rule because they have continued growing at respectable rates after the end of super-fast growth.

10. India grew at a fast (but not super-fast) per capita growth rate of a little above 4 per cent a year from 1993 to 2002. If we take the 17 years from 1993 to 2011, the growth rate of India's per capita income was around 5 per cent a year. From 2003 to 2011, the rate was nearly 7 per cent a year, i.e. super-fast, as defined above.

11. Another reason why sustained rapid growth is very difficult is that the nature of the growth challenge changes from one stage of development to the next. A country might grow by building initially on the advantages provided by resource endowment or cheap labour, and later on by developing industries that draw on technologies developed elsewhere. Even later, innovation has to become the name of the game. It is not easy to shift from one mode to another.

12. This section owes much to the excellent discussion in Chapter 15 of Ninan (2015).

13. Prime examples are the port of Hambantota (Sri Lanka), the deep-water facility in Colombo (Sri Lanka), the port of Gwadar (Pakistan), and the container facility in Chittagong (Bangladesh).

CHAPTER 2

1947–2016

A Tour d'Horizon

Two major accelerations of national income and output stand out in India's economic trajectory in the 20th century. The first took place a few years after independence in 1947. From around 1950, the growth rate of national income went up from the funereal 1 per cent a year (less than 0.2 per cent per head) that prevailed in the first half of the century to 3.5 per cent a year (1.4 per cent per head) for 30 years thereafter. This speeding up was certainly a welcome break from the past, and clearly related to the change in India's status from a British colony to a self-governing country. Even so, growth of 3.5 per cent a year for three decades from 1950 to 1980, mockingly dubbed the 'Hindu rate of growth', was a major disappointment. It was slower than the world average and the average for developing countries at the time; and it was also too slow to make any dent in the poverty ratio, let alone in the vast numbers of people in acute poverty. From around 1980, there was a second marked change of gear to a growth rate of more than 6 per cent a year (4 per cent per head) for the next 35 years (1980–2015). This was a major achievement that made India one of the fastest growing countries in the world and resulted in a considerable improvement in human welfare relative to the past. Towards the end of this period, however, there were worrying signs that long-term growth was faltering, and that conditions were not yet in place for a rapid ascent to first-world levels of prosperity. Table 2.1 shows the growth rate from 1900 to 1950 and the decadal growth rates thereafter.

Table 2.1 DECADAL GROWTH RATES OF GDP

	(1)	(2)	(3)
	Growth Rate (% per annum)	Investment (% GDP)	Capital-Output Ratio (col. 2 / col. 1)
1900/01–1950/51	1.0 (0.2)	n.a.	n.a.
1951/52–1959/60	3.5 (1.7)	11.5	3.2
1960/61–1969/70	4.0 (1.8)	14.6	3.7
1970/71–1979/80	3.0 (0.7)	17.5	5.8
1980/81–1989/90	5.6 (3.4)	20.4	3.6
1990/91–1999/00	5.8 (3.7)	24.3	4.2
2000/01–2009/10	7.3 (5.7)	31.3	4.3
2010/11–2014/15	6.1 (4.8)	33.7	5.5
1951/52–1979/80	3.5 (1.4)	14.7	4.2
1980/81–2009/10	6.2 (4.3)	25.3	4.1
1980/81–2014/15	6.2 (4.3)	26.5	4.3

Notes: Figures in brackets are per capita growth rates. Columns (1) and (2): Figures for 1951/52 to 2013/14 from the 2004/5 national accounts series; figures for 2014/15 from the 2011/12 national accounts series.
Sources: Column (1) 1900/01–1950/51 from Sivasubramonian (2000); 1951/52 onwards: same sources as Column 2. Column (2) 1951/52–2004/05 from Government of India, Central Statistics Office (2011); 2005/06–2014/15 from Government of India (2015a, 2016), and Government of India, Central Statistics Office (2012, 2013, 2014, 2015, 2016).

The broad division of India's post-independence history into two roughly equal halves, centred on 1980, is not intended to capture precisely when the second acceleration in national income began, but it is good enough for my narrative purposes.[1] That said, I am not implying that there were no variations within the two periods 1950–1980 and 1980–2015. One can certainly identify sub-periods with significant changes in the growth rate. Table 2.2 divides the two broad periods into several sub-periods of interest, though the periodization is inevitably subjective.

This chapter sketches with a broad brush the highlights of economic development and political narrative in the periods 1950–1980 and 1980–2015. It focusses principally on growth and poverty policies and outcomes.[2] In the first phase, 1950–1980, economic strategy largely followed a 'command and control model'. In the second phase, 1980–2015, economic strategy moved towards greater marketization, at first hesitantly, then more explicitly. The change in policy orientation was quite pronounced but it was also incomplete and lop-sided. As a result,

Table 2.2 SELECTED PHASES OF GDP GROWTH

	(1)	(2)	(3)
	Growth Rate (% per annum)	Investment (% GDP)	Capital-Output Ratio (col. 2 / col. 1)
1951/52–1964/65	3.9	12.5	3.2
1965/66–1979/80	2.9	16.6	5.7
1980/81–1992/93	5.2	20.5	3.9
1993/94–2002/03	6.0	24.6	4.1
2003/04–2010/11	8.5	34.5	4.1
2011/12–2014/15	5.4	33.0	6.1

Notes: In columns (1) and (2), the figures for 1951/52 to 2013/14 are from the 2004/5 national accounts series. For 2014/15, the figure used is from the 2011/12 national accounts series.
Sources: 1951/52–2004/05 from Government of India, Central Statistics Office (2011); 2005/06–2014/15 from Government of India (2015a, 2016), and Government of India, Central Statistics Office (2012, 2013, 2014, 2015, 2016).

towards the end of the period, rapid growth appeared to be running out of steam.

THE *ANCIEN REGIME*: A POLITICAL AND ECONOMIC NARRATIVE

From 1947 to 1980, the national political scene was largely dominated by two prime ministers, first Jawaharlal Nehru, and then his daughter Indira Gandhi. The first three years of Nehru's reign were taken up with stabilizing the country after the trauma of partition. Planned economic development on an indicative basis was initiated in 1950/51 but the shift to detailed, inter-sectoral, comprehensive planning came with the Second Five Year Plan that began in 1956/57. Moreover, early on during this Plan, there was an acute foreign exchange crisis that gave policymakers further justification, as they saw it, to control private sector activity. From 1951/52 to 1964/65, growth of GDP was 3.9 per cent a year, on the back of a rapid increase in public investment. But problems were building up due to the rigidities and inefficiencies of the control system, and already in the early 1960s, some observers diagnosed a 'quiet crisis in India'.[3]

Nehru died in 1964. He was succeeded by Lal Bahadur Shastri, who did not have a smooth ride: in 1965, there was a drought as well as a war with Pakistan. Shastri's tenure was cut short by his untimely death in January 1966 but not before he had made one lasting economic contribution. This was to support strongly the drive to promote a 'green revolution' to transform Indian agriculture by the injection of new seeds and technology. After intense political manoeuvring, he was succeeded by Nehru's daughter, Mrs. Indira Gandhi. There were two serious droughts in 1965 and 1966, with a sharp rise in inflation. In June 1966, the government carried out a large devaluation (combined with trade liberalization measures), under pressure from the US government, the IMF, and the World Bank, in order to deal with the ongoing 'quiet crisis'. Substantially increased foreign aid that was supposed to follow the devaluation package did not materialize. Politically the devaluation was a disaster. It was blamed for inflation and recession though these had mainly other causes such as the droughts and a fiscal squeeze that was imposed by the government. As a result, Mrs. Gandhi backtracked on liberalization, and was put off liberal economic policies for many years. She turned in a populist-socialist direction, all the more so because she needed to free herself from the old guard of the Congress. This paid off electorally, and together with the resounding military victory over Pakistan in 1971, handed her wing of the Congress Party, named after her as Congress (I), a landslide victory in the national election held that year. Encouraged by the election win, she moved even more firmly in the direction of controls and state ownership. There followed severe challenges in 1972–1974: two droughts, a quadrupling of the oil price, and raging inflation.[4] The government responded with a monetary and fiscal crackdown but this led to widespread discontent. In the ferment that followed, Mrs. Gandhi was challenged in the courts for some minor election offenses. In response, claiming that democracy and national unity were threatened, she imposed an Emergency in June 1975. Individual rights were suspended and the country acquired some of the characteristics of a police state.

In January 1977, Mrs. Gandhi, seeking democratic legitimacy, called an election, and Congress (I) was comprehensively defeated. A Janata Party coalition government took over but it was plagued by factionalism, and by 1979, virtually immobilized. In 1979, there was a severe drought, the worst since independence, and a doubling of world oil prices. As a result, inflation rose sharply. The Janata coalition split up; and in the election that followed, the Congress (I), led by Mrs. Gandhi, returned with a sweeping victory. Unsurprisingly, given the internal disturbances, the exogenous shocks, and the iron grip of controls on economic activity, growth fell to 2.9 per cent a year from 1965/66 to 1979/80, a full percentage point below what it was during Nehru's term of office (see Table 2.2).

Why did India fail to achieve rapid growth for three decades after independence (1950–1980)? The basic answer is that Indian policymakers acted with a mistaken conception of the role of the state. Convoluted regulation of economic activity created large inefficiencies and stifled business drive. At the same time, the state neglected to attend to areas where it should have been active. In particular, it failed to ensure that poor people could gain access to primary health care and education.

It is striking that growth was slow, even declined over time, despite a doubling of saving and investment rates. This clearly points to low productivity of investment as the main proximate reason for the poor performance (see the rising capital-output ratios in Tables 2.1 and 2.2). Low productivity in turn was the product of three features of economic policy: inappropriate and excessive state intervention in markets; the dominant role of the public sector; and neglect of critical social sectors. The origins of the first two features lay in statist doctrines, characterised by antipathy towards business, contempt for the price mechanism, and hostility to international trade that had a special resonance in many post-colonial societies. In India, a further twist was given to this kind of thinking by a 'heavy industry' strategy (based loosely on Soviet planning models), which was adopted in the Second Five Year Plan and used to justify the physical allocation of investment.[5] It was taken for granted that extensive government intervention and controls were necessary to subdue or supplant the market, and make the private sector's activities consonant with the planned trajectory of output.[6] Once the controls were established, the dynamic of rent-seeking took over and they proliferated to the point where no economic activity, unless of very small scale, could be legally pursued without obtaining dozens of permits and licences from different departments of government. Controls permeated every facet of business decision-making including investment, output-mix, pricing, credit, employment, entry, and exit. Especially harmful were the controls on foreign trade and investment that stemmed from the belief in 'self-reliance'. They resulted in India becoming something of a backwater, isolated from the benefits of international division of labour and diffusion of technology.[7]

Another aspect of the command and control strategy was the dominant role accorded to the public sector. The domain of the public sector extended well beyond the traditional utilities and included large swathes of manufacturing industry, many consumer goods, and even hotels. Public sector enterprises were expected to be highly profitable and to serve as the spearhead of investment. The reality was different. Returns in most public sector firms were abysmally low. Many of them not only made losses but became 'sick', a polite Indian word for bankrupt. Keeping them alive imposed a large fiscal burden. In retrospect, this is not surprising. Experience all over the world indicates that the 'agency problem' is far more severe in public than in private enterprises. Public sector managers are often faced with many conflicting objectives and many constraints on their freedom to manage, as well as no serious penalties for inefficient performance. There is an insoluble problem in reconciling managerial autonomy and public accountability. Some countries achieve a better compromise than others. India was among the worst.[8]

Neglect of the social sectors was the third feature of economic policy that led to slow growth; and it also contributed to making growth non-inclusive. It is now almost a cliché that the phenomenal success of the East Asian economies was based on solid achievements in education and health care (in addition to their outward-oriented trade policies).[9] India's performance in these areas was dismal; and in consequence, many people were denied the opportunity to enhance their principal income-earning asset, namely themselves. Part of the reason for this failure was of course low growth itself and the consequent shortage of revenues that could finance social expenditures.[10] Another reason for India's poor comparative performance is arguably that it started from a somewhat lower base than the East Asian economies (other than China).[11] But that defence does not really work since *changes* in human indicators such as life expectancy, infant mortality, and adult literacy were much faster in China and South Korea than in India (see Table 2.3).

Table 2.3 KEY SOCIAL INDICATORS: CHINA, INDIA,
AND SOUTH KOREA

Country	Life Expectancy (years at birth)			Infant Mortality (per 1000 births)			Adult Literacy (%, age 15+)		
	1960	1980	2010	1960	1980	2010	1960	1980	2010
China	41	64	73	165	56	16	43	69	93
India	43	52	65	165	123	48	28	36	63
S. Korea	55	65	81	78	34	4	71	93	98

Sources: 1960 and 1980 data from Statistical Appendixes in World Bank (1982, 1983); 2010 data from World Bank, World Development Indicators Online, except adult literacy in South Korea, for which the latest available figure is for 2000, from the Statistical Appendix in World Bank (2003).

Not surprisingly, slow growth and neglect of human development also led to a comprehensive failure in poverty alleviation. The headcount poverty ratio, which measures the proportion of poor people below an officially defined poverty line, was broadly constant between the 1950s and 1977/78 (see Table 2.4, and Datt and Ravallion 2010). In the 1950s, more than half the population was below the poverty line, a situation that remained unchanged throughout the first three post-independence decades. Since population growth was rapid, this implied large additions to the absolute numbers of poor people. The number of people in poverty rose by nearly 120 million over the period, from 210 million to 329 million (see Table 2.4).

Table 2.4 ALL-INDIA POVERTY AND INEQUALITY

Year	Headcount Poverty Ratio (%)			Inequality: Gini Coefficient (%)
	Old Definitions	Tendulkar Definition	Rangarajan Definition	
1950–1960	52.7 (210 million)	n.a.	n.a.	35.0 (RG: 33.7; UG: 38.2)
1960–1970	53.3 (262 million)	n.a.	n.a.	31.5 (RG: 30.3; UG: 35.3)
1973/74	54.9 (321 million)	n.a.	n.a.	29.2 (RG: 28.5; UG: 30.8)
1977/78	51.3 (329 million)	n.a.	n.a.	32.1 (RG: 30.9; UG: 34.7)
1983	44.5 (323 million)	n.a.	n.a.	31.3 (RG: 30.1; UG: 34.1)
1993/94	36.0 (320 million)	45.3 (404 million)	n.a.	30.7 (RG: 28.5; UG: 34.4)
2004/05	27.5 (302 million)	37.2 (407 million)	n.a.	34.7 (RG: 28.1; UG: 36.4)
2011/12	n.a.	21.9 (269 million)	29.5 (363 million)	35.9 (RG:28.7; UG:37.7)

Notes: In the "Headcount Poverty Ratio" part of the table, the figures in brackets show the absolute number of poor people in millions. In the "Inequality: Gini Coefficient" part of the Table, RG means Rural Gini and UG means Urban Gini.
Sources: Poverty, 1950s and 1960s: Datt (1997); poverty, 1973/74 to 2011/12 (except Rangarajan poverty in 2011/12): Planning Commission (2014a) and Planning Commission (2014c); poverty, 2011/12 (Rangarajan definition): Planning Commission (2014a); inequality, 1950s to 1993/94: Datt (1997); inequality, 2004/5 and 2011/12: Himanshu (2015).

ongress (I) and Mrs. Gandhi returned to power in January 1980 in the middle of a drought, an oil price shock, and a macroeconomic crisis. The crisis response was very different from what had happened in the previous crises in 1965 and 1973. The government tried, and largely succeeded, in undertaking an 'expansionary adjustment' without cutting public investment, with the help of a large IMF loan. Public investment rose as intended but the fiscal position deteriorated. Politically there was increasing tension, mainly because of a separatist movement in Punjab. This eventually led Mrs. Gandhi to order the army to storm the Golden Temple in Amritsar, which had become the militants' headquarters. In revenge, she was assassinated by two of her own bodyguards in October 1984. Congress (I), led by her son Rajiv Gandhi, won a national election, already scheduled, on a wave of sympathy, with a massive near-four-fifths majority in parliament.

Rajiv Gandhi had a modern, managerial style and wanted to shed the ideological baggage of the past. He took a number of liberalizing measures in his first two years in office. But the reformist phase did not last long. The turning point came in 1987 when his reputation was brought into question by allegations of corruption relating to the purchase of artillery from the Swedish firm Bofors. There were other difficulties too, including a massive agitation, led by the Bharatiya Janata Party (BJP), to demolish a 16th century mosque that had allegedly been built on the site of the birthplace of the Hindu god Rama. Faced with manifold personal and political problems, Rajiv Gandhi lost the impetus for economic reform. He called an election in late 1989, hoping to get a new and convincing mandate. The National Front, a combination of various opposition parties, campaigned successfully on the issue of corruption, and Congress (I) suffered a humiliating defeat. In December of that year, V. P. Singh formed a minority government with parliamentary support from the BJP and the Communists but its position was rickety. In August 1990, oil prices doubled following the Iraqi invasion of Kuwait. Given the fiscal position, which had been worsening throughout the 1980s, this shock affected not only the current account of the balance of payments but also the capital account. Acute difficulties began to be experienced in new commercial borrowing and even in rolling over existing short-term loans and credits, and reserves fell sharply. Communal and caste conflicts also grew apace, especially over V. P. Singh's attempt to implement the recommendations of the Mandal Commission, which had recommended in 1980 that 27 per cent of government posts should be reserved for 'Other Backward Castes', in addition to the 22.5 per cent constitutionally reserved for 'Scheduled Castes and Tribes'. The BJP decided that the time was ripe to bid for support from all Hindus by reviving the temple-mosque issue, and the V. P. Singh government collapsed when the BJP withdrew its parliamentary support. Rajiv Gandhi did not want to form a Congress government, preferring to bide his time and win a general election in due course.

The country staggered on with minority governments until a new election was called in May 1991. The day after it began, Rajiv Gandhi was assassinated. Congress (I) won 226 seats, 30 short of an overall majority, and formed a minority government, with P. V. Narasimha Rao as prime minister and Manmohan Singh, an economist–civil servant of wide domestic and international experience, as Finance Minister. The government's inheritance was grim. Inflation was 12 per cent a year and rising. The current account deficit was 3.5 per cent of GDP and 45 per cent of exports. Reserves were down to two weeks' imports. The consolidated fiscal deficit was more than 10 per cent of GDP. The external debt to exports ratio was 250 per cent, well up from 150 per cent in 1980. The new government moved swiftly to announce a programme of stabilization and liberalization. In 1991/92, fiscal retrenchment was undertaken, combined with a devaluation of the rupee, and supported by a standby credit from the IMF. Growth crashed to negative levels for a year because of the combined effects of erratic weather and fiscal contraction. But the recession proved to be temporary. There was a smart recovery in the following year, along with a reduction in fiscal and current account deficits.

In assessing economic performance in the decade of the1980s, it makes sense to extend the period to include the 1991 crisis and its immediate aftermath because the latter was caused in large part by the severe fiscal deterioration that preceded it. In the period 1980/81 to 1992/93, the growth rate averaged 5.2 per cent a year, a large rise compared with 3.5 per cent in the previous 30 years. In their 1994 book, Vijay Joshi and Ian Little attributed this acceleration to the following main factors: higher and more stable investment; an increase in efficiency as a result of some liberalization; and rampantly expansionary macroeconomic policies.[12] That judgement still holds good. Investment in the 1980s went up to an average of 21 per cent of GDP compared with 17 per cent in the previous 15 years. Both public and corporate investment rose, and public investment was far more stable in the 1980s than hitherto. Productivity increased as a result of various moves towards liberalization, hesitant though they were . But the higher growth was also based on large increases in government and foreign borrowing, so it contained the seeds of its own destruction.

The Narasimha Rao government began the process of liberalizing reform as soon as it took over in 1991, even before stabilization had been achieved. Though overdue, this was a bold move that aroused opposition. The fear that Indian industry would be unable to withstand foreign competition was articulated from both the Left and the Right, and it is to Rao's credit that he gave political cover to the small band of reformers headed by the Finance Minister, Manmohan Singh, to stay the course. In the event, the fears of the anti-reformers were belied. After a shake-out, liberalization led to a sizeable increase in economic efficiency. The Rao government's reforming zeal waned with the approach of national elections after its first three years in office. In the election of 1996, the BJP, whose strength had been steadily growing from the mid-1980s, emerged by a small margin as the largest single party. But it was a highly divided parliament, and a succession of short-lived governments ensued. The best that can be said for them is that they did not reverse economic reform. There was an election in 1998 in which the BJP increased its tally of seats and was again the single largest party. This government too lasted only a year, in which the main event was India's successful conduct of a nuclear test. Finally, in the election of 1999, the BJP was sufficiently ahead of the Congress Party to be able to form a stable minority government that lasted the full five-year term until 2004.

The BJP had the reputation of being a hard-line Hindu revivalist party. But during this term of office, it became respectable, under the moderating influence in domestic politics and foreign policy of the prime minister, Atal Behari Vajpayee. The BJP government carried forward the process of economic reform. There was some further liberalization of trade, finance, and foreign investment, and a beginning was made with privatization of loss-making public sector enterprises. There were also some advances in infrastructure provision, particularly roads, electricity, and telecommunications, though the shortfall remained large. A significant blot on the BJP's record was the reaction of the BJP-ruled state government in Gujarat to an unfortunate incident in Godhra where, in 2002, a railway carriage was set on fire and 59 Hindus died. In the communal riots that followed, there were more than 2000 deaths, mostly of Muslims, while the police stood by. Though this was a state government responsibility, many people felt that the central government did not condemn it strongly enough. (It could, for example, have dismissed the state government.)

The BJP fought the election of 2004 under the slogan 'India Shining'. To widespread surprise, it lost and Congress returned to power at the head of the United Progressive Alliance (UPA) coalition. Sonia Gandhi, the President of the Congress Party, wisely declined to be prime minister and installed Manmohan Singh instead. The UPA won again in the 2009 elections, so it had two consecutive terms of office (UPA-1 and UPA-2). Manmohan Singh's main achievement in UPA-1 was to negotiate a nuclear agreement with the United States. The time was propitious because the United States had begun to feel the need to insure against the growing power of a resurgent China. Even so, there was considerable domestic opposition to the deal and Singh had to fight a hard campaign to overcome it. (India has yet to see much benefit from the deal, however.)

Growth was 'super-fast' (around 8.5 per cent a year, 7 per cent per head per year) from 2003/4 to 2010/11. The UPA government cannot take much credit for this since there was not much supply-side reform during its tenure. (This was in part because it depended on parliamentary support from two Communist parties.) Crucially important for the successful growth performance was the fact that during the UPA-1's term of office, the global economic environment was highly supportive and enabled India to reap the benefit of the reforms of the previous 12 years. The global credit crisis broke in 2008. India's growth slipped to 6.7 per cent during 2008/9 but rebounded to more than 8 per cent for the next three years, driven by the pre-existing momentum of domestic consumption and investment. But there was a sharp slowdown thereafter: from 2011/12 to 2013/14, growth fell to around 5 per cent a year. Of course, the post-2008 global slowdown did not help. But there were also various purely domestic reasons for India's pronounced growth-recession (see below and, for a more extended discussion, Chapter 8). Inflation was also high for several years. The combination of inflation, growth slowdown, and various corruption scandals led to a collapse in the government's reputation for sound and effective governance.

By the time the elections of 2014 came round, it looked highly likely that the BJP would come to power, not because the country was enamoured of the party's advocacy of Hindu nationalism but simply because it was craving for clean, strong, and coherent leadership, and many people thought that the BJP's prime ministerial candidate Narendra Modi would provide it. In the election that followed, the BJP won enough seats to secure a small absolute majority on its own in the Lok Sabha (the lower house of parliament), and a sizeable majority in combination with its allied political parties. But it continued to be in the minority in the Rajya Sabha (the upper house of parliament). As this book goes to press in 2016, the BJP government has been in power for nearly two years. (Its performance is closely analysed in Chapter 13.)

THE PARTIAL REFORM MODEL: GROWTH SINCE 1980

Reformist ideas had begun to gather steam from the late 1970s onwards. By this time, the contrast between East Asian success and Indian failure was becoming hard to ignore. The first sign of change was that the Congress government enacted some business-friendly policy measures. By the time

Mrs. Gandhi returned in 1980, she had learned some salutary lessons from her previous 'left turn'. She also needed to cultivate new sources of support and the business community was one such source. The liberalization that she initiated, and Rajiv Gandhi furthered, was hesitant, piecemeal, and more 'business-friendly' than 'market-friendly'. But it worked because India was then far inside the efficiency frontier due to misguided past policies. Together with a sizeable fiscal expansion, it led to a rise in the growth rate to 5.6 per cent a year in the 1980s. This speeding up of growth, which occurred before the major reforms of the 1990s, has led some commentators to denigrate the importance of the latter. In my view this is quite wrong. Firstly, a contributory cause of fast growth in the 1980s was over-expansionary fiscal policy and foreign borrowing, as evidenced by the phenomenal rise in the consolidated fiscal deficit. This was around 5 per cent of GDP in the 1970s and rose to 8 per cent in the first half of the 1980s, and further to 10 per cent of GDP towards the end of the decade. This kind of expansion was manifestly unsustainable (and was unsurprisingly brought to an end by the full-blown macroeconomic crisis at the end of the decade).[13] Secondly, reform in the 1980s was very shallow. There was little in the way of introducing genuine competition, domestic or international. Without the more significant changes undertaken after 1991, output acceleration would have fizzled out.

The crisis of 1991 provided the occasion for a more decisive change of strategy. As part of the stabilisation programme, India borrowed from the IMF and no loans would have been forthcoming without the promise of structural adjustment. Meanwhile, the world had changed. Communism had collapsed in the Soviet Union and Eastern Europe and with it collapsed the respectability of India's earlier strategy. A programme of reform, more radical than anything attempted in the previous decade, was initiated in July 1991 by the Narasimha Rao government. The thrust of the reforms was to roll back controls in trade, industry, and finance, thereby increasing the market orientation of the economy. Quantitative import controls on capital goods and raw materials were abolished, import tariffs were slashed, investment licensing was scrapped in most industries, and significant moves were made to open up the economy to foreign direct and portfolio investment. The effects were fairly spectacular. Liberalization boosted productivity growth after an initial period of pain. Numerous old-style conglomerates (e.g. Mafatlal, Shri Ram, and some parts of the Birla clan come to mind) got swept aside as more nimble start-ups showed how business could be done. In due course, the majority of companies began to deliver a return on capital that exceeded its cost, so corporate savings and investment rose sharply. The response brought home the point that India possesses a dynamic entrepreneurial class whose energies had been stifled by the 'license raj'. For 10 years after 1993, growth was 6 per cent a year, higher than the 5.2 per cent rate achieved in the previous 10 years.

For eight years from 2003, there was a further acceleration in GDP to a super-fast growth rate of 8.5 per cent a year. This was so, even though the period included 2008/9, the year in which the global financial crisis broke. In the boom years prior to it, companies had borrowed up to the hilt, and they continued their capital spending in order to finish the projects they had started. There were some exogenous favourable factors that contributed to fast growth such as the strong tail wind from the world economy before the financial crisis, combined with low oil prices and a run of good harvests. But a significant part of the credit for the acceleration must also go to the cumulative effects of the reforms since 1991; given the favourable environment, they produced a phenomenal rise in corporate savings and investment, and overall productivity. Strikingly, nearly all the states grew faster from 2000 to 2010 than in the previous decade.[14]

Finally, the bubble burst. The proximate cause of the slowdown from 2011/12 was a collapse of corporate investment. This was to some extent a natural consequence of the need to deleverage after the over-borrowing of the boom years. But there was also another reason for the investment famine. This was the souring of the investment climate caused by 'governance failures'. The government was involved in several major scandals and scams, whose exposure led to a period of policy paralysis. Many projects that required various clearances to proceed came to a standstill. Another reason for the crumbling of investment was the worsening macroeconomic outlook. Inflation was around 10 per cent a year for six years from 2008. As a result, household savings were diverted to gold imports and the current account deficit widened to the dangerous level of 4.5 per cent of GDP in 2011/12 and 2012/13. Macroeconomic management was clearly not such as to inspire investor confidence. There was also the underlying problem that the lack of much meaningful economic reform for several years was taking its toll by lowering the potential growth rate. Since 2014, macro-stability has been restored but investment and growth continue to languish notwithstanding the new GDP numbers, which show a revival (see Chapters 8 and 13).

POVERTY, DEPRIVATION, AND INEQUALITY SINCE 1980

In a poor developing country, the touchstone of successful economic performance is poverty alleviation. Progress in reducing the headcount poverty ratio, viz. the proportion of the population below an officially defined poverty line, is shown in Table 2.4.[15] The definition of the poverty line was revised in 2009 by the Tendulkar Committee, and again in 2014 by the Rangarajan Committee, in a manner which raised measured levels of poverty. But the new and old estimates show a similar trend. In 1973, the poverty ratio (old definition) was 55 per cent. It fell significantly in the fast-growth period after 1980 but the rate of decline was disappointingly slow (compared with, say, China), even in the decade after the 1991 reforms. However, it speeded up during the period of super-fast growth (2003–2010).[16] The absolute number of poor people (Tendulkar definition) did not decline until 2004 but then fell quite rapidly. Even so, it remains large: 269 million in 2011 according to the estimate in that year on the Tendulkar definition and 363 million on the Rangarajan definition. The corresponding poverty ratios are 21.9 per cent and 29.8 per cent respectively. The former could be described as an estimate of the proportion of people living in 'extreme poverty'.[17]

Poverty ratios have also been falling in all states, but unevenly. In 2011, on the Tendulkar definition, they ranged all the way from 40 per cent in Chhattisgarh to 7 per cent in Kerala. In general, the Northern and Eastern states have worse poverty than those in the South and the West. Nearly half the poor are concentrated in four states: Bihar, Uttar Pradesh, Madhya Pradesh and Rajasthan. The incidence of poverty among disadvantaged groups (Scheduled Castes, Scheduled Tribes, and Muslims) is substantially higher than in the population as a whole. Poverty has fallen in these groups too, but the disparity between their poverty rates and the all-India average has remained unchanged between 1993 and 2010.[18]

Deprivation is not entirely captured by measures of income-poverty. India's record on wider measures of deprivation is unimpressive. Though indicators of broad deprivation have been falling, the levels are still very high, absolutely and comparatively (see Chapter 9 and Tables 9.1–9.4). India's performance is much worse than China's; more surprisingly, in some respects, it is worse than poorer and slower-growing Bangladesh, and no better than the average for 'low-income countries', hardly a recommendation for a country that has grown rapidly for 30 years, is classified by the World Bank as a 'lower middle income country', and aspires to be a major economic power. In health, notable black spots are wide prevalence of child malnutrition, low coverage of immunization, and severe lack of decent sanitation facilities. On child malnutrition, India does even worse than the average for low-income countries.[19] In education, progress has certainly occurred, but the shortfalls remain large. The literacy rate among young people (aged 15–24) is now 80 per cent but in China it is 99 per cent. Although 96 per cent of children between the ages of 6 and 14 are now enrolled in primary schools, dropout rates are high and a third of children leave before they reach the final grade. Moreover, in today's ٮ primary education is not enough to get by. The gross enrolment rate secondary schools is only 63 per cent, compared with 81 per cent in China, and around half of the enrollers drop out before completion. And, to make matters worse, in both primary and secondary education, the quality of provision is atrocious. Note also that many of the figures quoted above are overall averages; the figures are considerably worse for backward states, for poor people, and for socially-disadvantaged groups, including women.[20]

How about inequality in India? Inequality is not related to the goals of policy in any simple way but a rising trend of inequality would surely be a matter of concern.[21] India has the reputation of having a low level of inter-personal inequality of income by international standards. But this is an illusion created by the fact that it uses *inequality of per capita consumption expenditure* (calculated from National Sample Survey data) as a surrogate for inequality of income. For various reasons, including severe under-reporting of and by the rich, measured consumption inequality systematically underestimates true income inequality. Some attempts have been made to measure *inequality of incomes* in India directly. These turn up with calculated Gini coefficients above 50 per cent, which puts India in the same ball-park as high-inequality Latin American countries like Brazil.[22]

Measures of interpersonal inequality of consumption are good enough to indicate what is happening to the *trend* of inequality. On this measure, from the early 1960s to the early 1990s, inequality in India was roughly flat, with a broadly stable Gini coefficient in the low thirties.[23] But in the last two decades there has been a rise: the all-India Gini coefficient has gone up by about six percentage points from 1993 to 2011, from around 30 to 36 per cent (see Table 2.4).[24] This is mostly due to a rise in intra-urban inequality, and the urban-rural income differential; intra-rural inequality has not increased by much.[25] Other pieces of evidence are also suggestive of rising inequality, particularly in urban areas. Firstly, in the last decade, National Sample Survey data show that a) per capita urban consumption increased twice as fast as per capita rural consumption and b) within the urban sector, per capita consumption in the top decile has risen much faster than in other deciles. Secondly, there is plenty of evidence of a rising premium for higher education and skills. Thirdly, income tax data reveal that the share of the top 1 per cent of income earners in total income increased from 5 per cent in the early 1990s to 10 per cent by 2002. Informal evidence suggests that it has risen further since then.[26]

There has also been a politically salient rise in regional inequality. The gap between richer and poorer states widened significantly during the three decades after 1980. The Gini coefficient of state per capita incomes rose from 14 to 24 over this period. The ratio of per capita income in the richest state (Punjab in 1970/71, Haryana in 2004/5 and 2009/10) to that in the poorest state (Bihar in all three years), was 3.4 in 1970/71 but rose to 4.2 in 1993/94 and further to 5.0 in 2009/10.[27] This is so even though poorer states have shared in the output acceleration of recent years. The disparity between their growth rates and the higher growth rates of the richer states remains, though it has narrowed.[28]

OVERVIEW OF 1980–2014

In most respects, India's economic performance has undoubtedly been much better after 1980 than before. Fiscal management is the outstanding exception. Until the late 1970s, Indian fiscal policies were prudent. In the 1980s, fiscal deficits and foreign borrowing increased sharply, leading to a severe crisis in 1991, when the country narrowly staved off default on foreign loans. The fiscal slippage was in part a consequence of public sector losses and inefficiency but also of a massive growth in subsidies that occurred for various reasons grounded in political economy (see Chapter 11). Though the fiscal position improved after the 1991 reforms, it remains fragile, and enduring fiscal consolidation has not been achieved. This has had many untoward effects, not least the crowding out of essential public spending on infrastructure and the social sectors.

Since the 1980s, growth and 'inclusion' have improved greatly, the former more than the latter. This is not to say that everything is lovely in the garden. Far from it. The big question for the future is as follows. Are the changes that have occurred since 1991 sufficient for India to realize its goal of a rapid ascent to prosperity (which would require high-quality per capita growth of at least 6–8 per cent a year, i.e. aggregate growth of at least 7–9 per cent a year, for the next three decades)? I think not. As the ensuing chapters will show, the foundations for such an achievement have not been laid.

NOTES

1. There has been a spirited, even acrimonious, controversy about the precise point of inflection at which the second acceleration began. I do not think it is particularly interesting. A date 'sometime around 1980' is good enough for my purposes. For a survey of the controversy, see Corbridge, Harriss, and Jeffrey (2013), and the references cited therein.

2. Thus, I mostly omit discussion of policies and outcomes with regard to macro-stability and environmental sustainability. These are of course discussed in later chapters. For India's political and economic history, narrative and analytic, see Balakrishnan (2010), Bardhan (2010), Desai (2011), Guha (2007), Joshi and Little (1994, 1996), McCartney (2009) and Srinivasan (2011).

3. See Lewis (1962).

4. Macroeconomic crises in the period 1964 to 1991 are closely analysed in Joshi and Little (1994).

5. Nehru's role was critical. He was a Kashmiri Brahmin and also a Fabian socialist, sympathetic to elements of Marxist thinking. These attributes inclined him towards distrust of business and admiration for statist planning. However, it would be going too far to say that he imposed his ideas by force. Such views were widely held and in tune with the spirit of the times. The particular form that state planning took owed much to the influence of P. Mahalanobis, a leading statistician, who became, with Nehru's backing, the prime mover in economic strategy. The Second Five Year Plan (1956–61) was Mahalanobis's intellectual creature. In the 'Mahalanobis model', economic growth is driven by investment, which is limited by the availability of capital goods ('machines'). These cannot be imported freely since export possibilities, it is assumed, are highly limited; so machines have to be produced at home by expanding as fast as possible the capacity of the capital goods sector (the sector that manufactures 'machines to make machines').

6. A possible defence of the Indian planning strategy is that it overcame a major difficulty that is inherent in the early stages of development. This is that investment by any individual entrepreneur may be held back by uncertainty about the fruition of other investments (by other entrepreneurs). Arguably, planning solved this coordination problem. While this point has some merit, it is not inconsistent with the view that planning was excessively capital-intensive and autarkic.

7. For an authoritative analysis of the control system, see Bhagwati and Desai (1970) and Bhagwati (1993). Note that price, investment, and distribution controls under Nehru did not reach the draconian severity that they were to attain under Indira Gandhi. Foreign exchange controls were a slightly different story. They were quite relaxed until the mid-1950s but became increasingly tight after the foreign exchange crisis of 1957. By 1964, they constituted a serious impediment to production, part of the 'quiet crisis' that led to the World Bank sending the Bell Mission to report on the state of the Indian economy. Controls were greatly intensified during Indira Gandhi's prime ministership, after a brief liberalization episode surrounding the devaluation of 1966. The control regime included the Foreign Exchange Regulation Act of 1973, which restricted foreign investment in a comprehensive fashion.

8. As with controls, the policy of extending state ownership was pursued much more vigorously under Indira Gandhi than under Nehru. She took a 'left turn' in order to win popular support, after the political disaster of the 1966 devaluation. Her government nationalized all the major Indian-owned commercial banks and enacted the Monopolies and Restrictive Trade Practices Act to regulate closely the activities of business houses. After she came back in 1971 with a thumping parliamentary majority, insurance companies and the coal industry were nationalized and several failing textile mills were taken over by the government. Nationalization of the wheat trade was also attempted but given up when it failed to stem rising prices.

9. Arguably, another reason for the absence of inclusive development was the absence of radical land redistribution, in contrast to some East Asian economies. But this kind of reform generally happens in the aftermath of war or revolution, which was not how India achieved independence. Two other considerations were also relevant in preventing such a project in India. Firstly, India was a democracy from the very start, so compulsion was not possible. Secondly, India is a land-scarce country (the land-labour ratio is very low), so the major problem in Indian agriculture is extreme land fragmentation, not land concentration. Indeed, the largely futile efforts to carry out redistributive land reform in India diverted energy which would have been better spent in strengthening tenancy rights, and promoting education and health care.

10. Most states in India failed miserably in promoting education and health but there were some outstanding exceptions such as Kerala and Himachal Pradesh. This shows the importance of government focus and attention for successful social outcomes. See Dreze and Sen (1995, 2013).

11. China's starting point was little better than India's. South Korea had a somewhat higher adult literacy rate (40 per cent) than India (20 per cent) after the Second World War. But by 1960, the South Korean literacy rate was 71 per cent, India's was 28 per cent.

12. See Joshi and Little (1994), Chapter 13.

13. The causes of the crisis of 1991 are examined in depth in Chapters 7 and 8 of Joshi and Little (1994).

14. See Kumar and Subramanian (2011). Interestingly, the faster-growing states also tend to show better social outcomes, as shown in Subramanian (2012b).

15. The definition of the poverty line has changed from time to time. I ignore the early changes and concentrate mainly on the recent definitions introduced by the Tendulkar Committee and the Rangarajan Committee.

16. The rate of decline in the all-India poverty rate was 0.85 per cent per year between 1983 and 1993/94, 0.74 per cent per year between 1993/94 and 2004/5, and 2.18 per cent per year between 2004/5 and 2011/12.

17. The Tendulkar poverty line is roughly equivalent to the World Bank's poverty line of $1.90 a day at constant 2011 PPP dollars. On this basis, the World Bank estimates India's poverty ratio as 21.3 per cent of the population (very close to the Tendulkar Committee's estimate).

18. See Table 24.1 in Planning Commission (2013a).

19. Jean Dreze and Amartya Sen have pointed out that the figures for low-income countries are depressed by Sub-Saharan Africa (SSA), which has done badly for various special reasons. If we consider low-income countries outside SSA, India does worse than their average, not only in the three indicators mentioned above but in many others, e.g. life expectancy, under-five mortality, mean years of schooling, female literacy rate etc. (See Dreze and Sen 2013, Table 3.1.) Dreze and Sen also observe that Bangladesh was similar or worse than India in several social indicators in 1990 but overtook India by 2011 (Dreze and Sen 2013, Table 3.3), despite having had a much lower rate of growth.

20. For example, average female literacy (age 15–49) in India was 55.1 per cent in 2005/6 but in Bihar and Rajasthan, it was 37 per cent and 36 per cent respectively. The all-India under-five mortality rate (per 1000) in 2005/6 was 74.3 but in Madhya Pradesh and UP it was 94.2 and 96.4 respectively. The average proportion of fully immunized children was 43.5 per cent for India as a whole but in UP and Rajasthan it was 23 per cent and 26.5 per cent respectively

(see Dreze and Sen 2013, Table 3.8). Health and literacy indicators are also much worse than the national average among disadvantaged groups (see Tables 24.6 and 24.8 in Planning Commission 2013a).

21. Less poverty is unambiguously a good thing but the same cannot be said of less inequality. Inequalities may be 'good' if they are necessary to foster effort, innovation, and entrepreneurship. Inequalities may be 'bad' if they reward pre-existing social privileges and advantages or political connections and cronyism.

22. See Desai, Dubey, Joshi, Sen, Shariff, and Vanneman (2010).

23. See Table 2.4 and Weisskopf (2011).

24. See Himanshu (2015). A large part of the rise in inequality took place between 1993/94 and 2004/5. World Bank data show a more moderate rise between 1993/94 and 2011/12 from 30.8 per cent to 33.6 per cent, nearly all of which took place between 1993/94 and 2004/5.

25. It follows that poverty, especially urban poverty, would have fallen faster if inequality had not worsened.

26. See Banerjee and Piketty (2005). Data for wealth inequality also show a rise from 1991 to 2002. In 2002, the Gini for per capita land holding was 73 per cent (China's was 49 per cent). The Ginis for per capita asset holdings and per capita financial asset holdings were 65 per cent and 99 per cent respectively. See Himanshu (2015) and the references cited therein.

27. The numbers in this paragraph come from Purfield (2006) and Chapter 11 of Planning Commission (2013a).

28. See Kumar and Subramanian (2011) and Planning Commission (2013a), Chapter 11.

CHAPTER 3

Ends and Means, State and Market

Economic policy unavoidably involves explicit or implicit judgements about ends and means. In this book, I define the objective of India's economic development as *rapid, inclusive, stable, and sustainable growth of national income within a political framework of liberal democracy*. More fundamental objectives of development could be and have been posited but that is a philosophical minefield that I do not need to enter.[1] Successful attainment of the objective specified above is surely a prime requirement for fulfilling any of the more basic or 'fundamental' objectives that are likely to command acceptance on the basis of reasoned thinking.

Inclusive economic growth matters because aggregate income is of little value in itself, especially in a poor country. Growth has to be widely shared if it is to contribute to raising living standards across the board. (Needless to say, 'living standards' encompass more than income, narrowly construed, and include other aspects of well-being such as education and health.) *Rapid* growth is important because it contributes to 'inclusion' in a direct way by increasing employment and incomes rapidly, including those of poor people. It also helps inclusion indirectly because it leads to a rapid rise in tax revenues, which in turn can be used to reduce poverty, and to ameliorate the non-income aspects of deprivation. The political constraints on redistribution are also likely to be much weaker if growth is rapid. By *sustainable* growth, I mean growth that is environmentally-friendly. Pursuit of growth, without any regard to its consequences for the depletion of natural capital, would reduce the well-being of the country's citizens sooner or later.[2] *Stable* growth completes the quartet of development policy aims. Stability here refers to macroeconomic stability, in other words, prevention of high inflation, deep recession, and state insolvency. Instability can result in hardship, political and social unrest, even total chaos; and there is persuasive evidence that the long-run rate of growth is also reduced thereby.

I take it for granted that the above aims have to be realized in a liberal democratic framework. Liberal democracy involves not only periodic electoral competition but also the assurance of civil liberties and some basic individual and minority rights. Liberal democracy is a political choice that was made when India became independent. It has deep intrinsic value but also instrumental advantages and disadvantages for economic development. The main advantage is that, with free debate and contestation, changes that are agreed upon are likely to endure. The main disadvantage is that the very same process is liable to make desirable change slow and cumbersome. The aims I have outlined are compatible with what is sometimes called 'social democracy', which seeks to achieve the egalitarian objectives of socialism, while remaining committed to the values and institutions of liberal democracy.[3]

What about the means of attaining the above aims? The most fundamental choice concerns the balance between the state and the market in the organization of economic activity.[4] Post-independence India has always been a mixed economy in which private and state ownership of the means of production, as well as free and regulated markets, co-exist. But the mix has varied. In the first three decades after 1947, it moved quite sharply towards state ownership and state intervention in the market. Since then the balance has swung towards market liberalization and private ownership.[5] I believe this shift was wholly desirable. Is the balance now appropriate? This is one of the major questions running through this book, so a brief overview of the underlying principles is necessary.

The market is one of the most important methods of voluntary social cooperation. It has many virtues beyond the one emphasised in economics textbooks. The textbook virtue is that under certain well-defined conditions, in particular the prevalence of perfect competition, market interaction achieves economic efficiency. This is because competitive discipline ensures that whatever is produced is produced at the lowest feasible cost; and, in addition, whatever is produced meets consumer demand at prices which reflect costs of production. The overall outcome, brought about by an 'invisible hand', is an 'efficient allocation of resources', meaning a state in which all possibilities of making some people better off (without making others worse off) are exhausted.[6] This is a useful property, not to be despised. But its significance should also not be exaggerated. This is because an 'efficient' allocation of resources, in the sense defined, is compatible with any distribution of income, even one that is wildly inequitable.

Other virtues of competitive markets are equally, if not more, important. Firstly, they are a highly effective and undemanding way of coordinating information, far better in this respect than centralized planning.[7] In a market system, coordination of individual plans requires only that each agent knows market prices, and reacts to price signals. A central planner's task is immensely more complex and requires huge quantities of information (which individual agents have every incentive to conceal).[8] Secondly, markets can react flexibly to uncertain and changing economic circumstances but central planning cannot. Thirdly, market incentives promote a continuous process of risk-taking and innovation, disciplined by the test of profitability. (In other words, market economies tend to be better than planned economies in generating new ideas as well as discarding failed ideas.) No comparable mechanism exists in planned systems. These points have been well supported by evidence, for example, the enormous inefficiency, and eventual paralysis, of the centrally planned system of the former Soviet Union.[9]

Even so, all except a fringe of extremists would agree that free markets are not an unalloyed social good. There are two broad reasons for this: distributive justice and 'market failures'. As noted above, the distribution of income that a totally unrestricted market would throw up would not, except by fluke, be socially desirable. At a minimum, state intervention is necessary to provide a safety net for the poorest people. But a state may, and I think should, pursue a more inclusive concept of distributive justice and put in place some permanent income supplements for the poor, as well as establish substantive equality of opportunity, especially in access to education and health care.

If there are 'market failures', free and competitive markets do not achieve even economic efficiency (let alone distributive justice). This provides another rationale for state intervention. Markets can fail for several reasons. The market will not provide at all, or in adequate quantity, 'pure public goods', which have the property that if they are provided, they are by their nature available to all, and no one can be excluded from provision even if they wish to be excluded.[10] The standard examples are law and order and national defence but there are many others ranging from provision of macroeconomic stability to drainage of malarial swamps. The state has to raise tax revenue and pay for the provision of 'pure public goods' (which it may or may not produce itself).[11] Note that 'pure public goods' are only a part of what, in ordinary parlance, are called 'public goods' or 'public services', for example education, health care, and infrastructure facilities. Many of these can be supplied by the private sector and are not 'pure public goods'. They should more accurately termed 'private goods' but I am in no position to dictate common usage! In this book, I use the terms 'public goods' and 'public services' in the ordinary way but reserve the phrase 'pure public goods' for the narrower concept.

Markets can also fail when there are 'external effects'. These occur when production or consumption by economic agents has *unpriced* favourable or unfavourable effects on other agents. An example of an adverse external effect is pollution caused by a firm which, in the course of its operations, discharges toxic chemicals into a river and harms people downstream. Since the polluting firm does not pay for the damage it causes, there is a case for taxing it to make it cut back on its output. An example of a beneficial external effect is expenditure by a firm on training labour, which benefits other firms that can bid away the trained workers. Since firms that train labour cannot capture these external benefits of training, they would spend less on it than would be desirable from a national standpoint. It follows that there is a case for a state subsidy for labour training.[12] There are many such examples of positive and negative externalities.[13]

Another related case of market failure can arise when markets attempt to allocate resources that have ownership rights that are undefined or held in common. Relevant examples are minerals under the ground, fish in the sea, the earth's atmosphere, and telecom spectrum. Here, the state may have to act to prevent a 'tragedy of the commons'.[14] Unfettered markets are likely to lead to chaotic over-use, even exhaustion, of scarce resources that are un-owned or under common ownership. One solution is for the state to allocate private property rights (though it may quite properly appropriate the rents created thereby, for example by auctioning the resources). Sometimes this may not be possible and other kinds of state intervention would be called for.[15]

Taxes, subsidies, and sometimes mandates and prohibitions may at times be required to alter market outcomes by over-riding consumer desires for so-called 'merit goods' and 'demerit goods'. For example, the state may wish to ban heroin use and discourage cigarette smoking ('demerit goods'), and encourage child education and child nutrition ('merit goods'), for essentially paternalistic reasons.[16] (Obviously, such intervention can only be justified if it is practised on a limited scale. If the state goes too far in the direction of legislating consumption decisions, it can no longer be called a liberal-democratic state.)

It is of course obvious that markets will not lead to an efficient outcome if they are not competitive, and in that case, the remedy is for the state to restore competition (by anti-trust policy, trade liberalization etc.). But there are some activities in which monopoly is 'natural', in the sense that the scale of production required to achieve low costs is so large as to preclude competition. (Electricity transmission is an example.) In such cases, the state has to step in to nationalize the monopoly and run the operation itself or allow the monopoly to exist but regulate it to prevent monopolistic exploitation of consumers.[17]

A subtle but important case of market failure emanates from lack of equal access to information.[18] One of its important manifestations is misallocation of risk. Explanation of this is postponed to Chapter 9, which considers a glaring example of this type of market failure, viz. the failure of an unregulated market to provide health insurance. The state may be able to improve the situation by policy intervention, in this instance by making health insurance compulsory and universal.

Finally, markets may fail even in their prime function of coordinating information through price signals. Firstly, there is the phenomenon of generalized involuntary unemployment and output slack, i.e. the failure of the markets for labour and output to clear at a *macro* level. Macroeconomic policy is needed to maintain the level of aggregate demand at the right level to stabilize the economy.[19] Secondly, the market can fail to take account of the interdependence of investment decisions. Private investment decisions are taken on the basis of *present* prices but these prices may not be appropriate to the post-investment situation because the investments would themselves shift the economic configuration. So today's investment decisions would be optimal only if they were based on *future* equilibrium prices. How can the market generate the right investments for the future when future prices are unknown? This in essence is the argument for the state to step in to resolve coordination failures by means of sectoral or economy-wide planning. But the argument has been much abused (see below).

Does this litany of potential failures clinch the case for pervasive state intervention?[20] Not so, unless we take an idealized view of government as an omniscient, omnipotent, and super-benevolent entity.[21] In principle, there are innumerable 'external effects' and other market failures. But it is absurd to imagine that the state can intervene constructively to offset them all, since 'government failure' is also possible, indeed likely. This is because the government faces many constraints on beneficial action such as its own lack of information, competence, and technical expertise, as well as the unwillingness of citizens to comply with its wishes without extensive and intrusive surveillance.

Consider, for example, the case, sketched out above, for state coordination of interdependent investment decisions. This argument, or an even cruder version of it, was used in the Soviet Union and elsewhere (including India), to justify extensive state direction of the economy on the basis of multi-sectoral planning models that purported to calculate the future optimal path of the economy. The models were logically consistent but absurd nonetheless. Their implied claim that planners have the information to work out the economy's ideal trajectory, and the power to make it happen, was breathtakingly pretentious. Not surprisingly, they led to huge and costly errors. It has become clear that in the real world the investment interdependency argument can, for the most part, only justify 'indicative planning'. (The argument for indicative planning is probably strongest in coordinating investments, public and private, in infrastructure networks.)

The government also suffers from a 'principal-agent problem'. Its functionaries (legislators, bureaucrats) may pursue their own agendas rather than act in the public interest. They may shirk their duties or feather their own nests. They may make deals that benefit special-interest groups at the expense of the general good. State intervention can also cause losses due to 'rent-seeking'. This typically happens when governments intervene by requiring firms to obtain licenses, permits, and monopoly rights for the use of scarce resources. The attempt by firms to capture these privileges, granted by government discretion, diverts resources, entrepreneurial as well as physical, from constructive activities towards competition to secure government largesse, inflicting real economic costs on society in the process.[22] In other words, productive entrepreneurship is displaced by unproductive entrepreneurship, which gives more attractive payoffs.[23] Policy aspirations must evidently take account of these difficulties, and adopt a pragmatic approach to demarcating the economic borders of the state. The unsentimental conclusion has to be that government intervention should be based on a judgement that the realistic benefits from correcting market failure are likely to be greater than the realistic costs of government failure. And the balance between cost and benefit is likely to depend strongly on a country's institutions and culture, and on how they operate on the ground.[24]

The above discussion was concerned with the question: *When* should the state intervene? A second broad question remains: *How* should the state intervene, when there is a *prima facie* case for doing so? It could proceed by replacing the market altogether or by improving market functioning. Nationalization of private enterprises and comprehensive physical controls belong in the first category; taxes, subsidies, and 'regulation' belong in the second. In the post-war heyday of statist thinking in many parts of the world, wholesale replacement of the market was thought of as a good method of organizing the economy. The idea was that state ownership and production would be a simple and straightforward way of simultaneously avoiding market failures as well as pursuing equity and other social goals. Experience has not been kind to this view. One of the main problems turned out to be that public sector enterprises could not control costs or improve product quality. Since managers were given a multiplicity of aims, and were backed by the deep pockets of the state, they lacked the focus on efficiency that characterizes competitive, profit-seeking businesses. The incentive to cut costs, innovate, and respond to consumer preferences was absent or impaired. Efficiency was also compromised by the inevitably close relationship between nationalized industries and the government, which opened the door to political interference, cronyism, and manipulation. It was in recognition of these failings that there arose a wave of privatization in many countries (though it has barely lapped the shores of India).

Though the old nationalization dogma has broken down, it still casts its shadow in the widely held opinion that 'public goods and services' should be produced and delivered by the state, employing state-owned assets. In popular usage, 'public goods' and 'public services' mean goods and services that impinge on the welfare of large numbers of citizens but are likely to be underprovided by the market due to market failures or the existing distribution of purchasing power. (These include 'pure public goods', as defined earlier in this chapter, but also things like education and health care, and physical infrastructure services like transport, power, and communications.) The market may not supply enough 'public goods and services' because it fails to take account of positive external effects, or because of technological reasons such as increasing returns, or simply because the poor cannot afford to pay. Therefore, the argument often goes, such goods should be produced exclusively by the state. But this is a *non sequitur*. There is a crucial distinction to be made between on the one hand the state *paying for goods and services* and on the other hand the state *producing goods and services*.[25] For example, 'food security' may be thought of in common usage as a 'public good'. However, even if it is agreed that the state should pay for food security, it does not follow that the state should carry out the task of actually delivering food to people. The market may do the job of distributing food much more efficiently. The state could enable the poor to buy food in the market, at market prices, by transferring purchasing power to them directly in the form of cash or food vouchers. A system along these lines may be more effective in reaching poor people, and also less corrupt. This example is not chosen at random: it is highly relevant to the problems facing India's public distribution system (PDS) for food delivery.

The point has wide application. The state may pay for 'public goods and services', as popularly defined, for various good reasons, but it may still be cost-efficient to have them produced in the private sector. This may involve a contract between the state and a private entity that specifies what is expected of the latter. Paradoxically, the fact that contracts are necessarily incomplete (since they cannot possibly cover all contingencies) implies that private production is likely to be more cost-efficient than public production. The private entity will want to maximize profits. Since it will own all the profits that remain after fulfilling the requirements imposed by its contract with the state, it will have an incentive to innovate and to cut costs. In contrast, in the public sector, managerial incentives are blunted because all profits belong to the state. This is the rationale behind regulated privatization and the whole range of arrangements that go by the name of 'public-private partnerships'. They are all ways of harnessing the private profit motive for public purposes.

Of course, it does not follow that private production is always superior to public production. In a public-private contract, there is a danger that in the pursuit of profit the private partner will cut costs by reducing quality (particularly if competition is absent or weak and there is no fear of losing customers). To prevent that, the public-private contract would have to specify quality requirements, monitor producer performance, and penalize violations by producers of contract terms. None of this is easy, and it may well be extremely difficult. If quality is non-contractible, the only way to preserve it may be to leave production in the public sector with its soft and low-powered incentives. Another reason for keeping the production of 'public goods and services' in the public sector is that the state may be able to benefit from employing people with a 'public service motivation', who may work for it more cheaply and with greater dedication than they would for the private sector. These theoretical possibilities have to be tested against actual experience. Whether public or private provision is more effective cannot be settled a priori. For example, a plausible candidate for state provision is primary education since 'good education' is not easy to specify in a contract, and it is also possible that state schools may be better able to attract selfless teachers. Whether these abstract points have merit depends on the facts on the ground. The facts may not be supportive. For example, in India, government schools deliver education of very poor quality (see Chapter 9).

Another illuminating way to look at the difference between public and private provision is to think of it in relation to Albert Hirschman's famous distinction between 'exit' and 'voice'.[26] In competitive markets, the threat of customer-exit helps to keep price low and quality high, and induces producers to pay close attention to consumer wants. Since this mechanism is absent under monopolistic public provision, 'voice', i.e. complaints and protests, has to do the job. But the 'voice' channel faces several problems. Firstly, 'voice' generally requires collective action. This is difficult to organize because, from each individual's standpoint, it makes sense to free-ride on the efforts of others. (In other words, inaction is rational.) Secondly, even if 'voice' gets going, the government may or may not hear it and respond. It is not enough that the minister in charge wants to do the right thing. Functionaries on the ground will perform only if their incentives point in the direction of responding to the wishes of the consumers of public services. The implication is that voice and exit may work best in concert, so there is much to be said in favour of introducing competition between public and private providers in the provision of public services.

Thus, the circumstances in which the state should be the exclusive producer of goods and services are much narrower than the ones in which it should pay to ensure their provision. The state must, of necessity, pay for the provision of 'pure public goods' but it may also justifiably pay, wholly or partially, for other public goods and services, commonly so called, on a variety of grounds, such as to overcome external effects or offset an unequal distribution of income. But it should pay for *and* produce public goods, in either of the above categories, only when it is likely to be more efficient than the private sector in production.[27] This could be so when it is impossible or very complicated to contract production out to the private sector, or when contracting would involve the private sector in a very severe conflict between profit maximization and fulfilling the terms of the contract (in which case the profit motive is likely to win).

Are there then goods and services that the public sector, and only the public sector, should *finance as well as produce*, through civil servants and government employees? Yes, certainly. The list would surely include the following items among others: law and order; administration of justice; protection of contracts and property rights; external defence;[28] macroeconomic stability, including financial and banking stability; indicative planning and coordination, where justified; maintenance of competition and other 'rules of the road' for market functioning; administration of taxes and subsidies; income redistribution, including identification of the poor; environmental regulation; and the vast area of regulation of private sector activities, more generally.[29] Note that the above list does not include public goods and services, conventionally so called, such as health care, education, transport, and electricity. In these cases, public finance may be necessary (say, in education and health care, to subsidize the poor because they cannot afford to pay) but exclusive public production is not.[30] And if there is public production, the presumption has to be that it should compete with the private sector on an equal footing.

Let us now suppose that the boundary between the public sector and the private sector, in ownership and production, has been appropriately demarcated. That still leaves many choices about how to intervene in the market, when that is judged to be necessary. Should intervention take the form of taxes and subsidies, or price and quantity regulation? There are no simple answers to this question, only some rules of thumb that receive some support from theory and experience. Firstly, state intervention should be undertaken only in response to a clear market failure, and the bar of evidence should be set high since 'government failure' is also possible.[31] It is quite easy and very common for business and other lobbies to ask for and obtain government subsidies to correct supposed external effects but really to suit their own purposes. Indeed, one of important tasks of the government in many developing countries, including India, is to *remove* dysfunctional taxes, subsidies, and controls that come in the way of efficient market functioning. Secondly, in dealing with market failures, corrective taxes and subsidies that work with and through the market are to be preferred to price or quantity controls. This is because quantitative controls are major barriers to flexibility in the pattern of production and consumption, and are also more likely to lead to rent-seeking and corruption.[32] Thirdly, the state will quite properly wish to intervene to improve the distribution of income. But it should as far as possible avoid doing so by manipulating prices. Relative prices determine resource allocation, which can get thoroughly distorted if prices are set to achieve income-distributional goals. Direct income transfers are generally a much better way of alleviating poverty than price manipulation.

It should be clear to the discerning reader that I do *not* favour a minimal state. The state has to be strong and effective in its proper domain, which is wide and extensive. To deliver on its responsibilities, it needs to possess or acquire competence, honesty, independence, and transparency. Private sector competition can certainly help to improve the quality of government services. But there are many activities, including regulation of the private sector, which can only be carried out by the government or its agencies. This point is of crucial importance: any modern state is inescapably a regulatory state.

Each country has to work out for itself the appropriate balance between the state and the market. A central argument of this book, pursued in some depth in the following chapters, is that India has not yet achieved the right balance. Since the government has a wide range of indispensable core functions that cannot be outsourced, it is also clear that if the government is not up to performing them, reform of the state is essential for the success of economic development. This point too has a close bearing on Indian reality.

NOTES

1. For example, Amartya Sen defines the objective of development as 'expanding the real freedoms that people enjoy'. See the Introduction to Sen (1999).
2. The Expert Group on Green National Accounts (chaired by Partha Dasgupta) has recommended that GDP should be jettisoned as an indicator of economic performance and substituted by measurement of changes in a comprehensive notion of wealth (including natural capital). I am sympathetic to this point of view. But it is an impractical ideal at present since India lacks the data base for such an ambitious project. See Government of India (2013). I therefore stick to the convention of treating growth and environmental sustainability as separate objectives.
3. The defining principle of socialism is state ownership of the means of production, with central planning and control as its mode of operation. But this principle is pressed into the service of egalitarian aims. Social democrats accept the egalitarian aims but not the defining principle of state ownership and central planning.
4. A healthy democratic society also requires thriving civil-society institutions that operate outside the domains of the state and the market but serve to keep them honest. In addition, a strong civil society helps to develop the bonds of trust between citizens that are essential to the working of both the state and the market. The state should do all it can to allow civil society to flourish.
5. The relation between free markets and private ownership of the means of production is not entirely straightforward. It can and has been argued that the two are separable, i.e. that markets can work without private property. It is possible to imagine a 'socialist market economy' in which managers of state enterprises make decisions on the basis of optimal 'shadow' prices provided to them by the central planning authority (see Lange 1936). But this theoretical construct is highly unrealistic. Without the incentive of personal gain, managers are very unlikely to respond to shadow prices in their investment and allocation decisions. The implication is that markets can be expected to function well only in an economy that is largely under private ownership. Of course, 'largely' does not mean 'exclusively' or even 'predominantly'. There can be more or less state ownership of the means of production in an economy that is largely privately owned. Note that a quite separate argument for private property is its connection with individual freedom.
6. This outcome is called 'Pareto efficiency' in the jargon of economics. Pareto efficiency is ensured by the 'invisible hand' of competition, if there are no 'market failures'.
7. See Hayek (1940, 1945). Though better than central planning, the coordinating mechanism of the market is by no means perfect (see below).
8. Moreover, even if planning could somehow mimic a market system, the incentives of managers would not be such as to evoke efficient responses from them (see n. 5 above).
9. China is not a counter-example. Marketization was a major contributor to its rapid rise after 1980.
10. These conditions imply that consumers cannot be charged, so the market would not provide such goods. The temptation to 'free-ride' would defeat any attempt to undertake market provision. For example, national defence could not be provided by the market: no one would be willing to pay for it since, if it were

provided, any person would get the same amount of it as any other person, whether or not she pays for it.

11. Public finance and public production do not have to go together because production could be contracted out to the private sector though the government pays for it (see below).

12. Technical note: External effects may, in principle, be internalized by voluntary bargaining (see Coase 1960) but the feasibility of such internalization depends on the fulfilment of various stringent conditions, such as absence of transactions costs. State intervention to internalize externalities presents its own difficulties, however. For example, it may not easy to determine the rate of tax at which social marginal benefit and social marginal cost would be equated.

13. For example, negative externalities are very important in finance. The social costs of bank failures are much greater than the private costs to the managers of the banks that fail. So the latter would underinvest in the banks' safety from a systemic, social perspective. This constitutes one of the major grounds for financial regulation. An important example of a positive externality is research and development expenditure. As with labour training, firms may underinvest in R&D because they cannot fully capture the benefits, so there may be a case for a state subsidy. Another example of a positive externality is the provision of transport infrastructure. The social return to building a road may be higher than the private return.

14. See Hardin (1968). Sometimes, small communities can organize themselves to prevent a 'tragedy' by specifying the legitimate claimants of the scarce resource, and formulating and enforcing the rules for using it (see Ostrom 1990). When the number of potential claimants is large, this generally proves to be impossible.

15. For example, it would be impossible to define and enforce private property rights to fish in the open sea, not least because fish are mobile!

16. There may also be externality reasons for encouraging or discouraging these goods. But, strictly speaking, goods are 'merit goods' or 'demerit goods' only if the state believes that, in consuming them, individuals make consumption decisions they would later regret or, more generally, are not in their own best interests.

17. The natural monopoly argument needs two further comments. Firstly, the scope of natural monopoly is less wide than is often realized. Thus electricity generation and distribution are not natural monopolies, only transmission is. Railway tracks are a natural monopoly but not railway carriages. Telephone lines are a natural monopoly but not the telephones. Secondly, even a single producer may not have monopoly power if the market is 'contestable', i.e. if potential entry is very easy.

18. One of the seminal articles on this topic is Akerlof (1970).

19. This is the mainstream view, which I share. There is a 'new classical' school of thought which thinks otherwise.

20. Technical note: For the sake of completeness, another complication deserves mention. It is a standard proposition in welfare economics that correcting a market failure fully is not efficient if other market failures exist at the same time. Optimal state intervention then requires taking account of 'second best considerations'.

21. See Buchanan and Tullock (1962).

22. Correspondingly, the ability of a competitive market with free entry to prevent concentration of economic power and restrict rent-seeking activities is one of its major strengths.

23. For the distinction between productive and unproductive entrepreneurship, see Baumol (1990).

24. The Cambridge economist A. C. Pigou is widely credited with pioneering the rigorous analysis of 'external effects', and tax and subsidy policies to offset them. But Pigou was fully aware of the need to balance market failure and government failure: 'It is not sufficient to contrast the imperfect adjustments of unfettered private enterprise with the best adjustment that economists in their studies can imagine. For we cannot expect that any public authority will attain, or will even whole-heartedly seek, that ideal. Such authorities are liable alike to ignorance, to sectional pressure and to personal corruption by private interest. . . . The force of this argument for non-interference by the public authorities is, clearly, not the same at all times and in all places; for any given kind of public authority will vary, alike in efficiency and in sense of public duty, with the general tone of the time' (see Pigou 1920, Part II, Chapter 20.4).

25. See Hart (2003), and Grout and Stevens (2003).

26. See Hirschman (1970).

27. In other words, there are two important distinctions that cut across each other. One distinction is between a) 'pure public goods' and b) 'public goods and services' as popularly understood. Another distinction is between a) goods and services that should be financed and produced exclusively by the state and b) goods and services that should be financed by the state but not produced exclusively by the state. The two distinctions are not co-terminus with each other.

28. Defence via mercenary armies has obvious limitations! A mercenary army would be very difficult to organize and would not be able to call upon the patriotic sentiments of soldiers.

29. This is not a complete list because there cannot be one. Consider, for example, prison services. It has been found that prisons run by private companies may compromise to an undesirable extent on the quality of treatment meted out to prisoners. If so, it is better for prisons to be run by the state. The government may also decide to do some specific things, which it considers to be critically important (e.g. a child nutrition programme), 'in mission mode'. If it means what it says, it may be able to overcome the usual problems with government inefficiency and do better than the private sector. But if there are too many 'missions', the problems will reappear.

30. For example, should road building be thought of as exclusively a government activity? The fact that roads have strong positive externalities may suggest that the answer should be 'yes'. But the fact that government is not good at building roads suggests that the answer should be 'no'. These opposing considerations have to be weighed up.

31. For example, a cogent theoretical argument can be mounted in favour of governmental 'industrial policy' that identifies industries that a) have beneficial knowledge spillovers and/or b) are in line with the country's potential comparative advantage. Whether governments can do so successfully in practice is open to doubt. At the very least, caution is advisable in pursuing this path. For further discussion in the context of India, see Chapter 6.

32. There are some important exceptions to the presumed inferiority of quantitative controls. The information requirements of taxes and subsidies may be

excessively high relative to the importance placed on certainty of outcome. For this reason, price or quantity control is sometimes the right approach to take in financial regulation, regulation of monopolies, and environmental regulation. But the point that quantitative controls are usually undesirable remains true and is well illustrated by the miserable performance of India's 'license raj' in the first three decades after independence.

PART II
The Growth Challenge

CHAPTER 4

Capital Accumulation and Animal Spirits

Why does the growth rate of income matter? Consider where India would be 24 years from now at different rates of growth of income per head. At a growth rate of 3 per cent a year, income per head would *double*, and reach about the same level as China's per capita income today. At a growth rate of 6 per cent a year, income per head would *quadruple* to a level around that enjoyed by Chile, Malaysia, and Poland today. If income per head grew at 9 per cent a year, it would increase nearly *eight-fold*, and India would have a per capita income comparable to the average high-income country of today.[1] The 'power of compound interest' over long periods is such that even a small change in the growth rate of per capita income makes a big difference to eventual income per head. Of course, higher income per head does not automatically translate into widely shared prosperity. All the same, there is a strong empirical connection. This is not surprising since rapid growth not only improves the living standards of ordinary people *directly* through more employment and higher wages but also does so *indirectly* by providing the government with tax revenue that can be used to supplement their incomes.

THE SOURCES OF GROWTH: SIMPLE ANALYTICS AND THE INDIAN CONTEXT

India is not badly placed in terms of the 'deep' background conditions that favour growth. It is not afflicted by rampant macroeconomic instability (recurrent slumps or hyperinflations). It does not have pronounced geographical disadvantages, such as those faced by some landlocked or desert countries.

Though it has internal civil conflicts and occasional external wars, it is not racked or disabled by them. It does not suffer from a cripplingly extractive or authoritarian political or economic system. Indeed its democratic institutions are reckoned to be a source of strength over the long run, whatever their day-to-day inconvenience. If India has a growth problem, it is of its own making.

At a proximate level, growth of income and output needs rising supplies of basic resources ('factors of production') such as labour, physical capital, and human capital (i.e. education and skills), combined with improvements in 'total factor productivity'. Total factor productivity (TFP) is economists' jargon for the overall efficiency with which basic resources are used.[2] But TFP is an ungainly term and I shall often use the word 'productivity' instead; so, 'productivity' and 'total factor productivity' (TFP) are used as synonymous and equivalent throughout this book. (Note that they should not be confused with 'labour productivity', which means output per worker.) How does India measure up on these sources of growth?

Labour

Raw labour is not a constraint on growth in India. Indeed the opposite is closer to the truth: rapid growth of output is necessary to provide decent jobs for the growing labour force. Since a rise in the overall standard of living depends on *growth of output per head*, which can be approximated by *growth of output per worker*, it often makes sense to focus on the latter rather than the former in accounting for the sources of growth. Growth of output per worker, in turn, depends on a) accumulation of physical capital per worker, b) increase in human capital per worker, and c) improvements in TFP per worker. (An important qualification is that the equivalence between growth of output per head and growth of output per worker does not quite hold in India because the country is due to receive a 'demographic bonus': the working-age population is expected to increase faster than the population as a whole for the next three decades. While this 'bonus' lasts, output per head will grow somewhat faster than output per worker.[3] So long as this is kept in mind, growth of output per worker can serve as a proxy for growth of output per head.)

Physical Capital

Capital accumulation depends on how much the nation is willing to save and invest out of current output. In this respect, India has done well. Its people are thrifty and its companies are dynamic, as manifested by the country's impressive saving and investment record over the years, and especially so in the first decade of this century. Since the latter half of the chapter focuses on capital accumulation, further discussion is postponed at this point. Suffice it to say here that despite the shortfalls after 2010, savings and investment are unlikely to hold back India's growth, provided macroeconomic stability is preserved and the returns to saving and investment are restored and maintained at a satisfactory level.

Human Capital

Every country that has had sustained rapid long-run growth has put a major effort into increasing its stock of human capital by education and training. India has made some progress on this front but only at a modest pace. Half of the country's adult population is still illiterate or not educated beyond the primary level. The current level of educational attainment is no higher than China's was in 1980. ('Average years of schooling' of India's labour force is around 4.5 years now, compared with China's 4.8 in 1980 and 7.5 in 2010.) In the coming decades, India will have to raise sharply the proportion of the labour force that has secondary education or better. There is evidence that the private returns to secondary education are high (and social returns even higher) but poverty and credit constraints limit the ability of people to educate their children. Quality of education is as important as its quantity. Unfortunately, the quality of education in India is abysmal at all levels (see Chapter 9).

Total Factor Productivity

'Total factor productivity' (TFP) is the effectiveness or efficiency with which the supplies of factors of production (labour, physical capital, and human capital) are converted into output. Improvements in TFP are a critical ingredient in the growth process. In their absence, growth would slow down sharply because of 'diminishing returns' to the application of capital. TFP has a broad as well as a narrow meaning. In the advanced countries, TFP can be thought of narrowly as technical progress that pushes out the technology frontier. This happens at quite a slow pace, which is why their long-run growth rates of output per head are now rarely above 3 per cent a year. As a developing country, India is much better placed. It has a 'latecomer advantage': it does not have to discover new technologies but can increase productivity by imitating, adopting, and adapting those that already exist. So, there is an enormous potential for 'catch-up' with the advanced countries. Catch-up growth can be much faster than growth that pushes out the technology frontier.

There is more to TFP than 'technology' narrowly construed. In its broad aspect, growth in TFP can come about through all the various ways in which more output can be produced with a given amount of capital and labour. In a developing country, there is huge scope for increases in allocative and managerial efficiency: therefore, if the right policies are adopted to overcome these inefficiencies, TFP can rise very substantially for many years. The relevant point for India is that maintaining a high rate of growth of output per head requires a *rapid and sustained rate of TFP improvement*, not just a once-for-all change. Of course growth of TFP will eventually slow down as India approaches the world technology frontier and the manifold inefficiencies in its economy have been ironed out. But the 'long run' is decades away. Much of what goes by the term 'economic reform' in India has had broad TFP improvement as its object. India moved in a market-oriented direction precisely for this reason, and there is more to do along those lines. But it is as well to remember that economic reform does not mean liberalization, pure and simple. It is about finding the right balance between market provision, state provision, and state regulation. Thus reform of institutions, including the state itself, matters for growth of TFP.

One specific source of 'broad' TFP improvement, which needs to be highlighted, is reallocation of labour between sectors. A defining feature of underdevelopment is the presence of a 'dual economy' in which a large low-labour-productivity traditional sector coexists with a small high-labour-productivity modern sector.[4] This means there is a lot of scope for increasing TFP by shifting labour from the traditional to the modern sector.[5] In other words, labour reallocation can be a major contributor to rapid growth. Unfortunately, in India, this source of TFP improvement remains largely unexploited, which is also a major reason for India's failure to solve its 'employment problem' (see Chapter 5).

GROWTH ACCOUNTING FOR INDIA

Economists have found ways of empirically identifying the contributions of labour, capital, skills, and TFP to growth of output per worker. While the precise decomposition should be taken with several pinches of salt, it does throw light on broad orders of magnitude.[6] We have already seen in Chapter 2 that India's post-independence history can be divided into a slow-growth period followed by a fast-growth period, and that 1980 can be taken to be the approximate year of inflection. Tables 4.1–4.4 summarize the salient features of the change in the growth rate from the pre-1980 period to the post-1980 period, and the sources of the acceleration.[7]

Table 4.1 GROWTH OF OUTPUT, EMPLOYMENT, AND OUTPUT PER WORKER, 1960/1–2011/12 (ANNUAL % RATE OF CHANGE)

	Output	Employment	Output/Worker
1960–1980	3.4	2.2	1.3
1980–2010	6.2	1.5	4.7
2010–2012	5.6	0.8	4.8
1980–1990	5.4	2.0	3.4
1990–2000	5.7	2.2	3.4
2000–2010	7.7	0.3	7.4
2010–2012	5.6	0.8	4.8

Source: Bosworth and Collins (2015).

Table 4.1 shows growth in output, employment, and output per worker (i.e. labour productivity) in the two periods. Tables 4.2 and 4.3 show the contributions made to growth in output per worker by land, capital, human capital (proxied by education), and TFP. Table 4.4 decomposes growth in output per worker differently from Table 4.2 and shows how much of it can be accounted for by growth *within* agriculture, industry, and services on the one hand and shifts of resources *between* the sectors on the other hand.

The following trends can be seen clearly. Firstly, the growth rate of output and output per worker increased substantially after 1980, and dramatically so in the last decade. Secondly, although the acceleration is shared by all the three broad sectors of the economy, it is most pronounced in services.[8] This contrasts with the experience of China and the rest of East Asia where industry (led by exports) was the leading sector. Thirdly, from 1960 to 1980, growth was nearly all due to increases in factor supplies with only a negligible contribution from TFP; after 1980 more than half of growth came from TFP (and three-quarters of the *increase* in growth was due to faster growth of TFP).[9] Note also that TFP grew consistently faster in services than in agriculture and industry. Fourthly, growth of labour productivity, before as well as after 1980, is mainly due to capital accumulation and TFP *within* sectors rather than resource (especially labour) reallocation *between* sectors. This matters because value-added per worker is five to seven times higher in industry and services than in agriculture. This confirms the assertion made above that India has not yet exploited the huge potential gain in shifting labour out of low-productivity farming, unlike China and the rest of East Asia. Fifthly, growth of output and TFP slowed sharply from 2010. The growth accounting data do not extend beyond 2012 but we know from other evidence that the

Table 4.2 SOURCES OF ECONOMIC GROWTH, 1960/1–2011/12
(ANNUAL % RATE OF CHANGE)

	Output/ Worker	Contribution of			
		Capital	Land	Education	TFP
Whole Economy					
1960–1980	1.3	1.0	−0.2	0.2	0.2
1980–2010	4.7	1.7	0.0	0.4	2.5
2010–2012	4.8	2.3	0.1	0.4	1.9
Agriculture					
1960–1980	0.1	0.2	−0.2	0.1	−0.1
1980–2010	2.7	0.8	0.0	0.3	1.5
2010–2012	6.2	2.4	1.3	0.2	2.3
Industry					
1960–1980	1.6	1.8	0.0	0.3	−0.4
1980–2010	3.2	1.7	0.0	0.3	1.1
2010–2012	−2.1	1.7	0.0	−0.1	−3.6
Services					
1960–1980	2.0	1.1	0.0	0.5	0.4
1980–2010	4.6	1.1	0.0	0.4	3.1
2010–2012	3.8	0.2	0.0	0.4	3.2

Source: Bosworth and Collins (2015).

slowdown has continued thereafter (see Table 8.1). (All the numbers in this chapter are from the old 2004/5 series of national accounts. The new 2011/12 series of national accounts does not have any data prior to 2011/12, and there are also doubts about the reliability of the new figures from 2011/12 onwards: see Chapter 8.)

The marked speeding-up of growth in the first decade of the 21st century, and especially the sensational growth in its middle years, fooled many people into thinking that the growth rate had gone up permanently to around 9 per cent a year. And this euphoria was not dented by the global-crisis-induced slowdown in 2008, since growth rebounded to more than 8.5 per cent a year in 2009 and 2010 (see Table 8.1). However, from 2011, growth slowed sharply to around 5 per cent a year, with a large fall in domestic savings and investment (especially corporate investment). It will be argued in Chapter 8 that the five-year boom from 2003 to 2007 was fuelled by excessive debt, and helped by an exceptionally favourable world environment. The sharp slowdown post-2010 was partly cyclical and partly structural, caused by policy mistakes and mismanagement, but also by a decline in the

Table 4.3 SOURCES OF ECONOMIC GROWTH, 1980/1–2009/10
(ANNUAL % RATE OF CHANGE)

	Output/ Worker	Contribution of:			
		Capital	Land	Education	TFP
Whole Economy					
1980–1990	3.4	1.0	–0.1	0.3	2.1
1990–2000	3.4	1.3	–0.1	0.4	1.8
2000–2010	7.4	2.9	0.1	0.6	3.7
Agriculture					
1980–1990	2.2	0.3	–0.1	0.3	1.6
1990–2000	1.7	0.5	–0.2	0.3	1.1
2000–2010	4.2	1.5	0.3	0.5	1.9
Industry					
1980–1990	2.5	1.6	0.0	0.3	0.5
1990–2000	2.2	1.5	0.0	0.4	0.3
2000–2010	4.9	2.0	0.0	0.3	2.6
Services					
1980–1990	3.0	0.0	0.0	0.3	2.6
1990–2000	3.0	0.4	0.0	0.4	2.2
2000–2010	8.0	2.9	0.0	0.5	4.5

Source: Bosworth and Collins (2015).

Table 4.4 DECOMPOSITION OF GROWTH IN OUTPUT PER WORKER, 1960/1–
2009/10 (ANNUAL % RATE OF CHANGE)

	(1)	(2)	(3)
	Whole Economy	Weighted Sectoral Growth	Reallocation Effects (col. 1 – col. 2)
1960–1980	1.3	0.9	0.4
1980–2010	4.7	3.7	1.0

Source: Bosworth and Collins (2015).

pace of economic reform that reduced the potential growth rate. I think it highly unlikely that the underlying potential growth rate is currently much higher than the average for 1980–2010, say around 6.5 per cent a year. India is capable of inclusive growth at a sustained 8–10 per cent a year, but only if there is a second wave of major reforms to boost capital accumulation, education and skills, and TFP.

The rest of this chapter examines capital accumulation in India in greater detail. Other determinants of growth are examined closely in later chapters.[10]

CAPITAL ACCUMULATION, PAST AND FUTURE

India's domestic saving rate has risen substantially over the years, and especially so in the decade 2000–2010, when it peaked at the near–East Asian level of 37 per cent of GDP in 2007 (see Tables 4.5 and 8.4). However, it has fallen sharply to around 30 per cent since then, with an accompanying growth slowdown. Suppose, ambitiously, that India aims to grow at 10 per cent a year. If so, the saving rate will have to rise to around 41 per cent of GDP.[11] How is this to be done? To see what is involved, it is helpful to take a look at the components of the aggregate domestic saving rate, i.e. the savings of households, the corporate sector, and the public sector.

The collapse in the aggregate saving rate after 2007 was driven mainly by a decline in public savings and household financial savings (see Table 8.4). The fall in public savings was steep because the government increased its spending massively in the wake of the global credit crisis of 2008. Although some of this was natural, even desirable, its magnitude and duration were

Table 4.5 GROSS DOMESTIC SAVINGS, 1950/1–2009/10

	% GDP at Market Prices					
	1950s	1960s	1970s	1980s	1990s	2000s
Household	7.1	8.0	11.5	13.2	17.7	23.2
Financial[a]	1.8	2.6	4.4	6.5	9.7	10.8
Physical[b]	5.3	5.4	7.1	6.7	8.0	12.4
Corporate	1.0	1.3	1.5	1.7	3.7	6.3
Public	1.9	3.3	4.3	3.7	1.6	1.3
Government	n.a.	1.3	2.0	1.3	–2.1	–3.0
Public Enterprises	n.a.	2.0	2.3	2.4	3.7	4.3
Gross Domestic Savings	10.2	12.7	17.3	18.6	23.0	30.7
Foreign Savings[c]	1.1	1.9	0.2	1.8	1.3	0.5
Gross Capital Formation[d]	11.3	14.6	17.5	20.4	24.3	31.2

[a] Includes the financial savings of non-corporate business.
[b] Mainly own-account construction by households, which does not pass through financial institutions.
[c] Identically equal to the nation's current account deficit on the balance of payments.
[d] Identically equal to gross domestic savings *plus* foreign savings.
Sources: Government of India (2015a); Government of India, Central Statistics Office (2011); and Government of India, Central Statistics Office (2012, 2013, 2014, 2015, 2016).

excessive and unduly slanted towards government consumption rath
than investment. Raising public savings, therefore, is primarily a matt
of fiscal consolidation, especially eliminating the revenue deficit by cut
ting down subsidies and raising the tax-GDP ratio; and there is plenty of
scope to do this (see Chapter 8). Household financial savings have fallen
sharply from 12 per cent of GDP in 2009 to 7 per cent in 2013. This was
principally the result of high inflation and an over-relaxed monetary policy.
The decline in the real rate of return on saving to negative levels reduced
the incentive to save in the form of financial assets and diverted savings
towards holding gold instead. (This is an example of the close connection
between growth and macroeconomic stability.) Given the expected favourable effects of the demographic transition on savings, it should be possible
to restore a high level of the household saving rate, and then increase it
further, *provided* inflation is maintained at a moderate level of around 5
cent a year and financial sector reform continues to improve the efficiency
of intermediation.

Experience has shown that to avoid capital account crises, the current
account deficit should not average more than about 2 per cent of GDP. It
follows that the latter is also the safe margin by which national investment
can exceed domestic savings: total investment will have to rise to around
43 per cent over the next decade.[12] The current situation is not healthy.
Gross domestic investment peaked at 38 per cent of GDP in 2007. It has
been on a downward trajectory thereafter and now stands at around 32 per
cent (see Tables 4.6 and 8.5). Aggregate investment can be broken down
into public, corporate, and household investment. These three elements
are influenced by somewhat different forces. Public investment depends
on decisions by the government and by public enterprises, and is much less
dependent on 'sentiment' than private investment. Public investment has
fallen since the 1980s, when it averaged over 10 per cent of GDP, to around
7 per cent of GDP, partly due to fiscal compulsions and partly because of
an over-optimistic view of the private sector's ability to undertake infrastructure investment via public-private partnerships. The decline in public
investment, especially in infrastructure, needs to be arrested and reversed.
To do so, raising public savings is obviously critical since the leeway for
extra public borrowing, domestic and external, is strictly limited in view of
India's high fiscal deficits.

Private corporate investment has been the most dynamic element of
capital formation in recent years.[13] Corporate fixed investment was only
3.5 per cent of GDP in the 1980s but rose sharply in the fast growth
decade of 2000–2010, peaking at a spectacular 14 per cent of GDP in
2007. It has nearly halved since then. (It fell to 8.5 per cent of GDP in

Table 4.6 DOMESTIC CAPITAL FORMATION, 1950/1–2009/10

	% GDP at Market Prices					
	1950s	1960s	1970s	1980s	1990s	2000s
Gross Domestic Fixed Capital Formation	10.7	14.1	15.7	20.4	23.1	28.4
Public Sector	4.3	6.9	7.4	10.8	8.6	7.4
Private Sector	6.4	7.2	8.3	9.6	14.5	21.0
Corporate	1.3	2.0	1.6	3.5	6.7	9.0
Household	5.1	5.2	6.7	6.1	7.8	12.0
Change in Stocks	0.9	1.3	2.2	1.7	0.7	1.8
Investment in Valuables[a]	–	–	–	–	–	1.1
Errors and Omissions	–0.3	–0.8	–0.4	–1.7	0.5	–0.1
Gross Domestic Capital Formation	11.3	14.6	17.5	20.4	24.3	31.2

[a] In recent years, 'Valuables', i.e. the purchase of gold and other precious metals, has been identified in the national accounts as an element of capital formation (but it does not constitute productive capital).
Sources: Government of India (2015a); Government of India, Central Statistics Office (2011); and Government of India, Central Statistics Office (2012, 2013, 2014, 2015, 2016).

2012, and is doubtless even lower now.) Various factors were involved, including a more adverse global environment, high fiscal deficits and attendant crowding out, and a rise in the risk premium on investment caused by macroeconomic instability and policy paralysis in government (see Chapter 8). In the future, corporate investment will have to return to playing a vigorous role. 'Confidence' is a vital determinant of growth of business investment. The government will have to maintain a supportive investment climate by preserving fiscal prudence and macro-stability, promoting 'ease of doing business', enabling better infrastructure provision, and pressing ahead with economic reform. These are also the requirements for promoting the third category of investment, viz. investment by households.[14] Obstacles to higher investment are discussed further in Chapter 5.

THE NATURE OF INDIAN CAPITALISM

A high rate of investment is not enough to produce rapid growth of output. Other requisites, such as a fast pace of productivity improvement, are discussed in ensuing chapters. Even so, at this point, it would be convenient to touch on the following question about the process of capital accumulation that is highly relevant for advances in productivity: Does India's corporate sector have the competitive and institutional strengths associated with long-run dynamism?[15]

The vigour of the Indian corporate sector, so long suppressed by the stranglehold of controls, is now manifest to even the most cursory observer. In the wake of the liberalization of the 1980s and 1990s, many new companies, pioneered by outstanding businessmen, sprouted and blossomed, and went on to become market leaders and household names. Examples include Infosys and Wipro in information technology; Flipkart and Snapdeal in e-commerce; Sun Pharma and Dr. Reddy's in pharmaceuticals; Jet Airways and Indigo in civil aviation; Kotak Mahindra and Yes Bank in banking and finance; Zee and Sun Group in media; Bharti in telecommunications; and Vedanta in metals and mining. And though some old business houses declined or vanished, many others such as the Tatas, Ambanis, Mahindras, Bajajs, Jindals, and parts of the Birlas, raised their game and continued to flourish. Moreover, the Indian corporate sector did something that is uncommon in inter-country experience: it played a major part in building the country's infrastructure, on its own or in partnership with the government. Private companies are now prominent in roads, electric power, ports, and airports.

Though the dynamism of the corporate sector is evident to the naked eye, it is as well to check it against more rigorous quantitative tests. These yield some interesting insights.[16] The acceleration of growth from 2003 to 2011 clearly owed much to a remarkable rise in private corporate investment. And the speeding up of overall productivity (see Tables 4.2 and 4.3) shows *prima facie* that the liberalization of the economy that began in the 1990s paid off handsomely in terms of enterprise efficiency. Other obvious indicators such as entry, exit, and profitability tell a similar story. It is clear from the data that liberalization initially induced a substantial amount of entry of new firms, domestic and foreign,[17] and also led to a fall in concentration within industries. Profitability fell quite sharply after domestic liberalization and external opening-up before recovering to pre-liberalization levels, which conforms to the reaction that one would expect from exposure to greater competition. At the same time, other features of the liberalization process have not been quite so healthy. The first is that firm exit and 'shakeout' has been modest. In other words, India has experienced much more of the 'creation' than the 'destruction' part of Schumpeterian 'creative destruction'. Secondly, entry by new stand-alone firms, which had been strong in the 1990s, stalled in the next decade, and concentration rates went up again. Thirdly, although there has been some churning in the list of the top 20 firms, the dominance of incumbent privately-owned 'business houses' in terms of assets, sales, and profits has remained quite solid.[18] There are two possible interpretations of these tendencies.

One interpretation would be that India's corporate sector remains very concentrated but is nevertheless fiercely competitive. (Competition among the few can be as intense as competition among the many.) That many of India's large incumbents have survived and flourished could be put down to their having adapted and restructured, when exposed to internal and external competition. But another interpretation is also possible. This is that India's dominant incumbent firms have survived and made large profits by entrenching their monopoly power and cosying up to the state for special favours.[19] The fall in entry of new firms after 2000 could be cited as evidence; so could the revelation latterly of a large number of corruption scams and scandals in which many corporates have been implicated along with politicians and bureaucrats. It is not possible to discriminate rigorously between these two hypotheses. Very probably, both contain elements of the truth. There is plenty of evidence that India has a vigorous and dynamic entrepreneurial class that possesses the 'animal spirits' that are required to make risky investments in search of profits. But history all over the world shows that entrepreneurship can be directed to productive or unproductive uses depending on the context.[20] If the rewards are greater in unproductive rent-seeking than in productive activities, then that is where business energy will go.[21] There is no doubt that liberalization in India has very been successful in channelling the energy of firms into innovative and productive uses.[22] However, there is also evidence, especially in the recent past, that India's corporate sector is vulnerable to rent-seeking and unproductive entrepreneurship, a disease that could arrest the growth of productivity in the long run. The lesson is that while the state must redouble its efforts to liberalize, it must at the same time safeguard competition and restrain corruption and crony capitalism (see Chapter 11).

Another source of disquiet about dominant firms in India's private sector is that so many of them are 'business houses', i.e. conglomerates that are controlled by 'promoter' families and family trusts. It has been claimed, quite rightly, that the prevalence of conglomerates is not surprising, given the weakness of the state: it makes sense to do things in-house and in vertically integrated operations since the infrastructure is poor, the legal system is slow at contract-enforcement etc.[23] But is promoter/family control a healthy phenomenon? So far, overall, business houses have stood up to competitive challenges admirably. But family-controlled firms have well-known problems such as loss of efficiency over time due to an inability to prevent management falling into the hands of incompetent offspring. In the long run, the structure of corporate ownership in India will surely have to move in the direction of professionally managed, and widely-held firms, owned by diffuse institutional shareholders.[24]

NOTES

1. These calculations are based on measurements of cross-country per capita incomes at purchasing power parity (see Chapter 1).
2. Here, I ignore land as a factor of production. However, it is included in the empirical estimates of the sources of growth reported below.
3. This is true as a matter of arithmetic provided the labour force participation rate does not fall and the unemployment rate does not increase. But the demographic transition also has favourable effects on growth for more substantive reasons such as its positive effect on the rate of saving in the economy. Note, however, that the demographic 'bonus' will be reaped only if the growing labour force is productively employed (see below). The demographic bonus is examined more closely in Chapter 5.
4. Technical note: More accurately, the marginal productivity of labour is much larger in the modern sector because it has within it more capital and skills per worker, as well as higher TFP per worker, than the traditional sector does.
5. This increase is over and above any increase in labour productivity via capital accumulation or growth of TFP *within* the traditional and modern sectors.
6. Technical note: One of the problems with the standard method of identifying sources of growth is that it fails to recognize the interdependence of capital accumulation and TFP. The reason for the interdependence is that investment is generally embodied in better machines, not just more machines. As a result, the contribution of capital may be understated. There is no satisfactory solution to this problem. But it would also be wrong to attribute the whole or most of the contribution of TFP to capital because, as we have seen, TFP improvements can originate from a wide variety of sources, not just from 'more machines' and 'better machines'.
7. Tables 4.1–4.4 come from Bosworth and Collins (2015); see also Bosworth, Collins, and Virmani (2007). These articles contain a description of the 'sources-of-growth' methodology and its underlying assumptions. They also comment extensively on the sources and the quality of Indian data.
8. In particular, 'modern services' (communications, banking and insurance, business services, and education/medicine) grew at double-digit rates from 1980 to 2010. In the 2000s, they contributed more to overall growth than manufacturing. See Bosworth and Collins (2015).
9. Note, however, that physical capital accumulation also made a substantially bigger contribution in 2000–2010 than in the previous two decades.
10. Chapter 5 focuses on the growth contribution of labour, and the associated 'employment problem' in India. TFP improvement is the subject of Chapters 6 and 7 but it also figures strongly in Chapter 5 because, as discussed above, the allocation of labour is a critical determinant of TFP growth. Human capital accumulation is considered in Chapter 9, and institutions and governance in Chapter 11.
11. This is based on a crude calculation that takes a target growth rate of 10 per cent and multiplies that by a capital output ratio of 4.3. (4.3 was the capital output ratio in the decade 2000–2010.) That gives an investment rate of 43 per cent of GDP. Subtraction of a 'safe' level of foreign savings of say 2 per cent of GDP yields 41 per cent of GDP as the required domestic savings ratio.

12. Net foreign capital inflows would have to be higher than 2 per cent of GDP per year, say 4–5 per cent of GDP, to enable accumulation of a rising level of foreign exchange reserves.

13. Since public investment was contracting as a share of GDP, it is clear that the whole of the large rise in the aggregate investment ratio can be attributed to the private sector (corporate and household).

14. Note that 'household investment' includes investment by unincorporated enterprises that are mostly quite small. The investment constraints they face are discussed in Chapter 5.

15. In this section of the chapter, as in previous sections, the corporate sector is mostly taken to mean the *private* corporate sector. State-owned enterprises are extensively discussed in Chapter 7.

16. Empirical backing for the assertions made in this paragraph and the next can be found in Alfaro and Chari (2010) and Mody, Nath, and Walton (2011).

17. Notable examples of high-entry industries were consumer goods, automobiles, telecom, airlines, information technology, health care, and pharmaceuticals.

18. Incumbent business houses include well-known names such as Tatas, Birlas, and Reliance. From 1989 to 2008, the share of business houses in total sales of firms quoted on the Bombay Stock Exchange rose slightly from 41 per cent to 42 per cent. New stand-alone Indian firms increased their share from 4 per cent to 12 per cent, largely at the expense of state-owned and foreign firms. The shares of state-owned firms and foreign (including NRI) firms fell from 45 per cent and 10 per cent to 37 per cent and 8 per cent respectively. These numbers are from Mody, Nath, and Walton (2011), Table 1.

19. This is particularly so in 'rent-thick' sectors such as cement, real estate, infrastructure, construction, mining, telecom, and media. See Gandhi and Walton (2012) and Sen and Kar (2014). As T. N. Ninan has pointed out: 'It is not an accident that some of the more influential business families have focused on industries and sectors where the business-government interface is important— the terms of a mining lease, a highway franchise or a power purchase contract— or where heavy capital investment gets financed by government-owned banks, with the terms of the loan often structured midway. They have mostly kept away from technology-based sectors and branded consumer goods, where the marketplace usually offers a level playing field and where the rules are clearer' (see Ninan 2015, Chapter 5).

20. For the distinction between productive and unproductive entrepreneurship, see Chapter 3.

21. Not all rents are bad. Schumpeterian rents that arise out of innovation perform a productive role. Rents created by scarce government licenses are, in general, socially harmful.

22. In the Indian corporate sector, there is a robust correlation between improved profitability and larger market share (see Mody, Nath, and Walton 2011). Since this holds for both large and small companies separately, the causality is unlikely to be from larger market share to greater profitability.

23. See The Economist (2011).

24. Infosys and ITC are examples of companies with modern corporate institutional ownership and governance structures. Other problems connected with promoter-controlled business houses, such as disregard of the rights of minority shareholders, are usefully discussed in Ram Mohan (2014).

CHAPTER 5

Growth and the Employment Problem

Despite three decades of rapid growth, the employment situation in India remains alarming. A small minority of workers, mostly in the organized modern sector, have 'good' jobs in which wages and labour productivity are relatively high, and the work environment is fairly decent. The vast majority of workers are crammed into the 'unorganized sector' doing low-productivity work, with earnings that are paltry, and working conditions that are dire.[1] The future of employment looks even worse, because the labour force is expected to grow rapidly. Around a million new job-seekers will enter the labour force *every month* for the next three decades. As things stand, India is well on the way to perpetuating a two-tier economy.

This chapter argues that a more labour-demanding strategy of development could deliver faster growth that is also more inclusive. While a range of complementary measures will be required to encourage greater labour-use, one essential reform is likely to prove politically difficult. This is to make labour laws in the organized sector less rigid, less protective of the insiders in the organized labour market, and more open to the outsiders in the unorganized economy who stand and wait.

THE EMPLOYMENT PROBLEM

India has an 'employment problem' but it is nothing like what goes by that name in the advanced countries. To a Western audience, the phrase is likely to evoke images of open unemployment and dole queues. This would be misleading in the Indian setting. Poverty and the lack of a social security system see to it that most people have to scratch a living somehow, simply in order to survive. There are some openly unemployed people to be sure, including educated youth who can be supported by their families. The latter constituency is important because it is politically salient but a bigger problem by far is the prevalence of low-productivity employment in the enormous 'unorganised' sector of the economy. This can take the form of 'underemployment', in other words, too many people sharing work that could be done by fewer hands working a normal day at normal intensity.[2] But it can also manifest itself in people toiling long and hard for little return. Either way, it is reflected in low earnings.

We must be careful here. Is labour's low productivity not simply a manifestation of a shortage of complementary resources such as machines and equipment? This is certainly part of the overall picture. But there is more to it because there is another sector of the economy, viz. the 'organised sector', which provides 'good jobs' with more and better complementary resources, substantially higher labour productivity, and consequently much better pay. Strictly speaking, India has an 'employment problem' only in the sense that the workforce is *mal-distributed*: employment in the high-labour-productivity 'organised sector' is growing too slowly, and at the same time too much labour continues to be bottled up in the low-labour-productivity 'unorganised sector'. It is quite natural to describe the low demand for labour in the organized sector as constituting an 'employment problem'. However, it is a misnomer, strictly speaking, to use the same phrase to describe the low level of labour productivity and earnings in the unorganized sector. More accurately, the latter is a 'poverty problem', or a 'problem of underdevelopment' associated with a shortage of physical and human capital, and technology. Of course, I cannot legislate how people should employ words; and the use of the term 'employment problem' to cover both *low demand for labour in the organized sector* as well as *low quality of work in the unorganised sector* is probably here to stay. But it helps to keep the distinction in mind.

The dichotomy between the 'organized' and the 'unorganized' sectors, which corresponds roughly to the difference between the modern and the traditional parts of the economy, is fundamental to an understanding of the Indian employment situation. In the organized sector, labour productivity is high, and workers are likely to be unionized and receive various social security benefits; in the unorganized sector, productivity is much lower and workers are, on the whole, unprotected against shocks. For analytical and statistical purposes, the organized sector can be taken to cover the whole of the public sector *plus* private sector enterprises that employ more than 10 workers.[3] On this basis, in 2009/10, 84 per cent of the workforce was in the unorganized sector and 16 per cent in the organized (see Table 5.1). Note that even within the organized sector, only 'formal' workers receive the full range of social security benefits; 'informal' workers, such as contract workers, may or may not receive them and their employment can be much more easily terminated.[4] Even so, informal workers in the organized sector are considerably better paid on average than workers in the unorganized sector. Formal workers in the organized sector constituted only 7 per cent of the total workforce in 2010 (see Table 5.1).[5] The unorganized sector includes nearly the whole of agriculture; but it also includes a large amount of industrial and service activity. National output in 2005 was produced roughly 50:50 in the organized and unorganized sectors.[6] The share of the unorganized sector in non-farm output is a bit lower but significant nonetheless: around 30 per cent in industry and 45 per cent in services. When we come to employment, however, the unorganized sector dominates: almost all agricultural workers and 70 per cent of non-farm workers are crowded into it.[7] Put another way, the organized sector contains only 30 per cent of the non-farm workforce (and more than half of that consists of informal labour such as contract workers).

It is nearly an iron law that agriculture's share of national product contracts substantially in the course of economic development, and India has followed this general pattern (see Table 5.2). From 1950 to 1980 the share of agriculture in GDP fell from 55 per cent to 36 per cent; in the higher-growth period from 1980, it fell more sharply to 14 per cent by 2013. Until 1980, the space vacated by agriculture was occupied by industry and services equally, and since then largely by services alone. (Industry and services grew

Table 5.1 EMPLOYMENT IN THE ORGANISED AND UNORGANISED SECTORS, MILLIONS OF PERSONS (% OF TOTAL EMPLOYMENT IN BRACKETS)

Sectors	Employment		
	1999/2000		
	Informal	Formal	Total
Unorganised	341.3 (86.0)	1.4 (0.3)	342.6 (86.3)
Organised	20.5 (5.2)	33.7 (8.5)	54.1 (13.7)
Total	361.7 (91.2)	35.0 (8.8)	396.8 (100.0)
	2009/10		
Unorganised	385.1 (83.7)	2.3 (0.5)	387.3 (84.2)
Organised	42.1 (9.2)	30.7 (6.7)	72.9 (15.8)
Total	427.2 (92.8)	33.0 (7.2)	460.2 (100.0)

Sources: Table 22.5 in Planning Commission (2013), and National Commission for Enterprises in the Unorganized Sector (NCEUS) (2009).

faster than agriculture until 1980. Since then, services have been growing much faster than both agriculture and industry.) In the latter respect, India is rather distinctive; for example, during its early development, East Asia's growth pattern was industry-oriented. The position of manufacturing, a sub-sector of industry, presents a particularly striking contrast. In India, the share of manufacturing in GDP has increased very little since 1960, and has stayed nearly flat at around 15 per cent since 1980; in many East Asian countries, at comparable stages of their development, it was twice that level or even higher. Be that as it may, India has followed the historical norm as far as the shrinkage of agriculture's share of GDP is concerned.[8]

What about employment? India's relative contraction of agriculture in terms of output has not been matched by parallel changes in employment (see Table 5.2). In the first three decades after independence, the share of agriculture in total employment changed very little. Since then, it has fallen relatively modestly, from 68 per cent in 1983 to 49 per cent in 2011. The corresponding rise has been overwhelmingly in services and construction, not manufacturing; the share of manufacturing in total employment has been virtually constant at around 11 per cent. (The contrast with East Asia is again very stark. For example, in South Korea, the share of employment

Table 5.2 SHARES OF SECTORS IN OUTPUT AND EMPLOYMENT

	Output			Employment		
	1980/ 1981	1999/ 2000	2011/ 2012	1983	1999/ 2000	2011/ 2012
Agriculture	35.7	23.2	14.4 (18.4)	68.4	59.9	48.9
Industry	25.7	26.9	28.2 (33.1)	15.6	17.4	24.2
o/w Manufacturing	14.0	15.1	16.3 (18.1)	11.2	12.2	12.6
o/w Construction	7.6	6.5	7.9 (9.5)	2.2	4.4	10.6
Services	38.6	49.9	57.4 (48.5)	17.2	24.7	26.9

Notes: Output figures are at 2004/5 prices from the 2004/5 series of national accounts, except for the figures in brackets, which are at 2011/12 prices from the 2011/12 series of national accounts. Agriculture includes forestry and fishing. Industry includes mining; manufacturing; electricity, gas and water supply; and construction. Services includes trade, hotels and restaurants; transport, storage and communication; finance, insurance, real estate and business services; and community, social, and personal services.
Sources: Output figures from Government of India, Central Statistics Office (2011), and Government of India, Central Statistics Office (2014, 2015, 2016). Employment figures for 1983 and 1999/2000 from surveys of employment conducted by the National Sample Survey Office, in the 38th Round (1983) and the 50th Round (1999/2000). Employment figures for 2011/12 from National Sample Survey Office (2014).

in agriculture fell by 50 percentage points from 1960 to 1990 and went equally into manufacturing and services.)

What do these numbers imply? Since agriculture's share of output has fallen more than twice as much as its share in employment, it follows that the labour-productivity gap between agriculture and the rest of the economy, large to begin with, has increased further. In the early 1980s, output per worker in industry was three times higher than in agriculture, and in services it was four times higher. By 2011, the former multiple had risen to four times and the latter to seven times. This implies that there is a large potential gain to be reaped by a shift of labour from agriculture to industry and services. Huge labour-productivity differences exist not only between agriculture and non-agriculture but within industry and services as well. In industry, the unorganized sector produces around 30 per cent of output but employs 87 per cent of workers. Labour productivity in organized industry is six times that in unorganized industry. The unorganized sector in services produces around 55 per cent of output and employs 85 per cent of workers; labour productivity in organized services is three times that in unorganized services.[9]

The battery of numbers in the preceding paragraphs is intended to drive home a simple but crucial message: labour is India's most abundant resource but the organised sector, which should be the engine for creating good jobs, has been heavily biased against using it. And if ratios and proportions do not give a feel for what has been happening over time, consider the following eye-watering absolute numbers. In the 10 years from 1999/2000 to 2009/10, India's total workforce increased by 63 million. Of these, 44 million joined the unorganized sector, 22 million became informal workers in the organized sector, and the number of formal workers in the organized sector fell by 3 million.[10]

THE BIAS AGAINST USING LABOUR

Two glaring manifestations of the bias against labour are worth noting, both of which represent missed opportunities for growth and decent jobs. Firstly, over time, the pattern of production in organized industry has moved sharply towards capital- and skill-intensive sectors, such as chemicals, metals, electrical machinery, petroleum refining, automobiles, and engineering products, and away from labour-intensive sectors such as food products, textiles and apparel, leather, wood, furniture, and bicycles.[11] The same thing has happened in exports. Export composition has moved in favour of goods that intensively use capital and skilled labour such as engineering goods, chemicals, petroleum products, and gems and jewellery; the share of labour-intensive goods such as garments has fallen. This contrasts sharply with the erstwhile experience of the fast-growing countries of East Asia. They achieved rapid growth of output and decent jobs on the back of industrial expansion powered by exports of labour-intensive manufactured goods. This created a virtuous circle. Profitable exports spurred firms to invest more in such activities. The resulting demand for labour enabled the shift of surplus labour from agriculture and the unorganized sector to organized industry; and, in addition, the rising incomes of the new recruits to the industrial sector boosted the national savings required to finance investment. This was the road followed first by the 'Gang of Four' (Hong Kong, Taiwan, Singapore, South Korea), and later by China. (For example, China's export share in world markets for clothing and footwear rose from 1.3 per cent in 1980 to an astonishing 37.6 per cent in 2007. During the same period, India's share went up from 1.4 per cent to 3.2 per cent.) The lack of a vigorous labour-intensive sector has also meant that India, unlike China, has not been integrated into supply chains in global manufacturing. (In other words, India is a successful recipient of cross-border outsourcing in skill-intensive services but not in labour-intensive manufacturing.) But labour costs are now rising sharply in China. Though it would not be easy, India does have an opportunity to make inroads into world markets for labour-intensive goods (just as China once took over from the Gang of Four), if it takes steps to eliminate the bias against labour use.[12] Moreover, the export market is not the only destination for labour-intensive goods; there is also the potentially huge domestic market. The point I am making here is not that India should abandon producing capital- and skill-intensive goods. There is no reason why these activities should not continue to grow fast, provided they are efficient and internationally competitive, as many now are. But India could have *extra* growth by expanding production of labour-intensive goods in the organised sector.

What about services? They have certainly grown faster than industry. Some observers have lamented this on the ground that in the long run industry is more 'dynamic'. This old-style view has been overtaken by technical change. Services are now much more transportable and tradable than ever before and as capable of rapid improvements in productivity.[13] Much more relevant is the worry that the fast-growing service sectors (computer services, telecommunications, finance, and banking), which are mostly in the organized sector, make little use of low-skilled labour. A case in point is the information technology (IT) sector. It has become a byword for India's renaissance but it does not make much of a contribution to solving the employment problem. The output of the sector is about 2.5 per cent of

GDP. Employment in the sector went up by about 1.5 million in the last decade. An optimistic forecast would be that it will add another 1.5 million to employment in the present decade. But that number pales into insignificance compared with the forthcoming additions to the labour force, which run into tens of millions, over the same period.[14] In any case, the sector mostly employs skilled labour. It is not the answer to the employment needs of millions of low-skilled people with only primary and secondary education. They require industrial blue-collar work, with most training received on the job.

The second manifestation of the bias against labour is the highly peculiar employment-size-distribution of India's business enterprises. The economy has an inordinate number of tiny firms with very low productivity. The following data refer to 2005.[15] In manufacturing there were around 50 million workers. They worked in no less than 17 million enterprises. But 99.3 per cent of these were 'micro' enterprises (nine or fewer workers); and 99.8 per cent were 'small' (49 or fewer workers). The small firms (49 or fewer workers) employed 84 per cent of all workers in manufacturing; only 5.5 per cent were employed in medium-sized firms (50–199 workers), and only 10.5 per cent in large firms (200+ workers).[16] This extraordinary size-distribution of firms with a 'missing middle' is very different from what is found in East Asia (see Table 5.3), where the distribution is much more evenly spread (or increases with firm-size as in China).[17] The same story is repeated in services. In 2005, there were somewhat more than 100 million workers in services, employed in 16.5 million firms, of which 99.96 per cent were small (49 or fewer workers). The concentration of employment in small firms was even greater than in manufacturing: 96 per cent of workers were employed in small enterprises.

Table 5.3 SHARES OF MANUFACTURING EMPLOYMENT BY FIRM-SIZE IN INDIA AND SELECTED EAST ASIAN ECONOMIES, 2005 (PER CENT)

	Micro + Small	Medium	Large
	(1–49 workers)	(50–199 workers)	(200+ workers)
India	84.0	5.5	10.5
South Korea	46.5	23.9	29.6
Taiwan	38.9	21.3	39.8
Malaysia	27.5	19.7	52.8
China	24.8	23.3	51.8

Source: Asian Development Bank (2009).

The ultra-skewed distribution of firm size is significant because there is a close positive relation between firm size, labour productivity, and wages. For example, in the manufacturing sector in 2005, value-added per worker and wages per worker in large companies (200+ employees) were four to eight times the levels in the smallest organized sector firms (10–19 employees) and 10 to 20 times the levels in the smallest unorganized sector firms (one to four workers); and a very similar situation prevails in services.[18] None of this is surprising since the larger firms have higher capital per worker (as well as higher TFP due to scale economies) but it does strongly suggest that growth has been held back by the inefficiently high proportion of workers working in minuscule firms. Exports of labour-intensive mass consumer goods such as shoes, toys, and garments require production in factories that employ large numbers of people. There are many examples of this in China. In India, one of the obstacles to the formation of such companies was the reservation of hundreds of labour-intensive products for exclusive production by small firms. Small-scale industry reservations have been drastically pruned in recent years. But many obstacles to the growth of labour-intensive activities still remain, including strong disincentives to the use of low-skilled labour in both manufacturing and services.[19]

DEMOGRAPHIC TRANSITION: DIVIDEND OR DISASTER?

The employment scenario described above is distinctly unattractive but it promises to become even more so in future. To make the point, some explanation is necessary of the 'demographic transition' that India is going through. The 'transition' arises from the fact that mortality and fertility rates in the population do not change at the same pace. When economic development begins, child mortality rates fall rapidly in response to improvements in public health. Women's fertility rates fall too, but much more slowly, induced by the fall in child mortality (since fewer children are needed to achieve a desired family size), and by female education and birth-control policies. As a result, a 'baby boom' is created, which then works its way over time through the age-distribution of the population. As the larger young cohorts mature into adulthood, the share of people of working age in the population rises; and the share of 'dependents' (the old and the young) in the population falls. India entered this phase around 1980 but the change has now speeded up. According to UN figures, the share of working-age groups in India's population will rise from about 60 per cent in 2010 to peak at around 70 per cent in 2040, which implies a huge increase in the size of the potential labour force. Of course the actual increase in the labour force will depend on the 'labour force participation rate' (LFPR), i.e. on how many of the working-age people want to work. The chief joker in the pack is the 'female labour force participation rate' (FLFPR). This denotes the proportion of women of working age who want to work outside the home (note that 'domestic duties' do not count as 'work'). In India, the FLFPR is exceptionally low, around 30 per cent, less than half that of China. What will happen to it in the coming decades is not certain but if India follows the normal pattern in other countries, it will rise substantially.[20]

There is evidence that demographic transitions can deliver a growth 'bonus' or 'dividend'. Only to a small extent is this due to the availability of a larger proportion of the population for doing productive work. More important is the fact that working ages correspond to years of high saving, so the national rate of saving goes up. And since proportionately less has to be spent on feeding dependents, more is available for growth-promoting investment. Some estimates suggest that demography was responsible for one percentage point of East Asia's rapid growth. In India too, there is doubtless a potential gain to be garnered. But the 'bonus' will not fall like manna from heaven: the putatively marvellous effects on work effort, savings, and investment that are associated with the demographic transition are conditional on the influx of new workers finding productive employment, i.e. employment in which labour productivity is high.

The increase in India's labour force could average anywhere between 8 million and 12 million a year for the next 30 years.[21] On favourable assumptions, this large addition to the supply of labour could boost growth. In India's prevailing conditions, however, it may simply add more workers to the existing backlog of people in the unorganized sector with low-quality jobs. This brings me back from my brief demographic detour to the main theme of this chapter.

WHY SMALL FIRMS DON'T GROW

The organised sector, which is the location of most good jobs, employs too few people. Why should that be so? It could be because firms in the sector, particularly those that are small in size, do not grow larger and expand their operations. (It is important to note that even within the organized sector, there is a very large number of small firms. In 2005, the median firm in the organized sector employed only 20 workers.)[22] But it could also be because whether or not firms expand, they shy away from labour-intensive products and techniques of production. In India, both the reasons have force. This section addresses the first reason; the next section considers the second.

One way to find out why firms don't grow is to ask employers. Between 2000 and 2010, the World Bank conducted surveys of several thousand firms in the organized and unorganized sectors in India. In the organized sector, the 'benchmark firm' was an urban manufacturing firm of medium size (30 workers) that had not increased employment for three years (but non-benchmark firms were also surveyed). Each firm was asked the question: 'How much of an obstacle is item X to the operation and growth of your business'?[23] The top five reported constraints (other than access to finance, and tax rates) were electricity, corruption, tax administration, labour regulations, and 'inadequately educated labour'.[24] Deficient transport facilities, prevalence of crime, and lack of access to land were also important, especially in low-income states. Electricity figured very strongly everywhere: unreliable power supply dislocated production and forced firms to generate their own expensive electricity. (An astonishing 40 per cent of firms generated their own power.) Corruption was another constraint that received strong emphasis in all states. This involved direct costs in terms of bribes, especially in securing construction permits, operating licenses, and electricity connections, and in keeping tax inspectors sweet; there were also indirect costs in terms of time spent by managers in dealing with officials and inspectors. Interestingly, non-benchmark firms that had expanded jobs reported the same constraints (the only difference was that they put corruption ahead of electricity) but judged them to be of even greater severity.

One limitation of these surveys is that they do not identify all the constraints facing *potential entrants*. For this, the World Bank's 'Ease of Doing Business' reports are more useful. These are based on cross-country measures of business regulations, particularly as they apply to small and medium-sized enterprises, in ten areas: i) starting a business; ii) getting construction permits; iii) getting electricity; iv) registering property; v) getting credit; vi) protecting investors; vii) paying taxes; viii) trading across borders; ix) enforcing contracts; x) resolving insolvencies. The source of the data is informed judgements by local experts. Of course the coverage is narrow. (For example, no questions are asked about infrastructure other than electricity. And even within electricity, the questions relate mainly to getting a connection, not to reliability of supply.) Even so, the data are revealing. India's overall rank in the 2014 'Doing Business' report was 134 out of 189 countries, a slight demotion from the year before.[25] In some of the individual areas, including the first four items in the above list, which are clearly relevant to start-up firms, India's performance was even worse.

'Starting a business' involved 12 procedures, took 27 days, and India's rank was 179. 'Getting a construction permit' took 35 procedures and 168 days, and India's rank was 182. Getting electricity took 67 days, and India's rank was 111. 'Registering a property' took 44 days, and India's rank was 92. The same goes for some of the other items, for example, 'enforcing contracts' (rank 186) and 'resolving insolvency' (rank 121). Moreover, most of the above operations were very expensive (in relation to per capita income) compared with other countries. Very similar results come out of surveys conducted by other domestic and foreign bodies. For example, the CII/KPMG survey in 2014 recorded huge obstacles in 'starting a business' (especially getting approvals related to environmental clearances, land acquisition, construction permits, industrial safety permits, and power connections) and in 'contract enforcement'.[26] India also scores very low in the OECD 'product market regulation index', in particular for 'barriers to entrepreneurship' that take the form of administrative burdens involved in getting various permissions.[27]

These surveys and reports confirm what is obvious on the basis of casual observation: India does not offer an enabling environment for enterprises to enter the market and grow. The number of permits and no-objection certificates required, the delays in getting tax refunds, the large variety of inspectors who have to be faced (and paid off), the huge problems in land access and conversion, the enormous difficulties in securing essential services such as water, sewerage, and electricity, conspire to deter many incipient entrepreneurs. For years, there have been suggestions that there should be 'one-stop shop' clearance windows and other devices to make the bureaucratic wheels turn faster. But the pace of progress has been glacial.[28] Not all the blame can be laid at the door of onerous regulations, however. Problems with infrastructure, especially electricity and transport, also arise from more fundamental causes (see Chapter 7).

I now consider access to finance, which did not figure in the World Bank surveys. There is plenty of evidence that it is a major constraint for small enterprises.[29] Small firms often cannot provide collateral and banks do not find lending to them attractive for this reason, and because of the fixed costs involved. While there is certainly a market failure here, it is not obvious what to do about it. Blanket interest rate subsidies for small firms would be a bad idea. They are likely to be a waste of money since they do not get over the basic problem of identifying creditworthy borrowers and profitable projects. Availability of credit is a prime issue. If credit were available, a good project should be able to cover the true cost of lending. 'Directed credit' in India makes credit available but has a bad track record because it too does not solve the problem of identification. New financial institutions, including non-banking companies, have to be developed, and existing ones encouraged, which have the local knowledge to get over the collateral problem and identify creditworthy entrepreneurs and investments. The credit they provide would be costlier (interest rates around 2 per cent per month) than subsidized 'institutional credit' but it would be more easily available. Improvements in the credit infrastructure are also necessary. Creditor rights have to be strengthened to make lenders more comfortable with small-firm lending. Credit registries have to be developed to improve information about small borrowers. Commercial banks' methods of reaching small firms have to be improved, and that includes changing the incentives of their personnel.[30] The Reserve Bank of India is finally on the right track on these vital issues but there is a long way to go (see Chapter 6).

What about firms in the unorganized sector (which, by definition have fewer than 10 workers)? Do they provide a source of growth in productive employment? This is not on the whole a plausible scenario. Two-thirds of the firms in the unorganized sector are 'own account enterprises' without any hired worker, and are mostly hyper-unproductive. The vast majority of their owners are not 'capitalists in waiting' but people who would gladly switch into decent employment if it were available.[31] Another 15 per cent of firms employ less than six workers each; they too are highly unproductive. Even so, constraints to the growth of unorganized sector firms should certainly be removed (because there would be some firms which could make it to success). The World Bank surveys of firms described above did cover the unorganized sector (rural non-farm and urban separately). In rural non-farm enterprises, electricity and transport were identified as the principal constraints; in urban firms, electricity and land were. But there is also a lot of informal evidence that access to credit is a severe constraint. The remarks on this subject made above apply here too, with even greater force.

As noted earlier, the fundamental problem in the unorganized sector is low labour productivity. Rapid, labour-demanding growth in the organized sector is critical because it enables the movement of labour to more productive jobs, and provides demand for the products of the unorganized sector, directly as well as indirectly (via sub-contracting and out-sourcing). Even so, the number of workers in the unorganized sector will remain very large for many years. So policies that *directly* increase labour productivity would clearly be desirable. There is no simple or quick way to do this. Obstacles (listed above) to small and micro business should certainly be eradicated. Policies to boost agricultural productivity are hugely relevant. So is human capital formation via better nutrition, sanitation, education, skills acquisition, and health care. Social protection policies matter as well, beyond their purely redistributive role, because a safety-net against shocks increases the room for manoeuvre in taking small business risks. All this amounts to repeating that the 'employment problem' in the unorganized sector is a misnomer. The problem is one of poverty and low productivity whose solution depends on the entire development and reform agenda.

LABOUR MARKET AND LABOUR LAWS

While problems with 'ease of doing business' affect employment by imped-ing the growth of firms, they do not explain why medium and large Indian companies have shied away specifically from labour-intensive products and techniques. This feature of Indian growth can only be understood by focussing on the labour market.[32] This is characterised by excess supply of low-skilled labour and excess demand for skilled labour, of which one indication is the rapid rise in the skilled-unskilled wage-differential. (For example, the wage premium on tertiary education more than doubled between 2000 and 2010 despite an increase in the share of people with tertiary education in the labour force from 1 per cent to 8 per cent.) It stands to reason that the remedy has to be to increase the demand for low-skilled labour and the supply of skilled labour. Ameliorating skill shortages involves increasing the coverage and quality of secondary, tertiary, and vocational education, and on-the-job training. The asso-ciated problems are discussed in Chapter 9 but one important point is relevant here: raising the educational and skill level of the population takes decades. In 2030, even on very optimistic assumptions, a third of the labour force will have only completed primary education or less, and half of it will have completed only lower secondary education or less.[33] So raising the demand for low-skilled labour is a necessity, if unpleasant, even explosive, outcomes are to be avoided. This brings me to the subject of reforming labour market regulations. Surveys of existing firms in the organized sector (see above) indicate that these regulations are considered to be one of the major constraints on expansion. And this understates their importance because surveys by their nature exclude firms that would have existed if the regulations had been different.

India's labour regulations were enacted with the best of intentions but have ended up being profoundly anti-labour. Quite simply, they protect the interests of the small minority of workers in the organized sector at the expense of those outside. (Other worker-protection mechanisms such as unionization and social security also cover only the organized sector work-force and are, for all practical purposes, non-existent outside.) It is no part of my case that the labour market should be completely unregulated. Some regulations are undoubtedly necessary to counter the asymmetry of market power between companies and workers. In addition, regulations that force firms to make up for the large gaps in insurance markets have a point (for example, by making severance payments mandatory and by making firms contribute towards sickness, maternity, and other benefits). But India's labour laws go well beyond preventing exploitation of the workers that fall under their ambit. The main problem concerns 'employment protection laws' which govern job-security. In India, these laws are extremely rigid, more so than in the vast majority of countries.[34]

This was not always the case. When it was enacted in 1947, the Industrial Disputes Act (IDA) did not contain many of the rigid rules it later acquired. These were introduced by an amendment (Chapter V-B) to the Act in 1976, which made it compulsory for any firm employing 300 or more workers to obtain the authorization of the state government before closing down a firm, or laying-off or dismissing one or more its employees.[35] In 1982, this provision was further tightened by an amendment to widen its ambit to cover all firms employing 100 or more workers. In practice, permission to retrench is seldom granted even for legitimate reasons such as a drop in sales or a clear case of misbehaviour, for example chronic absenteeism. (Closure of a firm is even more difficult since it has, in addition, to run the gauntlet of the notoriously slow bankruptcy procedures, described in Chapter 6.) These clauses, applicable to both individual and collective dismissals, are among the toughest in the world, much tougher than in countries that compete with India in international trade.[36] There have been attempts to challenge the constitutionality of Chapter V-B on the ground that it violates the fundamental right to carry on business. These have been unsuccessful: the Supreme Court ruled in a landmark judgement in 1992 that Chapter V-B was constitutionally valid because 'it protected the interests of workers'.[37] Which workers? Evidently, the Court defined the category of workers narrowly to include only those employed in large firms. If, instead, the interests of the vast numbers of workers in the unorganized sector were brought into the reckoning, Chapter V-B would surely qualify as unjust law, whatever the legal merits of the Court's ruling. In addition to Chapter V-B, IDA has another pernicious clause of note, viz. Section 9A. This stipulates that employers have to give notice of three weeks for any rearrangement of labour tasks, an absurd requirement that clearly impedes enterprise flexibility and efficiency. And even when notice is given, workers can object to the changes by raising an 'industrial dispute' (see below). Workers tend to resist or litigate against any change in established service conditions, regardless of whether these have been rendered obsolete by technological change. There is little doubt that IDA, as it stands, is incompatible with creating an economy that responds flexibly to changes in tastes, technology, and international competition.

Flexibility is rather better in practice than on paper because state governments sometimes pass their own amendments that dilute IDA or turn a blind eye to violations of it; and employers can find ways round the letter or the spirit of the Act. A perfectly legal way round is to employ contract labour, and the number of contract workers in the organized sector has indeed increased substantially in the last decade. But this route also presents some problems for companies. The relevant governing act is the Contract Labour Act (CLA) 1970, which applies to all firms that employ more than 20 workers. The flexibility that contract labour offers is limited by the fact that much uncertainty surrounds its use; this is because the Act prohibits the employment of contract labour in 'core' or 'perennial' activities, and the definition of these is left to administrative discretion. Moreover, demands to make contract labour permanent are an issue over which trade unions frequently initiate strike action.

The rigidities created by labour regulations are accentuated by the parts of IDA that govern the settlement of industrial disputes. While the Act mandates 'conciliation' between employers and workers as the first response to a 'dispute', it places much greater emphasis on adjudication by labour tribunals and courts than on collective bargaining. Cooperation between workers and employers is additionally hampered by the tendency, encouraged by the Trade Union Act, to have a multiplicity of unions, with no provision for recognizing any one of them as 'representative' of workers. In consequence, the employer-worker relationship is excessively litigious, and in the overloaded labour courts, there are hundreds of thousands of pending cases, which linger for years. (The average time to settle a labour dispute is four years but it can be much longer.)[38] Lawyers benefit but the nation loses.

Another reason why compliance with labour laws is not straightforward is that there are too many laws: about 50 central laws and 150 state laws, many rules issued under various Acts, and a massive baggage of case law on top. They criss-cross, create ambiguities, and encourage corruption. Crucially, more and more laws kick in depending on whether a firm has 7, 10, 20, 50, or 100 workers.[39] Enforcement is subject to several different sets of inspections by labour inspectors who have to be paid off with 'gifts'. Not surprisingly, one of the objects of potential employers is to stay below the policy radars represented by the various employment thresholds.

India's labour laws hugely raise the cost of labour and were enacted without taking into account the reactions of employers and workers. The fact is that there is a strong disincentive to hire workers if they are impossible to fire. No doubt, employers can evade regulations, but only by incurring higher transactions costs, hassle, and uncertainty. So most companies quite rationally try and minimize the use of labour, remain small and uneconomic in scale, and expand in a capital-intensive manner. It is thus no surprise that the organized sector is lacking in enterprises that employ large numbers of workers producing labour-intensive products like garments, shoes, or toys for a mass market: employers would be reluctant to be stuck with a work-force that they could not trim in response to business conditions. Workers also respond strategically. Those who are lucky enough to gain entry to a formal job tend to hang on to it for dear life because if they lose it, getting another is very hard. Opponents of labour law reform say it does not matter because it would affect only the organized sector, which is very small. But a major reason it is small is *because* labour laws are highly restrictive.

Quantitative work by economists on India's labour laws is supportive of this judgement. This is not the right place for a detailed survey, so I shall be brief. The research method in many of these studies has exploited the fact that states have varied central labour laws, including IDA, by passing amendments. (In the Indian Constitution, labour is a 'concurrent subject', which means that both central and state legislatures have the power to make laws; and implementation of laws is *de facto* very much in the hands of state governments.) Tim Besley and Robin Burgess showed that states with more stringent employment-protective legislation have lower output and employment in organized manufacturing (and higher output and employ-ment in unorganized manufacturing) than states with less stringent legisla-tion. This study was criticized by Aditya Bhattacharjea on the ground that the classification of states by stringency of legislation was inaccurate. But further studies that have rectified this defect have confirmed the thrust of the Besley-Burgess results; and they have, in addition, made other intui-tively plausible findings. Ahmad Ahsan and Carmen Pages have shown that the output and employment costs of employment protection legislation are higher in states in which IDA procedures make industrial disputes more difficult to resolve. Poonam Gupta, Rana Hasan, and Utsav Kumar have found that after the liberalization measures in the 1980s and 1990s, gains in employment were higher in states with more flexible labour regulations, and that these states also had higher output of labour-intensive industries specifically. Rana Hasan and Karl Jandoc have uncovered a tendency for states with flexible labour regulations to have a greater share of employ-ment in larger sized firms, a tendency that is more pronounced in firms set up after 1982 when the IDA was tightened. Sean Dougherty and his co-authors have found that in states that have eased up on labour regulations, plants in labour-intensive industries have higher TFP than in states that have not eased up.[40]

Thus, it is imperative that India's labour laws be rationalized and recast to eliminate their current bias against employment. In practice this would be feasible only if organized sector workers were given some offsetting benefits in exchange. This would be the right thing to do. But it would also be expedient since there is little chance of labour unions giving away iron-clad job security for a mess of potage. The natural way to proceed would be to put in place immediately a robust system of severance benefits, as well as, in due course, unemployment insurance, employment services to assist job-search, and training schemes that respond to the requirements of employers. The main point is that protection of *jobs* can be weakened only by strengthening the protection of workers' *incomes*.[41]

The template for reform of labour laws should therefore include the following four elements. Firstly, both Clause Chapter V-B and Section 9A of the IDA need to be radically revised. The requirement to obtain prior government approval for retrenchment of workers (in firms with more than 100 workers) should go. In exchange, severance benefits and retrenchment compensation should be made more generous.[42] A possible staging post on the way could be to change the threshold for state authorization of dismissals to enterprises of more than 1000 workers. Another possible intermediate option would be to distinguish between existing workers and new recruits. Existing workers could retain their privileges but new workers could be moved to changed contracts, which allow termination of employment in the event of company distress or worker delinquency but have more generous monetary and non-monetary severance benefits. This is in accord with modern progressive thinking: the socially desirable labour contract is a compromise between 'permanent employment', with its inflexibility, and 'hire and fire', with its extreme insecurity and discouragement of training. Section 9A should also be amended to give companies more freedom and flexibility in the assignment and redeployment of labour tasks. Secondly, the CLA needs to be recast to reduce the scope for administrative discretion by clarifying the circumstances in which contract labour can be used.[43] Thirdly, the massive overload of labour laws should be streamlined and the inspections process made much more transparent.[44] Fourthly, the involvement of the state in industrial disputes should be curtailed and the role of collective bargaining increased.

The above reform agenda would obviously face political obstacles. Individual states would probably be able to make quicker progress, and a demonstration effect may lead others to follow suit. Article 254 of the Constitution permits states to pass laws (on subjects in the Concurrent List) that override central laws, provided they are permitted to do so by the President of India (who, in practice does whatever the central cabinet

decides). In 2014, the Rajasthan legislature passed bills to raise the employment threshold in Chapter V-B of IDA from 100 to 300 workers, and in the
CLA from 20 to 50 workers. This was shortly followed by the enactment
of similar legislation in Madhya Pradesh. Sensibly, in both cases, worker
compensation by employers in the event of retrenchment was significantly
increased.[45] Presidential assent has been obtained and the legislative
changes have been notified as law. This could set a significant precedent
for other states to follow though there has been very little further action
so far. At the central level, the Modi government has been able to do very
little, despite much talk.

I conclude that labour market reform is essential for increasing the
labour-intensity of the growth process. India's labour laws are job-
destructive and anti-labour. They need radical amendment in the direction
of greater flexibility, along with the introduction of more generous severance and unemployment benefits, and improved schemes for job-search
and training. There has been plenty of support for this view from economists but without any traction in the national political debate, until very
recently. A major reason is that trade unions, though small in membership,
are politically very powerful. Not only can they bring major enterprises
(especially public utilities) to a standstill but all the major trade union federations are affiliated to political parties, which are anxious not to displease
them.[46] So any reform initiative tends to be quickly scotched.[47] India awaits
central and state political leaders who have the courage and the powers of
persuasion to promote a policy package that increases employment for the
very many by reducing job security for the very few, while ensuring a safety
net for all.

NOTES

1. It would be wrong to claim that the standard of living of workers in the
   unorganized sector has not improved over time. The point is that it remains very
   low, and much below that enjoyed by workers in the organized sector.
2. In India, the National Sample Survey measures unemployment in four different
   ways. On the basis of the most generous definition of employment in terms of
   time worked during a reference period, the unemployment rate has consistently
   been very low, in the region of 2 per cent of the labour force. On the least
   generous definition of 'employment', the unemployment rate has been around
   6 to 8 per cent of the labour force. The wide difference between these two is
   suggestive of the presence of substantial underemployment.
3. The exact definition of the coverage of the organized sector is: government
   administration *plus* public sector enterprises *plus* incorporated private sector
   enterprises *plus* unincorporated, proprietary, and partnership enterprises in

the private sector that employ more than 10 workers. The unorganized sector constitutes the rest of the economy, viz. unincorporated, proprietary, and partnership enterprises in the private sector that employ less than 10 workers. This definition is used in the report of the National Commission for Enterprises in the Unorganized Sector (NCEUS) (2009). There are other definitions but they are rather less apposite. In any case they do not make much difference to the numbers.

4. Roughly half of the informal workers in the organized sector get provident fund benefits.

5. NCEUS (2009) introduced and quantified the distinction between formal and informal workers. In principle, there could be formal workers in the unorganized sector and informal workers in the organized sector; in practice, only the latter are quantitatively significant. On this basis, 93 per cent of the country's total workforce was 'informal' in 2010. This is higher than the proportion of the workforce that works in the unorganized sector because the organized sector contains many contract and casual workers who fall in the 'informal' category (see Table 5.1).

6. This estimate comes from NCEUS (2009). The share of the organized sector in total output is doubtless higher now, probably around 55–60 per cent, because we know that registered manufacturing has been growing faster than unregistered manufacturing, and the fast growing services sectors are largely in the 'organized' sector.

7. See NCEUS (2009).

8. Output figures in this paragraph are from the 2004/5 series of national accounts. The 2011/12 series of national accounts has different figures for 2011/12 but no available figures before that year. See Table 5.2.

9. It is even more informative to consider the huge differences in labour productivity across more narrowly defined sectors. In 2009/10, labour productivities in various sectors as a percentage of overall national labour productivity were in the following ascending order. Agriculture: 29; Unregistered Manufacturing: 58; Construction: 81; Community and Personal Services: 112; Trade and restaurants: 140; Transport, Storage and Communications: 208; Government: 266; Mining: 339; Registered Manufacturing: 395; Public Utilities: 632; Finance, Insurance and Real Estate: 723 (see Hasan, Lamba, and Sen Gupta 2013). The large scope for gain from labour re-allocation is thus glaringly evident. Of course, more investment would be needed in the labour-receiving sectors but output per worker would rise because they also typically have higher TFP.

10. These numbers were calculated from Table 22.5 in Planning Commission (2013a). Another astounding statistic is that while 157 million were added to the workforce between 1983 and 2009/10, formal employment in the organized sector increased by only 5 million (from 26 million to 31 million).

11. This paragraph is about the change in the composition of output away from labour-intensive *products*. It is also relevant that *techniques of production* have moved towards higher capital intensity in all industries, and in particular, in labour-intensive industries (see Chapter 7 of Bhagwati and Panagariya 2013).

12. So far, neighbouring Bangladesh has been more successful than India in doing so. It has to be admitted that India would face handicaps in the world market for labour-intensive manufactures. China still remains a formidable force and there are many other competitors such as Bangladesh, Mexico, Indonesia, Thailand, Philippines, Malaysia, and Vietnam, some of which have lower unit labour costs than India's organized sector (see Exhibit 37 in Dobbs, Madgavkar, Barton, Labaye, Manyika,

Roxburgh, Lund, and Madhav, 2012). It would not be easy to break into their existing marketing circuits. Moreover, India has so far been almost entirely absent in 'network trade' and 'global production sharing', which enable labour-abundant countries to specialize in the labour-intensive parts of the value chain.

13. See Eichengreen and Gupta (2011) on services in India, and Ghani (2010) on services in South Asia (including India).

14. Total employment created by IT sector may be twice as large as the above estimates because of downstream and upstream linkages. But the basic point remains.

15. More recent data are available in the Sixth Economic Census but without any disaggregation, so they are not of much use. The aggregate picture is essentially unaltered. The numbers in this and the two succeeding paragraphs come from World Bank (2011).

16. Moreover, of the workers employed in small firms, roughly two-thirds were 'self-employed' and/or ran 'own account enterprises' without any hired workers, and another 15 per cent were in enterprises employing less than six workers (see Hasan and Jandoc 2013).

17. Note from Table 5.3 that in China and Malaysia a majority of manufacturing workers are in firms employing 200+ workers. India's U-shaped distribution becomes more apparent if self-employed workers and those employed in establishments employing one to four workers are omitted from the calculation (see Figure 3.5 in Asian Development Bank 2009). Even so, India's distribution in Table 5.3 is more L shaped than U shaped, i.e. India lacks both medium-sized firms and large firms. Of course, firms have to pass through middle-size before becoming large-size, so the obstacles to the expansion of small firms are highly consequential. Note also that Dipak Mazumdar's work shows that 20 years ago, i.e. at a more comparable stage of development to India now, the East Asian countries had an evenly spread size-distribution of firms, very similar to what they have in Table 5.3 (see Mazumdar and Sarkar 2008, Chapter 5).

18. Note that the wage premium for workers in large firms remains even after allowing for the fact that they are more educated and skilled than workers in small firms. See World Bank (2011).

19. The poor state of infrastructure in India prevents employees being bussed in from long distances in large numbers (and in any case China's worker hostel system does not chime with India's social mores, particularly for women). In addition, in India, the lack of organized retailers with international links means that volume purchases that would encourage large-scale manufacture are missing.

20. From 2004 to 2011, the FLFPR in India fell significantly. One reason was that there were more females in education. But another was that an improvement in household living standards led to a withdrawal of females from the labour force (a consequence of the social stigma that still attaches to women working outside the home). See Rangarajan, Seema, and Vibesh (2014). This will surely change with increasing education and urbanization.

21. Average labour force growth will be about 10 million persons a year for the next 25 years on the assumption that the male LFPR remains constant and the FLFPR doubles. One of the challenges is that more than half of the national labour force increase will occur in five relatively backward states: Bihar, Jharkhand, Madhya Pradesh, Rajasthan, and Uttar Pradesh. Some states, especially in the South, have already had their demographic transition.

22. See Table 2.2 in Hasan and Jandoc (2013).

23. See World Bank (2011).
24. In such surveys, there are obvious problems with investigating tax rates or access to finance as constraints to the growth of firms. Companies always complain about high tax rates and do not take into account the social benefits of tax revenue. Companies may complain about access to finance but access *should* be more difficult for low-quality projects. Access to finance is examined below.
25. See World Bank (2014).
26. See CII/KPMG (2014).
27. See OECD (2007, 2011).
28. Note that as this book goes to press, there is news that in the World Bank's Ease of Doing Business Survey, India's rank has improved slightly from 134 in 2014 to 130 in 2016 (after having worsened in the interim to 142 in 2015). This represents some progress, which could perhaps be attributed to the efforts of the Modi government. But too much should not be read into this. For further discussion, see Chapter 13.
29. See Asian Development Bank (2009).
30. See Banerjee, Cole, and Duflo (2004).
31. See Hasan and Jandoc (2013).
32. India's labour laws and labour market reforms are illuminatingly analysed by Bhagwati and Panagariya (2013). Another important reference for the topics covered in this chapter is Srinivasan (2010).
33. See World Bank (2011).
34. Labour laws impinge more strongly on industry than on services. In particular, the Industrial Disputes Act (IDA) and its amendments (see below) are directed at industrial enterprises. But '(labour) regulations can impinge directly on the services sector through the broader application of laws such as IDA. . . . for instance, clauses in the Shops and Establishments Act sometimes overlap with those of IDA and some court decisions have extended the reach of the IDA to cover tertiary sector activities' (see World Bank 2010, 128). Even so, the weaker reach of labour laws is one of the reasons for the faster growth of organized services compared with organized industry.
35. Prime Minister Indira Gandhi broke a nation-wide railway strike in 1974 with some display of brutality. She may have been trying to make up to the trade unions by enacting the 1976 amendment.
36. According to the OECD's report on India (see OECD 2007), India's dismissal laws for permanent workers are tougher than all OECD countries except Portugal and all non-OECD countries except Indonesia.
37. Workmen of Meenakshi Mills Ltd. vs. Meenakshi Mills Ltd.
38. The Modi government has moved on some issues. For example, workers now have to have a single representative negotiating body to represent their interests. And the limit on overtime has been doubled to 100 hours in a month to suit industries with seasonal peaks of demand (e.g. garments).
39. For example, the Factory Act kicks in at an employment size of 10 workers (for enterprises using power) and 20 workers (for enterprises not using power). As soon as the Factory Act kicks in, the inspector raj kicks in too.
40. The studies referred to in this paragraph are listed in the bibliography: see Besley and Burgess (2004), Bhattacharjea (2006), Ahsan and Pages (2009), Gupta, Hasan, and Kumar (2009), Hasan and Jandoc (2013) and Dougherty, Frisancho, and Krishna (2014). These studies are concerned with the manufacturing sector.

Amin (2009) is about the retail sector; it too finds that stricter labour regulation leads to fewer organized sector jobs.

41. Note that a universal cash transfer scheme (see Chapter 10) would contribute to protecting workers' incomes.

42. The standard severance benefit in India is a lump-sum equal to 15 days of pay for every year of service. This is low by international standards and should be increased to 45 days or more for each year of service. In the longer run, India also needs a system of unemployment insurance, funded by contributions from employers, workers, and the state.

43. The contract labour system has the disadvantage that temporary employment reduces the incentive of companies to train labour. But this would be attenuated if Chapter 5B of IDA were revised since that would increase the incentive to employ regular workers. It would be unwise to wind up the use of contract labour since it does increase employment and introduce flexibility.

44. Some minor changes along these lines were made by parliament in the Winter Session of 2014. But there is still a long way to go.

45. The bills in Rajasthan and Madhya Pradesh also made some other sensible changes including a) raising the minimum threshold for registration of a trade union to 30 per cent of the total workforce (previously 15 per cent); b) raising allowable overtime; c) permitting women to work night shifts (with the state government responsible for security); d) freeing firms from having to comply with obsolete laws such as having to provide earthenware pots with drinking water.

46. For example, the Indian National Trade Union Congress (INTUC) is affiliated to the Congress Party, the Bharatiya Mazdoor Sangh to the BJP, and the Centre for Indian Trade Unions to the CPI (Marxist). The all-India trade union strike in September 2015 was probably one of the reasons for the Modi government backing off from reforming labour laws at the central level.

47. When Yashwant Sinha was Finance Minister in the first BJP government (1999–2004), he mooted the idea in one of his budget speeches that the requirement to obtain state authorization of dismissals should apply only to enterprises employing more than 1000 workers. The idea died a quick death.

CHAPTER 6

Productivity and Economic Reform

Advances in productivity are essential for achieving rapid growth of income and output. Where can India hope to find productivity improvements in the next two or three decades? The obvious source, apart from technological catch-up with the rich countries, is to eliminate, over time, inefficiencies in the allocation of resources. A flagrant example of inefficiency is the 'employment problem': too much labour is bottled up in activities and sectors in which output per worker is very low. That deformity, and how to correct it, was the subject of the previous chapter. But there are many other distortions that damage the effective working of the economy. Putting them right would speed up productivity growth over a medium-run time horizon. The present chapter is an extended discussion of this point and its implications.[1]

PRICE CONTROLS AND GOVERNMENT SUBSIDIES

A major source of economic inefficiency in India is that the markets for some commodities, especially some key inputs, are heavily distorted by government intervention in the form of price controls.[2] Their putative aim is to bolster the real incomes of the poorer sections of society; and to this end, the controlled goods are sold at prices well below their costs of production. The result is that the supply of these key goods is penalized and the demand for them is excessively stimulated. The difference between price and cost is sometimes met by explicit subsidies through the budget. More frequently, the subsidies are implicit or hidden, reflected in non-recovery of costs or reduced profits by government departments or by government and non-government enterprises. At the same time, targeting of the poor is a hit and miss affair, so the aim of benefiting the poor is at best very imperfectly achieved.

How should goods be priced? The basic rule for economic pricing is that the price of a good should equal the long-run (marginal) cost of producing it. Unless there are demonstrable external effects, or other coherent and compelling grounds, this is what the government should aim for.[3] In the case of tradable goods, the general rule can be further simplified: domestic prices should equal world prices, which represent the (marginal) opportunity costs for the economy of obtaining these goods.[4] Following these rules may involve raising prices above the current subsidized levels. Does that mean sacrificing the objective of protecting the living standards of poor people? Not so, if poverty could be alleviated more effectively in other ways, for example, by direct income subsidies. Manipulation of the price system is, in general, a very inefficient method of income redistribution.

There is another reason, apart from concern for the poor, for the persistence of price controls. This is quite simply the weight of the past. If a dysfunctional subsidy for good 'x' (say coal) gets established, then industry 'y' (say electricity), in which 'x' is a major input, comes to depend on a low price of 'x' to make profits or even to survive. And the same may apply in industry 'z' (say aluminium) which uses 'y' (electricity) and hence, indirectly, 'x' (coal) as inputs. It is easy to see, therefore, that inappropriate subsidies for several key inputs can result in an industrial structure in which inefficiency is pervasive. Starting from such a position, it is not easy to remove the counterproductive subsidies. But that is not a convincing argument for inaction; rather, it indicates the need for gradual change to unwind the subsidies, with sequencing that is carefully thought out.

In India, price and subsidy reform should certainly be a crucial element in the reform agenda. Consider, for example, the main energy inputs: oil-related products, coal, natural gas, and thermal electricity. They are all mispriced or, to put it plainly, too cheap. The subsidies have harmful effects. They encourage overconsumption, delay energy-efficient technologies, discourage investment in supply capacity, and crowd out high-priority government spending. Their supposed rationale is to shield poor people from high prices. In reality, most of the benefit goes to upper-income groups because they consume vastly more energy and energy-intensive products. For example, it has been estimated that the top decile of income-earners derives 7 to 10 times the benefit from fuel subsidies as the bottom decile.[5]

The main oil-related products are gasoline, diesel, liquid petroleum gas (LPG), and kerosene. Gasoline was deregulated in 2010. Until recently, domestic prices for diesel, LPG, and kerosene were well below world prices. In October 2014, the government took advantage of a fall in world oil prices to deregulate diesel. The test of the government's nerve will come if and when oil prices rise again. (In the past, the Vajpayee government deregulated diesel when oil prices fell but brought back the controls when the fall was reversed.) LPG and kerosene prices continue to be centrally administered. LPG is used for cooking by relatively well-off households but kerosene is used by the poor, mainly for lighting. Even so, it would be desirable to deregulate both LPG and kerosene.[6] The associated fiscal saving would be a multiple of the sum needed to compensate poor people by direct income transfers, leaving most of it for constructive purposes.[7] It would also eliminate the benefit to criminals that accompanies the current regime; they divert more than a third of subsidized kerosene for adulterating diesel.[8]

Coal is another mispriced input. There is a significant shortage of coal (despite growing imports) that is playing havoc with various activities, including electricity production. To put this right, many reforms are necessary in the coal sector, including repeal of the Coal Mines Nationalisation Act to allow private investment in coal mining, a fair but speedy process of obtaining land and environmental clearances, and clean and transparent auctions for coal blocks.[9] But coal-price reform is a necessary part of any policy framework to encourage supply and ration demand for coal. Domestic coal prices are generally only around half of world prices for coal of comparable quality. Unless this distortion is corrected, other supply-side measures are unlikely to work. Coal prices should gradually rise to trade parity. Of course this will have knock-on effects on the electricity sector. But in the long run, the electricity sector must surely be weaned off subsidized coal. Similar considerations arise with natural gas, whose price is fixed by the government at around a third of the import price. (In October 2014, there was a correction to bring them somewhat closer to import parity.) While many policy changes are required to stimulate investment in gas exploration and drilling, such as setting in place appropriate revenue-sharing arrangements, a necessary component of the policy framework has to be alignment of domestic and international gas prices.[10] Note also that in coal, gas, and fossil fuels more generally, environmental considerations suggest that taxes rather than subsidies would be desirable.[11]

Mispricing also bedevils the electricity sector, which has suffered for years from a fundamental problem. In most states there is still a single state-owned monopoly buyer, viz. the state electricity board (SEB), which is virtually bankrupt because it sells electricity at prices that do not cover costs (despite artificially cheap coal). Farmers and urban households are subsidized, the former heavily. The subsidy is covered by the industrial sector (which pays high prices), by large subventions from state governments, and by borrowing and payment postponements by SEBs to make ends meet. Charging economic prices is a political problem that has to be faced however the sector is organized but state governments continue to use cheap or even free electricity as a vote-winning device. As things stand, private investment in generation has to face a major hurdle, viz. that the SEBs cannot be trusted to pay their bills. Reform of electricity pricing is a necessary accompaniment of any successful restructuring of the power industry. Would that hurt the poor? Not really. Only 67 per cent of households have access to electricity, and even among these, electricity consumption is strongly related to income. Indeed it has been estimated that the bottom quintile receives only 10 per cent of total electricity subsidies, while the top quintile captures 37 per cent. Poor households could be protected from a higher electricity price by direct income transfers with a fraction of the money saved by subsidy abolition.

Another example of mispricing is fertilisers. Nitrogenous fertilisers (urea) are sold to farmers at fixed retail prices, which are not adjusted for long periods, and fertiliser companies are paid on a cost-plus basis. Fertiliser subsidies go partly to the fertiliser industry and partly to farmers but the former probably receive well over half of the total.[12] The system has resulted in underinvestment, and also misallocation by encouraging overuse of urea.[13] There is no sound economic argument for special protection of fertiliser plants. The subsidy should be abolished and high-cost plants closed down in a phased manner. For farmers, the incidence of fertiliser subsidies is regressive. Most of the benefits go to well-off farmers since they are the main users of fertilizers; so a universal subsidy is clearly undesirable. Prices should rise to import parity; small and poor farmers should be directly subsidized to enable them to buy fertilizers at market prices.

Other blatant cases of mispricing are rail services and water. Indian railways are unable to achieve reasonable standards of maintenance and capacity expansion because rail fares are politically determined. Rail pricing favours passenger traffic.[14] In order to keep passenger fares low, freight charges have been repeatedly raised, with the result that over the years there has been a massive substitution of freight traffic in favour of roads. Within passenger traffic, lower-class services are hugely underpriced in relation to cost. Three-quarters of passengers travel by the lowest class but they provide less than 20 per cent of passenger revenue. Even so, the bottom four-fifths of households provide less than a third of passengers on non-suburban routes, so low rail prices benefit the relatively wealthy much more than the relatively poor. Though many other reforms are necessary to make India's railways function better, the issue of economic pricing is crucial. Unless it is tackled, private investment will be deterred and public investment in railways will be constrained by lack of resources.

The issue of water-pricing is equally serious. Water is absurdly under-priced in both urban and rural use, given its present and impending acute shortage. And like other subsidies, water subsidies favour the better-off. Up to 85 per cent of price subsidies given to water utilities are spent on subsidizing private taps but 60 per cent of poor households get water from public taps. Water subsidies are discussed further in Chapter 7.

It is often claimed that in India final-output prices are free from controls though input prices are not. This is broadly true but with one glaring exception. The prices of some major foods, e.g. rice, wheat, pulses, sugar, are heavily controlled. The government buys cereals from farmers at administratively-set 'procurement prices' and sells them through the PDS at controlled 'issue prices'. The targeting is very poor and the leakages are huge. The subsidy for rice and wheat is enormous and amounts to 1 per cent of GDP. As explained in Chapters 8 and 10, it would be far cheaper and more effective to give poor people cash or vouchers to buy food at market prices, with government intervention restricted to running a price stabilization scheme.

NATIONAL GAIN FROM UNWINDING SUBSIDIES

The above account covers only some of the most conspicuous subsidies but there are plenty of others, even if they do not figure explicitly in the budget. Elimination of all dysfunctional subsidies deserves to be a prime component of an intelligent reform agenda. These subsidies distort efficient resource allocation, give rise to massive leakages to intermediaries and black market operators, and are regressive in the bargain (i.e. they benefit the relatively rich more than the poor).

What about the objection that since some portion of the subsidies does nevertheless reach the poor, unwinding them would hurt poor people? Fortunately, that possibility can be avoided. Recent technological developments have added greatly to the range of available instruments for income redistribution. Cash transfers to poor people are now a practical possibility. Biometric cards for individuals, combined with universal banking coverage, have the potential to address various inclusion and exclusion problems that have plagued all previous attempts at targeting. The necessary arrangements are not yet fully in place but that is surely the direction in which the country should move with all due speed.[15] This issue is discussed in some detail in Chapter 10. Suffice it to say here that elimination of dysfunctional explicit and hidden subsidies that serve no social purpose (along with some reduction in 'tax expenditures', increase in privatization receipts, and widening the income and value-added tax net) could save resources of around 10 per cent of GDP, of which only a small part would be needed to compensate the poor fully for subsidy elimination (and even to give a modest 'basic income' to the whole population). [16] The national gains would be large. In addition to some income redistribution to the poor, there would be a boost to growth, a) from improved resource allocation as a result of subsidy abolition, and b) from increased public investment made possible by the large fiscal savings. Of course, subsidy elimination is not easy and would take several years to be fully realized (see Chapter 10). An obvious difficulty is that subsidies are interrelated. For example, a reduced subsidy to coal would require an increased subsidy to electricity unless the electricity subsidy was reduced by raising electricity prices. Removal of subsidies is thus an exercise in sequencing and policy coordination. There is also of course the major political difficulty of overcoming resistance from the non-poor who stand to lose (see Chapter 10).

TAXATION, TRADE, AND COMPETITION

Tax reform is an essential step for raising productivity in India. The state taxes its citizens to pay for public goods and for other legitimate public purposes. The Indian government has rightly taken the view that a uniform goods and services tax (GST), or what comes to the same thing, a uniform value-added tax (VAT), provides the right balance between efficiency and administrative simplicity.[17] Trade policy is, in essence, an adjunct to the indirect tax regime; and it follows from the rationale of the GST as a destination-based tax that it should be charged on imports, but not on exports.[18] Any additional intervention, specifically directed to international trade, is hard to justify, with the possible exception of an across-the-board low tariff (of say 5 per cent), to exploit some generalized inelasticity of foreign demand. Trade and tax reforms in India have been a slow progression towards this ideal, which is yet to be reached.[19]

India's indirect tax system used to be a farrago of high import duties and cascading excise and sales taxes, levied by central and state governments at multiple rates. Many excises and sales taxes have now been converted into central and state VATs, and services brought under the VAT net, though all of this took over 20 years.[20] Even so, much cascading and complexity still remain. The final step in arriving at a uniform, nationwide GST, i.e. a uniform central VAT and a uniform states VAT levied on the same tax base,[21] still remains to be taken, though negotiations between the centre and the states have been in progress. Ideally, the move to a GST would subsume a host of other indirect taxes, surcharges and cesses, including several on inter-state trade.[22] It would at last make the country a single market, which at present it is manifestly not; and large benefits could be expected from such a change over time.[23] Unfortunately the politics of all this is not straightforward. A 'grand bargain' between the centre and the states is necessary to pass the requisite constitutional amendment.[24] The result promises to be a messy compromise, with too many tax rates and too many exemptions. If this is what happens, a huge opportunity will have been squandered, and the GST would become just a 'name-changer, not a game-changer'.[25]

What about taxes and restrictions specifically on international trade? As seen above, there is little justification for them. Worldwide experience confirms that trade openness is a crucial and necessary condition for rapid growth. Trade liberalization, especially for industrial goods, has been one of the signal achievements of India's reform programme so far; and it has made a big difference. The economy has become much more open[26] (though agriculture still remains highly protected, as in many other countries). Exposure to international competition has improved resource allocation and raised significantly the technological sophistication of the Indian economy. Further trade liberalization would be desirable. Whether this should be done unilaterally or as part of multilateral or regional agreements is a salient issue. Trade policies are discussed at greater length in Chapter 12, and so are policies towards foreign direct investment (FDI), an important channel for competition as well as technology transfer. Inward FDI has been substantially liberalized. There are now very few sectors where entry is capped or forbidden though investors still face too many administrative difficulties on the ground.

Domestic competition has also increased greatly, since many controls over production and investment in output markets (especially in industry and services) were abolished by the 1991 reforms. The churn in the corporate world provides striking evidence of this: several leading enterprises of 1991 have now lost their dominant position. Public sector enterprises have also been subjected to more competition. A potentially very significant development was the enactment of a modern competition law in 2009, and the establishment of the Competition Commission of India. After a slow start, the Commission has finally begun to flex its muscles. In the last couple of years, it has found evidence of cartelization or anti-competitive agreements in several cases and imposed heavy fines. In some of these cases it has made well-argued rulings against both state agencies and private companies (including some influential pharmaceutical distributors, carmakers, and realtors). It has thereby begun to acquire a reputation for independence. Its effectiveness will increase if, in future, it initiates inquiries on its own motion, as permitted by the Act.[27]

The removal of controls on industrial activity has unquestionably made the economic climate more investor-friendly than it was during the *ancien regime*. Even so, companies, domestic and foreign, still face many obstacles to the 'ease of doing business' (see Chapter 5).

FACTOR MARKETS AND FINANCE

Price reform and competition (domestic and international) in the markets for goods and services will not yield their full benefit in terms of productivity, if the underlying factor markets (labour, land, capital, and finance) are heavily distorted. This is very much the case in India.[28] It is not my contention that factor markets should be completely unregulated. Regulation will certainly be necessary but it should be directed to creating missing markets and correcting clear and specific market failures.

Labour

The labour market has already been examined in Chapter 5. It was argued there that various labour laws need to be radically revised to improve the flexibility of the labour market, and boost employment and productivity, to the benefit of the whole workforce that outnumbers its protected component in the organized sector by 15 times or more.

Land

The land market in India is thoroughly distorted. Part of the reason for this is that land titles are extremely unclear, especially in rural areas. As a result, it is not easy to transfer land, sell it, or use it as collateral for borrowing. Land cannot 'migrate' to its best use. There is a Land Records Modernization Programme which aims to put titles on a clear and secure basis by undertaking cadastral surveys, reconciling entries in various registries, and computerizing land records, but it has moved at a snail's pace. Completion of this process requires an energetic thrust from central and state governments, which has been missing so far.

In addition, the government's land acquisition regulations and arrangements are dreadful. Governments in all countries typically have powers of 'eminent domain' whereby they can acquire land for public purposes. This is also true of India where, until recently, the relevant statute was the Land Acquisition Act of 1894. There are some good justifications for 'eminent domain'. In a country where land rights are so murky, investments that serve public purposes, but need to acquire a large number of contiguous plots of land, may be deterred by the fear of litigation and 'holdouts'. So it sometimes makes good sense for the government to acquire land compulsorily and use it for the general good, on its own motion or through developers. Unfortunately, for several decades after independence, the Indian government typically acquired land very cheaply for infrastructure projects (especially dams and irrigation schemes) with little regard for the people who were displaced or whose livelihoods depended on the acquired land.[29] Sometimes, it was then sold on just as cheaply to developers who made large profits that were shared with politicians and bureaucrats. Such arrangements are now regarded, quite rightly, as unacceptable. The problem can only increase since the demand for land will explode in future due to the needs of urbanization, infrastructure investment, and mineral exploration.[30] The source of potential tension is obvious. On the one hand, land is required for industrial and infrastructure investments, and it would be desirable to have procedures for acquisition that are speedy and smooth. On the other hand, it is also clear that land should be acquired with fair compensation to all the stakeholders involved. This tension has now become highly charged. Civil society groups, and politicians (when it suits them), have taken up cudgels on behalf of the dispossessed and have succeeded in holding up investments for years or even preventing them altogether.[31]

To its credit, the UPA government did address this problem and after much consultation enacted the Land Acquisition, Rehabilitation and Resettlement Act (LARR) in 2013. According to the Act, land acquired by the government on behalf of private companies (for projects with a 'public purpose') has to pass four hurdles: a) a favourable 'social impact assessment'; b) compensation to landowners of at least four times the market price of land in rural areas and at least twice the market price in urban areas; c) consent by 80 per cent of affected families (70 per cent for public-private partnerships);[32] d) a relief and rehabilitation package for people affected by the project. Many layers of committees and bureaucracies were involved in the whole process, a recipe for delays and kickbacks. When the BJP government took power in 2014, it sought to amend the Act to abolish or weaken the 'social impact' and 'consent' requirements for specified categories of high-priority projects, while retaining the other two hurdles, but was able do so only by means of a presidential ordinance, because it did not have the requisite majority in the upper house. After two extensions of the ordinance, it finally gave up and left the matter to the states, which are constitutionally within their rights to amend the LARR (with presidential approval).

I am sympathetic to the Modi government's attempt to simplify the Act's labyrinthine procedures. Currently, it takes four to five years to acquire land under the LARR even when the effort is successful, which it may not be. This is surely far too slow for an industrializing country. Some states may now try to get round the LARR in one way or another but there will be no uniformity in their amendments. So the problems in land acquisition for inter-state projects, such as industrial corridors, will continue, and perhaps worsen.

In any case, since the states are not proposing to amend the rigid compensation provisions of the LARR, the whole approach to land acquisition promises to remain flawed. Simply doubling or quadrupling the 'market price' for land is a blunderbuss approach. Firstly, the prevailing 'market price' is a hopeless benchmark in India's highly imperfect land markets. Does it mean the price that is in the records, such as they are, or the up-to-date price, which, in turn, may rise greatly when news of the project is made known?[33] The scope for arbitrary judgement and corruption is obvious. Secondly, the formula does not allow for the heterogeneity of plots of land in terms of quality and much else. The prospect therefore is of continuing dissatisfaction and unrest as owners of better-quality land feel cheated.[34] What is needed is a method of price-discovery for different plots of land. The method proposed by Maitreesh Ghatak and Parikshit Ghosh has much to commend it.[35] This involves the government buying up land in the project region by accepting the cheapest bids in a transparent auction. Sellers whose land is needed by the project but whose prices are too high or who absolutely refuse to sell would then be assigned land of comparable quality that is not required by the project, but is nearby and within the region. This market-oriented solution, though not perfect, would be far better than formula-based prices dictated from above. As things stand, the resolution of the land acquisition problem is far from satisfactory.

Space precludes discussion of problems in urban land markets, other than government land acquisition policies. The urban land ceiling acts which froze up land markets in cities for many years[36] have now thankfully gone. But various distortions remain. To take just one example, the rigid 'floor space index' (FSI) requirements in cities encourage urban sprawl and hugely increase transport costs for residents. India's cities are far less dense compared with international good practice. It would make good sense to relax FSI requirements by charging those who wish to exceed them a price that reflects the extra burden they will impose on urban infrastructure (after allowing for the saving on transport costs).[37]

The Capital Market and Bankruptcy Arrangements

A competitive modern economy needs swift and efficient procedures to deal with company distress, insolvency, and exit. A distressed firm that cannot pay its dues but is basically sound should be restructured and given a chance to survive. A firm that is non-viable should be liquidated to enable the deployment of its assets to more productive uses. In this context, an unregulated market faces a collective action problem. Acute company distress is likely to result in a 'grab race' by creditors, which is not conducive to preserving value. Legal and administrative processes can help. In the ideal scenario, a distressed company files for bankruptcy and is put in the care of an independent expert body. The latter declares a moratorium during which the company is legally protected from its creditors and the decision is made whether to rehabilitate or liquidate it. Rehabilitation will generally involve a change of management, a write-down of the debt, and possibly some new 'senior' lending to get the firm going again. If this option looks hopeless, the company is wound up; the shareholders lose and the bondholders get what is left of the firm's assets. This is the kind of bankruptcy procedure that is followed in most advanced countries, and it works pretty well.

In India, insolvency procedures have worked very badly.[38] Company law and labour laws have acted in vicious concert to create the phenomenon of 'sick' industries—firms that are bankrupt but are not closed down. Creditors cannot sell the assets and labour is unpaid; the result is considerable waste of resources. To deal with this problem, the Sick Industrial Companies Act (SICA) was enacted in 1985 and, as required by the Act, a Board of Industrial and Financial Restructuring (BIFR) was set up. Both have effectively perpetuated the situation by putting an inordinate emphasis on rehabilitation of hopeless companies. The UPA government enacted a new Companies Act in 2013 but its insolvency provisions were not notified because they were contested in the courts, so the old system still continues to function. Soon after it assumed office, the Modi government announced that it would introduce 'a comprehensive bankruptcy code', and appointed a Bankruptcy Law Reform Committee (BLRC) for the purpose. The committee produced its report towards the end of 2015, together with a draft 'Insolvency and Bankruptcy Code' (IBC).

The SICA/BIFR procedures, which are still in force, are fine on paper but extremely unsatisfactory in practice.[39] Huge delays are common. The revival-liquidation decision takes many years. Moratoria are long and, in the interim, promoters and managers tend to siphon off corporate assets. There are then further delays in the revival process or in the courts, which are supposed to give effect to, or to review, BIFR decisions. The courts' role was intended to be minor but they have managed to erode the BIFR's powers by 'judicial innovations' whereby judges have taken it upon themselves to order additional moratoria and rehabilitation attempts, after the initial ones are exhausted. In other words, both the BIFR and the courts have leant over backwards to try and rescue even irreparably non-viable companies, thereby simply postponing the inevitable.[40] Another major problem with the SICA/BIFR provisions is that they apply only to the industrial sector, which leaves out large swathes of the company universe. (So a company such as Kingfisher Airlines, which recently had a high-profile bust, did not come within their purview.) As a result of these dysfunctions, creditors are relatively powerless when faced with defaults, and the credit market as a whole lacks width and depth.

The draft IBC addresses some of these problems. It covers both industrial and non-industrial companies. A new National Company Law Tribunal (NCLT) is to be set up as the adjudicating authority for the insolvency procedure.[41] If a moratorium is sought and granted by the NCLT, it would have a maximum term of 180 days. Importantly, 'debtor-in-possession' is abolished: the NCLT is mandated to dismiss the old management and replace it by a 'resolution professional' who administers the preparation of a revival plan, while the company continues to function. (This should help to stop asset-stripping by incumbents.) A revival plan has to be accepted by 75 per cent of the creditors for it to go forward to the NCLT for its sanction. If there is no acceptable plan, the NCLT has to make an order for liquidation. These are desirable changes. Whether they succeed in practice will depend in part on whether the intention to reduce the role of the courts works out. (The NCLT will be a quasi-judicial body, and its decisions are subject to appeal to an appellate tribunal, with the possibility of further appeal to the Supreme Court.)[42] That said, the immediate priority must surely be to embody the draft IBC in legislation as soon as possible.

More generally, India also needs a much more effective framework for creditor rights, which makes possible fair and reliable recovery of debt, outside of bankruptcy. Over the years there have been some minor improvements in the ability of banks to recover loans via statutory and non-statutory means.[43] (But the demarcation of lines of authority between the NCLT and the existing recovery schemes will have to be sorted out.) And the basic problem still remains of a culture in which promoters and tycoons feel they can get away with persistent non-repayment. Recently, there has been a welcome hardening of attitude and commercial banks, encouraged by the Reserve Bank, seem to be prepared to name and shame individual businessmen as 'wilful defaulters'.

Finance and Financial Inclusion

Finance is not traditionally regarded as a 'factor of production'. But it could be so called, and it is also an essential lubricant for the smooth running of the economy. Before 1991, India's financial sector was heavily repressed. Since then, many useful reforms have been made but an efficient financial system is still a long way off. An analytical survey of the unfinished tasks would require a volume on its own; and they have in any case been examined expertly in the landmark Raghuram Rajan Report on the financial system.[44] The Reserve Bank of India (now headed by Rajan) is clearly cognisant of what needs to be done though, as always in India, implementation remains a challenge. I confine myself here to discussing an issue of major importance for growth as well as inclusion, viz. the need to increase the access of the rural and urban poor, and of small enterprises and the unorganized sector, to the financial system.[45]

Previous attempts at financial inclusion have taken various forms, all more or less unsuccessful. Commercial banks have greatly increased the number of rural bank branches but without reaching most poor people. (The branches have been a financial burden, so the banks' motivation has been less than keen.) There has also been a big emphasis on cooperative banks. These have been a failure due to very poor loan recovery rates and a gross neglect of financial discipline. They have become little more than politicized agencies that distribute cheap credit to favoured clients, with direct or indirect refinancing from upper tiers of the banking system. Another channel for financial inclusion (with regard to credit) was 'priority sector lending' by banks, whereby 40 per cent of advances had to go to specified activities. But banks have tended to serve only the conventionally 'bankable' activities within the chosen sectors. The upshot is that the coverage of the formal financial system remains abysmally low. Only a fifth of the lowest quartile of income earners has a bank account, and while a third of the same quartile borrows, the borrowing is mostly from informal moneylenders who charge 3 per cent a month or more. Less than 5 per cent of those in the bottom quartile take bank loans. (The position may have improved somewhat of late due to the Jan Dhan drive—see below.)

The fact is that if financial inclusion is to succeed, there will have to be a departure from traditional models. Financial inclusion has to become profitable. This means that products have to be designed that genuinely address the needs of the poor. So, financial institutions have to offer services that are simple and cheap. This can be done only if costs of provision are low; so bricks-and-mortar bank branches are not the best way forward. Much more relevant is banking via mobile phones and local business correspondents. In other words, banks will have to rely on automation to reduce costs and, where necessary, use local employees paid at local rates. In this scheme, there would be scope for conventional banks using new technologies, newly licensed small and local banks with local knowledge, and microfinance institutions. Fortunately, this line of thinking is now the official policy of the RBI.

Several steps have been taken. Firstly, there has been an intensive, highly successful effort by the mainstream banks, as part of a flagship campaign (Jan Dhan) by the Modi government, to get people to open bank accounts. By December 2015, an astonishing 195 million new bank accounts had been opened. Though enthusiasm has to be tempered by the fact that more than a third of them were 'zero balance accounts' that showed no activity, the initial progress has clearly been impressive.[46] Secondly, the RBI has given approval for opening numerous new banks. Only two of them will be conventional universal banks (though the RBI has announced an intention to issue future licenses 'on tap' to any applicants that meet the regulatory conditions). Eleven will be 'payments banks' that can take deposits, and enable transfers to be made and received, but cannot lend. They are expected primarily to reach poorer customers through mobile phones. Twelve 'small finance banks' have also been licensed. These have to have a larger capital base than payments banks and will be allowed to lend, with the restriction that 75 per cent of lending will have to be for priority sectors such as agriculture and small and medium enterprises. Despite teething problems, these various moves have the potential to increase financial intermediation at the lower end of the market, shake up the sclerotic Indian banking system by increasing competition, and eventually spur economic growth. (Needless to say, increased competition will have to be accompanied by sensible regulation.)

AGRICULTURE

Agriculture now accounts for only 15 per cent of GDP but the sector still contains nearly half of the country's workforce and two-thirds of the country's poor. Industry and services have shaken off the 'Hindu rate of growth' but agriculture has not: trend growth in the sector has been stuck at less than 3 per cent a year for decades.[47] Increases in productivity due to technical progress (especially the 'green revolution') have been offset by pressure of population, fragmentation of land holdings,[48] and inept policy. Productivity levels are still very low in international comparative terms.[49] Agriculture should have been a prime focus of India's economic reforms because agricultural growth has a much stronger immediate effect on poverty reduction than growth in other sectors. (This is perfectly compatible with the view, which I share, that a necessary condition of economic development in the long run is a large shift of labour out of agriculture.) The social payoff from a rise in the growth rate of agriculture to 4 per cent a year would be very large. But reform has been neglected.

Though agriculture is almost wholly in private ownership, the presence of the state is pervasive. Until 1991, trade protection of industry resulted in high implicit taxation of agriculture, which was softened by subsidisation of agricultural inputs, notably fertilisers, irrigation water, and electricity. Unfortunately, since then, the subsidies have grown apace (though industrial protection has been cut back). They have created a large fiscal burden, and have also been very inefficient, for example by encouraging inappropriate usage of inputs. Less widely appreciated is the fact that there is extensive state interference in agricultural trade and marketing, through the antiquated Essential Commodities Act and other pieces of legislation. As a result, India remains a highly fragmented agricultural market and the supply chain in agriculture is extremely weak.

Policy reform in agriculture must focus on allowing market forces freer play, combined with well-aimed public intervention in those areas where unregulated market outcomes would be undesirable.[50] An essential element in the reform package is to dismantle the network of state controls on movement, storage, marketing, and processing of produce, activities in which the private sector has a comparative advantage. However, this is not enough. Competition has to be actively encouraged. The position in marketing is a good example. Agricultural Produce Marketing Committees (APMCs), putatively run by elected representatives of farmers, are in control of marketing.[51] According to the APMC Act, trade between farmers and buyers of produce (mainly wholesalers) is supposed to take place only in specified *mandis* (i.e. market yards) through an auction system. The original idea behind this was to protect farmers from exploitation. The system has evolved in such a way that trade takes place, in practice, through licensed intermediaries who have captured the APMCs, in cahoots with local politicians. The APMCs, contrary to intention, have become monopoly buyers who dictate terms to small farmers. These de facto monopolies need to be swept away.[52] Contract farming should also be encouraged so that Indian corporates get directly involved in agriculture. To some extent, this is happening. Some companies are trying to provide the 'cold chain' from farm to processing plant. Even so, the overall picture is unsatisfactory. More than half of the production of perishables such as fruits and vegetables goes to waste. The entry of multinational supermarkets would help to strengthen the supply chain. But it is held up by the reluctance of the government to displease the domestic retail trade.[53]

Another essential reform is to unwind the toxic mixture of price controls and input subsidies. The composition of government spending on agriculture is hugely counterproductive. In 1980, two-thirds of public expenditure on agriculture was investment and one-third was subsidies. Since then, the subsidies have grown massively; unsurprisingly, given the fiscal constraints, public investment has been crowded out. Now, four-fifths of public spending is subsidies and one-fifth is investment. (Amazing but true: the governments of Punjab and Andhra Pradesh spend more money on electricity subsidies than on health and education.) Cost-benefit calculations show that the economic return from a rupee spent on subsidies is well below the return from a rupee spent on public investment. Subsidies have other drawbacks too, including distortion of input use. For example, water and electricity subsidies lead to over-exploitation of scarce groundwater. In addition, they disproportionately benefit the larger, well-to-do farmers.

The current mix of government subsidies and public investment needs, therefore, to be turned on its head. Though the lion's share of investment in agriculture now comes from private sources, there is a crying need for more public investment in areas where the market will not invest of its own accord.[54] Rural roads, electrification, irrigation, extension services, and environmental protection are obvious examples but not the only ones. Some research spending also has a 'pure public good' character, for example the development of seeds which, once they are acquired by farmers, can be easily reproduced. Here, there is little incentive for private companies to innovate because they cannot capture the returns. ('Hybrid' seeds are different because they cannot be replicated.) Another strategic area for government action is the 'eastern question' in Indian agriculture. Too much reliance has been placed on a handful of Northern and Southern states for production and procurement of wheat and rice. (Punjab, Haryana, and UP together produce a quarter of the country's wheat and a third of its rice. Procurement is even more skewed. More than four-fifths of wheat procurement is from Punjab and Haryana, and around three-quarters of rice procurement is from Punjab and Andhra Pradesh.) But these states are suffering from groundwater stress and soil degradation. It would be wise to have a partial shift of wheat and rice production to Eastern states. These states have plenty of water and, given low current usage, plenty of scope for increased use of fertilisers. But they urgently need improvements in rural infrastructure, including roads and flood control. The Northern states, in contrast, need to diversify into vegetables and fruits which are less water-intensive. This strategic spatial shift in agricultural production cannot be left entirely to the market and will require some government investment, incentives, and disincentives. (Economic pricing of water and electricity would obviously help.)

Would removal of subsidies in agriculture evoke a negative supply response? Not so, if done along with the other reforms adumbrated above, since public and private investment would raise returns in agriculture. Moreover, supply would not be adversely affected if agricultural imports and exports were liberalized. India is competitive in wheat and rice; Indian producer prices are generally below world prices and free trade would raise them. This is also true of several other agricultural commodities like cotton.[55] (By the same token, prices of oilseeds will fall: here, India has a comparative disadvantage, so it makes sense for Indian production to contract over time. Output of pulses, however, is held back by production disincentives relative to cereals.) India has always exported tropical products like tea, coffee, cashew nuts, spices, and tobacco but it also has a comparative advantage in cotton, fresh fruits and vegetables, meat, and marine products. India has run a large trade surplus in agricultural products for years; with the right policies, it would have many further significant opportunities in this area.[56] Most farmers would gain from trade liberalization since they could more than recoup the loss of subsidies from the gain on higher product prices. However, two groups would be adversely affected. The first group is poor urban and rural consumers of food, including landless labourers, who would suffer, for a time, a loss of real income due to higher food prices. The second group is very small, self-sufficient farmers, who consume what they produce and do not have a marketable surplus. This means that an essential accompaniment of agricultural trade liberalization is a functioning system of income support for poor people (as strongly advocated in Chapter 10).

Needless to say, the role of government in agriculture extends well beyond reducing subsidies and investing in physical rural infrastructure. As discussed above, it has to create markets and enable them to function; and it also has a major role in correcting market failures. Agricultural research has been alluded to above. Water management is another obvious case. Careless use of water has lowered water tables in large parts of rural India, leading to the prospect of significant water stress. The market cannot deal with this problem without government action. It requires putting in place a system of water conservation by means of water charges and community-led ways of rationing, supervised by local panchayats. Another crying need which will not be met without government intervention is a system of crop insurance with a wide coverage, since droughts continue to be a major cause of agrarian distress.[57] It also goes without saying that the government has to set up poverty alleviation programmes, and enable the rural population to access health and education services. These are critical and necessary accompaniments of greater market orientation in agriculture.

Agricultural reform is thus a highly complex affair. It involves liberalization of input and output markets, replacement of subsidies by additional public investment in rural infrastructure, and some well-designed interventions in the market mechanism. The timing and phasing of these measures is a matter of considerable delicacy. Careful coordination involving different central and state ministries would be required. However there is at present no effective, over-arching institution to steer the process of agricultural reform.

INDUSTRY, SERVICES, AND 'INDUSTRIAL POLICY'

In thinking about industry and services, it is useful to return to basics. Rapid growth depends primarily on economy-wide improvement in TFP. Where is the latter to come from? A primary source is the shift of labour from agriculture and other traditional occupations to high-productivity modern industry and services. There are two growth payoffs from this shift. There is the increase in overall growth that comes from the increasing weight in national output of sectors with high labour productivity. In addition, as recent research indicates, high-labour-productivity manufacturing and services sectors, particularly those that are tradable, show 'unconditional convergence' to global, best-practice labour productivity. In other words, there is evidence that they are 'escalator' industries: once a country gets a toe-hold in them, there is a near-automatic tendency for labour productivity to improve, due to technical transfer and imitation.[58] Of course, the diffusion of this benefit to the overall economy depends on whether the escalator sectors absorb labour moving out of low-productivity traditional sectors.

In the last three decades, India has experienced rapid, even spectacular, growth of labour productivity in registered manufacturing and some modern services such as communications, banking, and business services. The problem is that these dynamic sectors have been virtual islands or enclaves that have not absorbed low-skilled labour, which is India's most abundant resource. That is a major obstacle to boosting the rate and inclusivity of growth. The lesson is not that India should abandon the capital- and skill-intensive sectors. There are two correct lessons. Firstly, India needs to reduce obstacles to the expansion of industries that are labour-intensive, and to increased labour use in all industries. This will certainly require changing labour regulations but that is not enough. It is equally important to break infrastructure bottlenecks, improve 'ease of doing business' and access to finance, and maintain a competitive exchange rate. Secondly, it needs urgently to raise the level of education and skills in the population so that the escalator industries do not run into a skills constraint. It is misleading to portray India's development challenge as a choice between two mutually exclusive strategies of industrialization, one labour-intensive and the other capital- and skills-intensive. India could and should 'walk on two legs'.

Is the above agenda too narrow? Should it be broadened or even replaced by 'industrial policy', i.e. policy that attempts to 'pick winners' by identifying, promoting, and subsidizing firms or industries that will generate beneficial spill-overs to the rest of the economy and capitalize on the country's *long-run* comparative advantage in world markets?[59] I would be very sceptical of such an approach. The empirical case is thin. 'State-led' development in East Asia is the prime example that is adduced but its accuracy is strongly contested.[60] Moreover, the arguments assume the presence of policymakers who are at once super-clever, dispassionate, and benevolent. In practice, 'industrial policy' is quite likely to encourage arbitrary and uninformed decisions, and cosy deals between business, politicians, and bureaucrats. Even if the East Asian example were factually right, its replicability to India is extremely doubtful. Indian authorities have not shown an aptitude for masterminding efficient strategies of industrialization; instead, they have shown marked tendencies towards corruption, rent-seeking, and crony capitalism. I conclude that India would be wise to avoid the primrose path of pursuing so-called 'industrial policies'. The right approach is to improve the environment in which structural transformation can take place.[61] This would also be the sensible way to pursue the Modi government's 'Make in India' initiative.

NOTES

1. For useful discussions of economic reform in India, see Acharya and Mohan (2010), Ahluwalia (2011), Desai (2010), Kelkar and Shah (2011), Mohan and Kapur (2015) and Singh (2010).
2. There is an excellent discussion of dysfunctional price controls and subsidies in Government of India (2015a), Volume 1, Chapter 3. Some data and numbers in this section are taken from this source.

3. Technical note: Other compelling grounds for departing from this rule could take the form of what economists call 'second-best considerations', if they were clearly demonstrable. A further reason for departing from the rule is in the few cases where there are genuine natural monopolies due to declining average and marginal costs. In such cases, setting price equal to marginal cost would lead to firms making losses. The state may then wish to cover the fixed costs by subsidy but that would involve raising extra revenue, which creates its own distortions. Regulators would have to balance the benefits of the price subsidy and the cost of the tax distortions. This would almost always involve setting prices that are higher than long-run marginal cost.

4. World prices should be taken to be c.i.f. prices for importables and f.o.b. prices for exportables. The world price rule assumes, realistically, that India cannot affect world prices of the vast majority of tradable goods. (The rule can be easily amended in the rare cases where India has monopoly power in world markets.) Note that free competition would tend to achieve the basic price rule automatically (provided there are no external effects). That is why full liberalization is often the right solution. But that may not be possible or desirable, especially when a gradual approach is called for.

5. See Anand, Coady, Mohommad, Thakur, and Walsh (2013).

6. The government has now quite rightly started to deliver the LPG subsidy by direct transfers into the bank accounts of beneficiaries. This will save money by cutting out leakages to fake recipients. But the larger problem is that the subsidy is regressive. The poorest 50 per cent of households account for only 25 per cent of consumption of LPG. The bottom three deciles of households enjoy a welfare gain of only Rs. 10 per capita per month from the LPG subsidy; the figure for the top decile is Rs. 80. The kerosene subsidy is more beneficial to the poorest since they account for half of kerosene consumption. But kerosene allocations greatly exceed kerosene use, which indicates massive diversion for nefarious activities.

7. It was estimated by Anand et al. (2013) that in 2012 the direct and indirect effect of correcting the price distortions in diesel, LPG, and kerosene fully would have been to raise the cost of living by around 5 per cent across all income groups. However, there would have been a fiscal saving of 2 per cent of GDP. Only a small proportion of that (estimated to be around a tenth, i.e. 0.2 per cent of GDP) would have been needed to compensate the bottom four deciles of the population by direct transfers. With the fall in oil prices and the deregulation of diesel, the figures will be different but the basic point remains valid.

8. The 'kerosene-mixing mafia' is not averse to murdering people who stand in their way. (A few years ago, this fate befell Yashwant Sonawane, a district official in Maharashtra, who tried to curb the mafia's activities.) The same mafia is involved in exporting low-priced Indian fuel products to Nepal and Bangladesh. Experience with the old 'smuggling mafia' is relevant. It was not eliminated until import restrictions were abolished (including those on gold imports). Similarly, the kerosene mafia could be got rid of by eliminating the universal subsidy to kerosene.

9. Towards the end of 2014, the Supreme Court cancelled many coal block allocations that had been made previously and enjoined the government to sell them by auction. This the Modi government proceeded to do.

10. This is not straightforward because there is no clear 'world price' for gas, so a sensible compromise would be to take the average of different regional gas prices.

11. See Chapter 7. Note that if both domestic use and imports are taxed at the same rate, the alignment of domestic with world prices remains intact.
12. Technical note: This is because the elasticity of farmers' demand for fertilizers is likely to be higher than the elasticity of producers' supply of fertilizers.
13. This is because other varieties have been decontrolled but the price of urea is administratively set. Over-use of urea has an adverse effect on soil quality.
14. Rail passenger fares remained practically unchanged for 10 years from the early 2000s. Note also that India's rail fares (adjusted for purchasing power parity) are exceptionally low by international standards (e.g. they are less than a third of fares in China).
15. Of course, biometric identification of individuals cannot solve the problem of identifying *poor* individuals. But that is a core function of the state, which it has to address one way or another unless universal subsidies are fiscally possible, which they may be. See Chapter 10 for an extended discussion.
16. The methodology for calculating hidden subsidies was suggested by Mundle and Rao (1991), and it has been replicated several times since then (see Chapter 10). On the pitfalls in using this methodology, see Rajaraman (2006).
17. For a detailed justification of this statement, see Joshi and Little (1996), Chapter 3. There is a case for taxes and subsidies outside a VAT but only to offset demonstrable 'market failures'. A clear case would be taxes on commodities that have adverse environmental effects, e.g. carbon taxes. It is also generally accepted that there should be some excise taxes over and above a VAT for 'demerit' reasons, e.g. on alcohol and cigarettes. An effective tax system also needs well-designed direct taxes. These are not my immediate concern here but are discussed elsewhere in the book.
18. Inputs are not taxed under a VAT and exports are 'inputs' into 'producing' imports. Exports should be 'zero-rated' for VAT, which means that an exporter does not charge VAT to the customer but can reclaim tax paid on inputs. Note that 'zero-rating' is quite different from a VAT 'exemption'. Being VAT-exempt means that the operator does not charge VAT to the customer and cannot reclaim tax paid on inputs.
19. It is now widely accepted that the only valid argument for trade intervention is to improve the terms of trade (if the country has monopoly power). See the seminal article by Bhagwati and Ramaswami (1963), and the response by Anand and Joshi (1979).
20. See Chapter 4 of Acharya (2006).
21. In contrast to India, many federations have a simpler system in which there is only a central GST, whose revenue is distributed to the constituent states. India's GST is going to involve the tax authorities of both centre and states separately taxing the same transaction. This more complicated system will take time to bed down.
22. At present, the tax structure is still very complex. At the central level, in addition to central VATs, there remain some excise and additional excise duties, service taxes, additional and special customs duties, surcharges, and cesses. At the state level, in addition to state VATs, there remain some sales taxes, entertainment taxes, luxury taxes, taxes on gambling and advertisements, and state surcharges and cesses. In principle, the GST should subsume all of these.
23. One benefit, among others, is that a GST would promote growth of laggard states since investment in them would no longer be deterred by the prospect of tax barriers to the movement of goods.

24. The Constitution does not allow sharing of tax bases by the centre and the states. A constitutional amendment would require a two-thirds majority in both houses of the national parliament plus approval by a simple majority of state legislatures.

25. Ideally, there would no exemptions to a VAT other than for unprocessed food and micro-enterprises, with turnover below a specified low threshold, that are administratively too difficult to tax. Non-rebatable excise taxes should be allowable only a few cases, as specified above (see n. 17). The consequence of allowing too many exemptions is that the revenue-neutral standard VAT rate would have to be so high as to erode compliance, and this would create pressure for even more exemptions. India seems to be moving towards a system in which there will be exemptions not only for petroleum products, alcohol, and tobacco but also for some important services and real estate transactions. There is also the possibility that the deal will include a 1 per cent tax on inter-state trade and movement of goods. This would be a thoroughly retrograde step that would involve a significant possibility of cascading, completely contrary to the logic of a GST.

26. For example, exports have more tripled as a share of GDP from 7 per cent in 1990 to 25 per cent in 2013. The (unweighted) applied average tariff has fallen from 144 per cent in 1990 to 14 per cent in 2013. See Chapter 12.

27. For a review of the framework and early working of India's new anti-trust regime, see Bhattacharjea (2012).

28. See Rajaraman (2012).

29. There are reliable estimates that around 50 million people were displaced over the years and 50 million acres of land taken over, mostly by the state for state purposes. A disproportionate share of the burden fell on the tribal population.

30. It is relevant to state here that India is one of the most land-scarce countries in the world. It is also a material fact that much of India's mineral wealth (90 per cent of its coal and 80 per cent of other minerals) is in forested lands occupied by tribal people, who have customary and ancestral rights.

31. The obvious example is of the Tata automobile plant at Singur in West Bengal, which had been built on land acquired by the state government but was abandoned following a fierce agitation. The Tatas moved the investment to Gujarat but the West Bengal government was brought down in the process. Other high-profile problematic cases include the investments by Vedanta and Posco in Odisha.

32. 'Consent' is not necessary for a wholly public project, i.e. one that is not awarded to or partnered with a private company. Why for one category and not for the other?!

33. It is also relevant that both urban and rural land prices in India have risen hugely in this century. India now has some of the highest land prices in the world, several times higher than countries such as the United States (see Chakravorty 2013). It is not surprising that investors balk at paying these land prices, which moreover spiral up further when news about impending projects becomes public knowledge.

34. This is what happened in Singur where farmers who sold land to the government were paid the *average* market price.

35. See Ghatak and Ghosh (2011, 2015).

36. See Joshi and Little (1996), Chapter 5.

37. Needless to say, changes in FSI policies have to fit into a whole new policy framework for urbanization. See Lall and Vishwanath (2014), and Ahluwalia,

Kanbur, and Mohanty (2014). See also the brief discussion of urban infrastructure in Chapter 7.

38. The World Bank's Doing Business Survey 2015 ranks India 137th out of 189 countries in the ease of resolving insolvencies. According to the survey, resolving an insolvency takes 4.3 years on average, costs 9 per cent of the debtor's estate, with an average recovery rate of only 25.7 cents on the dollar.

39. See Goswami (1996), Joshi and Little (1996), and Van Zwieten (2015).

40. It may be thought that this arises from concern for the workforces of the failing companies. But the obvious solution to this would be to make dues owed to the workers (plus redundancy payments) the senior-most debt.

41. The NCLT will deal with companies and limited liability entities. The IBC has separate arrangements for dealing with individuals and partnerships. I do not have space to outline these, which is not to say that are unimportant for increasing the 'ease of doing business'.

42. Success will also depend on whether other elements of the infrastructure proposed by the BRLC, and assumed in the draft IBC, work in practice. These include the development of a new profession of 'insolvency professionals' supervised by an 'insolvency regulator', and 'insolvency information utilities' to collate and disseminate information about listed companies and their creditors. Moreover, prescribing time-lines in legislation does not necessarily mean that they will be adhered to. (For example, the existing debt recovery tribunals are mandated to dispose of cases within six months. In fact, only a quarter of cases are concluded within a year.)

43. In 1993, the Government passed an Act to establish debt recovery tribunals for recovery of debts owed to banks. These tribunals have not worked well. More successful, but only slightly, have been asset reconstruction companies set up under the Securitization and Reconstruction of Financial Assets Act (SRAFESI Act) of 2002. There is also a non-statutory Corporate Debt Restructuring Framework based on voluntary debtor-creditor agreements, again largely for recovery of bank debts.

44. See Planning Commission (2009).

45. Other unfinished tasks in financial sector reform, some of which are discussed elsewhere in this book, have been clearly identified in the Raghuram Rajan report. Firstly, the country needs a clear and sound monetary policy framework to deliver macro-stability. I address this topic in Chapter 8. Secondly, there has to be a robust framework for financial regulation. India has rightly committed itself to adopting international best practices and prudential norms in banking (see Chapter 12). The Reserve Bank's supervision of the banking system is improving but has to be improved further. Other, more structural, regulatory issues have been addressed in the Report of the Financial Sector Legislative Reforms Committee though, in my judgement, not all its suggestions are persuasive. They have to be debated and an agreed framework put in place. Thirdly, India needs to deepen its financial markets to address the needs of individuals and businesses for liquidity, credit, and risk-diversification. (One example is the need to create an active market for long-term corporate bonds to support infrastructure financing.) Fourthly, efficiency improvements require more competition between banks on a level playing field. Particularly important is the need to change the competitive position of public sector banks. This will involve withdrawing their special privileges but also removing the special constraints that they face. This issue is discussed in Chapter 7. Fifthly, the country needs better mechanisms for

dealing with corporate distress and insolvency. This has been discussed in the preceding section.

46. Each account comes with built-in accident insurance of Rs. 100,000, and is eligible for an overdraft of Rs. 5000, on proof of satisfactory operation for six months. So far, less than 2 million accounts have passed that test.

47. Moreover, recent performance has been very poor. The 12th Five Year Plan (2012–2017) targeted a growth rate of 4 per cent a year but achieved only 1.7 per cent a year in the first three years.

48. The average size of farms in India is now only 1.15 hectares, and 85 per cent of holdings are under 2 hectares in size.

49. The comparison with China is revealing. China's foodgrain output is nearly three times India's, but with a smaller cropped area and a smaller average size of holding. Evidently, farm productivity is much higher in China.

50. See Gulati (2010) and Chapter 14 of Panagariya (2008).

51. For an excellent description and analysis of the working of APMCs, see Government of India (2015a), Volume 1, Chapter 8.

52. On paper, government monopoly of the conduit between farmers and wholesalers has now been abolished. Some states have enacted marketing laws based on a model APMC Act supplied by the centre in 2003, which allow private parties to enter the intermediation business freely. These laws also permit business firms to transact directly with farmers; farmers can thus even sell directly to supermarkets, in principle. On the ground, however, the overall situation continues to be as described in the text. One of the harmful features of the APMCs is the multitude of taxes and commissions that they impose on agricultural trading. The model APMC Act replaces these by a single market fee. Unfortunately, it retains the requirement that this fee be paid even for produce sold outside the APMC markets. This constitutes an entry barrier to the setting up of markets that compete with APMCs. The way forward has to be to phase out the commodities regulated by APMCs, and enable the creation of competitive markets by providing support for market infrastructure. The central government will have play a leading role in this, which it is constitutionally entitled to do in matters that have inter-state implications.

53. See Kohli and Bhagwati (2011) for a balanced analysis of foreign investment in the retail sector. See also Chapter 12.

54. During the 11th Five Year Plan (2007/8–2012/13), public investment in agriculture was only 3 per cent of agricultural GDP. Private investment in agriculture was four times public investment, and so were government subsidies to agriculture. See Tables 12.6 and 12.7 in Planning Commission (2013).

55. India is now among the world's largest exporters of rice. Over the last two decades, India has switched from being a large net importer of cotton to being a large net exporter (due to the emergence and spread of Bt cotton). It must be admitted, however, that both rice and cotton are highly water-intensive, so India is indirectly exporting scarce water. Rational water pricing may reduce rice and cotton exports but this is as it should be, given the scarcity of water.

56. Indian agricultural policies have been characterized by knee-jerk tariff increases and export bans to protect producers and consumers. This deters agricultural investment. The long-run objective should be to have low and stable trade duties that are altered by a predetermined formula if world price changes exceed certain prespecified thresholds. This would be possible since India's bound

agricultural tariffs are well above actual tariffs, and export restrictions are not proscribed by WTO.
57. Current schemes of crop insurance have very low coverage. A robust system would have near-universal coverage, up-to-date technology (using drones etc.) for assessing crop damage, actuarially determined premiums that are subsidized by the state (since a large majority of farmers are poor), and compensation paid quickly and directly into farmers' bank accounts. This could be done without adding much to the fiscal burden. For an excellent discussion, see Gulati (2015).
58. See Rodrik (2013) and Government of India (2015a), Volume 1, Chapter 8. The former is a seminal article that demonstrates the presence of 'unconditional convergence' in manufacturing. The latter provides some evidence that such convergence applies to modern services too.
59. For example, see Hausmann and Rodrik (2003). Bardhan (2015a) has a very useful discussion of recent arguments for industrial policy.
60. See Little (1999), Noland and Pack (2003), and Pack and Saggi (2006).
61. While I am against selective industrial policy, I am not against the government playing a coordinating role in indicative planning of infrastructure investments. An example of the latter is government leadership in building 'industrial corridors' in India, with both public and private investment playing a part.

CHAPTER 7

Ownership, Infrastructure, and the Environment

This chapter examines three crucial issues that are relevant for rapid and sustainable growth in India. The first is ownership. Is the substantial extent of state ownership of the means of production holding back productivity growth? The second is infrastructure provision. What should be done to lift the infrastructure constraint on growth? And does the locus of ownership matter for efficient production of infrastructure services? The third issue is the environment-growth relationship. How is India doing on protection of the natural environment? And how could its performance in this area be improved? The inclusion of environmental protection in this chapter may at first sight be surprising. But economic analysis makes it plain that ownership issues are as relevant for preventing damage to the environment as they are for providing material goods and services efficiently.

OWNERSHIP AND PRIVATIZATION

The Indian state is a large owner of companies and firms. There are 260 Central Government Public Sector Enterprises (CPSEs). (This figure includes only the 'non-financial and non-departmental enterprises'. It excludes the state-owned commercial banks and financial companies, as well as 'departmental' enterprises such as railways, posts, and broadcasting. Inclusive of these, the total is around 350. If regional rural banks are also included, the figure rises to around 500.) CPSEs are present in all sectors of industry and services; and in some, such as energy and power, they have very significant market shares. In the aggregate, they have a large footprint in the economy, and produce about 10 per cent of GDP and employ 1.5 million workers. In addition, there are 1000-odd State Government Public Sector Enterprises (SPSEs), especially in power, transport, and warehousing, employing 1.8 million workers. Typically, public sector enterprises (PSEs) underperform relative to private firms in the same industry.[1] All the same, CPSEs (including banks) produce 40 per cent of the profits of the country's 100 biggest listed firms. A few CPSEs are highly profitable: however, in some of these cases, for example Coal India Ltd., the profits are clearly due to monopoly position, not efficiency. What is indisputable is that the performance of CPSEs is highly variable. Around 60 CPSEs make losses, which sum to more than $5 billion a year (around 0.3 per cent of GDP), and a good many of these loss-makers have negative net worth. Hardy perennials among the large loss-makers are two public telecom companies (BSNL and MTNL) and Air India, the national airline.[2] The annual losses of these three enterprises together amount to more than $3.5 billion. On top of this, around two-thirds of the SPSEs (especially the zombie electricity distribution companies) make annual losses which add up to another 0.7 per cent of GDP.[3] Two questions arise quite naturally: Would public revenue not be better spent than in meeting the losses of PSEs? And would the resources tied up in loss-making and low-profit PSEs not be put to better use if they were in private hands?

One reason for the inadequate performance of many state-owned enterprises the world over is that it is very hard if not impossible for them to achieve an arm's length relationship with the government. The ultimate shareholder is the nation. But the national interest is interpreted by the minister in charge (and his friends and cronies), and the public sector manager is seldom given the clear objective of maximising profits. Moreover, rewards and penalties for managers are not tied to performance. So, the incentive to reduce costs and innovate is blunted. In private companies, managers' rewards are performance-related, and the threat of takeover tends to keep managers on their toes.

These considerations, which have a solid basis in experience in many countries, apply very forcefully in India. Political meddling is widespread in PSEs' business decisions. Appointments to managerial and board positions are also politicized since PSEs fall directly under the purview of various line ministries. (Occasionally, these concerns spill over into the public domain. In 2007, the Chairman of the Punjab and Sind Bank complained that Congress politicians had been appointed to four of the five 'independent' directorships of the bank's board.)[4] While managerial efficiency is not effectively monitored, there is a good deal of other kinds of scrutiny not only by parliament but other investigative bodies such as Comptroller and Auditor General (C&AG), Central Vigilance Commission (CVC), and Central Bureau of Investigation (CBI), which makes managers avoid legitimate business risks and opt for a quiet life. Labour relations tend to be fractious in PSEs since trade unions are generally stronger than in the private sector. The latter feature, added to government interference, may account for the fact that PSEs are often over-staffed and do not recruit at market wages: they pay far too much at junior levels and not enough at the senior.

Indian governments have not been unaware of these problems. One response has been to try and improve performance by reforms within the public sector. At various times, loss-making PSEs have been referred to bodies that were supposed to revitalise them or wind them up. But this initiative has gone approximately nowhere. Profitable enterprises too have been put under a form of supervision via 'memoranda of understanding' laying down targets to be achieved. In practice, these soft performance-contracts have turned out to be little more than just another bureaucratic burden. Two other responses have been more successful. The first was to open up entry of private companies into the sectors in which PSEs are operating, in other words, to increase competition. The second was to move in the direction of privatisation, accompanied by listing on the stock market.

Private sector entry has provided a competitive spur to PSEs and is the main reason for some improvement in the overall performance of PSEs over the years and the reduction in the number of loss-makers. (In 1991, around half the CPSEs made losses, now around a quarter do. The SPSEs, however, have faced little if any competition, and their condition remains financially desperate.) It could be argued that what really matters for efficiency is not ownership but competition, and if competition rules, privatization is unnecessary. Product market competition should keep managers on their toes; and this discipline would be reinforced by the threat of takeover if companies have to compete in the capital market. But this argument assumes that the government a) maintains a level playing field between PSEs and private companies and b) follows the logic of competition and is willing to see PSEs die if they cannot compete. In India, neither of these provisos has been fulfilled in practice. On the one hand, the playing field is tilted in favour of PSEs. They are not fully subject to market discipline. The large number of PSEs kept on life support speaks for itself, and the takeover threat is absent when the government is the majority owner. On the other hand, the playing field is in some ways tilted against PSEs because they are burdened with multiple objectives and subjected to the government's byzantine and intrusive practices. It follows that competition of the Indian variety will not be enough to improve productivity growth. Privatization has a major role to play.

So far, most of the privatization has been 'partial', i.e. disinvestment, not privatization. Since 1991, the government has sold minority stakes in 47 CPSEs, majority stakes in only 14. Around 50 CPSEs have been listed on the stock market, and seven of them are now among the top 20 companies by market capitalization. (Only six SPSEs are listed.) Research studies show that while selling minority stakes has improved the performance of PSEs, the improvement has been much greater when the government has divested a majority stake.[5] This is to be expected since the gains from managerial incentives and managerial autonomy can only fully accrue if the government cedes control. Incidentally, there is also a public finance aspect to this. The price a private investor would be willing to pay is bound to be adversely affected if the government retained majority control. It is quite likely, therefore, that the minority sales in India have been made at unfavourable prices.

There is more to be said about the relation between public finance and privatization. A well-known textbook proposition in economics states that there is no *purely fiscal* case for privatization. The proposition is correct in the sense that it follows from the assumptions on which it is based. If a public enterprise that is sold is identical in efficiency to the private enterprise that replaces it, the true intertemporal fiscal position will be unchanged because the sale price will equal the discounted value of future profits sacrificed by the government. But the assumption of 'identical efficiency' is false. The Indian government owns many enterprises that would evidently be more efficient and profitable under private ownership. In this realistic case, their sale prices would reflect the higher profits in private ownership, so there would be a fiscal gain to the government. This gain could be used in various productive ways. For example, the government could invest it in building rural roads, or other socially valuable projects that the private sector would normally shy away from, without any worsening of the fiscal position. The conclusion is that in the Indian context, a substantial privatization programme would be worthwhile on both efficiency and fiscal grounds.

Politically, privatisation has been a hard sell. Some apprehensions are more justified than others. It is understandable that there is opposition to selling off companies that are important to national security. It is also understandable that there would be legitimate concerns about strategic sales of profitable 'national champions' because of the likelihood that they would be bought up by a few leading business houses that are already very powerful economically and politically. But these considerations affect only a few enterprises. In fact, there tends to be resistance to any and all privatisation from trade unions, as well as from politicians and bureaucrats who stand to lose patronage. The first BJP-led NDA government (1999–2004) did make a serious effort to privatize. Though it was not very successful, it initiated all the majority sales that have taken place so far. The UPA government (2004–2014) gave up because it was hamstrung by internal divisions. Unfortunately, the current NDA government that took office in 2014 has been like its UPA predecessor, not its NDA predecessor, in its attitude to privatization.

What should the Indian government do with PSEs? There is a critical distinction to be made between sectors that can be made subject to competition and those that cannot. In the former category fall all tradable goods: these can be exposed not only to domestic competition (by allowing freedom of entry) but also to international competition by trade liberalization. This annuls the main argument for state ownership, which is to prevent monopolistic exploitation. There is thus a strong presumption in favour of privatization in the tradable sectors, which include large swathes of manufacturing industry, and some services too. (However, as argued above, competition by itself would not be enough. This is because, in the absence of privatization, there is unlikely to be a level playing field and a hard budget constraint. Air India is an obvious example. It has plenty of competition but it survives despite making large losses.)[6]

That leaves the activities, mainly infrastructure-related, in which it is not possible to have competition because they are 'natural monopolies' for technical reasons. (These sectors also almost always produce non-tradable goods, so external competition is absent.) But the domain of natural monopoly is much narrower than it appears at first sight: for example, in the electricity sector, the transmission grid is a natural monopoly but generation and distribution are not. Where monopoly is inevitable, the choice is perforce between a state monopoly and a private monopoly. Here, the case for privatisation is that in a state monopoly incentives may be even more unsuitable and autonomy even more compromised than in PSEs operating in competitive industries. The crucial point is that if the government chooses to privatize, and indeed even if it does not, the operation of a natural monopoly *must* be accompanied by regulation to prevent exploitation of consumers. Indeed, regulation is unavoidable in any network industry (e.g. electricity) that includes some natural monopoly element, even if other parts of the industry produce outputs which can be competitively produced. It follows that vertically integrated monopolies (like electricity) should be broken up, state or private monopoly being retained only where technically necessary, with the whole structure subject to an independent regulator.

Although the discussion in this section has focused on non-financial PSEs, it applies closely to financial PSEs such as public sector banks (PSBs). Banking is not a natural monopoly and there is plenty of evidence that Indian PSBs are performing very poorly. As documented extensively by the recent P. J. Nayak Committee Report, their profitability and productivity indicators are considerably worse than those of private banks and their asset quality is much weaker.[7] PSBs also need massive recapitalization (of which the government's share would be anywhere between 2.2 per cent and 5.9 per cent of 2013/14 GDP) over the next few years to support the credit needs of a growing economy and to meet international prudential (Basle 3) standards.[8] Poor performance is the result of the way the PSBs are governed. In the words of the Nayak Committee, 'It is unclear that the boards of most of these banks have the required sense of purpose . . . to steer the banks . . . the boards are disempowered, and the selection process for directors is increasingly compromised . . . board governance is consequently weak.'[9] It is clear that the situation cannot be salvaged without fundamental reforms in the way PSBs are governed. The Nayak Committee concluded that the government has two options: either to privatize the PSBs or to give them a radically new governance structure without full privatization. The Committee ignored the first alternative (which was not part of its remit) and opted for the second. It recommended that the government set up a holding company, the Bank Investment Company (BIC), to which it would transfer its holdings in PSBs, thereby distancing itself from bank governance. The BIC would, to begin with, be actively involved in various ownership functions including the professionalization of bank boards, but would, within three years, yield all ownership powers to these boards, while retaining a purely investor function on behalf of the government. Eventually, the BIC would reduce its holdings in each bank to less than 50 per cent in order fully to level the playing field between public and private banks.[10]

The Nayak Committee's recommendations make very good sense but they may run into the sand, like many previous attempts to distance the government from PSBs. My own preference would be for a two-fold approach. The government should implement a reform along the Nayak Committee lines for the stronger, more successful PSBs in which the Committee's approach has a fair chance of success. At the same time, it should take steps to privatize the weaker PSBs.[11] In any case, what is clear is that allowing the present situation to persist is an invitation to very serious problems down the road.

Though more than 20 years have elapsed since the reform programme began, infrastructure deficiencies remain a major obstacle to rapid growth. At the start of the reform process, India's physical infrastructure was thought of as a public sector preserve. Over time, it began to be understood that significant private sector participation is essential to address problems of incentives and efficiency. A further attraction of private investment was that it promised an escape from the fiscal constraints to increasing public investment. As a result, in recent years, in addition to inviting full private sector entry, the Indian government has also moved decisively towards promoting infrastructure investments via public-private partnerships (PPPs).

The fiscal case for PPPs is not in itself very strong and cannot be their main justification. A PPP seems attractive because the up-front capital cost of a project is wholly or in large part borne by the private investor. So it appears that the nation acquires infrastructure without the government having to pay for it. But this may be illusory if the cost to the government is merely shifted forward in time. Sometimes this is explicit: for example the private partner may be promised future 'availability payments' by the government, say an annuity in a road project that depends on how much the road is used.[12] Sometimes the government's liability is implicit. This would be the case, for example, when the private company builds and operates a road and recoups its costs, including capital cost, by charging a toll. Since the toll charges could have been earned by the government if it had built the road, they would have to be brought into the reckoning as a cost in any sensible cost-benefit analysis. The government also faces various contingent fiscal risks, including the risk that the private investor may walk away from an unsuccessful project and the government would have to take it over. Furthermore, private sector financing is generally more expensive than borrowing by the government. So PPPs are certainly not a free lunch, from the fiscal standpoint. Nevertheless, the fiscal case for PPPs is not without some merit. This is quite simply because fiscal constraints may imply that the alternative to a PPP is not public investment but no investment.[13]

The main justification for a PPP has to be that it provides better value for money than a wholly government-financed and government-run project. This it may well do, since the public sector has a deserved reputation for delays and cost over-runs. The basic idea underlying PPPs is that the bundling of finance, construction, and operation in private hands will reduce costs because of better alignment between incentives and performance compared with the public sector. For example, a private firm may build to a higher quality in the construction phase because it would gain from lower maintenance costs during the operation phase.[14] Lower costs are also supposed to result from risk-sharing between the government and private investors, since a good contract would allocate risks between the parties in line with their comparative advantages. For example, the government could acquire land and obtain environmental licences, and make sure there are no arbitrary regulatory changes, while the private party assumes the normal commercial risks, which it is better placed to handle.

The downside of PPPs is that they are highly complex arrangements. They can deliver substantial value but only if the various component parts work smoothly. India's experience has been far from perfect. While PPPs have delivered infrastructure that would not have been provided in their absence, they have also disappointed for various reasons.[15] Some major PPPs have failed altogether, for example the Delhi Airport Metro Project and the Tata-Mundra Power Generation Project, and have either reverted to government ownership or are being renegotiated. Many other projects have been adversely affected by lack of preparation by the government or lack of coordination between its different arms, resulting in long delays in obtaining land and environmental permits and making available essential ancillary facilities such as rail or road connectivity.[16] Another big problem has been lack of government competence in monitoring the bidding process and writing contracts. There have been several cases of bid manipulation by private parties in which project costs have been overstated or there has been aggressive bidding to win contracts followed by disputes, renegotiation, and downward revision of project benefits.[17] The need for greater professionalization in the government's approach to PPPs is manifestly clear. So also is the need for fairness and speed in the resolution of disputes.

I cannot, in the space available, present a detailed study of the main areas of infrastructure provision: telecommunications, roads, railways, ports, air transport, urban infrastructure, and electricity. What follows is a sketch of performance and problems. Private sector entry and competition has undoubtedly been beneficial, especially when it has been unencumbered by partnership with the public sector. This has been spectacularly so in telecommunications: coverage has increased phenomenally, prices have fallen, and quality has risen. The same is largely true of domestic air transport in which competition from private airlines has raised service standards greatly. Private investment has also resulted in some efficient new ports and power generation companies.

Infrastructure investment has come not only from public and private sources but from PPPs as well. PPPs have delivered infrastructure provision in the form of roads, ports, airports, power generation, and urban facilities but the volume has been less than desired and success has been more ambiguous. This, as already argued, is principally because the government has not acquired the requisite competence in managing the intricacies of PPP arrangements. It is also the case that incumbent government bodies involved in infrastructure services have not had their heart in the promoting PPPs. For example, the National Highway Authority is both the signatory of PPP contracts and the agency that monitors them. The conflict of interest is evident. A PPP programme for ports is way behind schedule, held up by resistance from Port Trusts and incumbent private concessionaires, who want to protect their monopoly positions.

Where full government ownership is present, the form it takes leaves a lot to be desired. Even when privatization is ruled out, corporatization and a more commercial outlook are essential, and so is independent regulation. Such arrangements are often missing. For example, most ports are still run by Port Trusts, which are in practice extensions of the government, and corporatization is held up by trade unions. The same is true of railways, which remain a government department (apart from corporatization in a few specific activities such as container train services), with a low premium on efficiency. There are no independent regulators in ports or railways to set tariffs. There are electricity regulators in 22 out of 29 states but they are mostly supine, superannuated civil servants who are loath to displease the government. The result of no regulation or ineffective regulation is that pricing remains hostage to politics. Electricity pricing, rail pricing, and pricing of bus fares are obvious examples.

The two main infrastructure black spots are electricity and urban facilities. The whole world now knows about the dire state of India's electricity sector after the sensational power failure that affected 600 million people in northern India in 2012. Power in India is erratic and there are frequent shutdowns. Peak demand exceeds supply by 15 per cent.[18] Many large companies therefore produce their own costly 'captive power'. Since small and medium-size enterprises cannot do so, their expansion is hampered. Underinvestment has caused inadequate generating capacity (until recently) but that is not the main problem, which is to be found in the distribution segment of the system. There is a political compulsion to give free or cheap power to the agricultural sector and to residential consumers—the two together constitute half of total sales. As a result, the state-owned distribution system makes massive losses and has great difficulty in paying its suppliers. This deters investment and modernization, not only in electricity distribution but in electricity generation too.[19] It does not help that the Constitution allows central and state governments to act at cross purposes since electricity is a 'concurrent subject'.

The Electricity Act of 2003 was supposed to change all this. On paper, it is excellent. It introduced a new framework requiring each state to unbundle its vertically-integrated SEB into transmission, generation, and distribution companies, privatise if desired, allow competition and private sector entry in generation and distribution, and set up a regulator to issue licences and set tariffs. 'Open access' was mandated by the Act. This meant that large consumers were supposed to be able to buy electricity from multiple sellers (including directly from producers).

That is not the way the system has evolved.[20] Unbundling has taken place in a bare majority of states (15 out of 29 states in 2011). There is competition and private sector entry in generation.[21] But the distribution sector remains largely unchanged, so there is still a single state-owned monopoly buyer and seller in each state.[22] 'Open access' does not exist or is hedged about with so many restrictions that it is ineffectual.[23] Electricity trading is allowed but only in a manner that does not threaten the monopoly position of the SEBs.[24] In the absence of competition, electricity distribution remains riddled with inefficiency. So-called 'transmission and distribution' (T&D) losses, of which a sizeable portion arises from electricity theft, are still in the region of 30 per cent of sales.

At the time of writing, there happens to be a 'power surplus', an extraordinary phenomenon in a country in which millions still lack access to electricity. This has arisen because recent governments have aggressively promoted electricity generation without reforming electricity distribution. The bankrupt SEBs cannot afford to buy power, so generators are forced to run at low capacity and the system is riddled with power cuts. The aggregate financial position of the SEBs is dire. Their accumulated losses amount to around Rs. 4 lakh crores (3 per cent of GDP), and their outstanding debt is of a similar magnitude; and they form a major component of the stressed assets of the banking system. Periodic partial bailouts of SEBs have not helped.

How is this tangled mess to be cleaned up? It seems to me that no enduring resolution will be possible without a gradual but firm and steady nation-wide reform that includes the following elements. Firstly, state governments will have to bite the bullet of charging cost-reflective prices. (Poor consumers will have to be protected by cash subsidies.) Secondly, a large part of the liabilities of the state distribution utilities must be written off so that they can start with a clean slate. Thirdly, these utilities should be broken up, privatised, and forced to compete, under the supervision of independent regulators, and 'open access' must become a reality.[25] Fourthly, the coal sector should be de-nationalized and opened up to competition. This is necessary to ensure an efficient and reliable supply of this vital input into electricity production. None of this is easy but in the absence of these radical steps, electricity promises to continue to be a drag on growth and development.[26]

Urban infrastructure also presents a huge challenge. At present about 30 per cent of India's population lives in urban areas; this share will rise to 40 per cent by 2030. (In absolute terms, this will mean a huge increase of around 250 million people in the urban population in the next 15 years.) India's urban infrastructure, especially for clean water and sewerage, is abysmal and the extra pressure on it will be massive. The required capital investment is far beyond what urban local bodies can afford. They have very limited tax capacity and there is a long tradition of fixing low user charges.[27] This will have to change. States will have to devolve more revenue to cities, and cost-reflective charges will have to be levied for urban services. Recourse to PPPs is obviously attractive in the urban context. There are around 150 currently in operation but they are beset by all the problems discussed above. I do not have the space here to discuss another important point: to develop urban infrastructure there will have to be far-reaching reforms to the governance of cities.[28]

It is blatantly clear that infrastructure shortages are holding growth back. Private investment in infrastructure has been growing and its role is envisaged to expand further. (In the 11th Plan, private investment in infrastructure was about a third of the total. In the 12th Plan, the share is supposed to rise to a half.)[29] Experience has made clear that there needs to be a considerable strengthening of the state's ability to contract, monitor, and regulate PPPs. At the same time, the shortcomings of PPPs indicate that the bias against public investment has gone too far. Public investment should be stepped up, with accompanying measures to improve the process of public sector project selection and implementation. The fiscal space for extra public investment should be created by rationalizing explicit and hidden subsidies (see Chapters 6 and 10). Private investment that is unmixed with public participation also needs more encouragement. And it is important to ensure that all sources of investment compete on a level playing field.

ENVIRONMENT AND NATURAL CAPITAL

Though it may seem eccentric at first sight, discussion of India's environment does belong in a chapter that focuses on ownership. Environmental problems are closely connected with the absence of well-defined property rights. Markets are efficient at trading resources that are owned privately.

But many environmental resources, for example the air that we breathe, have no property rights attached. A factory that discharges smoke and affects the lungs of those who live nearby does not have to pay for the harm it causes them. The harm is an 'externality' which is unpriced (or has a zero price) because the market in clean air is missing. This is an example of a one-way externality, from the factory to the nearby resident. But externalities can also be reciprocal, such that each party inflicts or confers an externality on all others. This is the case with many common property resources, in which 'open access' leads to over-use and over-exploitation. For example, unrestricted fishing can lead to depletion of fish stocks, and unrestricted use of the atmosphere as a sink for carbon emissions can lead to global warming. The remedy has to involve defining property rights. Sometimes it may be possible to set up private property rights and leave the allocation of the resource to private trading and negotiation. But in many cases this is completely unsuitable. Sometimes, it may be possible for the community to exercise the property right to the resource and organize its use sensibly. But community control is fragile and can easily break down. It then falls to the state to assume the property right and regulate use of the common property resource by taxation or controls.

In India, environmental issues were almost totally ignored for the first 25 years after independence. From the early 1970s, awareness has gradually grown and various regulatory policies have been introduced. Even so, it is obvious to the naked eye that the country is faced with degradation of the environment on a massive scale. This is confirmed by the authoritative Yale-Columbia 'environmental protection index' (EPI) ranking, in which India ranks 155th out of 178 countries in 2014.[30] The same index shows that India has a below-average score among countries with comparable income per head. The popular view is that China is much more environmentally challenged than India. This is not the case. China's EPI rank is 118 out of 178.

An imprecise but common-sense distinction can be made between two aspects of environmental damage: 'pollution' and 'resource degradation'. I have space only to discuss two aspects of each: local air and water quality as examples of pollution, and excessive water use and deforestation as examples of degradation. Air quality in India is extremely poor and has worsened markedly over the last 10 years. The country now boasts half of the world's 30 cities with the worst outdoor air pollution, including the top four (Delhi, Patna, Gwalior, and Raipur).[31] India ranks 177th out of 178 countries in the EPI air quality ranking, just ahead of China, the bottom country. On some other indicators, India is worse than China. For example, World Health Organization (WHO) data on particulate matter concentration (PM_{10}) in the air of urban centres show a highly dangerous score for India of 198 micrograms per cubic metre, compared with 121 for China and 18 for the United States. The same goes for the disease burden from outdoor air pollution.[32] Deaths of children from outdoor air pollution are much higher in India than in China, and massively higher than in the United States.[33] On water quality too, India does very badly: it is ranked well below half of the 178 countries in the EPI index, including China. In India, deaths of children under five from water pollution are 315 per 100,000 children compared with 56 for China and 0.1 for the United States.

What accounts for this appalling state of affairs? It is in part because India is a poor country and people's willingness to pay for environmental improvements is low. But that is not the sole reason. It is also because official policies take scant account of environmental externalities. Regulation is not lacking on paper. The Water Act and the Air Act were put on the statute book in 1974 and 1981, and Central and State Pollution Boards and a Ministry of Environment and Forests were established shortly thereafter. Even so, air and water externalities are not properly priced, and regulations are not enforced. Every now and then, when policy attention has been strong and consistent, progress has been achieved, only to fall back when the favourable conditions recede.

In the 1980s and 1990s, the drive to improve air quality was given a strong impetus by two judgements of India's Supreme Court. Firstly, it interpreted the fundamental 'right to life' in the Constitution to include the right to clean air and water. Secondly, it made it easier for people to engage in 'public interest litigation' (PIL) by weakening the usual requirement of *locus standi* in initiating a court case. Acting on a PIL that asked the Supreme Court to order the government of Delhi to implement the Air Act, the Court began in the second half of the 1980s an extended process of putting pressure on the executive to reduce several types of air pollution, monitored by an authority that it created for the purpose. The process included 'Supreme Court Action Plans' in various cities, beginning with Delhi, mandating regulations such as use of catalytic converters in cars, replacement of old auto-rickshaws and taxis with new vehicles using cleaner fuels, and conversion of city bus fleets to using compressed natural gas. As a result, air pollution levels in the chosen cities fell significantly for a time. The effort to improve water quality was far less successful despite a 'National River Conservation Plan' that covered many rivers including the Ganga. This is because there was much less public agitation for water quality than for air quality (presumably since it is easier for the vocal classes to take private action to purify the water they drink).[34] Also, in the case of water, lines of authority were muddled and steady backing by the Supreme Court was missing. More recently, air quality has again worsened steeply. For example, in Delhi, India's capital city, the hard-earned gains secured by PILs have been lost due to uncontrolled growth of diesel-guzzling cars, absence of congestion charges, neglect of building bypass roads to siphon off transport trucks from the city centre, and persistent deficiencies in public transport. The lesson is that the environment requires continuous policy focus and enforcement, if reversals are to be avoided.

The water situation in India is a dreadful combination of scarcity and pollution, and these two features have to be tackled simultaneously. Scarcity is caused by excessive use and depletion of water resources. In 1950, India had 5000 cubic metres of water per person annually; now it has 1200, and water is emerging as a major constraint on future growth. Recent estimates indicate that on a business-as-usual basis, national demand for water will be 50 per cent higher than supply in 2030. A whole of swathe of states in the western half of the country is suffering from water stress. In some regions the situation is already critical. Over-extraction of groundwater has lowered the water table and increased soil salinity to dangerous levels.

Water pricing has to be a key part of the solution (though certainly not the whole of it).[35] At present, water is absurdly under-priced, so there is little incentive for conservation and efficient water use. Supply of fresh water to industrial enterprises should be priced high enough to encourage them to treat and re-use water; and water supplied to urban households should be priced so as to cover the cost of both delivery of drinkable water and the cost of sewage treatment. (The latter is necessary to prevent pollution of fresh water sources. Fresh water must be treated to an acceptable level before it is returned to the ground. At present, large quantities of water are released into rivers untreated.) The affordability issue can be handled by ensuring a minimum supply on a universal basis, while water use above the minimum is priced at full cost. Needless to say, reducing water toxicity requires complementary policies on improving the quality of sanitation, which is one of India's major failings.

Agriculture accounts for four-fifths of total national water use but in a massively inefficient way. Water use in agriculture could be cut significantly by using better practices[36] and developing crop varieties that require less water. Canal water is priced at only 15 per cent of operating cost (capital costs are wholly uncovered). This leads to water wastage due to lack of maintenance, quite apart from making irrigation schemes financially unviable. It also 'encourages upstream farmers to use too much water for highly water-intensive crops, starving downstream farmers.'[37] Pricing of canal water will be necessary but exclusive reliance on it would be unwise because it would be unacceptable to raise prices to appropriate levels. Water rationing by regional and local water bodies will thus also be required, along with the use of cooperative methods.

Ground water is a common property resource but farmers are allowed to extract water at will from wells that are situated on their property, and electricity charges do not vary with water consumption. Water conservation thus requires grasping the nettle of raising electricity prices. Some states have shown the way forward. For example, in West Bengal, tube-wells are metered. Gujarat, when Narendra Modi was the chief minister, made higher electricity prices palatable by separating electricity feeder lines serving tube-wells from those serving villages, thereby improving availability of power.[38] But free power remains the norm in other states including Punjab, Karnataka, Andhra Pradesh, and Tamil Nadu.

Resource degradation is well exemplified by the condition of India's forests. In 1952, the Nehru government announced a target of one-third of land area to be brought under forest. Instead, for the next 30 years, there was extensive deforestation in the pursuit of 'development', and the area under forest cover fell to one-fifth of total land area. Though the decline has been modestly reversed since then, the initial target remains a distant prospect. Deforestation of course brings many ecological problems in its wake such as soil erosion, floods, and increased atmospheric carbon concentrations, in addition to endangering millions of people who depend on forests for their livelihoods. The Forest Conservation Act of 1980 and the National Forest Policy of 1988 said all the right things, including the suggestion that forest departments work with village communities who were to be given access to forest products in return for helping with forest protection.

Politically, as one might expect, the most sensitive issue has been the vetting of applications for diversion of forest lands to mining and industrial uses. Elaborate administrative procedures were set up for this purpose, with ambiguous guidelines, and they have worked badly. Decisions have often been extremely slow, with projects held up for long periods, sometimes for years. Political considerations are often alleged to cause delays. At the same time, the vast majority of projects have sooner or later obtained approval, which does not indicate judicious decision-making. In 2014, the Modi government set up a committee of senior bureaucrats, chaired by T. S. R. Subramanian, a former cabinet secretary, to examine the situation. Its report is forthright in its condemnation of the existing system: 'Legislation is weak, monitoring is weaker and enforcement is weakest'. In my judgement, the road-map set out by the Subramanian

Committee has much to commend it.[39] In order to speed up disposal of cases, it has recommended single-window clearance of projects by new central and state statutory agencies, manned by professionals and insulated from the political process (though the final decisions would still rest with environment ministries, subject to an appeal process). Project promoters would be bound by 'utmost good faith', whereby they would be expected to provide *all* information relevant to their projects, not simply that directly asked for, and would be made legally responsible for it, with severe penalties for misrepresentation of the facts. Both the fact-finding and the monitoring would rely less on inspectors and more on modern technology, with much tougher sanctions against non-compliance. The amount that successful applicants would have to pay for 'compensatory afforestation' would also be substantially increased. Unfortunately, the government appears to have shelved the report.

It is patently clear that India has yet to find the right balance between the claims of conventional growth and environment protection. The system works against growth because it is slow and cumbersome, against the environment because pricing and regulation are not tough enough, and against both environment and growth because it is excessively politicized. Win-win policies would be possible. The idea that protecting the environment entails a large growth sacrifice is not supported by research. Studies indicate both that the environmental costs of business-as-usual growth policies are high, and that remedial measures would be relatively inexpensive.[40] A policy that would have clear local environmental benefits would be a tax on fossil fuels. Such a tax would help moderate air pollution as well as promote water conservation (via a higher price for electricity). As it happens, it would also have the added benefit of helping to combat global warming.

GLOBAL WARMING AND CLIMATE CHANGE

Global warming, a gigantic reciprocal externality, has profound implications for all countries, including India.[41] The relevant science is now widely accepted, except by a dwindling band of cranks and 'climate deniers'. In brief, greenhouse gases (GHGs), mainly carbon dioxide, are emitted by the use of energy in conventional processes of production. They accumulate in the atmosphere, trap heat from escaping the earth's surface, and raise global temperatures. The scientific consensus is that if the global average temperature rose more than 2^0 C above a mid-19th century baseline, the associated climate change would have dangerously harmful effects, such as reduced water supplies and crop yields, more extreme weather in the form of heat waves and cyclones, sea-level rises, and large migrations of people. The consensus scientific projection is that by the end of the present century, on a business-as-usual growth path, global temperatures are likely to rise well beyond the 2^0 C threshold to a median estimate of 3.5^0 C, with a probability of more than 10 per cent of reaching 5^0 C. At 5^0 C, the changes in global climate could be so devastating as to make human life as we know it extremely difficult if not impossible. It follows that to insure against these dreadful, and possibly catastrophic, eventualities, global action should be taken to mitigate climate change by reducing GHG emissions.

Cooperative global action is necessary because each country has every incentive to free-ride; neither is cooperation helped by the fact that the costs of mitigation have to be incurred now while many of the benefits will accrue far in the future. However, it is also clear that business-as-usual growth would self-destruct in the face of untrammelled climate change. The only sensible way forward is to switch to low-carbon growth by reducing dependence on fossil fuels as sources of energy (since they are the principal source of GHGs). Moreover, this has to be done world-wide, not just by the advanced countries. Developing countries will have to play their part because they account for 80 per cent of the world's population and 50 per cent of world GDP, and these shares are expected to rise. Global estimates also show that a) the cost of climate mitigation to keep temperatures below the 2^0 C threshold would be modest[42] relative to the benefit; and b) the net benefit of climate mitigation would be far greater in poor countries than in rich countries.

Of course, who should pay for the costs of climate mitigation is a logically separate question from who should take climate-mitigating action. Though climate mitigation would have to be done universally if it is to be cheap and effective, there is certainly a persuasive moral case that the rich advanced countries (ACs) should pay for all of it since they bear 'historic responsibility' for expropriating and using up a large part of the safe carbon-capacity of the atmosphere.[43] The ACs have agreed, at least in principle, to step up climate-related transfers to poor developing countries (DCs) to $100 billion dollars a year from 2020. Of course this is far from sufficient and DCs should bargain hard for an increase in these contributions. At the same time, there is no doubt that DCs, like ACs, will have to make strenuous domestic efforts to achieve low-carbon growth if disastrous global warming is to be avoided, even if the ACs contribute less towards the costs of mitigation in DCs than they ideally should. Most DCs stand to lose heavily, and much more than the ACs, from excessive global warming, so their self-interest is vitally at stake.

How does India fit into this picture? It is a poor and populous country and its current per capita annual carbon emissions (1.5 tonnes a year) are well below the United States (17 tonnes), China (6 tonnes), and the world average (4.5 tonnes). However, in absolute terms, it has the third-largest emissions in the world. (At present, China leads the pack with 26 per cent of total world emissions, followed by the United States at 17 per cent, while India is at 6 per cent.)[44] And India's emissions are due to rise rapidly both in absolute terms and as a share of global emissions. India is thus one of the critical players for the future of global warming, which gives it some bargaining and deal-breaking power. But India is also one of the main potential sufferers from climate change, which could, if unchecked, cause it massive problems due to melting of Himalayan glaciers and disturbance to monsoonal patterns, and the resulting droughts, floods, typhoons, threats to coastal areas and major cities, and large population movements. Given its rapidly growing emissions, the country faces acute policy choices, for example with regard to electricity. At present, more than 300 million Indians lack access to electricity and have to cook in their homes with firewood, with attendant severe indoor pollution. Naturally, one of the country's aims is to achieve universal access to electricity. But electricity in India is mostly coal-based and thus highly carbon-intensive. How should this circle be squared?

A detailed discussion of the policies that India should follow would require a whole book on its own but the essential elements are clear enough. The crux of the matter is that growth has to be decarbonized, for which the critical policy requirement is to raise the price of carbon. The ideal policy would be a carbon tax that rises over time (coal as the dirtiest fuel would pay the highest tax).[45] Raising the price of carbon would signal to every consumer and producer that carbon-intensive goods and services should be used more sparingly. Just as important, it would provide a strong incentive for technical progress in developing 'clean' low-carbon products and processes. The costs of renewable energy sources, such as wind and solar power, are coming down rapidly. If fossil fuels were priced at a level that took account of the external effects of burning them, renewable technologies would become economic quite quickly. Of course, in the short run, electricity and transport prices would rise, but that is in any case desirable on various other counts. The main problem with raising the price of carbon that one has to worry about is that it would cut the real incomes of poor people. An income transfer that compensates them is thus an essential accompaniment of low-carbon policies. Setting up a cash-transfer mechanism for compensation is thus a matter of priority (see Chapter 10).

Since the price of carbon could only be raised gradually, there is clearly a role for other complementary policies, though none of these would work effectively without carbon pricing. One example is mandating energy efficiency standards for items such as refrigerators, air conditioners, vehicles, and buildings, since their proliferation will be a major source of rising energy demand. Another example is lowering the cost of finance for renewable energy, especially solar power, which is plentiful in India, by R&D subsidies. An important point to bear in mind is that there are many synergies between climate-mitigation policies, other environmental policies, and efficient growth policies more generally. Taxes on fossil fuels would also serve to combat air pollution. Rationalizing government spending in the agricultural sector (see Chapter 6) and charging economic prices for farm inputs would help to fight water scarcity as well as save energy. Changing the balance of domestic transport from road to rail would increase productivity and also reduce GHG emissions. More efficient urbanization policies, including energy-efficient public transport, would reduce urban sprawl and congestion while furthering climate mitigation.

Fears that climate mitigation policies would entail a major growth sacrifice are overblown. Consider, for example, the report of the Expert Group appointed by the Planning Commission on low-carbon strategies, chaired by Kirit Parikh.[46] This concluded on the basis of an economy-wide optimizing model that the growth-rate decline from 2007 to 2030 as a result of low-carbon strategies would be small (a decline of only 0.15 percentage points compared with the base case), while India's annual per capita carbon emissions would fall from a 2030 baseline of 3.6 tonnes to 2.6 tonnes. The total investment requirement of the low-carbon path would be roughly the same as the high-carbon path but there would have to be substantially higher investment in the energy sector (an extra 1.5 per cent of GDP annually, maintained over the period).

Of course, India's efforts would be pointless without accompanying global action. At the world level, the Kyoto Protocol of 1997 did not do much to curb emissions because it applied only to 'Annex 1 countries' (i.e. the advanced countries); and even within this group, the United States did not sign, and Russia signed but only adopted non-binding commitments. Large emitters such as China, India, Brazil, and Indonesia were exempt because they were 'Non-Annex 1'. But since 2009, the distinction between Annex 1 and Non-Annex 1 has come under pressure and it has finally been dropped in the recent Paris conference on climate change.

The achievements of the Paris conference of 195 countries in December 2015 should not be exaggerated. But they should also not be belittled. The outcome consists of a legally binding 'agreement' as well as a non-legally-binding 'decision'. In the 'agreement', countries signed up to the goal of holding the global temperature rise 'well below' the 2^0 C threshold and even to make an effort to keep it below $1.5°$ C. All countries, not just Annex 1 countries, have agreed to participate, on the basis of voluntary Intended Nationally Determined Contributions (INDCs) by each country. Only the advanced countries are expected to cut their emissions in absolute terms. The INDCs are not legally binding. What is binding is the 'pledge and review' framework, whereby countries are committed to participate in a transparent five-yearly stock-taking and goal-setting process in which they would also ratchet up their INDCs. (The first five-year cycle begins in 2020.) The 'agreement' itself makes no specific commitment on finance. However, the conference 'decision' 'strongly urges' advanced countries to provide financial support for developing countries (already agreed in principle) of $100 billion annually by 2020.

The Paris outcome has some obvious problems. There is no compulsion or enforcement of national targets declared in the INDCs. The provision of needed finance is an aspiration, not a bankable achievement. The procedures for measuring and monitoring emissions are as yet unresolved. Most important, there is no attempt to set a global carbon price. The INDCs at Paris are estimated to put the world on course for something like 3^0 C warming, so much will depend on whether countries become more ambitious as time passes. Even so, despite these difficulties, this is the first time that all countries, including the two main emitters, China and the United States, have come on board.

India's INDC for the Paris conference consisted of pledges to achieve the following goals by 2030: a) cut the carbon emissions intensity of GDP by 33–35 per cent relative to 2005; b) raise installed electricity power capacity from non-fossil fuel sources to 40 per cent of the total capacity; c) create a new carbon sink of 2.5–3 billion tonnes of CO_2 equivalent through expansion of forest cover. These are challenging goals at India's stage of development, as if not more challenging than those that China and the United States have set themselves. It is a pity that India did not try to persuade countries to put resources into bringing down the cost of 'clean coal', for example, by carbon capture and sequestration. Given India's large coal reserves, the availability of 'clean coal' technologies would make a big difference to the cost of climate mitigation policies in India. However, India does have the potential to develop solar power, and the Modi government is rightly targeting a huge increase in solar capacity from 2.3 GW in 2013 to 100 GW in 2022.[47]

It would have certainly been unwise for India to stand aside from the recent global deal on climate change. Climate mitigation is very much in India's interest. It is important also to avoid the danger that in due course the signatories to a climate agreement may practice trade restrictions and other discriminatory policies against those that do not join. India has rightly approached the issue of climate change mitigation as a diplomatic challenge of getting the right terms, not as a bugaboo to run away from. That said, there is no doubt that both climate mitigation and climate adaptation will pose significant challenges for India in its search for prosperity. That is all the more reason for embarking on radical economic reform.

NOTES

1. Supportive evidence is given in the OECD report on India (OECD 2007, Chapters 2 and 3), which concludes on the basis of a detailed study that the productivity of state-owned enterprises is a third less than that of private companies, and that the rate of return on capital is also much lower. See also Nayak (2012): 'Data from the Department of Disinvestment reveal that the profit margins of manufacturing PSEs are systematically lower than the figures for manufacturing firms in the private sector.' There is also the work of Gupta (2013), referred to below.
2. On Air India, see Roy (2015).
3. The state electricity distribution companies also have liabilities and arrears amounting to an astonishing 3 per cent of GDP.
4. Another familiar problem is delays in making appointments to board positions, including that of chief executive. There are many cases of PSEs remaining headless for months on end.
5. See Gupta (2013).
6. The rationale and modalities of privatization in India are ably dissected in Kelkar (2010).
7. See Reserve Bank of India (2014b) and Nayak (2015). PSBs have been losing market share to private banks. In 2013, the return on assets was three times higher in private than in public banks, and net profit per employee four times higher. In June 2015, impaired assets, i.e. non-performing and restructured loans, of PSBs were 13 per cent of all loans, as against 3.7 per cent for private sector banks.
8. See Table 2.9 in Reserve Bank of India (2014b).
9. PSBs suffer from having two regulators, the government of India and the RBI, and the government interferes extensively. (For example, in the 15 months from October 2012, the Ministry of Finance issued 82 circulars to PSBs.) The process of appointing members of bank boards is opaque and does not put professional competence at a premium. Bank executives are risk-averse because they fear being prosecuted by the Central Vigilance Commission for honest mistakes. See Reserve Bank of India (2014b) for an extensive discussion.
10. Setting up the BIC would require legislation, including repeal of the Bank Nationalization Act. While that is in process, the Committee's recommendation was that the government constitute an independent Bank Boards Bureau to

make top appointments in PSBs (so that the appointments process could be cleaned up).

11. In August 2015, the government came up with a seven-point proposal called "Indradhanush" (i.e. rainbow) to reform PSBs. It is grossly inadequate to the scale of the problem (see Chapter 13).

12. The government's liability could be even bigger. For example, in the Delhi-Noida toll bridge the government unwisely signed a contract that was very unfavourable to it by *guaranteeing* the private company a 20 per cent return on its capital investment. The projected traffic demand did not materialize and the government was left nursing a large loss.

13. Since a fiscal constraint can never be absolute at the margin, the implication is that the government may have a higher discount rate than the private sector. Note also that in some projects, the government may find it much more difficult than the private sector to appropriate the returns by levying user charges.

14. Another efficiency argument for PPPs is that since the private company owns the infrastructure asset during the life of the contract, all residual profits belong to it once it has fulfilled the contract terms. This gives it a strong incentive to cut costs and innovate (see Chapter 3).

15. See Lall and Anand (2014) and Pratap (2014).

16. For example, the central government may sign a PPP contract but the state government may hold up acquisition of land.

17. For example, in some ports in PPP-mode, faulty contracts have allowed private concessionaires to make excessive profits. A similar story applies to airports. Impressive modern airports, a welcome change from the past, have been built in PPP-mode in Delhi, Mumbai, Bangalore, and Hyderabad. But in Mumbai and Delhi, the concessionaires were allowed to charge an 'airport development fee' (not shared with the government and not part of the contract), which sharply reduced the value for money delivered by the projects.

18. This paragraph describes the normal state of affairs until recently. At the time of writing, there is a 'power surplus' for reasons outlined below.

19. At the time of writing, however, capacity is more than adequate; the main constraint on availability is the parlous state of SEB finances (see below). But this does not augur well for future investment in generation.

20. See Chatterjee (2015) and Sen and Jamasb (2012).

21. In addition to the large generating companies, captive and 'merchant' power plants can also supply surplus electricity to the system.

22. Orissa and Delhi have privatised their distribution but the result is private monopolies, each in its own licensed 'supply zone'. So, in effect, there is no competition in distribution.

23. For example, in order to protect SEBs, state governments have prevailed on regulators to impose very high 'surcharges' on trading.

24. Trading consists of traders acting as intermediaries between SEBs or between merchant producers and SEBs.

25. The various elements in the package are interdependent. For example, enforcing 'open access', in isolation, would be hopeless: the exit of creditworthy customers would simply drive the distribution utilities further into bankruptcy.

26. In November 2015, the government implemented yet another bailout of SEBs. But the accompanying package of reforms is not radical enough, so it is doubtful if the scheme will do more than serve as a temporary palliative (see Chapter 13).

27. Indian cities also have very low property taxes. Property tax reform is a first-order requirement for financing urban infrastructure.
28. See Ahluwalia, Kanbur, and Mohanty (2014).
29. See Tables 3.16 and 3.17 of Planning Commission (2013a).
30. See Yale Centre for Environmental Law & Policy (2014).
31. See World Health Organization (2014). Delhi's measured $PM_{2.5}$ levels are 15 times the WHO guideline. $PM_{2.5}$ pollution can lead to life-threatening heart and lung conditions.
32. Indoor air pollution due to the burning of solid fuels for cooking, especially prevalent in India's rural areas, is also enormously harmful and accounts for a million premature deaths a year in the country.
33. See Greenstone and Jack (2015), Figures 1 and 2, and the sources therein, for the much of the data referred to in this paragraph.
34. See Greenstone and Hanna (2014).
35. Australia and Singapore are examples to follow. They are both water-stressed but have addressed the problem effectively by price and non-price policies.
36. For example, in growing rice, the so-called 'system of rice intensification', combined with drip irrigation, would reduce water use.
37. See Ahluwalia (2013). My discussion of the water situation makes extensive use of this excellent article.
38. In Gujarat, the financial improvement made possible by higher prices enabled reliable power supply to be made available for agricultural uses for a stipulated eight hours a day, and for villages round the clock. Meters were made compulsory for new connections and power theft was curbed by lawsuits against thieves.
39. See Ministry of Environment and Forests (2014).
40. See Mani (2014).
41. The science, economics, and ethics of global warming are ably discussed in Dasgupta (2010), Nordhaus (2015) and Stern (2015).
42. A consensus estimate of the cost is that the growth path with mitigation would be below the business-as-usual path to the tune of 1.5 per cent of world GDP.
43. On the other side, it could be argued that the ACs did not expropriate knowingly. They acted in the belief, universally held until quite recently, that the atmosphere was an infinite resource. Moreover, the expropriators are mostly dead and gone. Their descendants, even if they could be identified, should not be held responsible for acts they did not commit. These points have some force but they do not entirely overturn 'historic responsibility'. For further discussion of this issue and the policy implications thereof, see Joshi (2009) and Joshi and Patel (2009a, 2009b).
44. However, India's cumulative emissions between 1850 and 2011 were only 2.8 per cent of the world total, compared with United States 21.2 per cent, Europe 18.4 per cent, and China 10.7 per cent.
45. An alternative policy would be to establish an emissions trading system, which would throw up a uniform price for carbon emissions. It would take me too far afield to discuss the relative merits of carbon taxes and emissions trading systems. The interested reader may consult Joshi and Patel (2009a, 2009b), Nordhaus (2015), and Stern (2015).
46. See Planning Commission (2014b).

47. India has also taken various other steps to put a price on emissions, such a) quadrupling the cess on coal, and b) eliminating diesel and petrol subsidies and taxing them instead. Indeed, as regards the latter, India stands out in not allowing a pass-through to consumers of the recent fall in world energy prices.

PART III

Stability and Inclusion

CHAPTER 8

The Requisites
of Macroeconomic Stability

What a huge difference a few years can make! At the end of 2007, India was riding high. The previous five years had been remarkably benign, with super-fast growth of close to 9 per cent a year, accompanied by moderate inflation of around 5 per cent a year. The consolidated fiscal deficit had fallen from 9.2 per cent of GDP in 2002 to 4 per cent in 2007. The current account of the balance of payments had been in surplus, or in small deficit of around 1 per cent of GDP, throughout the period. After 2007, there was a sea-change (see Table 8.1). Inflation doubled to 10 per cent a year for the next six years. The fiscal deficit doubled to 8.2 per cent of GDP in 2008 and remained at an average level of 7.7 per cent until 2013.[1] The current account deficit increased, moderately at first, and then alarmingly to 4.1 per cent of GDP in 2011 and 4.7 per cent of GDP in 2012, the highest since independence. The annual growth rate fell to 6.7 per cent in 2008 and recovered to 8.7 per cent in the following two years, but crashed to around 5 per cent for five years from 2011.[2] It would be tempting to blame the global credit crisis of 2008 for this change of fortune. In truth, the global crisis and all the other usual suspects, such as droughts and high oil prices, were less important in causing India's dramatic macroeconomic decline than various critical domestic policy failures. It has become clear that India has as yet much to learn in the art of maintaining macroeconomic stability.

Table 8.1 MAJOR MACROECONOMIC INDICATORS 2003/4–2015/16

Year or Average of Years	(1) Growth (% p.a.)	(2) Inflation (CPI) (% p.a.)	(3) Fiscal Balance (% GDP)	(4) CAB (% GDP)	(5) RER (2004/ 5 = 100)
2003/4–2007/8	8.7	5.0	−6.2 (−6.6)	0.3	102.2
2008/9–2013/14	6.9	10.0	−7.8 (−8.1)	−3.1	107.9
2007/8	9.3	6.2	−4.0 (−4.6)	−1.3	109.2
2008/9	6.7	9.1	−8.2 (−9.9)	−2.3	99.7
2009/10	8.6	12.3	−9.4 (−9.6)	−2.8	105.0
2010/11	8.9	10.5	−6.8	−2.7	115.0
2011/12	6.7	8.4	−7.6	−4.2	113.2
2012/13	4.5 [5.4]	10.2	−6.8	−4.7	108.7
2013/14	4.7 [6.3]	9.5	−7.2	−1.7	105.5
2014/15	5.5 E [7.1]	5.9	−6.6	−1.4	111.2
2015/16	5.5 E [7.3]	5.0 E	−6.5 E	−0.9 E	114.5 E

Notes: E denotes author's guesstimates in column 1 and author's estimates based on the first 10 months' data in column 5. Column 1: Growth of real GDP at factor cost, 2004/5 series. The figures in square brackets give growth of real GDP at factor cost, 2011/12 series. Column 2: Annual rise in the CPI (IW) until 2010/11 and CPI (NS) from 2011/12, measured on an average-of-months basis. Column 3: Fiscal balance of consolidated government (i.e. central and state governments combined), excluding off-budget subsidies, as a proportion of GDP (the figures in brackets include off-budget subsidies, which were discontinued after 2009/10). Column 4: CAB refers to the current account of the balance of payments as a proportion of GDP. Column 5: RER refers to the level of the real effective exchange rate (36-country index with export-based weights), with base year 2004/5.
Sources: Columns 1, 2, and 4: Government of India (2015a); Column 3: Ministry of Finance (2015a); Column 5: Reserve Bank of India (2015).

MACROECONOMIC STABILITY

Macroeconomic stability is a pure public good that ranks with law and order and defence as a necessary condition for advancing national well-being. It means primarily 'internal balance', i.e. keeping inflation low and output close to its potential maximum. In addition, three other features are now generally included in a wider and longer-run definition of macroeconomic stability. These comprise a sound fiscal position ('fiscal balance'), a sound balance of payments position ('external balance'), and a sound asset-liability position of financial institutions ('financial balance'). Failure on these three fronts is likely sooner or later to lead to high inflation or collapse of output or both, in other words to macro-instability narrowly defined. This chapter examines where India stands on internal, external, and fiscal balance. (Financial balance is discussed as part of 'internal balance' to keep the length of the chapter within reasonable bounds.) Tables 8.1–8.6 provide data on the major macroeconomic variables of interest from 2003 onwards.

INTERNAL BALANCE: PRICE AND OUTPUT STABILITY

Low inflation is a prime objective of Indian macroeconomic policy not only for reasons that apply everywhere[3] but because there is in India a well-grounded concern that inflation hurts the poor.[4] Inflation is also a highly salient issue politically, and plays a major role in elections. Opinion polls have routinely confirmed that people regard inflation as the economic issue that worries them most. In consequence, India exhibits in an acute form the tension that characterizes all democracies on the subject of inflation. On the one hand, inflation is unpopular and votes have to be won, so democracy has a built-in barrier against inflation. On the other hand, democracy gives voice to many competing groups, so the government is tempted to throw money at problems. In India, until recently, this tension has always been resolved in favour of low inflation. But there are signs that such an outcome can no longer be taken for granted.

Inflation in India averaged around 8 per cent a year from 1960 to the mid-1990s (though punctuated by occasional short bouts of galloping prices). This was low to moderate by the standards of the day in developing countries.[5] It then fell to 5 per cent for a decade or so. There has been a marked change since then. From 2008 to 2013, it averaged 10 per cent a year, and was above 8 per cent in each of the six years.[6] Moreover, the world has now moved towards low inflation. By today's global standards, India no longer counts as a low-inflation country. From 2008 to 2013, India's 10 per cent inflation rate was far higher than the advanced countries' average of 1.9 per cent; and it was also well above the developing countries' average of 6.6 per cent (5.3 per cent in Asia, 6.5 per cent in Latin America, and 9.1 per cent in Sub-Saharan Africa)[7].

There is nothing mysterious about the origins of India's high-inflation spurts. They are generally sparked off by two kinds of supply shock. The first is a drought or, worse, a succession of droughts. Failure of the rains reduces production in agriculture, and raises the prices of food grains, other food articles, and agricultural raw materials. (Even now, only about half the country's cultivated area is irrigated.) The second familiar supply shock is a rise in the price of imported commodities on the world market. Of these, the most important is crude oil: three-quarters of the country's requirement of this essential input is met by imports. One or both of these shocks have started most of the high inflation episodes in the last 50 years, including the most recent one that began in 2008.[8]

What sparks inflation is quite different from what keeps it on the boil. Though a supply shock raises the price of, say, food or oil products, this leads to a *persistent rise in the overall price level* only if it spreads and gathers strength due to the pressure of aggregate demand. If the economy is 'overheated', the inflationary impulse becomes generalized.[9] A wage-price spiral can then develop that is hard to break, especially if people begin to expect higher inflation and increase their wage and salary claims in order to protect their real incomes. To prevent these 'second-round effects', monetary policy has to keep excess demand and inflationary expectations in check. This is not easy because there can be unpleasant short-term trade-offs. A tight monetary policy can reduce growth for a time and put people out of work. This is painful but may be necessary to stop inflation getting out of hand. If a supply shock is the result of a temporary and reversible cause, for example a monsoon failure, there is obviously a case for doing nothing much except protecting consumers by importing more food or offloading it from a domestic buffer stock. Food prices may be kept reasonably stable thereby, and monetary and fiscal retrenchment avoided, until good harvests return to improve the supply situation.[10] But this may be a counsel of perfection. If the shock is severe, supply management cannot stem the tide of rising prices. Restrictive policies have to be introduced despite their unpopularity and their adverse effects on non-agricultural output, in order to curb inflationary expectations and prevent an inflationary explosion.[11]

In this simple sense, India's post-independence monetary policy has been quite sound. The authorities have tried to ride through supply shocks by increasing the availability of sensitive commodities via extra imports or releases from buffer stocks, but they have clamped down with monetary (and occasionally fiscal) retrenchment if there are clear signs that inflation is spreading to sectors not directly related to agriculture. Unfortunately, though this strategy served the country quite well in the past, it is no longer fit for purpose. This is because 'second-round effects' have become much more powerful than hitherto.

In today's world of low inflation, India's long-run inflation target should certainly be no higher than 4 or 5 per cent a year.[12] As in all countries, the primary responsibility for achieving this aim rests with demand management via monetary and fiscal policy. In India, fiscal policy is not a flexible instrument and the government tends to run large deficits. It follows that the burden of demand management has to be carried largely by monetary policy. Even so, demand management, on its own, will not achieve low inflation in India today (or at least not without intolerable cost). There are two systemic supply-side factors that create an inflationary bias. Firstly, there is the nature of state intervention in the food market. Such intervention is not necessarily a bad thing. In an economy that is subject to volatile swings in agricultural production, a price-stabilization scheme run by the government makes good sense. A responsible government may also quite rightly wish to protect the poorest people against food destitution. How would these tasks be organized in a rational system? The government would assure farmers a 'procurement price' (in other words a price at it which it stands ready to buy food from them) that is equal to an average of market prices expected to rule in good and bad years, thereby shielding them from price instability. It would buy from farmers in good agricultural years and add to a buffer stock. It would sell from the stock (and import more) in drought years in order to lower market prices. In addition, the government would enable the poorest people to buy food at the stabilized market prices, by giving them an explicit income subsidy in cash or in food vouchers.

The food market in India is a far cry from this desirable scenario. The procurement prices at which the government guarantees to buy food from farmers are raised from time to time by large amounts even in bad years, and especially before elections. This tendency was strikingly in evidence while the UPA government was in power. In the two pre-election years of 2007 and 2008, and the election year of 2009, procurement prices of the major cereals (rice and wheat) increased by an average of 60 per cent. From 2006 to 2013, they rose 113 per cent.[13] Admittedly, some of these increases were undertaken to compensate farmers for input-cost increases in previous years, but the speed and scale of the changes were bound to drive food prices higher. (Since the government is a major buyer, procurement prices tend to set the level of market prices.) As regards help to the poorest people, the existing system attempts to do that by issuing ration cards to enable them to buy food through 'fair price shops' at 'issue prices' that are well below procurement prices. Issue prices are changed very infrequently, which means that the food subsidy tends to rise and add to the fiscal deficit. This makes the government reluctant to disgorge its accumulated food stocks even in bad years.[14] It is a crazy system but it persists because there is method in the madness: it suits the interests of the powerful farm lobby. The combination of the propensity to raise procurement prices spasmodically by large amounts (and never to reduce them), and the reluctance to offload food stocks, implies that the government tends to administer upward food-price shocks to the economy that are of its own making.[15]

The second systemic supply factor that has a bearing on inflation is that rigidities in supply chains tend to generate spikes in the prices of food articles that are disproportionately sharp in relation to the shocks that trigger them. The public distribution system (PDS) deals mainly with the major cereals: rice and wheat. 'Food articles' is a much wider category than cereals and includes milk, fish, eggs, meat, sugar, and vegetables. These non-cereal foods are major sources of protein and are becoming a significant component of the typical consumption basket as incomes rise. Production of these items has not risen fast enough, and in several of the past few years, they have contributed more to the overall price rise than cereals. Like cereals, these commodities are vulnerable to negative supply shocks due to the weather and other factors. The food trade is cartelized, with many barriers to competitive entry erected by incumbent traders and the government.[16] Moreover, antiquated technology makes the conduit from farmer to retailer highly inflexible and inefficient. (It is estimated that half of the vegetables and fruits grown in the country rot before they reach the market.) As a result, supply shocks can have a large impact on retail prices and the cost of living. This makes it more likely that they will be passed on into wage demands and the overall price level, which increases the pressure on the government (and the central bank) to accommodate them by monetary expansion in order to avoid a slowdown of the economy.

How then should we think about the relative importance of supply factors, demand factors, and, as part of the latter, monetary policy, in achieving internal balance? It is useful to start with Milton Friedman's famous remark: 'inflation is always and everywhere a monetary phenomenon'. This is true in the restricted sense that the central bank can, with certainty, prevent inflation taking hold, provided that it is willing and able to tighten monetary policy *to any extent necessary, whatever the collateral damage.* But the stronger are the cost-push factors, and the demand stimuli that are not directly influenced by monetary policy, the fiercer the central bank has to be to rein in inflation, and the larger the short-run cost in terms of output and unemployment of doing so. And given these unpleasant side-effects, the bigger also is the temptation for the central bank not to clamp down and court unpopularity. This insight is important in understanding where India currently stands on the inflation issue.

High inflation from 2008 onwards had multiple causes. As usual, there were some adverse supply-side factors such as slow growth of agricultural production (compared with the previous five years), the sharp drop in production of food grains in 2009, the fall in production of food articles other than food grains in 2010, and the rise in oil prices from 2010, which was reinforced by rupee depreciation in 2011 and 2013. In addition, as noted above, government intervention in the food market, and rigid supply chains were inflationary forces in their own right. In the short run, these supply-side factors had to be taken as given. That shifts the focus to demand, which was also running high, as shown by several indicators. Firstly, large fiscal deficits, which had moderated in the five years before 2008, returned and continued thereafter. Secondly, the current account deficit widened significantly, which shows that home demand was strong. Finally, rural demand was booming as a result of a sharp increase in wage growth. Rural farm and non-farm money wages grew at 17.2 per cent and 14.9 per cent a year respectively during 2008–2012, compared with 7 per cent and 4.9 per cent during 2005–2008.[17] This must be attributed (partly) to the rural employment guarantee programme, which helps to set a floor to rural wages.[18] More generally, formal and informal indexation in the economy has increased in recent years. To the pre-existing indexation of the incomes of sections of the organized workforce (through dearness allowance payments) has now been added indexation of minimum wages in the employment guarantee programme. In addition, government salaries are more frequently and generously revised by pay commissions, and the incomes of farmers are protected by frequent revisions in procurement prices.

What about the policy response? Its course can be seen in Table 8.2. Since fiscal policy was expansive, the job of demand-side inflation control was left to the Reserve Bank of India (RBI). Given the strength of both demand and cost-push forces, monetary policy would have had to be tough to be effective. Put bluntly, the RBI muffed it. It took a softly-softly approach to raising interest rates. It is nearly an iron law of modern economic policy that to bring inflation down, the real policy rate of the central bank should be positive and higher than it was previously. The RBI's response departed massively from this canonical prescription. The average real policy rate, which was about 1.8 per cent in 2003–2008, fell to a *negative* 3.0 per cent in the high inflation period of 2008–2013. (See Table 8.2).[19] Moreover, the policy reaction was slow. Interest rate increases began late in the day and were very gradual. They did not send a clear signal that the RBI meant business. While this was doubtless because it feared hurting investment and growth, it is surely no surprise that inflation proved to be persistent.[20]

The above analysis shows that India's sharp slowdown after 2011 was not due to monetary tightening. Its true causes are to be found elsewhere. The 'double dip' in advanced countries was one factor because it reduced demand for Indian exports.[21] But the single biggest proximate cause of the growth-recession was the collapse of domestic investment. In the strong boom from 2003/4 to 2007/8, real gross fixed capital formation (real GFCF) rose rapidly at a rate of 15 per cent a year. This fell to 7 per cent a year from 2008/9 to 2012/13 and further to 3.6 per cent a year thereafter. While the rate of growth of public GFCF halved from 2008/9 onwards, growth of corporate GFCF crashed from 29.6 per cent a year to virtually zero during 2008/9 to 2012/13. Table 8.3 shows the movement of GFCF. Corporate

Table 8.2 INFLATION, NOMINAL INTEREST RATES, AND REAL INTEREST RATES

Year	2003/4–2007/8 average	2008/9	2009/10	2010/11	2011/12	2012/13	2013/14	2008/9–2013/14 average	2014/15	2015/16
CPI Inflation	5.0	9.1	12.4	10.4	8.4	10.4	9.7	10.1	6.0	5.0 E
WPI Inflation	5.5	8.1	3.8	9.6	8.9	7.4	6.0	7.3	2.0	-2.5 E
Nominal Policy Rate	6.8	8.0	4.8	6.0	8.0	7.9	7.5	7.0	7.9	7.0 E
Real Policy Rate (CPI)	1.8	-1.1	-7.6	-4.4	-0.4	-2.3	-2.0	-3.0	2.9	2.0 E
Nominal Lending Rate	12.4	14.1	13.4	8.9	10.4	10.0	10.1	11.1	10.1	11.5 E
Real Lending Rate (CPI)	7.4	5.0	1.0	-1.5	2.0	-0.2	0.4	1.1	4.1	6.5 E
Nominal Deposit Rate	6.9	8.3	7.0	8.5	9.1	8.9	8.9	8.4	8.6	8.2 E
Real Deposit Rate (CPI)	1.9	-0.8	-5.4	-1.9	0.7	-1.5	-0.8	-1.6	2.6	3.2 E

Notes: i) The CPI index used is the CPI (IW) General Index until 2010 and the All-India CPI (NC) thereafter; ii) The WPI index is the All Commodities index; iii) All real rates of interest are defined as nominal rate minus ex post CPI inflation; iv) the nominal lending rate is an average of the lending rates of five major banks; v) the deposit rate is for bank deposits of three to five years; vi) E stands for author's estimates, based on the first ten months' data.
Sources: CPI and WPI inflation from Government of India (2015a). All nominal interest rates from Reserve Bank of India (2015).

Table 8.3 GROSS FIXED CAPITAL FORMATION (GFCF)

	Increase in Real GFCF (% p.a. at 2004/5 prices)				GFCF at current prices (% GDP at market prices)			
	Public	Corporate	Household	Total	Public	Corporate	Household	Total
2005/6–2007/8 (average)	15.8	29.6	2.9	15.4	7.7	12.9	10.9	31.5
2008/9–2012/13 (average)	7.2	0.3	15.9	7.1	7.9	9.8	13.7	31.4
2007/8	12.5	27.7	5.3	16.2	8.0	14.3	10.6	32.9
2008/9	12.0	−21.9	33.2	3.5	8.5	10.3	13.5	32.3
2009/10	5.6	9.3	7.7	7.7	8.4	10.2	13.2	31.7
2010/11	5.0	17.6	9.2	11.0	7.8	10.4	12.7	30.9
2011/12	−1.3	−0.1	31.9	12.3	7.1	9.4	15.2	31.8
					(7.4)	(11.2)	(15.7)	(34.3)
2012/13	14.6	−3.6	−2.6	0.8	7.8	8.5	14.1	30.4
	(2.6)	(13.2)	(−1.4)	(4.9)	(7.0)	(11.8)	(14.6)	(33.4)
2013/14	n.a.	n.a.	n.a.	n.a.	n.a.	n.a.	n.a.	28.3
	(9.4)	(10.5)	(−5.4)	(3.4)	(7.0)	(11.7)	(12.9)	(31.6)
2014/15	n.a.	n.a.	n.a.	n.a.	n.a.	n.a.	n.a.	n.a.
	(14.5)	(13.7)	(−9.2)	(4.9)	(7.5)	(12.3)	(11.0)	(30.8)
2015/16	n.a.	n.a.	n.a.	n.a.	n.a.	n.a.	n.a.	n.a.
	(n.a.)	(n.a.)	(n.a.)	(5.3)	(n.a.)	(n.a.)	(n.a.)	(29.4)

Notes: Figures in brackets are from the 2011/12 series of national accounts. All other figures are from the 2004/5 series of national accounts.
Sources: Government of India (2015a); Government of India, Central Statistics Office (2011); and Government of India, Central Statistics Office (2012, 2013, 2014, 2015, 2016).

investment performance was particularly bad in 2011 and 2012, when real corporate GFCF showed an *absolute decline*; and informal evidence does not show much improvement thenceforth.[22]

What accounts for the corporate investment famine, given that tough monetary policy is clearly not an explanation? Some analysts have argued that excessive government spending and borrowing 'crowded out' private investment.[23] While it is true that fiscal deficits were high after 2007, crowding out should have shown up in a rise in real interest rates. As seen above, this did not happen. Moreover, while the public deficit (i.e. public investment minus public saving) rose substantially in 2008 and 2009, it fell sharply in 2010 and increased only slightly thereafter, not nearly enough to cause a severe collapse of corporate investment.[24] In my view, the fall in corporate investment was only to a minor extent the result of high fiscal or public deficits. It was mainly 'autonomous', caused by other factors unrelated to crowding out.[25] The evolution of domestic savings and investment is shown in Tables 8.4 and 8.5 respectively.

Why did corporate investment collapse? The main explanation is surely that companies were hobbled by an overhang of debt. In the go-go years of 2003–2008, they had thrown caution to the winds, and over-committed themselves to new projects. A slowdown of the scorching pace of investment was quite natural when the boom was stopped in its tracks by the global crisis. But a sustained investment recovery was made very difficult because much of the massive rise in investment had been financed by debt rather than equity.[26] When the bubble burst in 2008, many companies pulled back at first but continued borrowing and investing in 2009 and 2010 to try and finish the projects they had started earlier, becoming in the process progressively more weighed down by debt. In the end, the need to deleverage became urgent in the face of stagnant demand, and necessitated the abandonment of ongoing projects as well as cancellation or postponement of new investment.[27] Indeed, the debt burden became so high that it has not yet been worked off and continues to inhibit an investment recovery to this day.

Another reason for the investment slowdown after 2011 was that the risk premium on investment went up. Two identifiable factors were involved. Firstly, the deterioration in the macroeconomic situation did not help. New investment was discouraged by the persistence of high inflation and the rise in current account and fiscal deficits, which suggested that the economy was running out of control. Secondly, governance problems took their toll. From 2010 onwards, the government got tangled up in the fallout from the revelation of various scams, notably in telecom and mining. Their exposure was a good thing for the future of Indian democracy

Table 8.4 GROSS DOMESTIC SAVINGS (% GDP AT MARKET PRICES)

	2003/4–2007/8 (average)	2007/8	2008/9	2009/10	2010/11	2011/12	2012/13	2013/14	2014/15
Household	23.2	22.4	23.6	25.2	23.1	22.8 (23.6)	21.9 (22.5)	n.a. (20.9)	n.a. (19.1)
Financial	11.2	11.6	10.1	12.0	9.9	7.0 (7.4)	7.1 (7.4)	n.a. (7.7)	n.a. (7.7)
Physical	12.0	10.8	13.5	13.2	13.2	15.8 (16.2)	14.8 (15.1)	n.a. (13.2)	n.a. (11.4)
Corporate	7.2	9.4	7.4	8.4	8.0	7.3 (9.5)	7.1 (10.0)	n.a. (10.8)	n.a. (12.7)
Public	2.9	5.0	1.0	0.2	2.6	1.2 (1.6)	1.2 (1.3)	n.a. (1.3)	n.a. (1.2)
Government	-1.6	0.5	-2.8	-3.1	-0.5	-2.0 (-1.8)	-1.6 (-1.6)	n.a. (-1.3)	n.a. (-1.1)
Public Enterprises	4.5	4.5	3.8	3.3	3.1	3.2 (3.4)	2.8 (2.9)	n.a. (2.6)	n.a. (2.3)
Gross Domestic Savings	33.2	36.8	32.0	33.7	33.7	31.3 (34.7)	30.1 (33.8)	30.5 (33.0)	n.a. (33.0)
Foreign Savings	0.4	1.3	2.3	2.8	1.8	4.2 (4.3)	4.7 (4.8)	0.9 (1.7)	n.a. (1.2)
Gross Capital Formation	33.6	38.1	34.3	36.5	36.5	35.5 (39.0)	34.8 (38.6)	31.4 (34.7)	n.a. (34.2)

Notes: Figures in brackets are from the 2011/12 series of national accounts. All other figures are from the 2004/5 series of national accounts.
Sources: Government of India (2015a); Government of India, Central Statistics Office (2011); and Government of India, Central Statistics Office (2012, 2013, 2014, 2015, 2016).

Table 8.5 DOMESTIC CAPITAL FORMATION (% GDP AT MARKET PRICES)

	2003/4–2007/8 (average)	2007/8	2008/9	2009/10	2010/11	2011/12	2012/13	2013/14	2014/15
Gross Fixed Capital Formation	29.6	32.9	32.3	31.7	30.9	31.8 (34.3)	30.4 (33.4)	28.3 (31.6)	n.a. (30.8)
Public Sector	7.4	8.0	8.5	8.4	7.8	7.1 (7.4)	7.8 (7.0)	n.a. (7.0)	n.a. (7.5)
Private Sector	22.2	24.9	23.8	23.3	23.1	24.7 (26.9)	22.6 (26.4)	n.a. (24.6)	n.a. (22.3)
Corporate	10.7	14.3	10.3	10.2	10.4	9.4 (11.2)	8.5 (11.8)	n.a. (11.7)	n.a. (12.3)
Household	11.5	10.6	13.5	13.1	12.7	15.2 (15.7)	14.1 (14.6)	n.a. (12.9)	n.a. (11.0)
Change in Stocks	2.7	4.0	1.9	2.8	3.5	1.9 (2.4)	1.7 (2.1)	n.a. (1.6)	n.a. (1.8)
Investment in Valuables	1.1	1.1	1.3	1.8	2.1	2.7 (2.9)	2.6 (2.7)	n.a. (1.3)	n.a. (1.5)
Errors and Omissions	0.3	0.1	-1.2	0.2	0.0	-0.9 (-0.6)	0.1 (0.4)	n.a. (0.2)	n.a. (0.1)
Gross Domestic Capital Formation	33.6	38.1	34.3	36.5	36.5	35.5 (39.0)	34.8 (38.6)	n.a. (34.7)	n.a. (34.2)

Notes: Figures in brackets are from the 2011/12 series of national accounts. All other figures are from the 2004/5 series of national accounts.
Sources: Government of India (2015a); and Government of India, Central Statistics Office (2011); and Government of India, Central Statistics Office (2012, 2013, 2014, 2015, 2016).

but the short-term economic effects were unhelpful. The output of critical materials was adversely affected. (For example, mine closures by court order led to a significant fall in the output of iron ore.) The government entered a period of policy paralysis. Ministers and civil servants became cautious and unwilling to make decisions.[28] The spate of scandals heightened public sensitivities over land acquisition and environmental impacts but the government was not able to put in place fair, transparent, and speedy systems for dealing with these issues. As a result, project approvals came to a standstill, and so did progress on economic reform. On top of all this, the government shot itself in the foot by undertaking various silly initiatives that sent the wrong signals, such as retrospective taxation of some foreign companies. It is not surprising that faced with these manifold governance issues, in addition to a debt overhang and yet another global slowdown from 2011, new investment dried up.[29] Be that as it may, it is clear that the severe slowdown from 2011 had very little to do with 'crowding out' or the stance of monetary policy. The RBI misunderstood the nature of the slowdown and kept monetary policy loose despite the surge of inflation. The upshot was that the country got both high inflation and low growth.

I conclude that Indian policy towards internal balance needs an overhaul. India must decide whether it is serious about keeping inflation low. If it is, it would imply signing up to the view, which I strongly support, that there is no long-run growth advantage to be had from an inflation rate above 4 or 5 per cent. It follows, given the spread of indexation, that the Reserve Bank will have to be tougher than hitherto in responding to inflation. Of course, other supporting policies could help to reduce the burden that falls on the RBI. It would help if fiscal deficits were lower and fiscal policy flexible enough to play its part in demand management. It would also help if the government took steps to boost the growth rate of agricultural production (including protein foods with high income elasticity of demand), adopted a rational buffer stock policy, and promoted modernization of the rigid supply chains for farm products (for example by introducing more competition and allowing foreign direct investment in multi-brand retail). However, when the chips are down, the buck always stops with monetary policy in the fight against inflation. Does this mean that India should adopt 'flexible inflation targeting', as recommended by the landmark Report of the Monetary Framework Committee (chaired by Urjit Patel) in 2014?[30] I am in favour of such a step. Inflation targeting would be a helpful, even a necessary (though by no means sufficient), move to keep inflation within acceptable limits. The Appendix to this chapter surveys briefly the debate on inflation targeting.

In the past two years (2014/15 and 2015/16), the Modi government has been in the saddle. Inflation has been falling despite two bad monsoons in succession, and is now running at around 5 per cent a year. Several ingredients have contributed. The sharp decline in world commodity prices, particularly the collapse in oil prices, has made a major contribution. The weakness of economic activity since 2011 has had an effect in slowing the growth of money wages, including rural money wages. The government has wisely released food stocks and reined in increases in procurement prices. And last but not least, monetary policy has been credibly anti-inflationary. As soon as R. Rajan came in as governor of the RBI in September 2013, he signalled a tougher approach. The policy rate was hiked in three steps to 8 per cent and remained at that level for 15 months even while inflation was coming down. It has since been lowered to 6.75 per cent, but continues to be in positive territory in real terms.[31] The RBI has signalled that a further reduction in the rate will depend in part on the fiscal stance of the central government in its budget for 2016/17. The hand of the RBI was strengthened by its agreement with the Finance Ministry in February 2015 that in effect ushered in a regime of inflation targeting. The inflation target was agreed to be 6 per cent for January 2016 and 4 per cent (with a band of +/– 2 per cent) for 2016/17 and thereafter.[32] Other attributes generally associated with inflation targeting, such as the formation of a 'monetary policy committee' to make interest rate decisions, have yet to happen. (Until then, interest rate policy is in the hands of the RBI governor.)

Though the RBI has been successful in bringing inflation under control, monetary transmission has faced problems. For example, the commercial banks have passed on only about half of the rate cut that the RBI initiated in 2015. One reason for this is some long-standing distortions in the system. The government-administered rates on small savings are only changed annually, and set a floor to bank deposit rates, which in turn set a floor to bank lending rates.[33] Smooth transmission of monetary policy requires that small savings rates should move in tandem with the policy rate. Other factors that impede transmission include a) interest rate subsidies that are given for various selected activities and b) the high level of the statutory liquidity ratio (SLR), which stipulates the minimum share (currently 21.5 per cent) of bank deposits that has to be placed in government securities.[34] These are all features of 'financial repression' that clearly need to be phased out. But this would require coordination between the government and the RBI. For example, the SLR could not be reduced without reducing government borrowing, i.e. the fiscal deficit. The point to note here is that the smooth operation of inflation targeting depends on improving the transmission mechanism for monetary policy.

Overall, the performance on the inflation front has been commendable. What about investment and growth? In this area, the outcome has not been nearly as good despite the large terms of trade gain (more than 2 per cent of GDP) from the crash in global oil prices. The slowdown of the economy that started in 2012/13 still continues, though the new national accounts figures (2011/12 series) produced by the Central Statistical Office (CSO) give a very much rosier picture. If the new numbers are to be believed, the sharp slowdown lasted only a year: the economy recovered in 2013/14 and grew at more than 7 per cent a year in the next two years (see Table 8.1). I find this dubious (and so do many other economists) without in any way doubting the integrity of the CSO. The culprit is probably the CSO's new methodology, which has many problems including the use of inappropriate price deflators. The issues involved are highly technical and cannot be pursued here. However, it is incontestable that the new national accounts numbers are totally at variance with other indicators of economic activity, most of which are growing well below the rates that would be observed in a vigorously expanding economy (and were observed during past periods of rapid growth). Industrial growth, as measured by the index of industrial production, has been extremely weak, indeed barely positive. Exports have shrunk substantially in absolute dollar value. Imports, including capital goods imports, are also showing significant negative growth. Growth of bank credit, especially to industry, has been very sluggish. Employment creation in the organized sector is practically at a standstill. The company universe shows very slow, if not negative, growth of sales revenue, as well as strongly rising interest and debt burdens, and stagnating profits. Crucially, corporate capital expenditure and investment are subdued. Investment proposals are running at less than a quarter of their levels in 2010 and 2011. At the same time, there is not enough forward movement in the revival of stalled projects. Agricultural output has been nearly flat for the past two years and there is growing agrarian distress. In other words, if the economy has indeed recovered and is growing strongly, this is not visible anywhere except in the national accounts statistics.[35] I would guess that in 2014 and 2015 the economy has been growing around two percentage points less than indicated by the CSO, i.e. at about 5.5 per cent a year.

Revival of investment is critical but is held up by two interrelated problems: the debt hangover faced by major companies due to erstwhile reckless borrowing, and the corresponding rise in bad loans in the banking system. Corporate leverage is so high and the interest coverage ratio so low in some sectors such as steel, construction, and infrastructure, that companies therein can only think of survival, not fresh investment. (As of now, among the emerging market economies, India has the highest debt-equity ratio in the corporate sector.) The corporate sector accounts for three-quarters of banks' credit portfolios. So, as a mirror image of corporate weakness, the commercial banks, especially public sector banks (PSBs), have seen a steep rise in 'stressed assets' that has reduced their overall lending capacity, and their desire to lend, even to healthy companies.[36] Stressed assets of PSBs were 14 per cent of total advances in September 2015, accompanied by a sharp fall in bank profitability and the return on assets. This is not a good position for the banks to be in, if credit supply is to be available to finance rising investment.

The RBI has ordered the banks to clean up their books by March 2017, so they will have to 'recognize' bad assets and stop hiding them by accounting fudges. It has taken various other steps to deal with the bad loans problem such as allowing banks to take control of companies by converting unpaid loans into equity, and raising public consciousness about defaulting promoters. Thus far (December 2015), asset quality pressure has not eased at all, and the situation is likely to get worse before it gets better. The problem is so large and deep-seated that radical solutions may be required. Recognizing and providing for bad loans will inevitably mean losses for banks and a large blow to their equity capital; so, there will have to be a capital infusion (over and above what is required to fulfil the Basel 3 norms). Asking PSBs to raise more money in the market to shore up their equity will not be feasible until their balance sheets have been restored to normality. (These banks have been quoted at well below their book values for years: the market is only too well aware of their rank inefficiencies.) The government's planned capital infusions in the 2016/17 and future budgets are reckoned by knowledgeable observers to be grossly insufficient to meet the scale of the problem. However, if growth does not pick up soon, further recapitalization by the government will become unavoidable. It may help to set up a government-backed asset reconstruction company (a so-called 'bad bank') that would buy non-performing loans at a discount and get them off the banks' books quickly (but it would not avoid the need for recapitalization since the banks would take an equity hit) and focus on recovering value to the extent possible. A long-term solution would require not only recapitalization to solve the 'stock' problem of bad debt but also governance and ownership changes to deal with the 'flow' problem of improving the PSBs' income-earning capacity. Ways to do this have been discussed in Chapter 7.

An incidental lesson from the current macroeconomic situation is that 'microeconomic' inefficiencies can exacerbate macro problems. For example, corporate restructuring that is necessary for the revival of investment is more difficult than it needs to be because of India's highly cumbersome procedures for dealing with company distress, bankruptcy, and exit; and the asset quality problems in the banking sector have been brought about in part by governance problems in PSBs, which led to unwise lending.

EXTERNAL BALANCE

Overall, India has had a good record on external stability since the 1991 reforms although, or because, its balance of payments policy has diverged from economic orthodoxy in a constructive way. The hallmarks of this policy were 'managed floating' of the exchange rate, and the use of some focused controls on short-term capital movements. (Direct and portfolio equity investments have been largely unrestricted but there have been some controls on debt inflows, particularly of the short-term variety.) This regime has helped to keep the current account deficit at modest levels most of the time, and to preserve financial stability while the economy was integrating rapidly with the rest of the world.

The rationale of India's choice of external payments regime merits some explanation, since there are many regimes to choose from.[37] One extreme option is a permanently fixed exchange rate combined with 'capital account convertibility' (CAC), i.e. completely free and unrestricted capital movements. This alternative is clearly unsuitable since exchange rate changes may be necessary to maintain the country's competitive position in the face of adverse shocks.[38] Moreover, a fixed exchange rate plus CAC would deprive the country of 'monetary autonomy', i.e. the ability of policymakers to set interest rates to suit domestic conditions.[39] A diametrically opposite option is a regime with 'clean floating' of the exchange rate plus CAC: the authorities bind themselves to keeping their hands off both capital movements and the foreign exchange market. Monetary autonomy would then be partially restored but at the cost of losing all control over the exchange rate.[40] The danger is that the exchange rate may settle at an inappropriate level. For example, exuberant and imprudent capital inflows may drive up the exchange rate to an excessively high level only to be followed by a large current account deficit, a panicky capital flight, and a painful correction. A third possible regime is an 'intermediate' exchange rate, somewhere between fixed and floating, combined with CAC. The problem with this regime is that it is vulnerable to attack. Any targeting of the exchange rate, even an exchange rate band or crawl, gives speculators a target to shoot at.[41] This invites currency crises, of which there were plenty of examples in the 1990s in East Asia, Latin America, and Russia. Monetary autonomy would also be lost in the bargain.

India's regime of 'managed floating' plus capital controls has been helpful in avoiding these various pitfalls. It has enabled the authorities to target the exchange rate from time to time to preserve trade competitiveness, while letting the market dictate the level of the exchange rate most of the time. At the same time, since the capital controls have been specific, not pervasive, they have allowed the economy to enjoy many of the benefits of free capital flows (while protecting it against movements of 'hot money').

Foreign exchange reserves have also played a major role in buttressing the payments regime. Since 1991, India has aimed to maintain a comfortable reserve position for precautionary purposes, and has mostly succeeded in doing so. A large stock of reserves cannot prevent a currency crisis if macroeconomic policy is grossly irresponsible. But it can help to ward off self-fulfilling speculative attacks.[42] A reserve-related instrument that the Indian authorities have used quite regularly to target the exchange rate is so-called 'sterilized intervention', whose operation can be explained as follows. Exchange-rate targeting involves buying or selling foreign exchange reserves. For example, to prevent an appreciation of the exchange rate (and a consequent worsening of trade competitiveness), the RBI has to sell rupees and buy dollars in the foreign exchange market. But the newly created rupees could raise prices and thus worsen competitiveness by another route, thwarting the object of the exercise. The trick to get round this problem is to 'sterilize' the rupee creation by selling government bonds. But the solution has limitations. It imposes a fiscal cost because the interest rate that the government pays on the securities sold is likely to be higher than that earned on the dollar reserves that are bought. Sterilized intervention, therefore, can only be applied in moderation, as a supplement to capital controls, not as a substitute for it.

The main reason for managing the exchange rate is to help preserve trade competitiveness and ensure that the current account deficit is modest. (There is also some persuasive evidence that mild undervaluation of the exchange rate boosts growth.) A current account deficit has to be covered by foreign borrowing. There is nothing wrong with this up to a point, if there are good investment opportunities beyond those that can be financed out of domestic savings. But persistent and large deficits make it more likely that the borrowing will go into unproductive expenditure. They also make it more likely that foreign lenders will cut and run if doubts arise about the country's ability or willingness to repay, or simply due to sudden changes in investors' risk appetite. The safe magnitude of the current account deficit is not a hard and fast number. I think that a target deficit of 2 per cent of GDP is about right. This allows for shocks that may raise it occasionally to double that figure. (In 2011 and 2012, a deficit of more than

4 per cent of GDP raised acute financing concerns.) This is more conservative than the 3 per cent of GDP target that was assumed in the 12th Five Year Plan but is justified by the uncertain international climate and the well-attested propensity of international investors to take fright in the face of high current account deficits.

My overall view is that a) India's payments regime has been fit for purpose; and b) when the RBI has departed from this regime, the results have been less than favourable. A few examples illustrate the point. The first is the dramatic East Asian crisis of 1997 when capital flight toppled the mountain of foreign debt that many countries in the region had accumulated. For several years previously, they had experienced huge capital inflows, attracted by the so-called 'East Asian Miracle'. But capital flows are not all alike. Direct foreign investment is fairly stable and bolted down but that cannot be said of 'hot money' that flows into banks and short-term bonds.[43] East Asia had embraced free capital mobility and allowed hot money to pour in. When it poured out, upheaval and chaos followed. The interesting point is that India came out of the crisis unscathed, even though its 'fundamentals', such as inflation and fiscal deficits, were much worse than in the crisis countries. The critical differences were two. In the crisis countries, unlike in India, there was a huge amount of short-term debt in relation to foreign exchange reserves. (In South Korea, short-term debt was as large as the reserves, in Indonesia it was twice the stock of reserves; in India, however, it was only 30 per cent of reserves.) India averted the crisis by avoiding an unstable debt structure, an outcome that was a direct result of maintaining controls on the volatile element of capital inflows.[44] The other difference relates to exchange rate policy. The crisis countries kept their exchange rates fairly closely tied to the dollar. In the years leading up to the crisis, they lost trade competitiveness, since they had higher inflation than their trading partners. Moreover, their declared policy of exchange rate stability induced complacency about exchange risk, and encouraged dollar-denominated foreign borrowing. During the same period, India altered its exchange rate frequently to compensate for a higher rate of inflation relative to trading partners, thereby keeping it roughly unchanged in 'real' terms. The pressure for appreciation, caused by large capital inflows in the permitted categories, was resisted by sterilized intervention conducted by the RBI.

Another more recent illustrative episode was the period of super-fast growth from 2003 to 2007, when India attracted very large foreign capital inflows. The RBI governor Y. V. Reddy could have welcomed the inflows with open arms by relaxing capital inflow restrictions and letting the rupee appreciate in the foreign exchange market. This would have added to the prevailing 'feel good' sentiment by making imports cheaper.

A stronger rupee would have also been popular as a signal that India was on the way to becoming a major power. In the event, he was cautious. He retained the controls on inflows of 'hot money', so the debt structure did not become fragile. He did let the rupee strengthen, but nowhere as much as it would have in a free market. Instead, the RBI bought the dollars that were flooding in. India's reserves doubled between 2005 and 2007, from $150 billion to $300 billion. (The intervention was partially sterilized to prevent inflation.) When the global crisis broke in 2008, the reserves came in very handy. Not only did they serve to cover payments deficits but their very presence inspired confidence and prevented capital flight.

Since 2008, however, India's adherence to its payments regime has become more hesitant. D. Subbarao came in as RBI governor at a difficult time, only a week before the collapse of Lehman Brothers in September 2008. For India, the immediate effect of the global turmoil was that capital inflows dried up for six months. Subbarao responded with a mixture of running down reserves and letting the rupee depreciate. So far, his policy was entirely in consonance with Reddy's. Then, strong inward capital flows resumed because a) it looked as if the worst of the crisis was over and India had come out of it in better shape than many countries; and b) Western governments slashed interest rates to very low levels and started 'quantitative easing', which raised the relative return on Indian assets. At this point, Subbarao appears to have had a change of heart. Perhaps he thought that a stronger rupee would be good for damping down inflation. Perhaps he was persuaded by the reports of some government committees that had advocated moving towards a floating exchange rate. He turned away from Reddy's strategy of managing the rupee and allowed the exchange rate to be market-determined. In 12 months from April 2009, the rupee rose from $1 = Rs. 51 to $1 = Rs. 45, and remained around that level for another year. But Indian inflation was much faster than in other countries. The combined result of these two factors was that India's export competitiveness against its trading partners worsened sizeably. (Table 8.1 shows that the 'real effective exchange rate' [RER] appreciated by 10 per cent and remained at that level for two years. The RER measures competitiveness. A rise in the RER means a fall in competitiveness.) This contributed (along with other global and domestic factors) to the large widening of the current account deficit in 2011 and 2012 to well over 4 per cent of GDP,[45] and a slowdown in industrial growth.[46] Economic performance was also deteriorating for other reasons, as seen above. As a result, from August 2011, the rupee began to depreciate rapidly. Though a major crisis did not occur, the situation looked very threatening for a time, and a run on the rupee was on the cards. With the benefit of hindsight, it is clear that Subbarao erred in pursuing a 'strong rupee' policy for two years.

An even more recent episode of departure from the payments regime has occurred during the governorship of R. Rajan. The RBI quite rightly put up a defence of the rupee during the 'taper tantrum' of 2013 (when there was capital flight in response to market expectations of an imminent rise in US interest rates) in order to combat a destabilizing speculative dynamic. Since then, however, the real exchange rate has been allowed to appreciate by about 10 per cent (see Table 8.1). This has surely played a part in the precipitous collapse of Indian exports in 2014 and 2015 (though the slowdown in world trade has obviously not helped). In 2015/16, on the basis of figures for the first ten months, exports are expected to show *negative* growth of around 15 per cent.[47] As it happens, the current account deficit has been low because of the combined effect on imports of domestic recession and a fall in the oil price. But imports will and should pick up when the economy recovers, so the negative export growth is very worrying. It appears that the RBI is no longer managing the exchange rate with an eye to trade competitiveness (or it would surely not have allowed the recent substantial real appreciation).[48] Another concern is the strong trend since 2010 towards liberalization of capital controls on external commercial borrowing by companies and banks, and debt flows more generally, including inflows of foreign money into government securities. This kind of borrowing, unlike foreign direct and portfolio equity investment, makes the country more vulnerable to the roller-coaster of capital movements. It also makes exchange rate management more difficult. Further liberalization of capital inflows into bank loans or bonds would be a bad idea at this juncture.[49]

The bottom line is that India should be wary of abandoning its tried and tested policy of managing the exchange rate to maintain export competitiveness, with the help of targeted capital controls,[50] and sterilized intervention, as and when necessary. It would be unwise to change this policy framework until rapid export growth is more secure, and fiscal consolidation, financial regulation, and clean-up of the banking system are much further advanced.

FISCAL BALANCE AND FISCAL REFORM

India's fiscal problem has 'macro' and 'micro' aspects. The 'macro' part is about making the fiscal position sustainable by reducing the size of government deficits and debt. The 'micro' part, which is about moving towards a more efficient structure of taxes, and changing the composition and effectiveness of government expenditure, does not, strictly speaking, belong in a chapter about macro-policy. Even so, it is addressed briefly in this section (in addition to the macro-aspects of fiscal policy) because it arises naturally and is, moreover, critically important for inclusive growth.

The meaning and rationale of fiscal sustainability needs some explanation. Like any economic entity, the government has to be solvent if it is to function. It can borrow and go into debt to cover the 'fiscal deficit', i.e. the difference between revenue and expenditure. However, if the debt is excessive, or thought to be escalating rapidly, borrowing becomes more expensive. In the extreme, the government would find it impossible to borrow. It would then have to repudiate the debt directly, or print money at an ever faster rate to cover its deficits, which is tantamount to reneging on the debt indirectly by inflating it away. Hyperinflation and debt repudiation are of course classic recipes for social and political chaos. A wise government should keep deficits and debt low because any suspicion that it has a solvency problem can raise borrowing costs in the present and bring the day of reckoning forward.[51] But avoiding insolvency is not the sole reason for fiscal prudence. Large government deficits are undesirable, even if solvency is not in question, because they can result in lower growth via 'crowding out' of non-government activity. If the government's deficit goes up, its extra demand in the credit market raises interest rates. This discourages private investment spending, which in turn reduces the growth rate.[52] If net exports are crowded out, the economy gets into external debt; and if that becomes excessive, the country becomes vulnerable to a balance of payments crisis.

There is an important qualification to the above analysis. Running a fiscal deficit or surplus affects aggregate demand. Measures to cut the deficit may have a contractionary effect on national income and output. Indeed, it may be necessary to run a higher deficit in order to prevent or counteract a recession or slowdown in economic activity. (In a deep recession, 'crowding out' would not be an issue.) Thus, governments have to walk the tightrope of balancing short-run fiscal flexibility with long-run fiscal sustainability. Nonetheless, if the solvency position is in doubt, even the freedom to use the deficit for short-run demand management becomes restricted or disappears altogether.

Economic theory gives little guidance about the optimum level of government debt. But experience indicates that high public debt levels are associated with macroeconomic crises and low growth. India's net public debt ratio of around 70 per cent of GDP is not in safe territory.[53] Before the global credit crisis of 2008, the eurozone and the UK aimed at debt ratios of 60 per cent and 40 per cent respectively; and though these targets have been massively overshot during and after the credit crisis, they have certainly not been abandoned. It would be prudent to reduce India's public debt ratio to about 50 per cent of GDP over a time-horizon of, say, 10 years. The fairly slow adjustment is to guard against the danger that fiscal compression could have a depressing effect on growth of output.

Reducing the debt ratio is primarily a matter of controlling fiscal deficits. And in doing so, the revenue or current deficit is an object of special interest since capital spending has the virtue of being growth-promoting. Table 8.6 shows the course of revenue deficits and aggregate fiscal deficits in recent years. The Fourteenth Finance Commission (14th FC) has recommended, in its 'road map for fiscal consolidation', achieving a consolidated revenue surplus of 1 per cent of GDP by 2019/20.[54] This would, according to the Commission's calculations, reduce the consolidated debt ratio by about 7 per cent of GDP, while simultaneously a) accommodating an increase in consolidated capital expenditure of 2 per cent of GDP and b) reducing the consolidated fiscal deficit by about 0.6 per cent of GDP. The resulting numbers in 2019/20 would be as follows: consolidated fiscal deficit: 5.7 per cent of GDP (centre: 3 per cent; states 2.7 per cent)[55]; consolidated revenue deficit: –1.0 per cent of GDP (centre: 1 per cent; states: –2 per cent); consolidated debt ratio 58 per cent of GDP (centre: 36 per cent; states: 22 per cent).

The above road map looks quite reasonable, neither too lax nor too tough. However, adhering to it will not be easy. Firstly, the starting point is somewhat worse than assumed by the 14th FC. The central government deficit

Table 8.6 REVENUE AND FISCAL DEFICITS OF THE CENTRE, STATES, AND CONSOLIDATED GOVERNMENT (% GDP AT MARKET PRICES)

	Centre		States		Consolidated	
	RD	FD	RD	FD	RD	FD
2002/3	4.3	5.7	2.1	3.9	6.4	9.2
2007/8	1.1	2.5	–1.0	1.5	0.1	4.0 (4.6)
2008/9	4.5	6.0	–0.3	2.3	4.2	8.2 (9.9)
2009/10	5.2	6.5	0.4	3.0	5.7	9.4 (9.6)
2010/11	3.2	4.8	–0.2	2.0	3.0	6.8
2011/12	4.4	5.8	–0.3	2.4	4.1	8.2
2012/13	3.9	5.2	–0.2	2.1	3.7	7.2
2013/14	3.3	4.6	–0.1	2.5	3.2	7.1
2014/15	2.9	4.1	–0.5	2.3	2.5	6.4
2015/16	2.5	3.9		2.5 E		6.4 E

Notes. RD and FD refer to Revenue Deficit and Fiscal Deficit respectively. Figures in brackets show the consolidated fiscal deficit, inclusive of off-budget items, (these were brought on-budget from 2010). Negative figures denote surpluses. The figures for 2015/16 are estimates by the author.
Source: Ministry of Finance (2015a).

in 2015/16 was 3.9 per cent of GDP, not 3.6 per cent, because the government decided to depart from the 14th FC road-map in order to increase public investment, on the justifiable ground that private investment was weak. The combined debt ratio in 2015/16 was probably 70 per cent of GDP, not 65 per cent, as assumed by the Commission.[56] Moreover, the demands on the government treasury look formidable in the light of the recommendations of the Seventh Pay Commission, the recapitalization requirements of the banking system, and the takeover by the states of the debts of the electricity distribution companies ('discoms'). Secondly, the future environment promises to be different from the recent past in one major respect. From 2008 onwards, fiscal consolidation was meagre but this did not stop the debt ratio falling from 80 per cent of GDP in 2008/9 to 68 per cent in 2014/15. This is because high inflation eroded the value of the debt. Now, India has a formal inflation target. If inflation were maintained in the next five years at the targeted 4 per cent, the burden of reducing debt would fall very much on fiscal adjustment proper. The RBI's commendable efforts to maintain a positive real deposit rate, and to unwind financial repression, will tend to keep the government's real borrowing rate positive as well, say at around 3 per cent, unlike the six inflationary years from 2008, when it was zero or negative.

Reduction of the debt ratio will thus be more challenging than hitherto.[57] Even so, it is surely high time that India stopped its past practice of repeatedly postponing genuine fiscal consolidation. (For example, the Fiscal Responsibility Act of 2003 has been paused or amended several times. In effect, its fiscal deficit target of 3 per cent of GDP for the central government has not been reached 12 years after it was first adopted.)[58] It would be desirable to revamp the Fiscal Responsibility Act and define fiscal deficit goals not as fixed ratios to GDP but as bands within which these ratios must lie. Government action to achieve fixed targets runs the risk of being pro-cyclical. Permissible bands would allow cyclical considerations to be taken into account and give the government less of an excuse to breach fiscal road-maps. That said, fiscal consolidation is bound to be painful though necessary.

Reducing the fiscal deficit to a safe level is an important aim of a desirable fiscal policy but not its sole aim. Given the objective of inclusive growth, fiscal adjustment also has to be of the right quality. This has implications for both the tax structure and the pattern of government expenditure. In the pre-reform days, rates of direct tax used to be punitive. Now they are very reasonable (the top marginal rate is 31 per cent, which is below most European countries). As a result, compliance has improved and the yield of direct taxes has risen since 1991.[59] Even so, the ratio of overall tax revenue to GDP is only slightly higher than

20 years ago.[60] This is because of the sharp fall in tariff revenue in the last two decades: customs duties have been reduced, justifiably, to secure the benefits of trade liberalization. The rest of the indirect tax system is undergoing a major shift towards a uniform goods and services tax (see Chapter 6). This promises to be a big step towards making the country a single market, so the effect on revenue will be positive in the long run; but the near-term revenue effect is likely to be neutral, while the new system settles down.

An increase in the revenue productivity of the tax system will require widening of the tax base and reduction in the multitude of exemptions secured by special-interest groups. For this, enactment of a goods and services tax is of course a first-order priority. Another obvious, though politically difficult, avenue for widening the tax base is taxation of agricultural incomes, which is constitutionally a state subject. Powerful farm lobbies have seen to it that agricultural income is untaxed. In addition to depriving the government of tax revenue from agriculture, this has also led to tax evasion by people falsely declaring non-agricultural income to be agricultural. An agreement between the centre and the states to tax agricultural incomes is long overdue. Its absence is one reason among others for the appallingly low base of the personal income-tax, which is paid by only 40 million people (3 per cent of the population, and around 15 per cent of households). One of the objectives of tax policy must surely be to ensure in the next decade that at least a third of households pay income tax (even if many were to do so at a low rate). Though doing so is politically popular, finance ministers should resist the temptation to raise the minimum tax threshold faster than the growth rate of per capita GDP, as has happened regularly in the past. A broader tax base could also be obtained by pruning the multitude of exemptions and concessions in the tax code, which serve no useful purpose and cause evasion and avoidance.[61]

Reduction of government expenditure is essential for fiscal consolidation in India. But the objective of rapid and inclusive growth implies increased government spending on those aspects of infrastructure investment, social protection, and social enablement that should not be left wholly to private initiative. To achieve significant reduction in revenue deficits along with expenditure increase in these essential areas, two features of the economy have to be corrected that prevail even after more than 20 years of economic reform, and serve neither efficiency nor equity: a) a superabundance of dysfunctional subsidies and b) an excessive degree of state ownership of business enterprises.

Explicit subsidies mainly go to food, fuel, and fertilisers and currently constitute around 1.7 of GDP.[62] The need and scope for reduction, even abolition, of fertiliser and fuel subsidies was discussed in Chapter 6. Commendably, in 2013, the UPA government began the process of reducing diesel subsidies in small steps each month. The NDA government continued this policy and was able to eliminate the diesel subsidy in 2014 by taking opportunistic advantage of the sharp fall in global oil prices in that year. Subsidies on other fuel products such as cooking gas and kerosene still remain.

Food subsidies represent the difference between the cost incurred by the Food Corporation of India (FCI) in procuring, storing, and distributing food grains and the 'issue prices' at which they are sold to poor consumers through the 600,000 'fair price shops' of the PDS.[63] But it is widely acknowledged that the PDS leaks all over the place. Well over half the grain released by the FCI does not reach poor households because it is diverted to the open market or because many genuinely poor people do not have ration cards, while many non-poor people do. The food subsidy bill could be significantly reduced by directly subsidizing poor consumers to buy food at market prices by means of cash transfers (directly into bank accounts).[64] As discussed above in the section on 'internal balance', government buffer stocks could still be operated to moderate fluctuations in food prices, purchases, and sales being made through normal commercial channels. But most of the elaborate, inefficient, corrupt, and expensive machinery of the PDS could be wound up (except in remote areas). Unfortunately, the UPA government went in the opposite direction by enacting the Food Security Act. This has widened the category of food subsidy recipients to 67 per cent of the population. Even if this were justified on equity grounds, the introduction of a scheme that continues to rely on the leaky PDS to distribute food seems extremely unwise. Food subsidies, already close to 1 per cent of GDP, may thus rise further.

The explicit subsidies are only the tip of an iceberg. We must also take account of the massive hidden subsidies which permeate the provision of goods by the state (leaving aside genuine public goods where free provision is the appropriate course). If prices should reflect the true economic costs and benefits of different products and activities, the Indian subsidy system is a blatant denial of this principle. It is inefficient and regressive and leads to inappropriate usage of resources, and under-investment. As alluded to in Chapter 6, and discussed further in Chapter 10, very large fiscal savings could be secured by winding up the hidden subsidies on goods other than pure public goods, more than enough to compensate poor people for the loss of subsidies and, in addition, give them sizeable income supplements.

Another potential avenue for moderating the fiscal deficit is to reduce government interest payments, which are as much as 4 to 5 per cent of GDP, by retiring debt. The obvious way to do this is to sell central and state government public sector enterprises, with accompanying regulation, where necessary, to prevent abuse of monopoly power. The value of central PSEs alone is estimated to be 40–45 per cent of GDP.[65] Of course, privatisation of a PSE improves the true fiscal position only if the sale price exceeds the present value of future dividends foregone by the government, in other words if the enterprise would be more profitable if it were privately owned. In many cases, this would be virtually certain (see Chapter 7). It should easily be possible, over say five years, to shave at least 1 per cent of GDP off government interest payments by a well-designed programme of privatisation, even if government ownership were retained in appropriate areas. Other potential revenue-raising and expenditure reducing measures are discussed in Chapter 10.

Deep fiscal adjustment is critical for the success of India's search for prosperity. By 'deep adjustment', I mean one that embraces both a reduction in the fiscal deficit *and* a change in the composition of public expenditure towards social and environmental protection, social enablement, and investment in physical infrastructure. The technical possibilities are enormous but progress has been very slow. It is obviously the nature of the political system and its balance of forces that prevents India from achieving radical fiscal adjustment. The objective of rapid, stable, and inclusive growth will be gravely endangered unless this deadlock can be broken.

APPENDIX TO CHAPTER 8
Inflation Targeting

In this chapter, I have espoused the adoption of 'flexible inflation targeting' (FIT) in India. This appendix contains a brief discussion of the relevant issues.

The core rationale of inflation targeting is that there is no long-run growth benefit from inflation above a threshold rate. Many research studies have shown that in India this threshold rate is around 4 per cent a year. It makes sense, therefore, that the inflation target should also be 4 per cent a year (with a range of 2 per cent on either side for temporary deviations). The consumer price index (CPI) is a good index to define the inflation target because it is widely watched and understood, and acts as a major factor driving inflation via 'second-round effects' (see below). It also stands to reason that inflation targeting should be 'flexible' in the sense that the speed of approach to the inflation target should be left to the discretion (within limits) of a 'monetary policy committee' that oversees inflation targeting, acting via the RBI. This would enable the RBI to reduce the short-run output cost of hitting the inflation target. The monetary policy committee, chaired by the Governor of the RBI, would have on it independent economists and government representatives, in addition to RBI officials. As Chapter 8 explains, this regime is now effectively in operation in India, though statutory backing is yet to come, and a monetary policy committee is yet to be appointed.

Several objections have been levelled against FIT for India. The first objection is that around half of the CPI consists of food and fuel prices, which are driven by factors such as droughts, import costs, and administered prices. While this is true, the fact remains that increases in the CPI caused by exogenous factors can propagate an overall inflationary spiral because a) the CPI is used as a base for wage bargaining and indexation and b) the movement of the CPI strongly affects inflationary expectations, which are critical to the inflation dynamic, and these 'second round effects' *are* amenable to the influence of monetary policy. It may be prudent, therefore, to take pre-emptive monetary policy action to moderate 'second-round effects' as soon as the CPI registers a rise in inflation that threatens to breach the inflation target. Moreover, even food prices are not completely outside the reach of monetary policy since agricultural costs of production, especially rural money wages, are sensitive to the strength of demand for goods and labour in the non-rural economy.[66] In India's current environment of growing indexation, the traditional tactic of avoiding tough monetary policy, and simply waiting for the exogenous drivers to go away, will no longer suffice to combat inflation. (However, by the same token, the output cost of bringing down inflation may well be greater in the future than in the past. In other words, India will unavoidably face a sharper short-run trade-off between inflation and growth than hitherto.)

The second objection to FIT is that it would not work in the presence of the 'fiscal dominance' that arguably prevails in India. It is indeed true that if the government were profligate and regularly forced the central bank to print money to finance its deficits, inflation targeting would not work. But such an extreme scenario does not represent Indian reality. *Direct* monetary financing of deficits does not exist in India. It is the case, however, that fiscal deficits are excessive; and it is also true that, in the present dispensation, there can be *indirect* monetary financing of deficits since the RBI may be required to conduct open market operations to prevent a rise in the government's borrowing costs.[67] Other manifestations of indirect fiscal dominance in an extended sense (or equivalently of 'financial repression') are a) government capture of bank deposits via the statutory liquidity requirement, b) administered interest rates on small savings, and c) interest rate subsidies for selected activities. All these factors constrain monetary policy and/or impede its smooth transmission. However, none of them are significant enough to make monetary policy powerless, and they should and could be reformed while the inflation targeting regime is in operation. They are not reasons to give up on inflation targeting but reasons to improve its functioning by eliminating the distortions. As regards the fiscal deficit, if it were too expansionary, the logic of the regime implies that monetary policy would be tightened, if necessary, to hit the inflation target. This would also have the side-benefit of exposing the government to scrutiny. In other words, while it is certainly necessary to end fiscal dominance, inflation targeting may reinforce the pressure to end it.

The third objection to FIT is that it would be inconsistent with exchange rate management, which may be required to maintain export competitiveness and a safe current account deficit. It is true that if the short-term interest rate were the only monetary policy instrument, it could not achieve both an inflation target and an exchange rate target; so, if there is an inflation target, the exchange rate would have to float cleanly. But an inflation targeting regime for India would not be faced with this dilemma, if it retained sterilized intervention and focused capital controls on hot money movements as weapons of monetary policy. With these two additional instruments, inflation targeting would be compatible with managed floating.

The fourth objection to FIT is that it ignores financial stability (e.g. prevention of asset price bubbles), which is also an important objective. But financial stability is best pursued by using macro-prudential instruments. It is only on very rare occasions that it would be necessary to aim off-target on inflation to maintain financial stability, and the central bank could be given the power to do so (and explain itself).

Of these objections, the presence of fiscal dominance is the most pertinent. It is sometimes encapsulated in the view that FIT is 'either unnecessary or insufficient'. If there is a political and social consensus in favour of low inflation, FIT is unnecessary; and if such a consensus is missing, FIT is insufficient. But this view is much too extreme. The fact is that, in common with many countries, both the Indian public and the Indian government hold inconsistent views: they want low inflation but they are also reluctant to pay the price of getting inflation down. FIT is designed precisely to deal with such a situation by delegating monetary policy to the central bank, which is given an explicit inflation target. The idea, in other words, is that the government should tie its own hands the better to achieve its own objective of low inflation.

NOTES

1. Note that the fiscal deficit inclusive of 'off-balance sheet items' was 4.6 per cent of GDP in 2007 and 10 per cent of GDP in 2008. Many off-balance sheet items were brought explicitly into the budget after 2010.
2. According to the new (2011/12 series) of national accounts, the growth rate fell to 5.4 per cent in 2012 but recovered to an average of nearly 7 per cent in the next three years. I think, along with many other observers, that the new numbers overestimate growth since 2012 (see below).
3. For example, there is plenty of international evidence that high inflation is inimical to growth. One reason is that higher inflation also tends to be more volatile inflation, and volatile inflation makes investment riskier. Another problem with high inflation is that it worsens external competitiveness. Exchange rate depreciation could offset this but only by adding a further inflationary stimulus.
4. The poor tend disproportionately to have non-indexed incomes.
5. From 1960 to 1980, India's consumer-price inflation was around 7–8 per cent a year. The average for non-oil developing countries as a whole was twice as high, and it was even higher for Latin American countries.
6. This is inflation of the CPI (consumer price index). Average inflation of the wholesale price index (WPI) was somewhat less: 7.6 per cent a year. The divergence is accounted for mainly by 2009, a year in which the higher weight for

food in the CPI and the higher weight for fuel in the WPI made a big difference. In that year, food prices rose sharply and world oil prices fell sharply, so the WPI rose only 3.6 per cent but the CPI increased 12.4 per cent.

7. These numbers are from IMF (2014).

8. In this sentence, high inflation is defined as inflation of wholesale or consumer prices of 10 per cent or more for two or more successive years. For a close analysis of previous high-inflation episodes, e.g. 1965–66, 1972–74, 1979–81, and 1991–96, see Joshi and Little (1994, 1996).

9. This has been the case in most high-inflation episodes in the past. For example, in 1972–74, there was a rapid expansion of money supply and public expenditure, in part due to the war with Pakistan in 1971; in 1991, demand was running high due to large government deficits in the preceding years.

10. Of course, imports of food cannot check rising food prices if world prices of food also happen to be high.

11. Restrictive policies reduce non-agricultural output because wages and prices are not flexible downwards in modern industry and services. However, even though prices do not fall, the rate of rise in prices is checked.

12. A little inflation greases the wheels of the economy, and promotes growth, by facilitating relative wage and price adjustments without having to undergo absolute wage and price reductions that are very hard to engineer in modern economies. But there is also a lot of evidence that as inflation rises, it impedes growth, by introducing uncertainty into investment decisions. The above two opposing considerations lead to the notion of an 'optimal' rate of inflation, defined as the threshold rate of inflation beyond which the *net* growth benefit from inflation declines. Several studies have tried to identify the critical threshold for India. (For references to these, see RBI 2014a.) The consensus view is that the 'optimal' rate of inflation for India is around 4–5 per cent a year. A different and independent argument for low inflation is that inflation hits the poor hard, since they are less able to hedge against it than the well-off.

13. These numbers were calculated from data on minimum support prices given in Table 26 of Reserve Bank of India (2015). See also Bhalla (2011).

14. The underlying reasoning is nonsensical because stocks, once acquired, are a sunk cost; so, from a fiscal point of view, not selling is equivalent to selling at a zero price. Another reason for the reluctance to sell at a low price is the fear of round-tripping: traders could buy food cheaply from the government and sell it back to the government at the guaranteed procurement price. But this is a problem only because the government stands ready to buy at a high price in a bad year, which is plainly foolish.

15. There is also hard evidence that the present method of making cheap food available to the poorest is hopelessly ineffective in that the 'distributed' food does not reach the intended beneficiaries. This aspect is pursued below and in Chapter 9. Here, my focus is on the fact that government intervention in the food market creates an inflationary bias, quite apart from its ineffectiveness in subsidizing poor people.

16. This was all supposed to change with the reform initiated in 2003 of laws that regulate agricultural markets. But the states, under the influence of the vested interests of traders, have dragged their feet in making the appropriate amendments and implementing them. Agricultural Produce Marketing Committees, originally set up to protect farmers, have been captured by middlemen.

17. See Mohanty (2010).
18. Raghuram Rajan, governor of the RBI, made the important point that monetary policy is not irrelevant to moderating rural wage growth. A relative rise in rural wages has become necessary for the rural sector to compete for labour, which increasingly has non-rural opportunities. But this can result in a wage-wage spiral if the growth of non-rural wages is not kept in check by monetary policy to restrain non-rural demand (see Rajan 2014).
19. The real policy rate is defined here as the nominal policy rate minus ex post CPI inflation. A more appropriate definition would be the nominal policy rate minus expected CPI inflation. On the latter basis, the RBI's stance would look even looser since household expectations of inflation, as measured by RBI surveys, were above actual inflation. With a WPI measure of inflation, the RBI's interest rate policy would look somewhat less loose but nevertheless much looser than in 2003–2008.
20. In the immediate aftermath of the global crisis, the policy rate was reduced from 9 per cent in August 2008 to 4.75 per cent in April 2009, where it remained for a whole year though inflation was 10 per cent, perhaps because the RBI was taken in by the small rise in the WPI, as explained in n.6. It was then increased in 13 'baby steps' to 8.5 per cent from March 2010 to October 2011. Real lending rates charged by banks for company borrowing also fell (see Table 8.2): the average real lending rate fell from 7.4 per cent in 2003–2008 to 1.1 per cent in 2008–2013. The same story applies to bank deposit rates. Table 8.2 shows that the average real deposit rate (for three- to five-year deposits) fell from 1.9 per cent in 2003–2008 to *minus* 1.6 per cent in 2008–2013. All these reductions in real interest rates were the opposite of what was needed to cool demand, given the supply-side and demand-side rigidities in the economy. (Moreover, negative real deposit rates had another undesirable effect. They led to a reduction in household financial savings in favour of buying gold, as discussed below.) Note that in addition to the policy rate, the RBI has other instruments of monetary policy, e.g. the cash reserve ratio (CRR). The CRR was lowered from 9 per cent to 5 per cent in 2008. Thereafter its variations have been fairly minor. It has certainly not been used in a restrictive fashion.
21. Worsening competitiveness also played a part in the slowdown of Indian exports (see below).
22. This statement is at variance with the new national accounts figures (2011/12 series). But the new figures do not accord with most other evidence (see below).
23. See Kapur and Mohan (2014).
24. See Joshi (2014).
25. For further elaboration, see Joshi (2014).
26. See Nagaraj (2013). Nagaraj's otherwise excellent article overstates the direct importance of *foreign* capital in causing the debt-fuelled investment boom of 2003–8, as evidenced by the low level of the current account deficit during the period. Foreign capital inflows were certainly large (8 to 10 per cent of GDP annually) but they went mostly into reserve accumulation. They did, however, indirectly stimulate domestic investment by accelerating bank credit (since sterilization was inadequate). For another excellent analysis of recent macro-economic policy and outcomes, see Acharya (2012).
27. This suggests that it would have ideally been sensible to moderate the boom by a tougher monetary or fiscal policy before 2008.
28. One immediate result was a sharp increase in subsidies because necessary rises in administered prices of oil products and fertilisers were not implemented.

Infrastructure, particularly power, continued to be a major bottleneck. In the boom years, many power plants had been initiated. But when they came on stream, their customers, viz. the state electricity boards, were in even worse shape than before and could not afford to pay. Fuel linkages for power plants also continued to be a major problem. There were shortages of coal because the long-standing problems of coal pricing and the inefficiency of Coal India had not been corrected. Gas supply was inadequate because of an unresolved dispute between the government and Reliance.

29. Even so, these supply-side problems cannot all be blamed on post-2008 policies. It is tempting but wrong to regard the previous five years (2003–2008) as a model of good policymaking. Firstly, it would have been sensible to moderate the boom by sterilizing more aggressively the foreign inflows that were taken into the reserves. In the event, money supply expanded very rapidly. Secondly, the large fiscal consolidation was less impressive than it appears; it would look much less impressive if it were cyclically adjusted. Thirdly, there was not much supply-side reform: the boom bred complacency.

30. See Reserve Bank of India (2014a).

31. A major policy issue in 2015/16 was whether the RBI should have brought policy interest rates down still further to spur flagging investment. Its salience was sharpened by the fact that inflation, as measured by the wholesale price index (WPI), was negative throughout the year, implying sharply positive real interest rates on that basis. In my view, the RBI was right to stick to its guns. Firstly, the WPI is not a true producer price index. Secondly, the huge fall in the price of oil and other commodities implied that companies were facing much lower input costs and correspondingly better profit opportunities. Thirdly, the WPI is definitely not the relevant inflation index for producers of services, which constitute half the economy. Fourthly, the CPI is the right index to target as far as the RBI is concerned because it is CPI inflation that drives second-round effects. Fifthly, the RBI had targeted inflation lower than 6 per cent in January 2016, and the credibility of the new inflation anchor depended on achieving that target successfully.

32. According to the agreement, the RBI would be deemed to have failed if inflation were outside the band for three successive quarters. In the event of failure, it would have to explain itself to the government.

33. Banks fear that if they offered lower deposit rates than the rates on small savings, there would be an outflow of deposits.

34. See Reserve Bank of India (2014a) and Lahiri and Patel (2016).

35. See Aiyar (2016) and Shah (2015, 2016).

36. 'Stressed assets' = non-performing assets + restructured assets.

37. For a more detailed analytical assessment of India's external payments regime, see Joshi (2003a, 2003b, 2008) and Joshi and Sanyal (2004).

38. With a fixed exchange rate, any desired improvement in the competitive position would have to come about by price reductions across the board. This would be very costly and painful since it would, in practice, entail a drop in employment and output.

39. With a fixed exchange rate, capital account convertibility and perfectly mobile capital, home interest rates cannot differ from foreign interest rates.

40. The restoration is only partial. Evidence shows that domestic financial conditions are strongly affected by global financial cycles through credit

channels, whatever the exchange rate regime. See Rey (2015) and Klein and Shambaugh (2013).

41. By targeting the exchange rate, the authorities commit to buy or sell foreign currency in unlimited amounts to defend the target. But international speculators have much greater resources in their hands than a country's authorities, so a defence is unlikely to work against determined speculation.

42. How large should the stock be? There is no precise answer. But old benchmarks like 'reserves equal to three months' imports' or 'reserves equal to all debt due to mature in a year' do not provide an adequate margin of safety in today's world of highly mobile capital. In 2007, just before the global crisis India's foreign exchange reserves were around 25 per cent of GDP and proved to be an adequate and safe level. On this basis, the safe level would now be around $500 billion, compared with the existing stock of about $350 billion.

43. Inflows into equity markets are betwixt and between. They are less unstable than hot money because changes in the prices of equities act as a brake on large sales, but they are less stable than direct investment. In the event, they proved to be highly unstable in the East Asian crisis.

44. For details, see Joshi (2003a).

45. Another important contributing factor was the fall in household financial savings and their diversion to holding gold (gold imports increased enormously). This is because inflation was high and the RBI's interest rate policy led to a negative real rate for financial savings. The fall in financial savings can be seen in Table 8.4. The rise in 'investment' in gold can be seen in Table 8.5 under 'valuables'.

46. Technical note: It is often claimed on the basis of econometric estimation that the price elasticity of demand for Indian exports is quite low (for example see Rangarajan and Mishra 2013 and Kapur and Mohan 2014). In my opinion, this result is the result of estimating export equations that mix up demand and supply. Robust elasticity estimates require a structural model in which export demand and supply equations are estimated in a simultaneous equation framework. Joshi and Little (1994) did this for the period 1960–1990 and found a short-run price elasticity of demand for exports greater than one, and a long-run price elasticity of demand of three (with 80 per cent of the long-run effect coming through within two years), across a wide range of specifications. Admittedly, these estimates are now quite old and need to be updated.

47. Growth of non-oil exports is also negative, although not quite as bad. More generally, export growth has been dismal for the past four years. While the world trade environment has been unfavourable, part of the explanation surely lies in the bias towards appreciation of the real exchange rate from 2010.

48. Admittedly, this would have placed a somewhat greater burden on interest rate policy in fighting inflation but in my view that would have been a price worth paying.

49. See Subramanian (2009, 2012a).

50. Capital controls overlap with prudential regulatory instruments and there is no hard and fast distinction between the two.

51. A solvency problem would also lead to capital flight and a sovereign credit downgrade in global capital markets.

52. This assumes that growth receives a bigger boost from private investment than from government expenditure. This is often, though not invariably, the case.

53. The combined domestic and external debt of central and state governments is about 70 per cent of GDP in 2015/16. This figure *understates* public debt because it excludes a) the domestic debt of non-financial public sector enterprises and b) non-government public and publicly guaranteed external debt. (Indeed, one could argue that a large part of the entire external debt of India, which is around 20 per cent of GDP, is a contingent liability of the government.) But it also *overstates* public debt since India's foreign exchange reserves count as public assets and should arguably be subtracted to give an accurate estimate of public debt. I ignore these complexities here and assume that the net public debt ratio is the same as the government debt ratio: around 70 per cent of GDP.

54. The 'revenue deficit' means total revenue minus current expenditure. According to the 14th FC, the adjustment would have to be done by the centre because the states were reckoned to be in revenue surplus already (see Fourteenth Finance Commission (2015), Chapter 14, and Table 14.1). 'Consolidated' means 'the aggregate figure for centre and states combined'.

55. The 14th FC road map brings the centre's fiscal deficit to 3 per cent in 2016/17, i.e. well before 2019/20. But the centre departed from the road map in 2015/16 with a fiscal deficit of 3.9 per cent rather than 3.6 per cent, postponing the date by which a 3 per cent deficit would be reached to 2017/18.

56. The consolidated debt ratio in 2014/15 was estimated to be 68 per cent of GDP in Ministry of Finance (2015a). It would be somewhat higher in 2015/16 because, in that year, the consolidated primary deficit was about 2 per cent of GDP, and the real interest rate on government borrowing in that year exceeded somewhat the real growth rate of the economy.

57. Even so, it should not be massively challenging because the real growth rate of the economy will almost certainly exceed the real rate of interest on government borrowing (2015/16 was an aberrant year in which the GDP deflator fell and, in consequence, the real rate of interest on government borrowing was unusually high). With moderate fiscal consolidation, e.g. as envisaged by the 14th FC, the debt ratio would fall.

58. Between 2001 and 2003, India's consolidated fiscal deficit averaged 9.4 per cent of GDP, even higher than in the crisis year of 1991. In 2003, the Indian parliament passed a Fiscal Responsibility Act, which required the central government to balance its revenue budget and bring its fiscal deficit down to 3 per cent of GDP in five years; and many state governments passed similar such Acts. The timetable was roughly on track from 2004 to 2007, helped by an unexpected speeding up of growth to 9 per cent a year, which boosted tax revenues substantially. But it was then blown apart by a pre-election public spending spree in 2008, when subsidies, social expenditures, and government salaries were raised and rural debts waived. (A further stimulus came from fiscal expansion undertaken to combat the headwinds from the global crisis, but that was quite small.) The consolidated fiscal deficit (inclusive of off-balance-sheet items such as oil bonds) ballooned to 9.9 per cent of GDP in 2008, the year of the global crisis. This relaxed fiscal stance must have helped to limit the fall in the growth rate of GDP to 6.7 per cent in that year. Growth rebounded to 8.7 per cent a year for the next two years but the average deficit remained high at around 8 per cent of GDP. While the increase in the deficit in the crisis year of 2008 was understandable, even desirable, its continuation at a high level along with the growth rebound was not. As a result, when growth fell sharply in 2011–14, there

was not much space left for expansionary counter-cyclical policy. This shows the importance of low deficits and debt to enable the government to 'keep its powder dry'.

59. The tax authorities have also made some progress in deploying information technology to increase the efficiency of direct tax collection.

60. The ratio of total tax revenue to GDP was around 16 per of GDP at the end of the 1980s and is about 17.5 per cent now.

61. See Govinda Rao (2016).

62. These three subsidies amounted to 2.5 per cent of GDP until quite recently. The decline is largely due to the fall in world oil prices, which has enabled a painless reduction in fuel subsidies. All food subsidies, and most fertilizer and fuel subsidies, are now shown in the budget. 'Off-budget' subsidies were significantly reduced in 2011 but some remain.

63. Issue prices are infrequently revised and bear little relationship to the costs incurred by FCI. One of the reasons for the FCI's high costs is that it carries excessive stocks (see the section on 'internal balance' above).

64. This issue is examined further in Chapter 10.

65. See Kelkar (2011). In addition, there are state PSEs. Central and state governments also own a lot of underutilized prime land, which could be sold.

66. See Rajan (2014).

67. Simple explanation: A higher fiscal deficit adds to the demand for credit and therefore raises the interest rate on government borrowing. If the government wants to prevent the latter, it can ask the RBI to conduct an 'open market operation' whereby the RBI prints money and uses it to buy government bonds in the market. The result: an unchanged interest rate but a larger money supply.

CHAPTER 9

Education and Health Care

A Question of Quality

For an individual, education and health are major determinants of employment prospects and, more generally, of the good life; for a nation, they are among the crucial drivers of economic growth and inclusive development. In India, they also happen to be large blots on the country's performance. Seventy years on from independence, India's education and health indicators remain grossly unsatisfactory. The problems are complex, and not amenable to a quick fix. Even so, I take a definite position in the analysis below. It has been too readily taken for granted in India, despite a large presence of private providers, that the state should deliver education *balance* and health care. I argue that solving India's education and health quandary will require a much greater role for the market and the private sector than assumed hitherto. Unquestionably, the state must *ensure* access to education and health care for even the poorest people. But it does not follow that these public services have to be *delivered* by the state and its functionaries.

EDUCATION

There has been progress in education but not nearly enough (see Table 9.1). Illiteracy has fallen. In 1960, two-thirds of the population aged 15+ was illiterate; now one-third is (but that means the absolute number of illiterates is the same). Of course, the overall adult literacy rate is a slow-moving number. The literacy rate among young people is higher: for example, in the 15–24 age group, it was 86 per cent in 2014. School enrolment has taken large strides: 96.5 per cent of children between the ages of six and 14 are now enrolled in primary schools.[1] But enrolment is not the same as attendance; studies show that only two-thirds of children are in school on a random day. Dropout rates are also high: a third of children leave primary school before they reach the final grade. Moreover, in today's world, primary education is not enough for employability. The gross enrolment rate (GER) in secondary schools was around 43 per cent in 1999 and went up to 71 per cent in 2012.[2] Despite the improvement over time, education performance is not impressive when compared with other developing countries. In China, an obvious comparator, the overall literacy rate is 95 per cent, the literacy rate among 15- to 24-year-olds is nearly 100 per cent, and the GER in secondary education is 92 per cent. The average length of education enjoyed by India's labour force is 4.4 years; in China it is 7.5 years. China is clearly well ahead of India in education. What is more galling is that in some respects India's performance is not up to scratch in comparison with some South Asian countries such as Sri Lanka and Bangladesh, and even countries in Sub-Saharan Africa.[3]

Table 9.1 COMPARATIVE EDUCATION INDICATORS

Indicator	India	China	Bangladesh	Low-Income Countries
Adult Literacy Rate	69	95	60	57
	(2011)	(2010)	(2013)	(2010)
Youth Literacy Rate (male)	90	100	79	74
	(2011)	(2010)	(2013)	(2010)
Youth Literacy Rate (female)	82	100	83	63
	(2011)	(2010)	(2013)	(2010)
Net Enrolment Ratio (primary)	93	98	92	79
	(2012)	(1990)	(2010)	(2012)
Gross Enrolment Ratio (secondary)	71	92	54	40
	(2012)	(2012)	(2012)	(2012)
Gross Enrolment Ratio (tertiary)	25	30	13	8
	(2012)	(2012)	(2012)	(2012)
Mean Years of Schooling	4.4	7.5	4.8	n.a.
	(2012)	(2012)	(2012)	
Public expenditure on education (% GDP)	3.9	n.a.	1.9	3.8
	(2013)		(2009)	(2010)

Note: For exact definitions of various indicators, see the sources below.
Sources: i) World Bank (2015); ii) mean years of schooling from UNDP (2015): data refer to '2012 or nearest year available'.

How should educational progress be measured? In India, the tendency has been to focus on *education inputs*. Of course, education needs school buildings, textbooks, trained teachers, and amenities such as drinking water. And there has been a big increase in such inputs in the last decade, as a result of government expenditures on education programmes such as *Sarva Shikshya Abhiyan*, and the Mid-Day Meals scheme. (These expenditures, in turn, were made possible by the rising revenues that flowed from rapid growth.) Things could doubtless be better: for example, there still remain large numbers of primary schools with only one teacher. Nevertheless, if we go by the quantity of inputs into education, financial and physical, there has been a definite improvement.[4]

However, a different and more pertinent measure of educational progress is *actual learning outcomes*. Measured by this yardstick, India's progress has been utterly dismal, indeed shameful. A major source of evidence is surveys of primary education in rural India, done annually by Pratham, a respected non-government organization. In these surveys, children in all the districts of rural India are tested on their skills in reading, writing, and arithmetic. The results are chilling (see Table 9.2). For example, in the Pratham survey of 2014, it was found that 52 per cent of children in Grade V (aged 10–11) were at least three grades behind where they should be in reading ability. Performance in mathematics was equally shocking: 74 per cent of children in Grade V could not do simple division (of a three digit number by a one-digit number). Equally worrying is the fact that learning achievement has not improved since the Pratham surveys began in 2006; indeed there appears to be a marked worsening in recent years.[5] Such results have been corroborated by many other studies, using nation-wide representative samples of both rural and urban India, and of both public (i.e. government) and private schools.[6]

It is not easy to compare educational standards in India with other countries, using common tests, because the government has been very reluctant to allow such data to be collected. But there are a couple of exceptions. In the 2009 round of the regular Programme for International Student Assessment (PISA) survey conducted by the OECD, two Indian states (which are among the better states educationally) participated: Himachal Pradesh and Tamil Nadu. Students aged 15 were asked test questions in reading, science, and mathematics. The two states were placed respectively 72nd and 73th out of the 74 countries that took part, just above Kyrgyzstan.[7] And the average child in the two states was at the same level as the bottom fifth percentile of children in the OECD countries. (Three

Table 9.2 PUPIL EDUCATION ACHIEVEMENTS IN RURAL AREAS OF SIX INDIAN STATES, AND OF ALL INDIA, IN 2014

	In Standard V Who Are Able to:			In Standard IV Who Are Able to:
	Read[a] Vernacular	Read[b] English	Divide[c]	Subtract[d]
Himachal Pradesh	72	53	38	53
	(83)		(64)	(74)
Kerala	61	69	26	43
	(71)		(50)	(64)
Tamil Nadu	50	33	26	43
	(40)		(26)	(57)
Bihar	45	19	31	36
	(88)		(72)	(81)
Madhya Pradesh	28	10	10	15
	(58)		(29)	(46)
Uttar Pradesh	27	21	21	18
	(61)		(39)	(53)
All-India	41	24	21	32
	(63)		(39)	(59)
All-India[e]	48	24	26	40

Note: Percentage of children in government schools, and in private schools (in brackets).
[a] Read a Standard II level text (short story in vernacular).
[b] Read easy English sentences. The figures in this column are weighted averages for government and private schools combined.
[c] Divide three-digit number by one-digit number.
[d] Subtract two-digit number from two-digit number, with carryover.
[e] This row gives weighted averages for government and private schools combined.
Source: Pratham Educational Foundation (2015).

East Asian countries were among the top five scorers in the survey.) Similar dire results were found when the mathematics questions from the well-known Trends in International Mathematics and Science Study (TIMSS) test were done by 6000 Class IX students in Odisha and Rajasthan. The states were ranked respectively 43rd and 47th out of the 49 countries that took part.[8] The average student in the two states performed at a level three standard deviations below the mean in OECD countries.

Most of the hard evidence presented above is about primary education. Secondary education has been much less researched but informal evidence indicates a similar picture.[9] The big question that arises is why expansion in educational inputs has not been translated into better educational outcomes. There has been quite a lot of high-quality research on this, based on econometric work with nationally representative data sets, and on 'randomized control trials'. (Again, the rigorous scholarly studies are mostly about primary education.)[10]

My reading of what these studies show is that the poor educational outcomes are the product of inappropriate incentives. The faulty incentives relate partly to prevailing pedagogic practice. Teaching in Indian schools is curriculum-driven to an absurd degree; the over-riding objective of teachers is to 'finish' the curriculum of each year even if the majority of students are falling behind. As a result, children move into upper classes without having learned the basics. Only students at the top of the distribution keep pace with the curriculum; the rest become progressively less able to cope and lose interest.[11]

Even more critical for poor education quality is lack of teacher effort, which again is the product of wrong incentives. Several studies, based on unannounced visits, have found that teacher-absenteeism (around 25 per cent) is a pervasive feature in government schools, and that even when present, many teachers while away the time doing things other than teaching.[12] (Since student-attendance rates are also poor, it follows that actual learning time for a typical student is way below normal.) Strikingly, it also turns out that teacher absence is negatively correlated with pupil-teacher ratios. In other words, if more teachers (per pupil) are hired, teacher absence increases![13] It seems quite clear that the major reason for teacher absence is an incentive structure that engenders lack of 'accountability'. Government teachers have completely secure jobs. They are strongly unionized and have considerable political clout; and it is, in practice, almost impossible to fire a teacher whatever the degree of delinquency. At the same time, they are generously paid, irrespective of performance.[14] Salaries of government teachers have risen sharply in recent years on the back of recommendations by Pay Commissions. (In China, the average teacher's salary is about the same as per capita GDP. In India it is three times per capita GDP.) Another research finding is that modestly-trained 'contract teachers' who have lower pay and less job security than regular teachers are less likely to be absent and more likely to produce better learning outcomes.[15] This suggests that the sharper incentives they face more than make up for lack of formal training.

What is to be done? How should India ensure that the majority of children are educated to a decent standard? It is clearly essential that government schools should be made to function better. But change from within government is monumentally difficult. One suggestion is that decentralization and 'bottom-up' governance could do the trick. If teachers were controlled by village-level parent committees, they would be more accountable. Research has not been kind to this hypothesis. Village education

Private choice
public → improve

committees work badly.[16] Another possibility is that competition from private schools would be helpful (just as private competition has forced public sector enterprises to raise their game).

Private schools may be 'aided' or 'unaided'. Aided schools receive government grants and have over the years become very much like government schools. Unaided schools receive no government subsidies but they have been growing apace. In primary education, they now have a 31 per cent share in rural areas and 50 per cent in urban areas. In secondary education, the share is 21 per cent in rural areas (up from 7 per cent in 1993) and 56 per cent in urban areas (up from 11 per cent in 1993). By 'private schools', I shall, hereafter, mean 'unaided private schools'.

The rapid growth of private schools is indicative of relative quality as perceived by parents. More objective evidence about quality is available from Pratham, whose survey data show that private schools produce markedly better learning outcomes than government schools in primary education.[17] Of course, this finding cannot be taken at face value since students at private schools are more likely to come from economically and educationally advantaged backgrounds, and also to have had some pre-school education. There have been several studies comparing public and private schools, while controlling for the confounding factors. It would be fair to summarize the three main conclusions as follows.[18] Firstly, private schools produce somewhat better learning outcomes than government schools: the 'private school premium' is small but positive, and statistically significant. Secondly, private schools show a marked and statistically significant advantage over public schools with regard to teacher effort. Thirdly, private schools achieve their somewhat better performance than public schools at a much lower unit cost; in other words, they are considerably more cost-efficient.

It is not surprising that teacher effort is greater in private schools. That is what one would expect from the closer alignment of performance and incentives. The finding on unit costs is explained by the amazing fact that teachers' salaries in private schools are anywhere between a third and a tenth of the level in the public sector. It means that, at the margin, expansion of education would be much cheaper in the private sector, without loss (and perhaps some gain) of quality. On private versus public school quality in secondary education, there is not much hard evidence. Again, raw data show that learning levels are better in private schools. But this may or may not reflect parental background; there has been no careful research on this. However, what is clear is that, as in primary schooling, unit costs of education are much lower in private schools. This again is largely because the salaries of teachers are only a third of the level in government schools.

losers in privat- isation

Of course, we have to be cognizant of the fact that though private schools are cheaper than public schools from the national standpoint, they are not so for the average citizen, whose child has to pay fees in a private school but can attend a government school for free. Indeed, one of the main arguments for public education is that it ensures universal free access (at the expense of the taxpayer) and makes up for the effects of income inequality. But this is a deficiency that could be corrected by offering all parents, or poor parents in particular, the option and the means to choose private or public schools for their children, by giving them 'education vouchers'. Under such a scheme, both public and private schools would charge fees but students would 'carry their school fees with them' in the form of vouchers that are paid for out of general taxation. A voucher scheme would thus match the equity objective of free public education but would have the additionally important feature of enabling competition between public and private schools. In the Indian context, it is hard to imagine that government schools could deliver greater teacher effort and better education outcomes solely on the basis of reform *within* the public school system, in response to the 'voice' of citizens. Or to put it another way, 'voice' alone would be ineffective if parents did not also have the possibility of 'exit'.

Thus the case for education vouchers in India is not ideological but pragmatic: competition and the threat of student-exit are necessary conditions for public education to improve. There are two counter-arguments. The first is that if vouchers were introduced, the children of parents in vocal elite-groups would leave government schools, which would lead to further deterioration of these schools by reducing the pressure for reform. But there is little point in locking the stable door after the horse has bolted: not merely the top elite but also the broader elite, including panchayat leaders and teachers in government schools, already send their children to private schools. The second counter-argument is that parents, especially those who are themselves uneducated, cannot make sensible decisions about schooling. There is little evidence for this patronizing view. It is high time India got away from treating consumers of public services as idiots who have to be saved from themselves. Is it really better to give poor parents no alternative except sending their children to a poor-quality government school?

The big recent news on India's educational system is the coming into force of the Right to Education Act (RTEA) in 2010. The Act mandates, as a matter of right, 'free and compulsory education' of children at the primary level; and as a corollary, it requires expansion of the number of public schools to cover every neighbourhood. It sets norms regarding school infrastructure and pupil-teacher ratios with which schools have to comply. All private schools have to be 'recognized' by the government to be allowed to practice; and to be recognized, they have to satisfy the specified norms. Private schools are also required by the Act to reserve 25 per cent of places for children from 'economically weaker sections' of society; the cost of doing so in any particular private school is to be reimbursed by the government at the average unit cost per child in government schools as a whole or the actual unit cost per child in that private school, whichever is lower. Pedagogically, the most significant innovation is that board examinations are prohibited: children advance automatically to higher grades, though there is supposed to be continuous assessment of students to maintain quality standards. A lot of the detail is left to be formulated by the states, which have to implement the Act.

Has RTEA put India's educational system on the right track? Far from it. Firstly, there is a pedagogic point. In the context of abysmally low and declining standards, the automatic progression of students that the Act mandates is surely a bad idea and needs to be revisited. It is likely to exacerbate the existing problem of the curriculum moving faster than actual learning, which leads to a large underclass of students who are completely at sea in the higher grades. At the very least there should be a certificate that students can obtain if they clear a minimum hurdle in core skills such as reading, writing, and arithmetic.

Secondly, the Act stipulates bringing down the pupil-teacher ratio from 40:1 to 30:1. (This applies mainly to government schools; private schools in general already satisfy this requirement.) But all the evidence shows that employing more regular government teachers is very expensive and does not improve learning outcomes. At the same time, one of the most robust results from empirical studies is that contract teachers, hired cheaply and with only modest amounts of training, to provide supplementary instruction to children (at their level of learning rather than as dictated by the curriculum), are very effective in improving learning levels. But employment of contract teachers has raised hackles. Resistance comes from the feeling that having a large number of untrained teachers would de-professionalize teaching as a vocation. The solution, as Karthik Muralidharan has suggested, is to place contract teachers in a career progression to becoming regular teachers, subject to satisfactory performance as well as training and experience over several years as 'teaching assistants'.[19] The funds that would have been spent in hiring more regular teachers could be used to hire teaching assistants instead. This would enable a dramatic reduction in the pupil-teacher ratio to well below 30:1 and permit extra teaching of pupils at their level rather than where they ought to be to keep up with the curriculum.

Learning levels, especially of the weaker students, would be substantially improved thereby.

Thirdly, the Act has nothing to offer on measures to improve the accountability of regular teachers in government schools, despite the glaring need for this. For example, it may help to make part of each teacher's salary a bonus related to performance. Another useful step could be to devolve appointment, retention, and bonus payments of teachers to local governments who may be much better able to monitor teacher effort. (Of course, all such measures would be opposed by teachers' unions. This is precisely why competition from private schools would help. But RTEA does very little to increase competition.)

Fourthly, the Act's treatment of private schools is counterproductive. A large majority of these schools are cheap 'budget schools' that operate with lean infrastructure. The imposition of rigid input norms (such as teacher qualifications, size of library, and size of playground) will raise their costs, and may lead to a large number of them closing down. This would not be to anyone's benefit: what matters is quality of the outcome, not the satisfaction of inflexible qualifying norms. (As of December 2015, these fears would appear to be justified. According to the National Independent Schools Alliance, several thousand schools have either closed down or have received notice to close.) Another danger that must be avoided is extension of the over-generous salary structure of government teachers to the private sector. Such a development would be disastrous; it would sharply increase the cost to the nation of expanding primary education.

Finally, the benefits of opening up private schools to disadvantaged children, funded by the state, would be greatly diluted if schools were able to cherry-pick them. They should be chosen by lottery, with responsibility for the administration thereof shouldered by state governments.[20] The benefits of the scheme are also conditional on state governments reimbursing fees to the private schools promptly and fully. There are credible reports that these provisions are not working well due to difficulties in identifying disadvantaged children and the niggardliness of state governments in reimbursing private schools.

In sum, the RTEA does not address the underlying reasons for the low quality of education in India. High pupil-teacher ratios and lack of physical facilities are not the main issue. The core problems are to do with curriculum-driven teaching practices and pervasive lack of teacher accountability. The former could be put right by regulation. The latter, which is about having motivated teachers who actually teach, is a much harder nut to crack. I find it hard to believe that it could be addressed without adopting some of the features of a voucher system, such as funding public schools on a per-student basis rather than a block grant. (The implication would be that if public schools could not attract students in competition with private schools, they would to have to contract or close down.) Without some such threat, the performance of public schools is very unlikely to improve.

HIGHER EDUCATION

To keep the length of this chapter within reasonable bounds, my treatment of higher education will have to be brief.[21] Expansion in recent years has been sizeable. In 2011, total enrolment in higher education was about 22 million students (26 million inclusive of students in 'distance learning'), and the GER was 18 per cent of the relevant age group.[22] There were 660 universities or 'degree-awarding institutions' (of which 30 per cent were private), 33,000 colleges (60 per cent private) affiliated to the universities, and a further 12,750 'diploma institutions' (75 per cent private).[23] The 12th Five Year Plan set a target of increasing the GER to 25 per cent (an extra 10 million students) by 2016 and to 30 per cent by 2030. As with school education, the problem is not so much quantity as quality (of both public and private provision). Though there are a few excellent centres of learning such as the IITs and IIMs,[24] the unfortunate reality is that the average university or college produces 'unemployable' students with inadequate skills and knowledge.[25]

The problems of the Indian university system stem in large part from its poor governance structures. A statist control mentality is pervasive, and politicization is rife. Higher education is one of the most regulated sectors in the economy, indeed a throw-back to the full panoply of the license raj. The main regulators are the University Grants Commission (UGC), the All India Council for Technical Education, and bodies such as the Medical Council of India and the Bar Council for specialized professions. Entry of new universities or colleges requires many clearances, as well as government legislation or permission from the relevant regulator. Private universities have a hard time getting approval, and if they succeed, they have to remain unitary: private colleges are obliged to affiliate with public universities. All universities suffer from heavily centralized regulation and micro-management by the regulators of admissions, faculty recruitment and promotions, course curricula, student fees, and staff salaries. In public universities, salaries are tied to civil service scales and seniority is the criterion for promotion.

The higher-education license raj has had dire consequences. Extensive bureaucratic controls and lack of competition have killed creativity, teaching and course innovations, and quality improvements generally. Instead, they have led to rent-seeking behaviour. The system has deterred serious educators and education entrepreneurs and encouraged sharks and manipulators. Crooked politicians have got into the education business on a large scale. There is a lot of corruption; many senior officials, including heads, of regulatory bodies have been indicted.[26] Some universities and colleges have been found to sell doctoral degrees to defray their operating expenses.

India's university system needs a 'regulatory revolution' that removes the heavy hand of the state and replaces it by much greater decentralization and autonomy. The tyranny of central and state governments, and regulatory bodies like the UGC, should be curtailed and their powers confined to making broad policy and certifying that some basic norms are followed. Subject to that, both public and private universities should be given much more autonomy in internal governance, including personnel selection and salaries of staff. Tuition fees should not be controlled. The private returns to higher education justify economic user charges as a general rule; problems of access should be handled by loans (to be paid out of a 'graduate tax' on future salaries) and scholarships. More competition should be encouraged to raise standards. Ironically, authoritarian China has allowed its universities much greater autonomy than democratic India, and has reaped the benefits in the superior quality of its universities.

In addition to academic higher education, India also has a huge need for vocational and technical education and training (VTET) for the millions of young people entering the job market in the two or three decades to come. Space considerations prevent extended discussion of this topic here, except for a few brief remarks. Firstly, while VTET is indeed important, an effort to extend it on a large scale is likely to be fruitless without the basic foundation of good-quality primary and secondary education, which is lacking in India. Secondly, the need for skills is so huge that meeting it without private sector participation is completely unrealistic. While this is now appreciated in government circles, the country still lacks a workable model of public-private participation in this area. The ultimate objective must be for the state to make funds available to enable indigent young people to acquire training, provided competitively by training institutes, public or private, that are able to attract applicants, with the state playing a regulatory role. Thirdly, apprenticeship schemes that offer on-the-job training are a critical element of the VTET architecture. Since firms tend systematically to underprovide such training because of the fear of staff being poached, there is a case for a subsidy to training financed by a small payroll tax on all companies.[27]

India's health status and nutrition indicators have improved over the years. However, the levels achieved are very low, absolutely as well as comparatively (see Tables 9.3 and 9.4). China has outstripped India by a huge margin.[28] Moreover, outcome indicators such as rates of life expectancy, infant mortality, and prevalence of underweight and stunted children, are worse in India than in some South Asian countries that are poorer, such as Bangladesh. India has also done worse or not much better, on average, than the 36 poorest countries in the world (the World Bank classifies these as 'low-income countries').[29] An important reason for India's miserable health outcomes is that it has neglected 'traditional public health', whose domain covers items such as immunization, access to safe water and decent sanitation, and nutritional support for children. Evidence of the poor progress on these fronts can be seen in Tables 9.3 and 9.4. Once more, India is well behind China; it has also done worse than Bangladesh, and worse or not much better than 'low-income countries' in general.[30] And this is not necessarily because India started from a lower base. For example, in 1990,

Table 9.3 COMPARATIVE HEALTH INDICATORS 2014

Indicator	India	China	Bangladesh	Low-income countries
Life Expectancy at Birth (years)	68	75	71	61
Infant Mortality Rate (per 1000 live births)	39	10	32	55
Under-Five Mortality Rate (per 1000 live births)	50	11	40	79
Maternal Mortality Ratio (per 100,000 live births)	181	28	188	512
Births Attended by Skilled Staff (% total)	52 (2008)	100 (2008)	34 (2013)	52 (2008)
Child Immunisation Rate—Measles (% children aged 12–23 months)	83	99	89	77
Child Immunisation Rate—DTP3 (% children aged 12–23 months)	83	99	95	78
Access to Improved Water Source (% population)	94	95	86	65
Access to Improved Sanitation Facilities (% population)	40	75	60	28

Note: For exact definitions of the various indicators, see the source below.
Source: World Bank (2015).

Table 9.4 COMPARATIVE NUTRITION INDICATORS

Indicator	India	China	Bangladesh	Low-income countries
Prevalence of	15	11	17	28
Undernourishment	(2012)	(2012)	(2012)	(2012)
(% of population)				
Low Birth-Weight Babies	28	2	22	12
(% of population)	(2006)	(2010)	(2006)	(2011)
Underweight Children	44	3	33	20
(% children under five)	(2006)	(2010)	(2014)	(2014)
Stunted Children	48	9	39	36
(% children under five)	(2006)	(2010)	(2014)	(2014)
Prevalence of Anaemia	59	19	56	60
(% of children under five)	(2011)	(2011)	(2011)	(2011)
Consumption of Iodized Salt	71	97	58	51
(% of households)	(2009)	(2011)	(2013)	(2010)
Vitamin A Supplementation	59	n.a.	99	68
(% children, 6–59 months)	(2012)		(2012)	(2012)

Note: For exact definitions of the various indicators, see the source below.
Source: World Bank (2015).

Bangladesh was in a position similar to or worse than India but it has made bigger strides since then.[31]

India spends 4.1 per cent of GDP on health, which is not low in comparison with South Asia and 'lower-middle-income countries'. But it has one of the world's lowest shares of *public* spending in total health spending (29 per cent). Correspondingly, the share of private spending (71 per cent) and the share of out-of-pocket private spending (61 per cent) in total health spending are remarkably high, among the highest in the world.[32] It would be natural to infer from this that India needs to increase public spending on health substantially. But this conclusion should be approached with caution. It would be valid only if the quality of the spending was wiser than hitherto. As argued below, there is little to be said in favour of a business-as-usual expansion of government health expenditure.

The case for state intervention in health care is *prima facie* very strong. This is so not only because of powerful equity considerations but also because market failures are much more prevalent here than in many other sectors. Three different potential areas of health care can usefully be distinguished: 'traditional public health' (TPH); 'primary care', i.e. low-cost, routine, predominantly out-patient care; and 'secondary care', i.e. high-cost, specialized, predominantly in-patient care. The strength of the case for intervention, on market-failure grounds, is very different in these three areas. It is absolutely decisive in TPH, strong in secondary care, and fairly weak in primary care. Of course, the challenge, as always, is to weigh the efficiency and equity considerations in favour of state intervention against the possibility of 'government failure'.

'TRADITIONAL PUBLIC HEALTH' (TPH)

TPH consists, firstly, of state intervention in activities that the market will not finance at all, or to an adequate extent, because they are 'pure public goods' (for example, drainage of swamps, eradication of pests such as rats and mosquitoes) or have very large externalities (for example, immuniza-tion, clean water, and sanitation). Secondly, TPH is also concerned with state action to encourage consumption of so-called 'merit-goods' (such as appropriate nutrition for children) and to discourage consumption of 'demerit-goods' (such as smoking). Much of TPH thus relates to preven-tive as distinct from curative care. It certainly requires spending public money and it often requires public delivery as well, since there are likely to be severe limits on contracting for delivery by the private sector. It may also involve over-riding of consumer sovereignty. Thus, state intervention in TPH is essential because it fills a clear gap in market functioning; on top of that, there is also an equity angle because absence of state action in this sphere is likely to hit poor people particularly hard. (For example, there is clear evidence that the poor suffer disproportionately from infectious diseases.) Historically, TPH has been of enormous importance in bringing about health improvements in the advanced countries, much more so than curative care. As Angus Deaton has noted, 'The major credit for the decrease in child mortality and the resultant increase in life expectancy must go to the control of disease through public health measures. At first, this took the form of improvements in sanitation and water supplies. Eventually, science caught up with practice and the germ theory of disease was understood and gradually implemented ... through ... scientifically based measures. These included routine vaccination against a range of diseases and the adoption of good practices of personal and public health based on the germ theory. The improvement of public health required action by *public* authorities ... (and) could not have been accomplished by the market alone ...'.[33]

In India, TPH has been systematically neglected and takes up less than 10 per cent of government health expenditure. Ironically, the situation was better in this respect when it was a British colony. In the colonial period, there was a separate civil service cadre for public health, distinct from medical services. Sanitation departments were active in monitoring local sanitation conditions and disease trends. After independence, things changed. By then the advanced countries had achieved high standards in public health, and glamour and status in the health profession had shifted to curative medicine. Unfortunately, these developments infected India before it had achieved adequate public health standards. Government funding was diverted from public health, and public health services were merged, to their detriment, with medical services. The experience and knowledge that India had acquired in this field withered away. (It should be noted here that the state of Tamil Nadu bucked the trend and resisted the dismantling of public health services. It has reaped the reward in its superior health indicators compared with most other states in India.)[34]

Nutritional support for children is an important component of TPH because it cannot be left to the wisdom and means of parents. India has a major programme, viz. Integrated Child Development Services (ICDS), to provide health and nutrition services to children under six years of age through *anganwadis* (child-care centres). It needs to be pursued with more determination and vigour than hitherto, with increased financial assistance from the government. However, recent research strongly suggests that malnourishment among children has more to do with lack of sanitation than lack of food. Poor sanitation leads to frequent infections. In order to fight these and survive, children's bodies divert energy and nutrients away from bodily growth and brain development. This leads to physical and mental stunting, not just temporarily but permanently. Within sanitation, open defecation is a first-order issue. Half of India's population, i.e. 600 million people, defecate openly without access to a toilet or latrine, with disastrous consequences for health and human capital. In recent years, India's governments have made considerable efforts to deal with this problem. But the emphasis has been too much on constructing latrines, not nearly enough on getting the beneficiaries to use them. Given the attitudes to purity and pollution in Indian society, behavioural change will not happen without an intensive public education campaign at the village level.[35]

SECONDARY CARE

This aspect of curative health care covers a) major health events that are infrequent and unpredictable (such as surgery requiring in-patient hospital treatment) and b) chronic conditions (for example hypertension or diabetes) that require specialized attention. Such conditions are expensive to treat and can bring financial ruin to families, so there is a clear-cut equity case for subsidizing poor people. There is also a more general 'efficiency' case for state intervention for the following reason. The combination of the uncertain need for care, and its high expense, makes major health events natural candidates for risk-sharing via health insurance. But unregulated markets in health insurance are notoriously subject to market failure. One of the causes is so-called 'adverse selection'. There is a tendency for unhealthy people to demand more health insurance relative to healthy people, which bids up the average premium. This reinforces the tendency for less healthy people to stay in the market and healthier people to quit, which pushes up the insurance premium still further, and so on, in a vicious cycle that can, in the extreme, cause the market to break down altogether. Insurance companies tend to respond to this by excluding people with a prior history of health trouble or excluding certain services from coverage, with the consequence that many people are left uncovered by health insurance. In the presence of 'adverse selection', the government can improve overall welfare by universal compulsory health insurance. (Equity considerations can be handled by state subsidies to pay the insurance premiums of poor people.) Another cause of the failure of insurance markets is 'moral hazard', the tendency of insurance to change the behaviour of the insured in ways that are hard to monitor. With insurance, people do not have to bear the full cost of treatment, so they have an incentive to take fewer health precautions. (However, the incidence of this problem can be exaggerated in the field of secondary care since many of the conditions that are insured against are unpleasant enough to offset the moral hazard effect.) More importantly, since insurance is paid by a third party, there is a tendency for patients to demand, and health providers to supply, unnecessary care and more expensive care, which leads to cost and price escalation. Moral hazard cannot be addressed by state intervention. But adverse selection constitutes by itself a sufficient ground for the state to step in and regulate the insurance market.

Countries differ in their response to market failures in health care. The UK and Southern European countries have mostly chosen to deliver health services through a national health service. This is, in effect, a combination of in-kind universal state insurance with state provision of care; private health insurance and provision are only voluntary add-ons. In Canada and many Northern European countries, the choice has been to offer a uniform state health insurance package to all, but to allow public as well as private providers of care; private insurance markets are purely supplementary. In contrast, the United States relies mostly on private insurance markets, which is why there are large numbers of uninsured people, a situation which the recent introduction of 'Obamacare' has begun to correct.[36]

India has begun to introduce a state insurance system for secondary care, viz. the Rashtriya Swasthya Bima Yojana (RSBY) scheme, which takes roughly a single-payer, Canadian–North European track.[37] The scheme covers those below the poverty line (BPL) as defined by the Planning Commission, i.e. around 60 million families (300 million individuals). The insurance package, available via a smart card, is capped at Rs. 30,000 per family per year and can be used for a wide range of hospitalizations, including maternity and pre-existing conditions. Patients can choose public or private providers (hospitals). The premium price is currently around Rs. 550 per family per year. The premiums are paid by the central and state governments in the proportion 75:25, out of general tax revenues. The scheme was initiated in 2008, and around 180 million individuals (36 million families) had been enrolled by October 2015; and by then the number of hospitalizations was running at a rate of more than a million annually. Insurance is managed by insurance companies that bid for the right to do business; each district is allocated to one insurance company. Enrolment is done by the insurance companies; they have an incentive to increase enrolment since their premium-revenue from the government depends on the number of enrollees. Hospitals have to be empanelled on the basis of various criteria to qualify as care providers. The cost of care is controlled by price packages for specified conditions that are fixed in advance by the government's controlling agency.

In my view, the RSBY constitutes a good way forward in the provision of secondary care. It separates government finance from provision. It is right that the government should insure poor people and gather them in a single risk pool, with enrolment that is available independently of health status (to prevent adverse selection). This will guard against the scandal of exclusion from insurance that has plagued the United States. At the same time, it is also right to harness both public and private suppliers in the delivery of care. In India, a UK-style national health service would be a mistake. (The UK too is having acute difficulties with it, as regards quality and fiscal cost.) Public hospitals are currently not in a position to supply the quantity of care required; neither is there is any realistic prospect that the quality of care they provide will improve without the discipline of competition.

PRIMARY CARE

In primary care, market failures are of much less significance than in TPH and secondary care. Primary care is clearly not a 'pure public good' and, in India, it is indeed largely supplied by the private sector. External effects, while present, are not pervasive. So the case for state intervention is not decisive. (There remains, however, one plausible source of market failure in primary care. This arises from the fact that patients are ill-informed in medical matters. Doctors know much more about medicine than patients, so there is a potential for supplier-induced demand: patients may be inveigled into buying unnecessary, and possibly even harmful, treatment.)[38] There is of course an equity case for subsidizing primary care for poor people. But this is an argument for public finance, not necessarily for public provision. Whether public provision is a good thing depends on the quality of public provision. Ultimately, the relative desirability of government and private provision can be settled only by comparing their performance on the ground. In other words, a judgement has to be made on the relative importance of market failure and government failure.

On paper, India's public primary care system is comprehensive. There are more than 25,000 primary health centres (PHCs) and more than 150,000 'sub-centres' serving India's 600,000 villages, so the typical village has a health facility that offers free health care within fairly easy reach.[39] Nevertheless, it is clear that people prefer to pay and go to private providers who are often unqualified: surveys indicate that around 75 per cent of primary care is supplied by the private sector. This suggests *prima facie* that the private sector offers a better quality of care. Of course, this should not be taken for granted without closer scrutiny. Fortunately, there has been a great deal of careful research in the last decade investigating the quality of primary care in India, both public and private.

The results of the research are depressing. They can be grouped under three headings that are relevant to the quality of care given by providers: physical presence, competence, and effort.[40] *Physical presence* of the provider is obviously a necessary condition for provision of health care. But rates of absenteeism in public facilities are extremely high.[41] A nationwide representative sample survey of public facilities by Chaudhury and others in 2003, based on unannounced visits by surveyors, showed an average absenteeism rate of 40 per cent for both doctors and other health staff.[42] A more intensive survey around the same time by Banerjee and others in rural Rajasthan showed an absenteeism rate of 45 per cent in sub-centres and 36 per cent in primary centres.[43] More recent studies show an unchanged picture.[44] Another study by Banerjee and others documents an attempt to reduce absenteeism among health workers by making camera recordings of attendance. The attempt failed because it was subverted by machine tampering (which, the authors convincingly argue, could not have happened without the connivance of the government health administration).[45]

One way to gauge the *competence* of health providers would be to consider their medical qualifications. By this standard, the public sector is far superior since a medical degree (MBBS) is a pre-condition of employment as a doctor. Among private providers, around two-thirds of those who call themselves 'doctors', especially in rural areas, have no qualifications at all. (Some of them may be 'registered medical practitioners' [RMPs] but this does not mean they are properly qualified, though they may have acquired some knowledge by some other means such as doing a few months of a long-distance course.) Only 10 per cent of private providers are properly qualified, i.e. have MBBS degrees, and of the rest around 20 per cent are practitioners of traditional medicine (*ayurveda*, homeopathy, etc.). It would be tempting to conclude from this that public health facilities provide better, high-quality care. But the only way to investigate the actual quality of care is to see what goes on between doctor and patient. Several careful studies have done this. I commend, in particular, various papers by Jishnu Das, Jeffery Hammer, and their collaborators who have studied medical interactions in both rural and urban India.[46] I cannot here describe their work in detail but the following few paragraphs give an outline.

One way to study *competence* is to interview public and private providers and ask them questions about diagnosis and treatment based on 'vignettes' or hypothetical cases, with the answers graded by a team of experts. This was the method used by Das and Hammer in their well-known study in Delhi. There were five 'vignettes': diarrhoea in a baby; simple cold; tuberculosis; depression in a young woman; pre-eclampsia in a pregnant woman. Knowledge was found to be very low and in four out of the five vignette-cases the average provider was more likely to harm than help the patient.[47] Though public doctors are supposedly more qualified, the average level of competence of public and private doctors was not very different. The ranking by knowledge was in the following descending order: private qualified doctors, doctors in public hospitals, doctors in public health clinics, private unqualified doctors. (As important as this ranking was the fact that doctors, both public and private, were far more competent in rich than in poor neighbourhoods.)

Quality of care does not depend on knowledge and competence alone but on what use the doctor makes of it, in other words, on *effort*. To investigate this aspect, the interviews with health providers were followed up by a spending a day with each provider, observing how he or she dealt with patients (length of consultation, number of questions asked, examination of the patient, medicines prescribed, advice on medicine-use etc.). In this case, the results were even more disturbing. Not only were the average length of consultation, number of questions asked, and number of examinations done, very low (3.8 minutes, 3.2 questions, and examinations 60 per cent of the time) but the average provider in a public health clinic was much worse than average (two minutes, one question, and no examinations). The study also compared providers' actual performance with their responses to the vignettes. There was a huge difference. On average, doctors did far less than what they knew should be done. Private unqualified doctors asked all the questions they knew to ask; in other words, they were putting in a lot of effort. Private qualified doctors put in less effort than they knew to be appropriate. In the public health facilities, especially the PHCs, the difference was dramatic: doctors did very little, much less than they knew to be necessary. Das and Hammer summarize as follows: 'Private doctors without an MBBS, which include RMPs and all sorts of other degrees normally bunched together in the 'quacks' group, provide better care than public sector doctors, all with an MBBS, primarily because of the abysmally low effort of public sector doctors outside the large hospital setting'.

It could be argued that the 'vignette-studies' were defective because knowledge that they were being interviewed would have altered the doctors' responses and behaviour. This criticism has been met in the recent study of 60 rural villages in Madhya Pradesh by Jishnu Das and others, which used 'standardized patients' (i.e. individuals from the local community trained to act the part of genuine patients and present a consistent case of illness) to study doctor-patient clinical interactions regarding three medical cases: unstable angina, asthma, and dysentery (of a child not present).[48] The results were very similar to the 'vignette-studies'. There were serious shortcomings in the quality of care. Interactions were brief (an average of less than four minutes) and there was little in the way of patient-questioning or patient-examination. On average, only a third of the essential questions and examinations were asked or done.[49] The correct treatment was followed only a third of the time, while an unnecessary or harmful treatment was prescribed about 40 per cent of the time. Notably, there was a large difference in adherence to the check-list of essential questions and examinations between the public and private sectors: even unqualified private doctors performed better than the public doctors, and qualified private doctors performed much better.

All the studies find, however, that private doctors are worse than government doctors in one important respect: they tend to over-prescribe antibiotics, injections and drips. So patients with self-limiting diseases may be better off going to a public clinic, and the rest may be better off going private. Even if she knew this, however, a typical patient may well prefer going private since she would not know in advance the nature of the disease that affects her.

Recent official thinking in India has emphasized universal health care (UHC) as a major objective of policy.[50] In the government's vision, UHC is defined as universal public health insurance for both primary and secondary care, with primary care delivered mainly by the public sector, and secondary care provided by a combination of public and private hospitals. Universality can only be a long-term objective. The need of the hour is better health care for poor people. But even for this category, my review suggests that the vision needs to be modified.

I think that the RSBY is the right way to go in secondary care. (Note that some states currently have their own insurance schemes. These need to be integrated with RSBY. The obvious way to do this would be to make them 'add-ons' that offer more than the basic RSBY package, e.g. complex tertiary care.) While the conception of the RSBY is sound, it will doubtless have to contend with significant managerial and regulatory challenges. Management of the scheme has been devolved to insurance companies who, in turn, use third-party administrators. The government will have to learn to monitor these bodies. Quality and cost control will also be tricky issues.[51] Regulation will have to see to it that private hospitals do not make money by performing unnecessary operations. The scheme assumes competition between private and government hospitals but the latter will have to be given much greater autonomy to enable them to compete. As of December 2015, the RSBY covers around half of all below-poverty-line families. Enrolment needs to be stepped up. Obviously, the economics of the scheme would be improved if its coverage were expanded to include people above the poverty line (though they would have to pay their own premia until fiscal constraints ease sufficiently for the state to take over payment).

On primary care, the official vision needs correction. Evidence, noted above, indicates that both supply and demand in primary health care are grossly dysfunctional or distorted. On the supply side, the overall quality of care is very low. And though the government spends a lot of money on primary care infrastructure and personnel, it delivers care that is no better in competence and much worse in effort than the private sector. On the demand side, patients much prefer going to fee-charging, private, often unqualified doctors, who treat patients with much more consideration and courtesy than government doctors, and make up in effort what they lack in qualifications. But they also offer antibiotic and steroid treatments for ordinary, often self-limiting, conditions. There is surely an element of supplier-induced demand in this; unfortunately, it appears now to have become ingrained in consumer preferences. People do not feel they are being properly cared for unless they are prescribed antibiotics.

Given this dismal scenario, what are the policy implications for primary care? It is clear that a business-as-usual expansion of the public sector would be a waste of money. The public health care system suffers from a deep lack of accountability and this problem has to be solved first. But there is no quick or easy way of doing this. Public insurance to cover primary care (say as an extension to RSBY) would be extremely unwise in the current environment. Abhijit Banerjee has it right when he says that, 'in such an environment, insured outpatient care will be extremely expensive to offer. It would be heavily used and might increase over-medication'. He goes on, 'We have created a health care culture that is profoundly cynical. Most government doctors are absent and practice (privately) after hours in government facilities. All rules are bent and everyone knows it. It is hard to imagine there would not be collusion between doctor and patient to charge the health system.... Given the enormous corruption on the ground in India, the implications are frightening. Hence it would be wise to stay away from any (insurance) system that offers outpatient care'.[52] I agree.

The government has announced its intention to increase public health funding sharply higher from the present 1 per cent of GDP over the next few years. While this would indeed be desirable, it is the composition of spending that is at issue here. The top priority must surely be a substantial increase in spending on TPH. Immense health benefits would follow from increasing immunization, child nutrition, safe water, and sanitation. On secondary care, there should be a concerted effort to achieve the RSBY target of insuring, at the very least, the entire population of poor people. (The states could be encouraged to have their own add-on schemes for tertiary care.) On primary care, the government should accept that improvement will come only by pursuing several complementary steps. Firstly, the government must accept the reality that most primary health care is already in the private sector and give up trying to replace it by public care. Secondly, a programme should be put in place a) to provide training courses for unqualified private doctors and b) to make certificates of training a condition of being allowed to practice. Thirdly, in India almost any drug is available across the counter. This must change: drugs should be sold only for prescriptions from those who are certified to prescribe them. Fourthly, steps should be taken to make public medical personnel perform their duties. This is part of the very general and difficult problem of making government functionaries more accountable. It is hard to see how this could be done without moving to a system where 'the money follows the patient'. Ideally, providers in public facilities should be paid on a capitation, not a salaried, basis, depending on how many patients they attract in competition with private doctors. Finally, in pursuing equity, there is much to be said for a system in which the government gives each poor household a 'basic income', part of which it can use for primary health care, with freedom to go to a public or private medical facility.

NOTES

1. An alternative way of looking at this is that at least 7 million children are out of school.
2. The overall GER is 71 per cent but this is an average of lower and upper secondary education. In the latter, the GER is significantly lower.
3. See Dreze and Sen (2013). Dreze and Sen also point out (in their Table 3.1) that India's female literacy rate among 15- to 24-year-olds is below the average of 16 countries (outside Sub-Saharan Africa) that are poorer than India. The same is true of mean years of schooling in India (4.4 years in India, 5 years in the same 16 poorest countries, and India's rank is 12 out of 17).
4. There does remain an acute shortage of teachers. Regular teachers in government schools are well-paid, so they are expensive to hire. A far more serious problem is the quality of teaching, as discussed below.
5. In 2010, 46 per cent of children in Grade V could not read a Grade II text, and 64 per cent of Grade V children could not do simple division, i.e. the results were better than in 2014. Most of the major states show a drop in test results in mathematics between 2010 and 2014.
6. Test results are somewhat better for urban than for rural schools, and for private schools than for public schools. The latter feature is discussed in greater detail below.
7. See Walker (2011).
8. See Das and Zajonc (2010).
9. Note that since the PISA and TIMSS tests were administered to students during or after the first year of secondary education, they do provide some evidence about its quality.
10. Muralidharan (2013) and Mukerji and Walton (2013) provide excellent, policy-oriented surveys of this literature.
11. See Banerjee and Duflo (2011), Chapter 4, and Pritchett and Beatty (2012).
12. See Chaudhary, Hammer, Kremer, Muralidharan, and Rogers (2006).
13. See Muralidharan, Das, Holla, and Mohpal (2014).
14. See Pritchett and Murgai (2007), Kingdon (2010), Kingdon and Muzammil (2010).
15. See Muralidharan and Sunderaraman (2013) and Goyal and Pandey (2013).
16. See Banerjee, Banerji, Duflo, Glennerster, and Khemani (2010).
17. For example, only 41 per cent of children in Grade V in government schools could read a Grade II level text; the corresponding figure for private schools was 63 per cent. Only 21 per cent of children in Grade V in government schools could do simple division; the corresponding figure in private schools was 39 per cent. See Table 9.2.
18. See Desai, Dubey, Vanneman, and Banerji (2009), French and Kingdon (2010), Muralidharan and Sunderaraman (2013), and Singh (2015).
19. See Muralidharan (2013).

20. My discussion has focussed on primary schooling. But India has reached a stage of development in which expansion of secondary education is also a critical need. Several similar considerations apply as for primary schools. Firstly, affordability is a very serious problem for poor people. Secondly, private schools are no worse in quality than state schools but have much lower unit costs per pupil. It follows that India should aim to give people the means to acquire secondary education for their children (by vouchers or cash transfers) but allow them to go public or private schools, which compete with one another.

21. I am aware that brevity may give my views in this section the air of *ex cathedra* pronouncements. More comprehensive treatments of university education, which provide the background for my position and judgements, can be found in Kapur and Mehta (2007), Kapur (2010c, 2011, 2014), Panagariya (2008), and Bhagwati and Panagariya (2013).

22. India's GER for higher education is about average for lower-middle-income countries but lower than China and East Asia.

23. See Planning Commission (2013a), Chapter 21.

24. Even at the top end, the picture is not particularly good. Not a single Indian university is to be found among the world's top 200 universities, according to reputable global rankings (see, for example, the Times Higher Education rankings in 2015).

25. Various industry bodies, as well as the Planning Commission, have reported that a very high proportion of university graduates are ill-prepared for employment. See also Blom and Saeki (2011).

26. See Kapur (2011). Kapur also points out that a review committee found that the UGC, which has the power to 'deem' educational institutions to be universities, had conferred the status on 88 'unfit' and 'deficient' institutions, half of which had links to politicians.

27. Good discussions of VTET can be found in World Bank (2008), Mehrotra (2014), and Mehrotra and Ghosh (2014).

28. For example, in 2014, India's life expectancy at birth was 68 years, China's was 75 years. India's infant mortality rate was 39 per 1000 while China's was only 10. In India, in recent years, around 45 per cent of children have been underweight; in China, the proportion is less than 5 per cent. In 2014, child immunization rates for measles and DPT were between 80 and 85 per cent in India; by the same year, China had attained a rate of 99 per cent. See Tables 9.3 and 9.4.

29. Note that India is a 'lower-middle-income country', according to the World Bank classification. India's absolute levels of performance in life expectancy, infant mortality, and under-five mortality are somewhat better than the average for 'low-income countries'. But this is because the 'low income countries' include many in Sub-Saharan Africa, which perform badly on these counts due to special factors, such as the prevalence of AIDS. Dreze and Sen (2013) point out that India does worse than the average for 17 poorest countries outside Sub-Saharan Africa.

30. India looks even worse compared with low-income countries, if Sub-Saharan African countries are excluded.

31. For example, India's infant mortality rate fell from 81 per 1000 live births in 1990 to 39 in 2014; the fall in Bangladesh was from 139 to 32.

32. The level and composition of India's health spending is different from most countries but similar to the rest of South Asia.

33. See Deaton (2013), 93.

34. See Das Gupta (2012).

35. On open defecation, see Spears (2013). Building latrines is not enough. There is evidence that a large proportion of newly built latrines are lying unused. Steps have to be taken to ensure water supply, proper maintenance, and refuse collection.

36. Some writers have contrasted the American model of private insurance and provision on the one hand, and the Canadian and European model of state insurance and provision on the other hand. This slides over the important point that Canada and several European countries have state insurance combined with either private provision or a mix of public and private provision.

37. There are some differences, however. In some European countries, notably Germany, there is mandated 'social insurance', financed by payroll taxes on employers. In India, this cannot be chosen as the basic method because the organized sector is small. RSBY premiums are paid out of general taxation. The RSBY resembles the Canadian–North European model in that the state does the insurance but health care provision is by both state and private providers.

38. This kind of market failure affects secondary care as well but is less important in that context because there is some peer-monitoring in hospitals.

39. See, however, Rajaraman (2014) for inequalities in the spatial distribution of public services.

40. I owe this classification to Das and Hammer (2005, 2012)

41. Another reason for absence, separate from absenteeism, is unfilled positions in public health centres. Medical personnel are reluctant to serve in poor and remote rural areas.

42. Chaudhury, Hammer, Kremer, Muralidharan, and Rogers (2006).

43. Banerjee, Deaton, and Duflo (2004).

44. For example, see Gill (2009).

45. Banerjee, Duflo, and Glennester (2008).

46. For example, see Das and Hammer (2005, 2007), and Das and Hammer (2012) for a summary of various relevant studies.

47. For example, two-thirds of the observed providers did not ask questions or perform examinations that would diagnose pre-eclampsia in a pregnant woman, a serious condition that can lead to death of the mother or the child.

48. See Das, Holla, Das, Mohanan, Tabak, and Chan (2012). The study also covered urban Delhi. These results were also very bad (but slightly better than those of rural Madhya Pradesh).

49. The check-list of essential questions and examinations was a sub-set of those recommended in the guidelines of the National Rural Health Mission, and it only contained items that could easily be done in primary facilities, e.g. asking relevant questions about the patient's history, and carrying out examinations such as checking the pulse or taking the temperature.

50. India's health policy is comprehensively assessed in Mahal and Fan (2012).

51. So far the RSBY seems to be alive to quality issues, as exemplified by the disempanelling of a sizeable number of hospitals. Cost control has also been effective so far. The annual benefit cap per family obviously helps. So too do the fixed rates for medical procedures; these are clearly better than fee-for-service payments in controlling costs. Even so, over the longer run, there will be pressures from providers to increase rates for their services, and from insurance companies to re-price premiums.

52. See Banerjee (2012).

CHAPTER 10

Safety Nets and Social Protection

O ne of the defining features of social democracy is the presence of robust social support systems. These can be *enabling* or *protective* (admittedly, the distinction is not entirely clear-cut). Social enablement aims to provide people, including the poorest among them, with the *earning capacity* to obtain decent incomes and lead fulfilling lives. Public services such as education, nutrition, health care, and sanitation are among the main components of an enabling agenda. The protective aspect of social support is rather different. Social protection is concerned with guaranteeing every individual or family an acceptable minimum standard of living *regardless of earning capacity*, by state-financed insurance mechanisms to alleviate temporary poverty caused by adverse contingencies, and state-enforced redistributive real income transfers to keep chronic poverty at bay.[1]

There are also many policies that can combat poverty indirectly. These include the whole range of measures to raise productivity, and more specifically, to encourage employment and labour use. Unquestionably, these growth-promoting and labour-demanding policies have the greatest quantitative impact on poverty in the long run. Social protection policies are different. They are about policy interventions to reduce poverty *directly*, here and now. They aim to provide cushions, buffers, and safety nets, contingent as well as permanent, to relieve poverty and deprivation among those who lose or do not gain during the hard slog that a development transition normally involves.

How should we judge the quality of social protection policies? We must ask (a) whether they fulfil their primary purpose, which is to benefit poor people; (b) whether they do so as cost-effectively as possible; and (c) whether they are fiscally affordable, given many other legitimate claims on the budget, including public investment and 'enabling' social expenditures. The previous chapter has assessed India's main 'enabling' policies in some depth. This chapter takes a cool and critical look at India's social protection framework and concludes that it is inefficient as well as ineffective. Its aims are laudable but the means it employs are seriously defective. Radical changes of policy design are called for.

INDIA'S SOCIAL PROTECTION FRAMEWORK

unfortunately these systems are already in place.

Historically, the poor were left largely to fend for themselves during the early phases of industrialization in the advanced countries. Quite rightly, this is no longer regarded as acceptable in any social democracy, rich or poor. Moreover, in the advanced countries, social enablement mostly predated social protection. Now all social democracies are rightly expected to do 'enablement' and 'protection' simultaneously though the exact balance between the two is a matter of choice.

India has several social protection schemes. But two of them take pride of place as pillars of the protection architecture: a) food subsidies; and b) rural employment guarantees. Food subsidies work through the Targeted Public Distribution System (TPDS).[2] The FCI procures food grains (mainly rice and wheat), from farmers at pre-set 'minimum support prices' and supplies them to the TPDS, which has more than 600,000 'fair price shops' scattered across the country. Those in possession of a 'below-poverty-line card' (BPL card) can buy specified quantities (currently 5 kilogrammes of grain per head per month) from these shops cheaply, at 'issue prices' that are a fraction of minimum support prices and prices on the open market. The problem is that the selection of BPL card-holders, which is done by state governments, is extraordinarily haphazard: fake cards are common, and so is systematic over-registration. The coverage of BPL cards has large exclusion errors, i.e. many poor people are left out, as well as large inclusion errors, i.e. many non-poor people get in. Moreover, the leakages into the open market are huge. This is not surprising given the large difference between market prices and issue prices. Agents all the way down the supply chain, including traders who run the fair price shops, are strongly tempted to divert food from the TPDS; and in this activity they are often hand in glove with local politicians. The system is expensive and costs around 1 per cent of GDP annually. In 2013, the UPA government passed the Food Security Act, which mandated that the coverage of the TPDS should be widened to include 67 per cent of the population. So the cost is due to rise further when state governments have fully expanded their BPL lists.[3]

Various estimates have been made of the leakages from TPDS. Ten years ago, both the Planning Commission and the National Sample Survey estimated that well over half of the food distributed did not reach the intended beneficiaries.[4] The latest estimate made by the Shanta Kumar Committee suggests that the figure is still around 47 per cent.[5] Defenders of the scheme have claimed that some states, for example Tamil Nadu and Chhattisgarh, show low leakages of around 10 per cent. But two states do not a country make. And one's confidence in these claims is not strengthened by the exposure of a scandal in the same much-praised Chhattisgarh, where 94 per cent of households had been listed as BPL, and more ration cards had been issued than the total number of households in the state.[6] (This obviously implies that the true leakage in Chhattisgarh was very much larger than the touted 10 per cent.) Another reason for the high cost of running the TPDS is the sheer inefficiency of the operation. One symptom of this is that the salaries of its functionaries, inclusive of so-called incentive payments, are extravagantly high. Various malpractices are also rampant.[7] A recent scholarly examination of the TPDS shows that after allowing for the excess costs from inefficiency, only 10 per cent of the food subsidy is an income transfer to the poor.[8]

The TPDS has another serious shortcoming. It is founded on the principle of providing poor people a specified quantity of calories. But the relationship between calories and good nutrition is quite weak,[9] so choice is restricted to no good purpose. It distributes mainly rice and wheat but diets, even of poor people, are changing in favour of other foods. After years of public distribution of cereals, India remains a byword for malnutrition; and as many commentators have pointed out, this is more due to lack of balanced diets, and the prevalence of disease and poor sanitation, than low calorie intake. It is hard to resist the conclusion that the TPDS is ripe for abolition if a more efficient substitute could be found; and this leads to the thought that the objective of ensuring food security would be better achieved by making cash transfers to people, which they could use to buy food in the market. The state could continue with price stabilization via buffer stocks but it could get out of the business of distribution, in which the private sector has a comparative advantage. Up to two-thirds of government spending on food subsidies could thus be saved and used for other socially desirable purposes.

The second pillar of the social protection framework is the Mahatma Gandhi Rural Employment Guarantee Scheme (NREGS), initiated by an Act in 2006 and rolled out across the country by 2008.[10] It guarantees, as a legislated right, up to 100 days of employment a year to any rural household at a specified minimum wage indexed to the cost of living. The work has to be made available within 15 days of application or the worker becomes entitled (in theory but not in practice) to unemployment benefit. One-third of the workers have to be women. Village councils (*gram panchayats*) are closely involved in selecting projects and administering the programme. The focus is typically on labour-intensive works that improve rural infrastructure and land productivity such as rural roads, soil conservation, flood control, groundwater recharge etc. It is mandated that wages have to be at least 60 per cent of the total cost. Total expenditure on the scheme was Rs. 33,000 crores (0.45 per cent of GDP) in 2011/12. Since then, it has fallen to 0.3 per cent of GDP.

The scheme has not delivered on the '100 working days a year' promise. Even so, it has provided a substantial amount of employment: an annual average of 40 days per household to about 50 million rural households (one-third of the rural total), but with significant variation across states.[11] There is evidence of excess demand for employment in states where the administrative machinery is not up to running the programme competently. The inclusion of women and socially disadvantaged groups (scheduled castes and tribes) is impressive. But the scheme is by no means problem-free. Household surveys and social audits reveal the incidence of delayed payments, payment of less-than-full wages, and other such irregularities. Corruption and leakage of funds undoubtedly exist, though there is encouraging recent evidence of major improvement in cases where wages have been put directly into workers' bank accounts (see below). Planning, implementation, and monitoring by local bodies are weak and variable, with the result that project selection is poor and the quality of assets created is low. Despite this, for its primary purpose as a scheme of social protection, the programme is quite successful. It does provide a safety net for rural landless labour in the lean periods of the agricultural cycle when wages fall and work is scarce.

An important argument against the NREGS is that it is not a cost-effective method of poverty alleviation. At best, the whole of the wage component of expenditure is a transfer to workers in the scheme; the actual transfer is likely to be less since they would be giving up some alternative earnings. In any case, the non-wage component of expenditure is wholly wasted, if poverty alleviation is the sole aim. It would be cheaper to make cash transfers equal to the net wage component of expenditure and use the rest of it for more productive purposes. This is a strong argument but not strong enough to justify the government ditching the scheme. Firstly, the alternative earnings lost by NREGS workers would be low, perhaps close to zero, in the slack season, which is when the scheme mainly operates. So the argument that the scheme diverts labour from productive work is not strong. Secondly, there is research-based evidence that the scheme has a small positive effect on rural wages, and even on urban unorganized sector wages (since rural-urban migration is negatively affected) because it improves the bargaining power of labour. Thirdly, the NREGS has the critically advantageous feature of 'self-selection' by workers (since only the very poor would turn up for arduous work).[12] The alternative of a cash transfer scheme would face the acute problem of identifying the poor. Only the adoption of a *universal* cash transfer scheme with a sizeable per capita transfer could justify dispensing with the NREGS. As shown below, even a transfer that raises the average income of India's poor population to the poverty line would not be quite enough since the income of the poorest people would be below the average. In my judgement, the NREGS should be continued for the next decade as a fall-back safety net for the poor (together with the adoption of technologies to reduce malfeasance), alongside the cash-transfer 'basic income' scheme advocated below. It will continue to do much good if it remains self-selecting (and since this will require that it remains a low-wage scheme, minimum wages in the NREGS will have to be kept in check). The present government's neglectful attitude towards the scheme is unwise.

Besides food subsidies and the employment guarantee scheme, there is a whole range of other 'poverty programmes'. Classifying them into 'enabling' or 'protective' is inevitably arbitrary. Some social assistance, pension, and insurance programmes fall clearly in the 'protective' category. Of these, the following four are probably the most important. The *National Social Assistance Programme* makes cash transfers (pensions) to specified vulnerable groups such as the elderly, the widowed and the disabled who are below the poverty line. The *Aam Aadmi Bima Yojana* provides life insurance for poor people: the insurance premiums are paid by central and state governments on a shared basis. The *Rashtriya Swasthya Bima Yojana*, discussed in the previous chapter, provides health insurance to cover poor people against the costs of hospitalization in public or private hospitals, for a nominal fee. The *Janani Suraksha Yojana* offers women cash rewards to deliver babies with proper public or private medical care. All these programmes are small; the aggregate sum of money spent on them is only around 0.1 per cent of GDP; they are completely dwarfed by food subsidies and the NREGS, which together account for around 1.3 per cent of GDP and are set to rise to 1.5 per cent of GDP.[13] However, if we widen the definition of social protection programmes to include a) subsidies, which are *intended* to help the poor (even if they fail to do so) and b) programmes which are ambiguously 'enabling' or 'protective', social protection expenditures are very much higher, probably more than 10 per cent of GDP. As regards (a), the extensive network of price subsidies, explicit and hidden, covers many goods and services such as fuels, fertilizers, water, and electricity that are supposed to help the poor but are in fact highly regressive (see Chapter 6). Expenditure on these subsidies, either directly in the budget or in the form of foregone revenue, accounts for several percentage points of GDP. As for (b), the Statistical Appendix to the 2014/15 Economic Survey (pp. A141–145), lists around 50 poverty programmes, many of them so-called 'centrally sponsored schemes'.[14] Even if we do not count the main education and health care schemes as falling clearly in the 'enabling' class, that still leaves a great many others. They are a mixed bag. Some such as the *Integrated Child Development Scheme*, for early childhood development, and the *Mid-Day Meals Scheme* for school children have a reasonably good track record. Many others such as the *Indira Awas Yojana*, a housing scheme for the poor, and the *National Livelihoods Mission*, a micro-credit subsidized lending scheme, are known to be to be very badly targeted. Many government reports have pointed out the failings of the multiplicity of India's poverty programmes: unnecessary proliferation, large leakages and corruption, lack of accountability of government functionaries, lack of implementation capability etc.[15] They raise the same overwhelming question that food subsidies do: Would their objectives not be better served by straightforward cash transfers?

THE TECHNOLOGY OF CASH TRANSFERS

The dispiriting reality of social protection schemes leads naturally to the proposal that some of them, especially the price subsidies, could be substituted by cash transfers to the poor, thereby saving money as well as increasing the effectiveness of income redistribution. It may be feared, however, that cash transfers may be no better than existing methods in reaching poor people. Recent developments in technology have gone a long way to answering such an objection. It has now become possible to have cash transfers delivered by a secure payments infrastructure. The Manmohan Singh government took some major steps down this road and its successor has wisely built on this foundation.

The technological package has three components. Firstly, it is now possible to provide people with a biometrically-authenticated unique identity in the form of a smart card (named the *Aadhar* card in India). The project of persuading all citizens to acquire such a card (the unique identification or UID programme) has made enormous headway. By the end of 2015, the number of Aadhar cards issued was around 900 million; and it is expected that the coverage will be near-universal by the end of 2016. Secondly, there is the drive to persuade people to open bank accounts. This too was begun under the UPA regime but the Modi government has put real energy into it, under the so-called *Jan Dhan programme*, which has proceeded rapidly. The number of bank accounts that have been opened has already reached 195 million (by December 2015), and the expectation is that all 240 million of India's households will soon have them. The essential step of linking the bank accounts to the unique Aadhar cards is also well under way. The third element of the package is 'mobile banking' that adds to the convenience of operating the Aadhar-seeded bank accounts. This is made possible by the amazing spread of mobile phones: there are now 900 million mobile phones in India. These three developments will have multiple benefits. In the present context, the main advantage is the feasibility of making cash transfers to the intended recipients, not to fake or 'ghost' recipients, and to prevent the money being stolen somewhere along the way. Parts of the technology package have already proved their worth in the payment of sub-sidies for cooking gas. These used to take the form of price subsidies; now they are put directly into the bank accounts of beneficiaries. The change has resulted in significant fiscal savings as a result of the discovery of 30 mil-lion bogus gas connections.

Scepticism about the cost-effectiveness of the technology package in making cash transfers is nevertheless quite natural. There are complex tech-nical and logistical issues to be sorted out. It may also be feared that rent-losers from the process would stymie the operation of the package in one way or another. It is very pertinent, therefore, that the merits of harnessing the new technologies have been demonstrated by Karthik Muralidharan and his associates in a randomized control trial that examined the delivery of NREGS wage payments into bank accounts via the introduction of 'smart cards', in a setting large enough to be policy-relevant, viz. 158 sub-districts (*mandals*) of Andhra Pradesh with 19 million people.[16] In the 'treatment' mandals, the new system was introduced two years before it was in the 'control' mandals (in which payments continued to be disbursed in the old way). Since the mandals in which the scheme was introduced were chosen by lottery, they were on average identical to those that received it two years later. So the difference made by the programme in the 'treatment' mandals could confidently be attributed to the programme itself. Among the many encouraging results of the experiment were those which showed defini-tively that a) delays in wage payments, as well as 'leakages' and corruption were substantially reduced and b) the change to the new system was highly cost-effective, with benefits ten-fold higher than the costs of setting-up and operating the smart-card operation. This research, and the experience with delivering cooking gas subsidies (see above), give persuasive grounds for believing that the new technologies make cash transfers a real practical possibility. So, are cash transfers the way to go? The next section assesses this important issue. Note that 'cash transfers' should be understood to mean 'technology-enabled cash transfers'. Without the new technologies, the advantages of cash transfers would be much diluted.[17]

THE CASE FOR TECHNOLOGY-ENABLED CASH TRANSFERS

The general case in favour of cash transfers as a means of poverty allevia- tion starts with one unquestionable fact: the present system, which relies mainly on price subsidies, fails to reach the intended recipients, makes them excessively dependent on the tender mercies of unaccountable state functionaries, and is riddled with patronage and corruption. Unconditional cash transfers would empower recipients and give them much greater flex- ibility and freedom of choice. (For example, they could obtain a more varied and balanced diet than subsidized rice and wheat.) Cash transfers would also be far less subject to leakages and corruption: once the beneficiaries were selected, the transfers could be put into their bank accounts in an authenticated manner. And, in addition, if cash transfers were financed by eliminating subsidies, the change would have a significant growth- enhancing efficiency effect by aligning prices more closely with costs.

Various objections have been made to cash transfers as a means of social protection. Some of them are unimportant. For example, there is the objec- tion that the real value of cash transfers would be eroded by inflation. The obvious answer is to index the transfers to a relevant cost of living index. But other objections are more germane. The first, and in my view the most significant, is that cash transfers do not in any way solve the problem of identifying eligible poor people. Technology can eliminate impersonation, 'ghost' recipients, and fake ration cards, but not flaws in the inclusion or exclusion of people from BPL lists. There are two possible ways forward. One possibility is to bypass the problem altogether by making the cash transfers universally applicable. Identification of the poor would then be unnecessary, and there would also be the added advantage of undercutting resistance from those citizens who would otherwise be deemed ineligible. The downside is that this option may be fiscally too demanding. (However, this should not be assumed without further examination. India could afford a universal transfer, as I shall show in the section below.) Another option is to decide eligibility on the basis of 'rough justice' by applying proxy means tests; obviously, the likelihood of excluding the poor would decrease as the fraction of the population made eligible for transfers increases. A third option would be to make the transfers universal but add a small cost to obtaining them such as having to go in person each month to a specific location for biometric confirmation to receive a cash transfer. The introduction of this cost may reduce significantly the number of households who claim, perhaps by as much as half of the total number of households. In the context of India's political economy, any of these alternatives would be better that retaining the present system.

Another objection to cash transfers is that consumer choice is not always a good thing. The recipients of cash may fritter it away on getting drunk rather than spending it on worthwhile purposes. Evidence does not support this fear. A pilot study conducted by SEWA, and funded by UNICEF, in the state of Madhya Pradesh is relevant here.[18] In six 'treatment' villages, each individual was given an unconditional monthly cash sum of Rs. 200 per day per adult and Rs. 100 per day per child (paid to the mother/guardian) for 18 months. In six other 'control' villages, individuals were given nothing. The results were interesting. In the treatment villages, spending increased, but the money was spent on 'good' things like health care, toilets, walls, roofs, more nutritious diets, better seeds, sewing machines, repaying debt, etc. This study has its limitations because households were given the extra money *on top* of existing benefits such as subsidized food from TPDS.[19] So, strictly speaking, it is not possible to draw definite conclusions about what would happen if these were *replaced* by cash transfers.[20] Even so, the results are highly suggestive at least on the question of the quality of spending that cash transfers bring about. Households need protection but not from themselves. The picture of the representative household as one that fritters away money on drinking and gambling is very far from the truth.

Even so, I would not want to take an extreme stand on consumer sovereignty. There are occasions when paternalism is justified. People may suffer from myopia or incomplete altruism even towards their own families. It may be necessary to compel them to do certain things, e.g. send their children to school, as is done in many countries (including India). And even if compulsion were thought to be a step too far, it may be necessary and desirable to strongly induce or nudge people to do certain things like use mosquito nets, and have vaccinations, peri-natal maternal care, and health check-ups for children. Conditional cash transfers (CCTs) are a possible solution; in such arrangements, cash transfers are made conditional on recipients doing specified things. Brazil and Mexico are known for their successful CCT programmes. India has conditional programmes too, e.g.

CCTs for pregnant women attending health clinics, and even conditional in-kind transfers, e.g. mid-day meals conditional on school attendance. The NREGS is also a CCT programme, with cash payments conditional on work, though it does have, in addition, the 'self-selection' property that many CCTs lack. Of course, conditional transfers face another problem in addition to selection of eligible candidates: there has to be monitoring to make sure that the conditions are satisfied, which is often easier said than done. Other areas where unconditional cash transfers may not be suitable are health insurance and education. To take advantage of risk-pooling, state help for hospitalization is best given in the form of an entitlement to payment cover if a health event arises, rather than as an unconditional cash transfer. And if the state decides to give people the means to educate their children at public or private institutions of their choice, this may best be done by giving them 'education vouchers' rather than unconditional cash transfers (which they might not spend on the designated purpose).

In sum, cash transfers are not a magic potion that cures all maladies. They may not always be suitable instruments for social protection. But I do think they must be a major, perhaps even the primary, element in a social protection framework. It is true that while they put purchasing power in the hands of people, they cannot ensure that the supply of the relevant goods will be forthcoming. Suppliers, public or private, would have to respond. But it is hard to see why they would not, except in remote areas where markets are very thin or non-existent. (For such areas, more conventional arrangements would have to continue for the time being.) For most of the country, and for command over most ordinary goods and services, cash transfers would work well for poor people. This does not in any way imply that the state should renege on its responsibility of financing pure public goods and other public services, and, in appropriate cases, of producing or delivering them.[21]

'BASIC INCOME' SCHEME: SCOPE AND FINANCING

Despite the existence of various social protection schemes, India clearly has a huge poverty problem. The two most recent national measurements of the incidence of poverty pertain to the year 2011. One of these, carried out by the Planning Commission, was based on a poverty line defined by a committee chaired by the late Suresh Tendulkar. It found that there were 269 million people (21.9 per cent of the population) below this poverty line.[22] The Tendulkar poverty line was criticized as being too low, and hence as understating the extent of poverty. In response, another committee was set up, this time under the chairmanship of C. Rangarajan.[23] It reported that there were 363 million poor people (29.8 per cent of the population in 2011), so it obviously used a higher poverty line than the Tendulkar line. For the purposes of setting up an income support scheme in a poor country with severe fiscal constraints, a relatively austere poverty line that measures the number of people in *extreme* poverty is surely the right one. In the rest of this section, I shall use the terms 'poor' and 'poverty' to mean 'extremely poor' and 'extreme poverty', which I assume to be correctly measured by the poverty line as defined by the Tendulkar Committee.[24]

It would obviously be a good thing if all poor people in India could be assured a 'basic income', defined as an annual cash grant large enough to raise their incomes to the poverty line. Would that be possible? Surprising as it may seem, the answer is, yes, it would be feasible and fiscally affordable.[25] The first step in demonstrating this is to estimate the total cost of lifting poor people to the poverty line by cash transfers. The cost would obviously be minimized if targeting of the poor were 'perfect' in the sense that all the poor could be individually identified, and each poor person was given exactly the right amount of extra income to reach the poverty line. These conditions are of course hopelessly unrealistic. It is impossible to identify poor people with precision. Not only are the objective facts not known, they may even be unknowable given the obvious incentive to conceal the truth, and the inevitable politicization that would attend any such effort. Moreover, even if the poor could be identified, their individual incomes would not be known with any precision. Two conclusions follow. Firstly, any administratively feasible scheme would have to make a *uniform* cash transfer to individuals or households (the head of the household or senior woman of the household would have to be the recipient in practice). Secondly, since it is enormously difficult to identify a constituency that has all the poor and only the poor, cash transfers would in practice have to be given to a wider group than the estimated number of poor people in order to be sure of including all of them. One obvious alternative is to cut through the identification problem altogether by making the transfers *universal*, in other words, extending their coverage to the whole population. Another alternative is to use proxy means tests to identify the poor, e.g. by excluding people who pay income tax and/ or have the obvious markers of high income such as ownership of land above five acres, ownership of houses with more than three rooms, and possession of relatively expensive consumer durables such as automobiles, bearing in mind that some of these categories would overlap.[26] In this way, one might be able to isolate say 67 per cent or 50 per cent of the population containing all poor people with a high degree of certainty. My view is that any such effort would be politically very contentious and divisive. A universal transfer would be preferable if it were fiscally possible because it would arouse much less resistance.

The Appendix to this chapter estimates the cost of universal 'basic income' provision, taking account of the realistic constraints identified above. The scheme envisaged therein would raise the average income of poor people to the poverty line by making the requisite uniform and universal cash transfer. The Appendix shows that at 2014/15 prices, this would involve making a cash transfer of about Rs. 17,500 a year per household (i.e. around Rs. 1450 per month per household) which, if it covered all households, would cost 3.5 per cent of GDP annually. Of course, it would cost less if the transfer were paid to only a fraction of the population. For example the cost would be 2.5 per cent of GDP and 1.9 per cent of GDP if the coverage were limited to 67 per cent and 50 per cent of the population respectively, though that would of course raise all the problems of deciding whom to include and exclude.

The next step in judging the feasibility of the scheme is to determine whether there is fiscal space for it, taking into account other competing objectives. At first sight, it looks hugely expensive. In actual fact, it would be perfectly viable, if it were combined with a fiscal restructuring programme that is in any case justified for several other reasons. India has large unexploited fiscal resources. The first such resource is the extensive network of dysfunctional subsidies, which could be wound up. 'Subsidies' here refer not only to the explicit subsidies that are recorded in the budget but to the implicit or hidden subsidies that arise from the sale of goods by the public sector at prices below their costs of production. The Ministry of Finance has estimated in the Economic Survey for 2014/15 that subsidies amounted to 4.2 per cent of GDP for the following items alone: food, fuels, fertilizers, iron ore, water, electricity, and rail fares.[27] The full extent of subsidisation is surely much higher. The most recent estimate of explicit and implicit subsidies granted by the central and state governments combined was carried out by the National Institute of Public Finance and Policy (NIPFP) in 2003 for the year 1998/99. It estimated that 'non-merit subsidies' were 7.7 per cent of GDP;[28] one would expect subsidies in 2014/15 to be of the same order of magnitude.[29] The NIPFP subsidy estimate of 7.7 per cent of GDP excluded government expenditure on pure public goods such as law and order, defence, and administration; and it also excluded 'merit subsidies', which were defined as subsidies to goods with large externalities such as education, health, nutrition, environment, rural development programmes, roads and bridges, and urban development. Food subsidies were also counted as 'merit subsidies' in the NIPFP study but we have seen that they are a prime candidate for being wound up. Since food subsidies are around 1 per cent of GDP, the NIPFP figure of subsidies that could be eliminated goes up to a possible 8.5 per cent of GDP, without touching so-called 'merit goods'.[30]

Even 8.5 per cent of GDP is, however, an underestimate of hidden fiscal resources for several reasons. Firstly, the NIPFP calculation excludes implicit subsidies that take the form of 'tax expenditures', i.e. foregone revenue as a result of tax exemptions to various favoured activities. Tax expenditures are close to 6 per cent of GDP annually for the central government alone, with a further unknown amount for state governments. Though, for various reasons, this figure cannot be taken at face value,[31] there is little doubt that there are many counterproductive exemptions whose elimination would be pure gain. A conservative estimate of annual fiscal savings from this source would be, say, 1.5 per cent of GDP. Secondly, privatization of PSEs would make further fiscal savings possible, with an efficiency gain in the bargain. It has been estimated that the value of PSEs owned by the central government is around 40–45 per cent of GDP.[32] (In addition it would be possible to sell PSEs owned by state governments, as well as prime land in government ownership.) With a determined effort, privatization could raise net resources of, say, 1 per cent of GDP annually for the next decade. Thirdly, a courageous government that grasped the nettle of taxing agricultural incomes could raise around 0.5 per cent of GDP annually. Fourthly, one of the advantages of a basic income programme is that many dysfunctional social welfare expenditures could be wound up. As already explained, I would recommend retaining the NREGS as an important back-up safety net, especially since it has the cardinal virtue of being 'self-selecting' in its coverage. But expenditure on central and state programmes *exclusive of* health, education, explicit and implicit subsidies, and the NREGS, is around 2.5 per cent of GDP. Around 0.5 per cent of GDP could surely be shaved off these programmes as cash transfers are brought in.

The upshot is that if action is taken on the fronts alluded to above, resources of at least 10 per cent of GDP and perhaps up to 12 per cent of GDP could be liberated annually for public purposes. Suppose that 2 per cent of GDP is set aside to increase public investment and another 2 per cent of GDP to reduce the fiscal deficit. That still leaves at least 6 per cent of GDP that would be more than sufficient to finance a basic income scheme. As shown in the Appendix to this chapter, it would take up 3.5 per cent of GDP, leaving a further large excess for extra public investment and enabling social expenditures, as well as further reduction of the fiscal deficit. Note also that with growth of national income over time, the absolute real amounts of resources available for redistribution would rise for any given percentage of GDP earmarked for the purpose (or a given amount of redistribution could be done with a smaller percentage of GDP). So in a few years, the resources required to pay for a universal basic income set at a fixed absolute real level of income would fall to well below 3.5 per cent of GDP (or the universal basic income transfer could be increased at the given share of 3.5 per cent of GDP to eliminate any residual poverty that remains after the implementation of the scheme).[33]

Needless to say, a basic income scheme would face some challenging difficulties. One difficulty is that winding up subsidies would raise the cost of living since the prices of the previously subsidized items would rise. So any given cash transfer would be worth less in real terms. But many of the subsidies, other than food, are thoroughly regressive, so this point is less important than it appears. And crucially, my estimates (see Appendix) of the cost of providing a basic income explicitly include compensation to offset the increase in the cost of living that the 'extreme poor' would face due to subsidy abolition. Elimination of subsidies would also have powerfully positive effects on the allocative efficiency of resources; this would increase growth, and with it the resources available for poverty alleviation.

Of course, unwinding subsidies is not straightforward. It has to be done gradually, so it is a multi-year project. Some subsidies are interdependent and the sequencing of their removal would have to be worked out carefully. (For example, raising the price of coal could not be done in isolation since that would only increase the subsidies that would have to be granted to the electricity sector.) Thus, subsidy removal would have to be a coordinated long-term programme that cuts across line ministries, and central and state government responsibilities, very much an exercise in 'cooperative federalism'. A further point is that since removal of subsidies would raise some prices, monetary policy would have to see to it that the change in relative prices does not trigger an inflation spiral. Accomplishment of the 'basic income' scheme would also depend on successfully implementing the project of universalizing Aadhar and Aadhar-linked bank accounts to enable the disbursement of cash transfers directly to individuals/families. Fortunately, this is well on the way to completion.

The most serious non-fiscal problem with any 'basic income' scheme is the identification and targeting of beneficiaries. A top-down effort to select recipients would probably unleash a torrent of resentment. Therefore, in my judgement, a *universal* cash transfer would be the best route to follow. I would therefore recommend the adoption of the scheme adumbrated above and in the Appendix, which involves disbursing a 'basic income' of Rs. 17,500 per household per year (about Rs. 1450 per household per month) into the bank accounts of all households, as soon as this becomes feasible. Such a scheme would go all the way to lift the incomes of even the poorest people to the poverty line, since they would retain the additional option of earning an income from the NREGS, which I propose should be continued. In consequence, extreme poverty would be very nearly eliminated, while the universality of the scheme would avoid resistance from the better-off sections of society. (Since the 'basic income' would be universal, all households would benefit, though at a rate that falls progressively with income. Apart from the abolition of extreme poverty, a large majority of the population would be wholly compensated for the rise in the cost of living due to the elimination of subsidies, and, in addition, some of the non-poor would receive an income supplement over and above the compensation.) The full scheme would also yield growth benefits since a) subsidy abolition would better align prices with costs and b) the fiscal savings would be sufficient to permit an increase in both public investment and social expenditure on education and health care. Moreover, establishing a robust safety net would make it easier to undertake other reforms such as labour market reform and liberalization of agricultural markets.

A possible way to reduce the cost of providing a universal basic income scheme merits consideration.[34] This is to introduce an element of self-targeting or self-selection by introducing a small cost to using the scheme. The obvious way to do this would be to make people pick up their monthly transfer by personally going to a specified location for biometric identification rather than having the money automatically deposited into their bank accounts. (Once the identification is done, the money could be sent to their bank accounts or paid in cash for those who do not yet have a bank account. If they do not pick up the money within a specified time they would forfeit the monthly payment.) The number of locations would have to be neither too many (in which case the cost would be too low) nor too few (in which case it would be too troublesome to collect). One would expect rich people to opt out of receiving a basic income because it would not be worth the trouble (though if an individual or family fell on hard times, they could go and get it).[35] This modification would certainly reduce the fiscal cost of the basic income scheme, though by how much is not clear. My guess would be that somewhere between 50 to 67 per cent of the population would use it at any one time. (The estimates in the Appendix indicate the reduction in cost that would follow in consequence.) Whether such a scheme would be desirable and feasible is a matter of judgement. My personal preference would be for a universal basic income scheme that is available as an entitlement unless individuals/households voluntarily chose to forego the benefit.

Estimate of the Cost of Providing a 'Basic Income'

1. The calculations below pertain to the year 2014/15. For some items, hard data were available only for 2011/12. These were projected forward to 2014/15, in the manner indicated below.
2. Note the following facts, approximations, and plausible assumptions:
   i) GDP at market prices (new series) in 2014/15 is roughly Rs. 125.4 trillion = Rs. 125,400 billion = Rs. 125.4 lakh crores.
   ii) The population in 2011/12 according to the Census of 2011 was roughly 1200 million of which 69 per cent was rural, and 31 per cent was urban. It is assumed to be 1250 million in 2014/15, with the identical rural-urban split as in 2011/12. So the rural population in 2014/15 is 862.5 million, and the urban population is 387.5 million.
   iii) In line with Census data, the average size of household is taken to be five individuals, so there are 250 million households in 2014/15.
   iv) Poverty is taken to mean 'extreme poverty', and is assumed to be measured by the Tendulkar Committee's poverty definition. The national headcount poverty ratio was 21.9 per cent in 2011/12, with rural and urban poverty rates of 25.7 per cent and 13.7 per cent respectively. There were 269 million poor people, 216 million rural and 53 million urban.[36] It is assumed that the above poverty ratios are unchanged in 2014/15. So the number of poor people in 2014/15 is 274 million, composed of 222 million (rural) and 52 million (urban).
   v) The 'poverty gap index' in 2011/12 was 5.05 per cent (rural), 2.7 per cent (urban), and 4.32 per cent (overall), using the rural-urban weights 69:31.[37] (The 'poverty gap index' is defined as the mean shortfall of individual incomes in the population from the poverty line, counting the non-poor as having a zero shortfall, expressed as a proportion of the poverty line.) It is assumed that the poverty gap indexes are unchanged in 2014/15.
   vi) The poverty line in 2011/12 was Rs. 816 per head per month (rural), i.e. 9792 per head per year (rural), and Rs. 1000 per head per month (urban), i.e. Rs. 12,000 per head per year (urban);[38] so the national weighted average poverty line was Rs. 873 per head per month, i.e.

Rs. 10,476 per head per year, using the weights 69:31. The consumer price index shows a rise in prices from 2011/12 to 2014/15 of around 30 per cent, so the poverty lines in 2014/15 are calculated by raising the 2011/12 poverty lines by 30 per cent. Therefore, the poverty lines in 2014/15 are: Rs. 12,729 per head per year (rural); Rs. 15,600 per head per year (urban); and Rs. 13,619 per head per year (national).

3. A rough calculation can now be carried out to estimate the total cash transfer required to raise 21.9 per cent of India's population in 2014/15 to the poverty line in 2014/15. As a first cut, the calculation assumes that targeting is perfect, i.e. i) all poor people are perfectly accurately identified and ii) each poor person's income shortfall in relation to the poverty line is covered exactly, no more no less. It then follows from the definition of the poverty gap index that the total annual cost of perfect targeting is (poverty gap index) × (poverty line) × (total population), i.e. $(0.0432) \times (Rs. 13,619) \times (1250 \text{ million}) = Rs. 735,426 \text{ million} = 0.59$ per cent of GDP.

4. Of course, the assumption of perfect targeting is grossly unrealistic. I now drop the assumption in 3(ii), and impose the realistic condition that there should be a *uniform* transfer to all poor people (still assumed to be perfectly identified) so as to exhaust the total cost already estimated. It follows that this uniform transfer is equal to $(Rs. 735,426 \text{ million} \div 274 \text{ million}) = Rs. 2684$ per head per year (i.e. Rs. 234 per head per month). This uniform transfer is also identically equal to the gap between the poverty line and the average income of poor people without the transfer. The average income of the poor is thus Rs. $(13,619 - 2684) = Rs. 10,935$ per head per year.

5. I now drop the assumption in 3(i) and assume, realistically, that perfect identification of poor people is not possible and that a larger fraction of the population than the poverty ratio has to be paid the above uniform transfer to ensure that all poor people are in fact covered. What would be the cost of making the transfer of Rs. 2684 per head per year to various fractions of the population? This can be calculated quite simply. I focus on four possibilities: a) 21.9 per cent of the population; b) 50 per cent of the population; c) 67 per cent of the population; and d) 100 per cent of the population, i.e. a universal transfer. The total annual cost in these four cases is as follows:

   a) 21.9 per cent of the population: [Rs. (2684) × (274 million)] ÷ GDP = 0.59 per cent of GDP, as above.
   b) 50 per cent of the population: [Rs. (2684) × (625 million)] ÷ GDP = 1.34 per cent of GDP.

c) 67 per cent of the population: [Rs. (2684) × (837.5 million)] ÷ GDP = 1.79 per cent of GDP.

d) 100 per cent of the population: [Rs. (2684) × (1250 million)] ÷ GDP = 2.68 per cent of GDP.

6. Some adjustment has to be made to the above figures if, as recommended in the text of the chapter, the above transfers are financed by removal of subsidies. When subsidies are removed, prices of the previously subsidized items will rise. The real-income impact of subsidy removal would, as a simple approximation, equal the proportion of the subsidized items in household budgets *times* the rise in their prices. As a maximal estimate, suppose that 30 per cent of the household spending of the 'extreme poor' is on the previously subsidized items, and that the prices of these items rise by 20 per cent.[39] Then it follows that the cash transfer would have to be increased by (30 per cent) × (0.2) = 6 per cent of poverty-line income to maintain the real value of consumption at the poverty line.[40] Therefore, the uniform transfer required to raise the average income of the poor to the poverty line has to be Rs. 2684 + [(0.06) × (Rs. 13,619)] = Rs. 2684 + Rs. 817 = Rs. 3501 per head per year = Rs. 17,505 per household per year. Therefore, the total transfers required in cases (a)–(d) would be as follows:

   a) 21.9 per cent of the population: [(Rs. 3501) × (274 million)] = Rs. 959 billion = 0.76 per cent of GDP.

   b) 50 per cent of the population: [(Rs. 3501) × (625 million)] = Rs. 2188 billion = 1.74 per cent of GDP;

   c) 67 per cent of the population: [(Rs. 3501) × (837.5 million)] = Rs. 2932 billion = 2.34 per cent of GDP;

   d) 100 per cent of the population: [(Rs. 3501) × (1250 million)] = Rs. 4376 billion = 3.49 per cent of GDP.

7. Some allowance should be made for the administrative costs of the scheme. These are hard to estimate but an annual cost of 0.01 per cent of GDP would surely be enough for a universal transfer, which does not involve identification of poor people, and perhaps 20 times that, i.e. 0.2 per cent of GDP, for transfers to fractions of the population. The cost of making Aadhar and bank accounts universal should not really be attributed to the scheme since they are required in any case for various purposes.

8. The upshot is that the following conclusion holds for 2014/15: To lift the average income of poor people to the national poverty line, financed by removal of subsidies, the uniform transfer would have to be Rs. 17,505 per household per year (i.e. a little more than Rs. 1450 per household per month). The total cost (inclusive of administrative costs) would be 0.96 per cent of GDP, 1.94 per cent of GDP, 2.54 per cent of GDP, and 3.50

per cent of GDP for transfers to 21.9 per cent, 50 per cent, 67 per cent, and 100 per cent of the population respectively. On various grounds, as discussed in the text, I recommend a universal transfer or basic income scheme, which, as seen above, would cost 3.5 per cent of GDP annually.

9. Note the following important consideration. Since the scheme involves a transfer that brings the average income of poor people up to the poverty line, it may be feared that it would not suffice to lift the *poorest* people to the poverty line. I would make two rejoinders to this. Firstly, any such shortfall in their incomes could be made up by income from employment under the NREGS, which I suggest should be continued as a safety net for another decade or so. Secondly, if the poverty line is thought of as fixed in absolute real terms, a fixed percentage share (say 3.5 per cent) of a growing real national income would enable, within a few years, a rise in the annual transfer to considerably more than the Rs. 17,500 per household at 2014/15 prices that is suggested above. This would eliminate, within a short period, any residual poverty that might remain after the implementation of the above basic income scheme.

NOTES

1. Social protection has both an efficiency aspect and an equity aspect. In its efficiency aspect, it offsets market failures in credit and insurance markets that prevent people from taking adequate self-protection measures. In its equity aspect, it makes up for the market's indifference to poverty and deprivation.
2. Originally, the public distribution system was open to all. It became 'targeted' to those below the poverty line in 1997.
3. Social activists, of whom some were on the National Advisory Council, had originally proposed that the coverage of the TPDS should be 75 per cent of the population, with each person entitled to buy 7 kg of subsidized food per month. But this was watered down in the Food Security Act to 5 kg per head per month for 67 per cent of the population.
4. The Planning Commission estimated the leakage to be 57 per cent of the foodgrains intended for distribution: 36 per cent due to illegal diversion and 21 per cent due to mis-targeting. See Planning Commission (2005).
5. See Government of India (2015b).
6. See 'Fake ration cards pile up in 'model' PDS state', *Indian Express*, 1 August 2014.
7. See Government of India (2015b).
8. See Jha and Ramaswami (2012).
9. See Deaton and Dreze (2009).
10. There has been quite a lot of scholarly work on the NREGS and its impact. See for example the useful books by Khera (2011) and Shankar and Gaiha (2013). For an excellent survey of research articles, see Mookherjee (2014) and the references cited therein. In 2014, there was a fierce debate between some leading economists

on the merits of the NREGS: see Bhagwati and Panagariya (2014a, 2014b) and Abreu, Bardhan, Ghatak, Kotwal, Mookherjee, and Ray (2014a, 2014b).

11. The relatively well-governed states such as Tamil Nadu, Kerala, and Andhra Pradesh show better performance than less well-governed states such as Bihar, Odisha, and Jharkhand.

12. The idea behind 'self-selection' is to require the beneficiary to undertake some costly action to qualify for the benefit (with NREGS it is eight hours of hard work per day). This procedure screens out those who do not really need the benefit.

13. For a useful account of India's social protection schemes, see Kapur and Nangia (2015).

14. Note that according to Government of India (2015a), Statistical Appendix Table 9.9, expenditure on social services *excluding* health and education was 2.6 per cent of GDP in 2013/14. This estimate also excludes all price subsidies, and spending on NREGS (which is budgeted under 'rural development').

15. Some of the problems of poverty programmes are deep-seated, and rooted in India's clientelistic politics. For an excellent analysis of the failure of India's poverty programmes and why India seems to prioritize specific-purpose poverty programmes over provision of public services, see Kapur (2010b), and Kapur and Nangia (2015).

16. See Muralidharan, Niehaus, and Sukhtankar (2014). The paper explains the technology of the smart card programme, which had the 'same functionality as intended by UID-linked direct benefit transfers'.

17. Note that the Aadhar programme currently faces some legal obstacles. Some civil society activists are hostile to it because of 'invasion of privacy' issues. They have taken the matter to the Supreme Court, which has made an interim ruling that a) Aadhar cannot be made mandatory for receipt of government benefits; and b) voluntary use of Aadhar is permitted only in some specified schemes such as PDS, NREGS, National Social Assistance Programme, and the Jan Dhan programme. The government urgently needs to put Aadhar into a statutory framework that permits compulsory use of Aadhar but safeguards privacy.

18. For an account of this experiment, see Davala, Jhabvala, Standing, and Mehta (2015). For the first three months, the money was paid in physical cash, after that into bank accounts. After a year, the grants were increased to Rs. 300 a day for adults and Rs. 150 a day for children.

19. However, the study did find that a high proportion of the poor did not have BPL cards.

20. Another SEWA pilot in Delhi did not suffer from this problem. In the treatment group, families were given a cash transfer but were not entitled to take anything from PDS ration shops during the pilot period. In the control group families did not receive any cash transfer and continued to use PDS ration shops. The results showed that cash transfers did not reduce spending on food and increased other forms of spending, including health care and education.

21. An excellent discussion of cash vs. in-kind transfers can be found in Banerjee (2015).

22. See Planning Commission (2013b).

23. See Planning Commission (2014a).

24. The Tendulkar national poverty line, as a weighted average of rural and urban poverty lines, is Rs. 873 per head per month at 2011 prices, i.e. about Rs. 29

per head per day. The Rangarajan poverty line, again as a weighted average, is Rs. 1107 per head per month, i.e. about Rs. 37 per head per day, at 2011 prices. Incidentally, the Tendulkar poverty line is very close to the World Bank's poverty line of $1.90 a day per capita at 2011 purchasing power parity (PPP) prices and produces a very similar poverty ratio for 2011 as the Tendulkar Committee. The World Bank also computes poverty with higher, less stringent, poverty lines of $2 a day at 2005 PPP prices and $3.10 a day at 2011 PPP prices and these produce poverty ratios of 69 per cent and 59 per cent respectively.

25. The authoritative source of a 'basic income' scheme for India is Bardhan (2011). I have tried to improve on his formulation in various particulars but I am indebted to him for the idea.

26. See Ninan (2015), Chapter 11.

27. See Government of India (2015a), Volume 1, Chapter 3.

28. See Srivastava et al. (2003). The methodology originates from a pioneering article by Mundle and Rao (1991), which calculated explicit and implicit government subsidies for 1987/88. Note that the 1998/99 estimates turned out to be very similar to the 1987/88 estimates. (See also the important article by Rajaraman (2006), which points out the pitfalls in assuming that this measure of subsidies also measures the fiscal savings that would result if the subsidies were removed. In my judgement, taking account of Rajaraman's qualifications would not reduce the estimate of fiscal savings greatly though it would be useful to have a research project to confirm this.)

29. My confidence in this statement is increased by a private communication from Sudipto Mundle who is currently in the process of repeating the Mundle-Rao 1987/88 exercise (see n. 28) for 2011/12. In the eight states so far studied, the estimate of total explicit and implicit subsidies as a proportion of the states' GDP is remarkably close to the 1987/88 estimate (and thus to the 1998/99 estimate as well). Mundle goes on to say: 'the overall picture is one of remarkable stability of subsidy incidence. . . . I don't think the picture will change after we complete the remaining states and the union government estimates . . . though the level will be even higher for the union government'.

30. Note that NIPFPs' definition of 'merit goods' is quite different from the standard definition used in Chapter 3. Note also that soon after the Modi government took office in 2014, it appointed an Expenditure Commission. One would have thought that it would have looked into the extent of non-merit explicit and implicit subsidies but no such analysis has seen the light of day.

31. See Govinda Rao (2011) and Kavita Rao (2013).

32. Kelkar (2010).

33. This is an important point. The scheme is designed to bring the average income of the poor up to the poverty line. But what about those poor people whose incomes are well below the average? Their income shortfall would be made up by income from employment in the NREGS scheme. But some poverty may remain, especially among the urban poor, who are not covered by NREGS. This is why, as pointed out in the text, the universal basic income may have to be increased as national income grows over time. But complete abolition of extreme poverty within say five years is an entirely feasible idea.

34. See Banerjee (2015).

35. In addition, the government could campaign to exhort well-off people to forego the 'basic income' voluntarily, the way it is doing for the LPG subsidy.

36. See Planning Commission (2013b).
37. See Appendix Table 2 in Government of India (2014).
38. See Planning Commission (2013b).
39. This is a guesstimate. Note that many non-merit subsidies are thoroughly regressive, so withdrawing them would not affect the poor greatly.
40. This is a maximal estimate because it ignores substitution effects. Higher prices would increase the supply of the previously subsidized products and switch demand away from them. The eventual rise in prices would thus be lower than the maximal estimate.

PART IV

Political Economy

CHAPTER 11

The State of the State

States do not function in a vacuum but in specific social and political settings. This chapter begins with some general reflections on the Indian state, the context in which it operates, and the implications thereof for economic policy. This is followed by an examination of two systemic flaws in the quality of the state's functioning that threaten to set back economic progress in India. The overall message of the chapter is that if the Indian state is to be successful in promoting inclusive economic development, it will have to take urgent steps to reform itself.

POLITICAL ECONOMY OF THE INDIAN STATE

For diehard Marxists, the state is just a committee for managing the affairs of the bourgeoisie.[1] For diehard public choice theorists, the state is simply an instrument used by individuals and groups in power to pursue their self-interested goals. Neither of these extreme positions gives a true characterization of the Indian state. Though there is much to criticize in the way it functions, the post-independence history of the state in India lends no credence to the view that it is devoid of autonomy.[2] The Indian state does have some scope for independent action and, in consequence, a critical and potentially beneficial role to play in economic development. Of course the state's autonomy is not unlimited; it is constrained by several factors, some external, and others that are internal and arise from within the state itself.

The fundamental constraint on state action in India is that the country is a democracy as well as an extremely diverse society. That India is a democracy is of course a cause for celebration because democracy has intrinsic value, and there are also persuasive grounds for thinking that it is conducive to long-run stability. (In contrast, the long-run stability of the Chinese political system is far more doubtful.) But in the day-to-day functioning of India's democracy, as in all democracies, the state's actions and policies are constrained by electoral considerations. In addition, the latitude that the state enjoys is limited by the heterogeneity of Indian society. Despite a cultural unity, India has many deep divisions and inequalities based on caste, religion, language, region, ethnicity, and economic status. These cleavages make it more difficult to agree on national goals, and on sharing the costs and benefits of pursuing them, than would be the case in relatively homogeneous societies. One of the state's functions is precisely to coordinate 'collective action' in the face of competing interests. But a democracy has to operate mainly on the basis of persuasion rather than force; and the complexity of Indian society makes it hard to gain support and consent for state intervention to resolve collective-action gridlocks. A related difficulty is that the diversity of Indian society makes it a fertile ground for 'identity politics': individuals are susceptible to appeals to put their group identities ahead of their national identity.

The magnitude and impact of these 'givens' has been amplified in the course of time by two major changes in the nature of Indian democracy, which may be characterized as 'social and political awakening' and 'institutional decay'.[3] 'Social and political awakening' is the growing self-assertion of many hitherto disadvantaged groups in democratic bargaining and contestation. 'Institutional decay' is the weakening of the state's capacity for effective and beneficial intervention. To put it crudely, 'social and political awakening' has sharpened the external constraints on the Indian state's freedom of manoeuvre, while 'institutional decay' has tightened the internal constraints on its ability to act purposively.

The most salient manifestation of 'social and political awakening' is the dramatic arousal of India's historically subordinate groups. In the immediate aftermath of independence, upper caste Hindus dominated politics. Over the years, their ascendancy has been eroded by an upsurge of middle- and low-caste Hindus (but Muslims and the 'scheduled tribes' have remained largely in a subordinate position). The dilution of traditional social hierarchies was of course one of the objectives of the independent Indian state. What was not foreseen was the extent to which caste identity would become politicized. The position of the middle-level castes, e.g. the *yadavs* in Bihar and UP, *jats* in Punjab, *marathas* in Maharashtra, and *vokkaligas* in Karnataka, was immensely strengthened, at first by the abolition of *zamindari* and the success of the green revolution, and later by the implementation of the recommendations of the Mandal Commission on job reservations for 'other backward castes'. The leaders of these caste-groups, such as Lalu Prasad Yadav in Bihar and Mulayam Singh Yadav in UP, formed or cultivated new political parties (RJD in Bihar, Samajwadi Party in UP) that appealed directly to the interests of the communities they represented. A similar course was later followed by the leaders of the *dalits* (i.e. former 'untouchables' or members of the 'scheduled castes') such as Kanshi Ram and Mayawati (both low-caste *chamars*). Kanshi Ram started the Bahujan Samaj Party, which subsequently became a major force in UP under the leadership of Mayawati. Another focus of political mobilization was regional identity. Parties emerged in Punjab, Kashmir, Andhra Pradesh, Assam, Tamil Nadu, Maharashtra, and elsewhere, that sought to marshal regional loyalties and fight for regional concerns and benefits.

This fragmentation of the party system has had major political conse-quences. From independence until 1989, the national government was formed by the Congress Party (with the exception of the Janata Coalition from 1977 to 1979). It regularly got around 40 per cent of the votes and 60 per cent or more of seats, giving it an absolute majority in the Lok Sabha. (This discrepancy between votes and seats is made possible by India's 'first past the post' electoral system.) Significantly, the Congress also controlled the Rajya Sabha. Moreover, from 1971 to 1989, and particularly for much of the time that Indira Gandhi was prime minister, the Prime Minister's Office (PMO) acquired great power over other institutions. From 1989, these centralizing forces have been reversed. The trend has been for the Congress to lose its share of votes as well as seats, and for the BJP to gain at its expense. Strikingly, however, the Congress and the BJP together have never won more than 60 per cent of votes (the rest have been shared between the regional and caste-based parties), with the result that for 25 years until 2014, no party was able to win an absolute majority of seats. National governments with parliamentary majorities could be formed only by arranging formal party coalitions or securing informal support in par-liament from parties outside the coalition, much as in systems with pro-portional representation. Every government had to rule with the support, formal or informal, of well over a dozen parties. Ideology played little or no part in these alliances, which were mostly marriages of convenience. (For example, the DMK and AIADMK, the two regional parties in Tamil Nadu, have each allied with the Congress and the BJP at one time or another.) In 2014, the BJP succeeded in breaking the trend towards fragmentation by securing a bare majority in the Lok Sabha on its own; even so, it is strik-ing that the combined vote share of the BJP and Congress did not increase much, and there remained a very large number of parties in the house. Moreover, the BJP lacks a majority in the Rajya Sabha, so legislation still requires much compromise and negotiation. Another important development is in the relation between the centre and the states. During the Nehru era, Congress ruled in both tiers of the Indian federation.[4] Now it is very common to have state governments of a different party from the one ruling at the centre. Some of the state parties are nationally significant, so in the last two decades they have often had the power to make or break the government at the national level. As a result, the federal balance of power has shifted markedly towards the states.[5] (The central government's power over state governments is likely to be further weakened in due course by the dilution of its financial control that will come about as a result of the award of the 14th Finance Commission.) In sum, the trend towards political fragmentation is unmistakable. It may be hailed as a movement towards deeper democratization but it would be hard to deny that it has created difficulties for cohesive national policy-making.

The fragmentation of political power has been accompanied by a similar fragmentation in economic power. Class politics in the Marxist sense has always had little application in India since the manifold divisions in Indian society are not conducive to the formation of class consciousness. Power has traditionally been held by a small 'dominant coalition' of big industrialists, rich farmers, and the top echelons of the salariat in the public and private sectors. However, even this narrow elite has, in the main, been too divided to act collectively.[6] What 'awakening' has done is add greatly to the number and diversity of groups that have influence within and outside the dominant coalition. An obvious manifestation of this is increased pressure on the fisc because so many groups have to be bought off with subsidies and sweeteners. It is notable that India was a fiscally conservative country until the late 1970s. Since then, 'awakening' has made populist expenditures a running problem. In the states, revenues are regularly used for giveaways (for example free colour television sets), and for distributing patronage to clients. The increased political salience of various groups that do not trust each other also goes some way to explaining why the Indian state has a poor record on the provisioning of mass public services. Of course, the failure is in part due to problems on the supply side. But it is also due to lack of strong demand for service provision, even from poor people who have most to gain. 'Awakening' seems to have led primarily to a demand for dignity and self-respect on the part of disadvantaged groups. So, politicians have often been able to get away with satisfying this demand by purely symbolic measures such as building statues of past and present leaders. In other words, 'awakening' has strengthened identity politics as well as clientelism.

While political awakening has greatly complicated the mechanics of state intervention, it has certainly had desirable effects on the uplift of disadvantaged people; and it may even have contributed to political stability.[7] But there are no such redeeming features in the other notable change that has affected the character of the Indian state, viz. 'institutional decay', which has degraded the quality of governance. A major aspect of 'decay' that is germane to solving collective action problems is that intra-party democracy has nearly vanished in all political parties. The rot began with Mrs. Indira Gandhi. When she was prime minister and Congress Party president, she bypassed the party's democratic procedures, and started personally appointing state chief ministers and cabinets, and local party leaders. The practice has over time infected all other parties. Loyalty to the party chief has become the passport to power; and ironically, as power has dispersed from the centre, it has become more concentrated in the hands of chief ministers of states.[8] In many states, parties are entirely subservient to the party leader and his family. One consequence of this development is the silting-up of the channels of compromise between competing groups. Any democracy needs mediating institutions that can resolve differences. In the old days, the Congress Party with its 'broad tent' performed this function. The party had deep roots in Indian society and was a complex, subtle, and resilient network of patronage and bargaining. Now, political parties lack the well-oiled mechanisms that can deal with settlement of claims outside the budgetary process. The atrophy of party organizations has meant that such demands have to be managed by handouts and other populist measures that increase government expenditures or reduce tax and non-tax receipts. Another institution that is needed in a well-function-ing democracy is a relatively neutral and impartial civil service, that can 'stand above' competing demands. In India, the civil service has lost these virtues over time (see below).

'Awakening' and 'decay' have created major problems for securing con-sensus on economic reform measures. Labour market reform is supported by employers but opposed by trade unions though it would benefit the vast majority of the labour force. In agriculture, market liberalization would be to the benefit of farmers as a whole but it is opposed by rural interests that run the agricultural price marketing committees that profit from admin-istering the existing restrictions. Liberalization of foreign direct invest-ment in multi-brand retail would be to the benefit of consumers but it is opposed by retail traders who stand to lose. In land policy and environ-mental protection, there is a conflict between the interests of industrialists and landowners and displaced communities (and the NGOs that support them). In education, students in government schools would greatly benefit if attendance of teachers was improved but reform is held up by powerful teachers' unions. Such examples could be multiplied. But perhaps the most important systemic obstacles are to the kind of wide-ranging reform of the network of subsidies that has been advocated in earlier chapters. As I have argued, elimination of subsidies could open the door to considerably higher levels of public investment (which would be to the benefit of all), while also benefiting poor people directly. But the government is fearful of going down this road because it knows that there will be strong resistance from groups that would lose, even though they happen to be relatively well-off. A vicious circle is involved. Resistance is not irrational in the absence of a credible promise from the state that it would invest in infrastructure. But the state finds it very difficult to make credible promises and firm commitments in India's 'awakened' polity. As a result, governments in India have so far had to practice reform by stealth, ambiguity, and playing off one group against another. But that kind of reform may not be enough to usher in the systemic changes that are called for to secure rapid growth and poverty abolition.[9] The scenario cries out for political leaders who believe in reform but can also persuade, inspire, communicate, and marshal collective energies.

There is more to 'institutional decay' than the wasting away of the mechanisms for conflict resolution. 'Decay' has also taken two other forms which are detrimental to economic development. Firstly, the competence of the state has declined in relation to the increased demands on it, manifested for example in the dire condition of the provisioning of public goods such as education and health care. There is a glaring 'administrative deficit', which needs to be corrected. Secondly, money and crime have taken over politics to a growing extent. Corruption in public life has increased manifold: the prediction of some analysts that it would abate as a result of the 1991 reforms is now seen to be hopelessly optimistic. Bribes and graft have become ubiquitous in dealings between companies and the government to obtain contracts, and licenses to exploit scarce national resources. Ordinary citizens find that backhanders to police and government officials are necessary to get even the simplest things done. Neither of these two types of decay bodes well for the future of Indian development. The following two sections focus on these problems.

STATE COMPETENCE AND ACCOUNTABILITY

Commentators on India have often remarked on the puzzling contrast between some of the spectacular achievements of the state and its everyday incompetence. The Indian state has conducted national elections for an electorate of 800 million people with barely a hitch. It has run an extensive and impressive nuclear programme. It has sent a spacecraft to Mars more cheaply than any other country. At the same time, it fails miserably in delivering public services to its citizens. One way of understanding the contrast is that the state has delivered when it has been in 'mission mode' or when exceptional individuals have been given charge of specific projects. But these recipes cannot be generalized. It is impossible to do everything on a war footing and with unusually able people in charge. Consider education and police services, for example. These are activities that involve thousands of teachers or police officers interacting with millions of students and citizens every day. Changing the behaviour of these state employees cannot be done by compulsion or exhortation. It can only be done gradually by changing incentives and structures.

As of now, despite the occasional eye-catching accomplishments, India clearly suffers from weak state capacity. One reason for this failure is simple neglect. India began as an independent country with an administration that was excellent by developing country standards. But there has been no attempt to build on this platform, with the result that the administrative system is no longer fit for purpose. This may not have mattered when a growth dividend could be reaped simply by the state 'getting out of the way' of business activity. But that phase is over. Inclusive growth in future will be hampered, even arrested, without better delivery by the state of its core functions.

A good illustration of the short-sightedness of neglecting administrative matters is provided by the operation of the rights-based agenda that has been pursued in recent years.[10] Under the influence of an active civil society, the state has legislated in rapid succession justiciable rights to information, work, education, and food. In some ways, this has been a laudable endeavour to increase the state's accountability to citizens; and it has certainly opened up an important space for civic engagement. But in some other ways, it has also been a diversion from the real problems involved in service delivery. Without accompanying political and bureaucratic change, how can the newly legislated rights be made effective? The right to food was enshrined in the Food Security Act (FSA). But it is obvious that enactment of a law cannot by itself ensure that food reaches the targeted beneficiaries if the distribution system remains unchanged. Why would the enactment of a legal right to food get over the problem of leakages and diversion? And is it realistic that a citizen who does not receive the stipulated quantity of food through state channels would or could sue the government?[11] The right to education is now on the statute book via the Right to Education Act. Even if the state ensures 'free and compulsory education' at the primary level, can the establishment of a justiciable right ensure education of good quality? Can it make teachers turn up for work, and put in the requisite effort? Will it deliver good educational outcomes? The same goes for the right to work under the National Rural Employment Guarantee Act. A guarantee of employment does not solve the corruption problems in employment schemes. The basic point is that enactment of justiciable rights is far from sufficient to ensure that the rights are made effective. It may even distract from the hard task of improving state capacity to deliver the substance of the rights.[12]

What can be done about India's administrative shortcomings? There will have to be action on two fronts simultaneously. At present, the state's ambition vastly exceeds its capabilities. So, solutions will have to focus on moderating the former as well as enhancing the latter. Moderating the state's excessive ambition requires redefining the scope of desirable state activity. The basic point, as discussed extensively in this book, is that conventional ideas about the economic boundary of the state need to be questioned. Many infrastructure services, physical and social, have often mistakenly been considered to be exclusively the state's preserve. In fact, many of them could be produced more efficiently by the private sector, along with arm's-length regulation by public authorities. When the public sector does produce, it should do so in competition with the private sector and on a level playing field. This means the state has to be ready, over time, to get out of production if it cannot do so efficiently. Since the Indian state is over-extended and over-burdened, it needs to open up production to the private sector more than it has done so far, while at the same time improving its capacity to regulate private sector activities (in other words, learn 'to steer, rather than to row').

That said, the scope of desirable government activity is bound to remain large, so the issue of improving administrative competence, motivation, and accountability remains. One potential way forward is greater decentralization. There are various services currently administered by state-level authorities that would be monitored better if they were controlled by local governments. Teachers in government schools provide a good example. One reason for their legendary lack of job-commitment is that they are not accountable to the local community: they are employees of state governments which could be hundreds of miles away. There are good reasons to think that more democratic decentralization would both improve information flows and make state functionaries more responsive to the needs of citizens. The relevant constitutional amendments (73rd and 74th Amendments) were enacted in the early 1990s. Unfortunately, they only *suggested* that state governments transfer powers and funds to local governments but did not *require* them to do so. Naturally, the local democracy experiment has had highly mixed results. On the one hand, the induction of three million elected local councillors (half of whom are women) is surely a good thing for democracy. On the other hand, the decentralizing intentions of the constitutional amendments have been neutered by state governments, which have succeeded in preserving tight control over local governments (both *panchayati raj* institutions in villages and municipal governments in towns and cities) and the resources made available to them. So, India has not so far had a fair experiment in increasing local governance and accountability. The equilibrium is unlikely to change without effective devolution of adequate fiscal powers to local governments. Even so, a caveat is in order. Change is necessary but it will have to proceed gradually. This is because local governments are themselves bedevilled by lack of adequate administrative capacity, and elite capture is also a major issue.[13] State capacity at local levels needs attention and massive improvement.

While a greater role for the market, and more devolution to local rural and urban bodies, are necessary to enhance state effectiveness, they are by no means enough. Internal reforms are essential at both the central and state tiers, and in all branches of government: executive, legislative, and judicial. They would have to go beyond introducing information technology to simplify procedures and cut red tape (though that would be useful too).[14] For reasons of space, I shall focus here principally on the civil service, the police, and the courts.[15] The top civil service, once called the 'steel frame' of India, has traditionally been regarded as a source of strength. But it has not changed with the growing complexity of government and remains generalist if not amateurish. It has often been suggested that there should be regular lateral entry (say at 'joint secretary' level) but this has not happened. Promotion relies too much on seniority and too little on performance appraisal by persons other than the immediate superior in the hierarchy. In addition, the civil service is excessively politicized.[16] The tendency to favour 'loyal' civil servants that began with Mrs. Gandhi has been continued by all governments thereafter. Things are much worse in the provincial civil services, which are below par in quality.

The lower levels of the civil service comprise front-line staff for the delivery of core services such as education, health care, and law and order. But they are in urgent need of reform. Several problems stand out. There is severe under-staffing because salaries are relatively high and fiscal constraints are tight.[17] At the same time, the productivity of government workers is low. Productivity is not easy to measure directly. But there is plenty of indirect evidence as detailed in Chapter 9. Absenteeism is rife: teachers, doctors, and nurses do not turn up, and when they do, do not work purposively. Untrained para-teachers on low pay improve student learning more than regular teachers with high pay. Fee-charging private providers in education and health have a large and growing market share despite the presence of free public provision. There is no simple way of making government functionaries more accountable, when the problem is as deep-seated as it is in India. There will have to be movement on three different fronts simultaneously: more market, more decentralization, and more internal reform that changes incentives. What should internal reform consist of? One example is Karthik Muralidharan's proposal that envisages employing many more apprentice teachers at much lower rates of pay than regular teachers (which would make the scheme fiscally feasible). These apprentices would not be stop-gap add-ons; they would fit into a career structure, with training and skilling, and performance-based credits that would count for regular employment as teachers in due course, with exit payments for those who are not successful.[18] The scheme is certainly radical but that is the kind of change that is needed to break out of the current quandary.

The police force, apart from the small elite Indian Police Service (IPS), lacks proper training and equipment, and is stuck in the colonial tradition of law-and-order enforcement and crowd control rather than crime prevention and citizen protection. There are too few police officers per head of population, and too many vacancies (at present 25 per cent of police posts are unfilled).[19] Ordinary citizens do not trust the police, who have a reputation for brutality and rampant corruption. The police force is deeply politicized both in the sense that its recruitment policies are based too little on merit and too much on satisfying caste 'reservations', and in the sense that it is subject to systematic political meddling. The problems are not to be found only at lower levels. They are also present in top-level investigative agencies such as the Intelligence Bureau (IB), the Central Board of Investigation (CBI), and the Central Vigilance Commission (CVC). The current vacancy rate in CBI executive posts is 15 per cent; in CBI law-officer posts, it is 32 per cent. These agencies are used as much for partisan politics to suit the government of the day, and to gather intelligence on political opponents and harass them, as for legitimate purposes.[20] The needed reforms to make the police force more professional, autonomous, and accountable have been outlined by many bodies, e.g. by the National Police Commission in 1977, and by the Supreme Court at various times, but nothing much has been done. It is hard to avoid the conclusion that politicians are unwilling to reform the police service because they want to use it for their own ends.

The condition of the courts is in no better shape. While the Supreme Court has earned some well-deserved plaudits for judgements that have compelled the executive to promote the public interest, the judiciary as a whole has grave weaknesses. There is a huge backlog of cases and a large number of vacancies in judicial positions at all levels. (There was a backlog of 32 million cases in 2011 of which 24 per cent were pending for at least five years and 9 per cent for more than 10 years. In 2012, the Supreme Court had a vacancy rate of 13 per cent and the High Courts and District Courts of 29 and 21 per cent respectively. Even if we ignore vacancies, India has only 12 judges per million people; the United States has 108 per million.) The Indian legal system places a very low value on time, so there are frequent delays and adjournments of court cases. There is an urgent need for streamlining the judicial process, cutting down on adjournments, and economizing on time more generally. Institutions to speed up judicial processes such as arbitration tribunals (*lok adalats*) and village courts (*gram nyayalayas*) suffer from inadequate physical and human infrastructure. The reputation of the judiciary as a 'clean' institution has also suffered in recent years, even at top levels, and certainly lower down the chain. In 2012, the Congress government introduced the Judicial Appointments Bill, which sought to allay some of these concerns by mandating that judges publicly declare their assets, creating a judicial code of conduct, and laying down processes for dismissing judges who violate the code. But the bill lapsed (before being passed by parliament) when the government left office. Many useful suggestions to reform the legal system have been made by Law Commissions but with little effect so far.

CORRUPTION AND CRONY CAPITALISM

Another manifestation of weak state capacity is corruption.[21] It is sometimes argued that both society and the state should ignore corruption because it has the virtue of making bureaucratic wheels turn faster ('speed money'). But that argument has severe limitations: a bribe culture may have precisely the opposite effect and induce bureaucrats to create more red tape, licenses, and other barriers to entry in order to increase their own take. It might also be argued that corruption is a force for good because it enables the most profitable, and hence the most efficient, firms to prosper (because they would be the ones able to pay the highest bribes!). This argument is too clever by half. The firms that pay the highest bribes may not be the most efficient but simply the best 'connected' or the most monopolistically powerful. In any case, private profitability may not be a reliable indicator of economic efficiency. For example, a firm that evades a pollution tax by bribing an inspector may increase its profits but at the cost of economic efficiency (properly defined to allow for the social cost of pollution). Corruption should also be combated for a deeper reason: if allowed to rise unchecked, it can end up destroying social trust and delegitimizing the state.

Why has the incidence of corruption risen in India despite the 'dismantling of the license raj' over the last three decades? Although some channels of corruption (such as smuggling of imported consumer goods) have closed, others remain open, and new channels have opened up. Despite overall liberalization, many essential goods are still subject to price control, which inevitably creates dual markets and the possibility of arbitraging between them. Politicians and bureaucrats retain a lot of discretion in the allocation of national resources such as land, minerals under the ground, and telecom spectrum. The value of these resources, and of the rights to exploit them, has shot up as a result of rapid growth. There has also been a sharp increase in various transfer programmes such as the rural employment guarantee scheme, which increase the scope for corruption. Though these government interventions are well intended, they are often not well designed. Beneficial regulation in a modern economy needs regulators who are competent and independent, but in India they are in short supply. In addition, India's anti-corruption laws have many loopholes; and the adjudication and enforcement authorities are not up to the task of preventing, investigating, and punishing corruption.

Corruption takes several forms.[22] It may be 'facilitative' when an official has to be paid speed money to persuade him to do what his job requires of him. It may be 'extractive' when an official has to be paid a bribe to stop him harassing a citizen on a trumped-up charge or when an official simply steals government money that is on its way to designated beneficiaries. It may be 'collusive' when an official connives with the bribe-giver to look the other way when a law is broken or to actively help in its violation. And each of these three types of corruption could be 'petty', involving small amounts of money in the ordinary everyday dealings of citizens with street-level bureaucrats, or 'big-ticket', involving huge government contracts worth billions of dollars. By their nature, corrupt activities do not yield hard data. Nevertheless, investigative journalists, statutory agencies, and innovative academic researchers have managed to throw some light on this dark corner of public life. They have found more than enough evidence to confirm the popular perception that corruption is rife in the country, and a major problem that needs to be addressed.

Big-ticket corruption takes place mainly in government procurement, state allocation of scarce resources, and electoral finance; and often these three channels are inter-connected. Procurement by government departments or public enterprises involves choosing between suppliers, which obviously creates scope for kickbacks and 'collusive corruption'. This is fiscally expensive since the government treasury is over-charged thereby; and it may also reduce efficiency if incompetent firms win the contracts. Similarly, the allocation of valuable and scarce resources such as land or mining rights can be done in such a way as to cream off huge sums of money for individual politicians and bureaucrats or political parties. Sometimes, big-ticket corruption is not collusive but 'extractive', involving blatant flouting of government regulations or embezzlement pure and simple.

Sukhtankar and Vaishnav have listed 28 major collusive and extractive scams that have hit the headlines since the year 2000, in which the average sum involved was about Rs. 36,000 crores ($6 billion) and the median around Rs. 12,000 crores ($2 billion).[23] A few examples will suffice here. Of the *collusive* scams, perhaps the most notorious was the telecom spectrum scam. In 2008, the Union telecom minister Andimuthu Raja decided to allocate 2G wireless spectrum on a 'first come first served basis' at 2001 prices, with the allocation allegedly rigged to benefit some favoured companies, which then sold the licenses to others at much higher prices. The loss to the government was Rs. 56,000 crores (about $9 billion).[24] Other infamous collusive scandals that have come to light include several cases of corrupt issuance of mining licenses, e.g. in Goa and Orissa, at giveaway prices, and without the necessary environmental licenses, with the subsequent profits shared by crooked tycoons, politicians, and bureaucrats. Prominent examples of *extractive* scams are a) the Uttar Pradesh food grain scam that involved a large number of government officials and private traders, in which food grains destined for distribution to poor people were allegedly diverted to the open market and sold abroad; and b) the Maharashtra irrigation scam in which half of the money spent on more than 30 irrigation projects allegedly went into the pockets of state political leaders.

Electoral finance in India is a prime locus of collusive corruption.[25] Path-dependency matters here. One of the watershed moments in the history of corruption was the ban on corporate donations to political parties imposed by Mrs. Indira Gandhi in 1969 because she was concerned about the money that would flow into the coffers of the right-wing parties that opposed her. The effect was to drive political donations underground into 'black money'. It was only in 1985 that the ban was lifted. This move did not work because by then the reliance of political parties on black money was well entrenched. Granting tax credits for corporate donations also made little difference. Tax credits do not work because corporates prefer secrecy: they are risk averse and fear reprisals from parties that win elections for donations given to their opponents. With increasing democratization, the number of elections has increased; with higher growth, winning elections has become much more lucrative and fighting elections has become much more expensive.

Many politicians use a seat in the legislature or a ministerial position to make money to enrich themselves or their parties. In some states, illicit money raised from industrialists (in exchange for licenses, mining approvals etc.) goes directly to chief ministers who spend it on funding their own election campaigns or those of their associates, buying off politicians in opposition parties and inducing them to defect, and other such 'political purposes'.[26]

Indirect evidence cleverly gleaned by various research studies confirms the connection between corruption and electoral finance. It is an open secret that the construction and real estate industries are used by politicians to deposit and invest black money, which then gets used for election expenditures, as and when necessary. Devesh Kapur and Milan Vaishnav have found indirect evidence of such corruption by uncovering an electoral cycle in cement consumption: they show that there is an identifiable tendency for cement consumption to fall before elections (since builders divert money to fund election campaigns).[27] A similar phenomenon has been discovered by Sandip Sukhtankar who shows that mill-owners pay lower sugar cane prices to cane farmers during election years to enable them to funnel more money into politicians' election campaigns.[28] Another disturbing feature of electoral corruption is the rise of criminal politicians. In the 15th Lok Sabha elected in 2009, 30 per cent of MPs had pending criminal cases against them, and for 14 per cent of MPs the charges were of a 'serious' nature such as murder, attempted murder, kidnapping etc. In the 16th Lok Sabha elected in 2014, the figures are even higher: 34 per cent for criminal charges and 21 per cent for serious criminal charges. Parties supply such candidates because they bring money and muscle. Since elections have become much more expensive than hitherto, criminal candidates are attractive because they can be expected to be self-financing. But election data show that criminality is also associated with a higher chance of winning, which is a *prima facie* indication that there is also a demand for criminal candidates. This is confirmed by opinion surveys: they reveal that many voters are not put off by criminality, especially of candidates from their own ethnic or caste group, presumably because criminality signals a credible ability to be a representative who can deliver physical protection and access to public services and benefits for his 'clients' and supporters.[29]

'Petty' corruption is especially prevalent in three areas. The first is the simple and routine business of getting things like a ration card, a birth certificate, a caste certificate or a driver's license. This aspect is well-known to anyone familiar with India: it is impossible to get the lower bureaucracy to act without the greasing of assorted palms. Rigorous confirmation has been provided by various studies, including the famous experiment by

Marianne Bertrand and others investigating driving licenses in Delhi.[30] The results were disturbing and showed that the process of getting a license is pervasively corrupt. Nearly all the people employing agents (who paid bribes) got a license quickly and without taking the required driving test; those who applied in the regular way had to take the test and most of them failed. (Around 75 per cent of license-getters did not take the driving test; about 60 per cent of the license-getters failed an independent driving test arranged by the experimenters.) In this case corruption was collusive, clearly more than just speed money: by letting loose bad drivers on to the roads, it subverted the regulations in a positively harmful way.

A second major area in which petty corruption is common is transfer and safety-net programmes, which distribute food, money, medicines etc. to poor people. The benefits which are supposed to reach the poor end up lining the pockets of intermediaries en route. This kind of corruption is extractive: it is theft at the expense of both beneficiaries and taxpayers. Examples are the huge leakages from the PDS and the scheme for guaranteed rural employment (NREGS). The corruption that permeates the PDS is of course well-known. A report by the Planning Commission found that 57 per cent of the food grains issued by the FCI did not reach the poor; and the same report also reckons that for every rupee transferred to the poor, the government spends 3.65 rupees.[31] A recent study of districts in Orissa and Andhra Pradesh compared the officially recorded disbursements of NREGS wages against what the workers actually received and reached the sobering conclusion that about three-quarters of the labour budget was embezzled.[32] A third aspect of petty corruption is absenteeism and shirking from work by government employees, which is tantamount to a 'theft of time' from the state. As explained in Chapter 9, this is a ubiquitous phenomenon in state-provided education and health services. Teachers are absent around 25 per cent of the time, and even when present, actually teach only half the time. Absence among health care workers is even worse; and, in addition, doctors put in very little effort, especially in poor neighbourhoods. Though petty corruption sounds less serious that grand corruption, it imposes huge economic and human costs because it is so pervasive. For example, it has been estimated that teacher absence alone costs the government about Rs. 8000–10,000 crores ($1.2–$1.5 billion) annually.[33] And on the conservative assumption that leakages account for 25 per cent of spending on the NREGS scheme, they amount to another Rs. 20,000 crores ($3.5 billion) annually. So, in its totality, petty corruption involves sums that are comparable with big ticket corruption, and perhaps larger.

Corruption is not of course a purely Indian problem. It exists in all countries to a greater or lesser extent and totally eliminating it would be virtually impossible. There is evidence that it is negatively correlated with per capita income: richer countries tend to have less corruption than poorer ones. That leads to the thought that corruption in India should be left to its own devices in the expectation that it will decline spontaneously as incomes rise. This thought should be resisted because corruption, if it gets out of hand, has the potential to seriously impede the development process. (Indonesia and Russia are obvious examples.) A close reading of US history also supports this view. The so-called 'gilded age' of the United States in the second half of the nineteenth century was a heyday of corruption and crony capitalism. 'Robber barons' such as Andrew Carnegie, John D. Rockefeller, Cornelius Vanderbilt, and others, built up huge monopolies in steel, oil, railroads etc., and then used their wealth to manipulate the political system for their own ends. (At one time they 'owned' a large majority of US senators.) While the 'robber barons' were certainly dynamic entrepreneurs and contributed to the country's rapid growth, they also initiated an unhealthy trend which, if it had continued, would have made the growth unsustainable. This decay of the US political and economic system did not stop of its own accord. It was controlled in the late 19th and early 20 centuries by deliberate public policy choices, such as legislation to curb the power of large monopolies, instigated by the executive[34] and the legislature, working in alliance with political and social movements, especially the Progressive Movement. India, likewise, cannot afford to treat corruption in cavalier fashion. This raises the tough question: what can be done to defeat corruption or at least keep it within acceptable bounds?

The obvious place to start is to find ways to reduce the scope for discretionary action by government officials, together with measures to change their incentives to act corruptly. More information and transparency can help because they shift the balance of power in favour of citizens (provided officials who do not comply have reason to fear that they would be penalized). So the Right to Information Act (RTIA), enacted in 2005, is a step forward. Streamlining of procedures can also be very useful. Thus, the recent initiative to replace multiple inspections of compliance with numerous laws by self-certification combined with random checks is a good idea, since 'inspections' are a fertile ground for corruption. New technologies of e-governance also have a lot of potential. For example, there is good evidence that direct transfer of NREGS wages into workers' bank accounts has considerably reduced the scope for stealing by intermediaries.[35] The combination of transparency, streamlining of regulations, and adoption of information technology can be strengthened by legislation that reduces the incentives for corrupt actions either directly or indirectly. Several bills have been passed by central and state governments in the recent past to do exactly that (at least on paper). How effective they will be in practice remains to be seen.[36]

The anti-corruption moves described above can affect all varieties of corruption. But fighting 'big ticket' corruption, mainly associated with government allocation and procurement, and electoral finance, needs more specific action. Corruption in allocation and procurement can be reduced by adopting impersonal devices such as auctions in place of discretionary decisions. The Public Procurement Bill, which was introduced in 2012 but is still pending in parliament, would be a major step in the right direction since it would make an open bidding process the default option for procurement in government contracts. Some other moves also augur well. For example, the NDA government, under pressure from the Supreme Court, recently passed two bills that require the government to allocate mining leases by auction.[37]

An important qualification is necessary at this point. While reducing the scope for bureaucratic discretion is generally desirable, there are also severe drawbacks to 'too much zeal' in this regard. Administrative discretion cannot be totally eliminated, for good reasons; at the very least it will be required for regulating markets. Moreover, many bureaucratic actions involve decisions under conditions of uncertainty. The problem with over-zealous measures against corruption is that they may result in hounding officials for honest mistakes. Apart from being morally wrong, this would also stifle bureaucratic initiative, drive, and leadership, an outcome that would be very costly for economic development. It is not easy to make laws that balance these different considerations but it has to be done as best as possible.

Stamping out electoral corruption and criminality will require fundamental reform of the financing of political parties and elections, and of election laws that are shot through with holes. At present, 75 per cent of the income of India's six major political parties comes from undocumented sources.[38] One loophole that makes this possible is that political parties are only required to reveal political contributions that are larger than Rs. 20,000. As a result, it has become standard practice to divide each large donation into numerous small amounts that are just short of the threshold. The expenditure side is no better. Current election laws impose limits on election expenditures by individual candidates but these limits are flouted on an industrial scale. This is because political parties do not have to reveal expenditure on 'propagating party programmes.' In practice, this means that there are no effective limits on candidates' election spending. As regards the supply of criminal candidates, the Supreme Court has issued some helpful judgements. In 2003, it ruled that candidates must file affidavits declaring their assets and liabilities as well as their criminal convictions and pending cases. In 2013, it went further and decreed that a sitting MP or MLA, if convicted in a court of law, should face immediate disqualification.[39] The Election Commission (EC) would like to go further: it has recommended that any person against whom charges have been framed by a court should be disqualified from standing for election. This has not received much support because it is thought to be too difficult to guard against trumped up charges. It would surely not be beyond the wit of woman or man to formulate appropriate safeguards. (For example, there have been suggestions that 'fast track' courts should be set up to deal speedily with cases against politicians.) Of course, the above measures only attack the *supply* of criminal candidates. As explained above, there is evidence that there is also a *demand* for such candidates because they are seen as better able to deliver various benefits for their voter-clients than law-abiding candidates. This will change only if and when the state becomes better at ensuring provision of public goods for citizens so that clientelistic arrangements are no longer perceived to be necessary or useful.

It is also beyond doubt that there is an acute need for political parties to become more accountable in their operations. It would be right to compel them to accept monitoring and regulation by the EC that includes oversight of their audited annual accounts. Of course, regulation by the EC would not be credible and effective in the absence of enforcement powers, such as the power to de-register a party for flagrant violations of the law.[40] In the longer run, India needs to enact legislation a) to make political parties internally democratic and b) to fund elections from the public purse, as in some European countries.

I have focused above on informational, technical, and legal remedies for corruption. But how are these to be implemented? India has weak administrative and judicial systems. So the success of anti-corruption policies is dependent in part on making good these deficiencies. An even more basic problem is that in so far as anti-corruption measures have to be instigated by politicians, they face a glaring conflict of interest since many of them gain from corruption. Why would politicians act against their own interests? The silver lining is that they do have to respond to waves of popular feeling. It helps that there are social movements in the country that have mobilized a demand for clean government and made it into a major electoral issue (though many people, schizophrenically, continue to vote for corrupt politicians). In other words, the reaction to corruption in India has some similarities to the reaction in the United States to the excesses of the 'gilded age'. A related hopeful possibility is that the growing middle class in India will agitate to strengthen the rule of law, as has happened historically in some countries. Some recent departures from past electoral patterns also bode well. Automatic anti-incumbency in elections seems to be on the wane. Since 2000, there has been a tendency for state governments that have delivered on economic development to be re-elected.[41] Voting on caste lines still continues, and identity politics is still going strong, but economic development and corruption are gaining ground as issues of electoral salience. These are all promising straws in the wind.

NOTES

1. This section has benefited from Pranab Bardhan's path-breaking analysis of India's political economy (see Bardhan 1984). See also his more recent reflections in Bardhan (2010, 2015b).
2. The state has often acted against the interests of one or other of the groups or 'proprietary classes' that could claim to have a major influence on the state. Sometimes it has done this by playing off one group against another. See Bardhan (1984), Chapter 5.
3. Manor (1983) introduced the evocative terms 'political awakening' and 'political decay'.
4. The exception was Kerala. It elected a Communist government in 1957.
5. A striking example of this shift is the sharp decline in the frequency of the use of presidential power to dismiss state governments. Mrs. Gandhi used this power repeatedly.
6. See Bardhan (1984) and Chapter 10 of Bardhan (2010).
7. It can be argued that India's caste cleavages keep a desirable check on political mobilization on the basis of religion since political parties are forced thereby to seek support from all religious groups. In other words, caste politics may have the beneficial side-effect of undermining confessional politics.
8. See Manor (2015), Chapter 14. Manor estimates that in May 2014, 40 per cent of Indians lived in states where a single leader dominated state politics, and another 20 per cent in states where one leader had near-complete dominance.
9. It would be wrong to draw the conclusion that economic reform is impossible in India. A very similar analysis to the one above led Pranab Bardhan to the view he expressed in his 1984 book (see Bardhan 1984) that India was in stasis, caught in a trap of competing interests. But even as the book was being written, changes were taking place that culminated in the reforms of 1991. Of course these reforms were partly crisis-induced. But they were not reversed even after the crisis was resolved. Note also that they were introduced by a minority government. The right conclusion to draw is that reform is difficult but not impossible. There is certainly room for adroit political agency.
10. See Aiyar and Walton (2014).
11. Note also that the FSA does little for malnutrition, which is now a more critical problem than hunger. Moreover, it focuses on delivery of cereals in the face

of mounting evidence that the pattern of consumption is shifting away from cereals to other food items.

12. The Right to Information Act was enacted in 2005. It has increased the transparency of state operations somewhat, and various studies show that making an information request tends to achieve results. But there has also been a backlash. Civil servants tend not to express opinions on file. More is done by way of removable 'post-its' and private phone conversations.

13. For a concise review of the experience with decentralization, see Manor (2010). For further discussion, see Chapter 13 below.

14. Two articles that provide very useful discussions of the relevant issues are Kapur and Vaishnav (2014a) and Debroy (2014). I have drawn on them liberally in the rest of this section.

15. For example, I ignore here the sorely needed reforms to improve the functioning of parliament. The top executive has problems too. During the previous Congress government, there was, in effect, a dyarchy at the centre, with power shared between the cabinet and the party president. This did not make for resolute government. There was also a tendency, caused by coalition politics, for cabinets to be excessively large, with resulting diseconomies of scale.

16. One of the main instruments of political control is postings, promotions, and transfers of civil servants.

17. There are acute shortages of teachers, police, health care workers, and staff for childhood nutrition programmes. There is also enormous variation between states. See Muralidharan (2016).

18. See Muralidharan (2016). His scheme would make it possible to expand the number of staff in a manner that is fiscally feasible, while also improving their quality. Improving accountability and motivation of existing regular staff is a more difficult nut to crack.

19. Muralidharan (2016) reports that the government of Tamil Nadu has instituted a 'Special Youth Police Brigade', which employs low-paid police apprentices to assist regular police with peripheral tasks. As he points out, this scheme could serve as a building block for a full-fledged apprentice scheme.

20. J. S. Verma, a former Chief Justice of the Supreme Court, is on record as saying that 'It is too much of a coincidence that in sensitive matters the outcome of the CBI's investigation depends on the political equation of the accused with the ruling power, and it changes without compunction with changes in the equation.' See Singh (2012) and Srivastava (2013).

21. In this chapter, I restrict myself to corruption that involves the government and the public sphere, thus leaving out purely intra-private-sector corruption. India has plenty of the latter as well (for example in private medicine) but it would take me too far afield to pursue that topic.

22. The distinction between 'facilitative', 'collusive', and 'extractive' corruption is made by Sukhtankar and Vaishnav (2015). This article contains a marvellous analytical review of the literature on corruption in India and I have made extensive use of it in this section. See also the excellent analysis in Ninan (2015).

23. See Sukhtankar and Vaishnav (2015).

24. Rs. 56,000 crores ($ 9 billion) was about 10 per cent of central government revenue in 2009/10. According to the CAG report the loss to the fisc was Rs. 1.76 lakh crores ($29 billion) but it is generally agreed that this is an over-estimate

based on assuming that the licenses could have been sold by the government at (predicted) 3G auction prices. A more reasonable estimate of the loss to the government, based on the actual premium that the eventual buyers paid to the initial buyers, is $9 billion. As it happens, in this instance, the direct loss to consumers was negligible because they paid the same prices for telecom services as they would have paid if the licenses had been sold by auction to the eventual buyers (see Sukhtankar 2015). This illustrates the important point that corruption may result in very different losses to consumers, the government, and other parties involved.

25. See Gowda and Sridharan (2012) for a useful analysis of corruption in electoral finance and political parties.
26. See Manor (2015).
27. See Kapur and Vaishnav (2011).
28. See Sukhtankar (2012).
29. See Kapur, Sircar, and Vaishnav (2014), Vaishnav (2014), and Sridharan and Vaishnav (2015).
30. See Bertrand, Hanna, Djankov, and Mullainathan (2007).
31. See Planning Commission (2005).
32. See Niehaus and Sukhtankar (2013a, 2013b).
33. See Muralidharan, Das, Holla, and Mohpal (2014).
34. Much credit goes to Presidents Teddy Roosevelt and William Taft.
35. Relevant here is the rigorous study by Muralidharan and others on the Andhra Pradesh Smartcard Initiative, which showed that leakages in NREGS and Social Security Pension payments fell sharply after the initiation of the programme. See Muralidharan, Niehaus, and Sukhtankar (2014).
36. Some of the relevant bills, other than the RTIA, are as follows. The Right of Citizens for Time Bound Delivery of Goods and Services Bill, 2011, sets timelines for delivery of public services and decrees the appointment of grievance officers, with powers to impose fines on defaulting government functionaries. Many states have similar 'right to service' laws. The Prevention of Corruption (Amendment) Bill, 2013, and the Prevention of Bribery of Foreign Public Officials and Officials of Public International Organizations Bill, 2011, contain provisions criminalizing both giving of bribes to and acceptance of bribes by public officials. The Whistle Blowers' Protection Bill, 2011, seeks to protect persons making public interest disclosures related to acts of corruption. The important Public Procurement bill, which is pending in parliament, is discussed below.
37. These are the Coal Mines (Special Provisions) Bill and the Mines and Minerals (Development and Regulation) Bill. It is important to note that auctions must guard against problems such as collusion among bidders. Auction design requires expertise, which the government will have to develop.
38. See Sridharan and Vaishnav (2015), based on figures gathered by the Association of Democratic Reforms.
39. The Congress government was minded to repeal this law in parliament but in the end changed its mind as a result of public indignation. It did, however, pass legislation which nullified another Supreme Court ruling that would have disqualified persons in jail or custody from standing for election.
40. Efforts to make party finances transparent have signally failed so far. In 2013, the Central Information Commission (CIC) made a ruling that political

parties were subject to the RTIA. But this initiative got nowhere. The Congress government immediately introduced a bill in parliament to exempt political parties from the Act (though the house was dissolved before it could be passed). Soon thereafter, the CIC ruefully admitted that its ruling was not 'implementable' in the face of opposition from all political parties.

41. See Gupta (2014), Gupta and Panagariya (2014), and Vaishnav and Swanson (2013).

CHAPTER 12

India and the World Economy

Ten years after independence in 1947, India embarked on an autarkic path of development, with the avowed objective of building its industrial base on the basis of import-substitution and 'self-reliance'.[1] Convinced that it had been exploited by foreign capital during its colonial past, it also closed itself off from international investment. As things turned out, the second half of the 20th century coincided with a sensationally rapid growth of global trade and investment, and the emergence in East Asia of trade as a growth engine. The consequence was that while India did build a diverse industrial base, it became one of the world's most inward-looking countries, and paid a steep price in foregone trade, investment, technology flows, and productivity growth. A major goal of India's historic reforms launched in 1991 was to reintegrate India into the global economy and reap the economic benefits thereof. Since then, India's globalisation has proceeded apace. This chapter begins with an examination of the evolution and extent of India's global engagement in recent years. I then discuss the impact of India's global engagement on India and on the world. I end with an analysis of how India should position itself on global economic issues.

INDIA'S GLOBAL ENGAGEMENT: EVOLUTION AND EXTENT

Even as late as 1990, India had one of the most closed economies in the world. Indeed, by some measures (for example, the ratio of exports of goods and services to GDP), the economy was more closed in 1990 than it was in 1950 (see Table 12.1). A crucial element of the 1991 reforms was the reduction of barriers to international trade and foreign investment. Thereafter, though the pace has varied, the broad thrust of trade policy has been quite firmly in a liberalizing direction. Tariffs in the manufacturing sector have been slashed: the average applied tariff fell from 145 per cent in 1990 to 10.2 per cent in 2013 (see Table 12.2).[2] Even more important, quantitative import controls on manufactured goods have been almost entirely swept away. Though agriculture still remains fairly highly protected, as in most countries, the average applied tariff on agricultural products has come down from 134 per cent in 1990 to 33 per cent in 2013.[3] Restrictions on inward and outward foreign investment have been substantially reduced. Liberalization has also extended to the exchange rate regime. In the old days, the exchange rate used to be fixed for long periods; since 1993, it has been a managed float.

These changes have brought about a remarkable increase in the openness of the economy and a radical shift in the structure of the balance of payments (see Tables 12.1, 12.3, and 12.4). Exports of goods and services have more than tripled as a proportion of GDP from just 7 per cent in 1990 to 25 per cent in 2013. Naturally, imports of goods and services have shown a roughly similar rise. The country has become a more attractive destination for foreign investment, so inflows of capital have increased significantly. Capital outflows have also grown but net capital inflows have been substantially positive (see Table 12.4). In the present century, the overall balance of payments has generally been in good health, with a modest current account deficit outweighed by a large capital account surplus.[4] As a byproduct, the country has accumulated a sizeable stock of foreign exchange

Table 12.1 INDIA: INDICATORS OF OPENNESS (% GDP)

	1950	1980	1990	2007	2013
Exports (goods)	6.5	4.9	5.8	14.2	17.1
Exports (services)	1.9	1.3	1.4	7.7	8.1
Exports (goods + services)	8.4	6.2	7.2	21.9	25.2
Imports (goods)	6.5	9.5	8.8	22.0	24.8
Imports (services)	1.3	0.2	1.1	4.5	4.2
Imports (goods + services)	7.8	9.7	9.9	26.5	29.0
Trade (goods + services)	16.2	15.9	17.0	48.4	54.2
Current Account (receipts)	n.a.	n.a.	8.0	26.8	29.4
Current Account (payments)	n.a.	n.a.	11.2	28.3	31.2
Capital Inflow	n.a.	n.a.	7.2	36.9	27.2
Capital Outflow	n.a.	n.a.	5.0	27.7	24.7
Gross flows (current + capital)	n.a.	n.a.	32.4	119.7	112.5

Sources: Reserve Bank of India (2009), and Reserve Bank of India (2015, and various earlier years).

Table 12.2 INDIA: STRUCTURE OF APPLIED TARIFFS (UNWEIGHTED AVERAGES, %)

	1990	2006	2013
All Goods	144	16	13.5
Agriculture	134	43	33.5
Manufacturing	145	14	10.2

Note: Bound tariffs remain much higher than applied tariffs. Unweighted averages of 'bound' tariffs in 2013 were as follows. All Goods: 48.6; Agriculture: 113.5; Manufacturing: 34.6.
Sources: World Trade Organisation, Trade Policy Review (India), various years; and World Trade Organization, Tariff Profiles (various years).

Table 12.3 INDIA: STRUCTURE OF THE BALANCE OF PAYMENTS ON CURRENT ACCOUNT (% GDP UNLESS OTHERWISE INDICATED)

	1960	1990	2007	2012	2014	2014 $ billion
Current Account	-2.4	-3.1	-1.3	-4.8	-1.6	-26.8
Trade Balance	-3.0	-3.0	-7.8	-10.7	-7.1	-144.9
Exports	3.8	5.8	14.2	16.6	15.5	316.5
Imports	6.8	8.8	22.0	27.3	22.6	461.5
Invisibles Balance	0.6	-0.1	6.2	5.8	5.8	118.2
Software Services	0.0	Neg.	3.0	3.5	3.4	70.4
Private Remittances	Neg.	0.7	3.4	3.5	3.3	66.3
Other Items	0.6	-0.8	-0.2	-1.2	-0.9	-18.6

Source: Reserve Bank of India (2015, and various earlier years).

reserves, currently about $350 billion (around seven months' imports). Aggregate gross external receipts and payments (current and capital combined) have more than tripled as a proportion of GDP from 32 per cent in 1990 to 112 per cent in 2013. India is thus more open than ever before.

On the current account, the most striking feature is the huge surge in invisible exports, particularly exports of information technology (IT) services. India's net IT exports grew from virtually nothing in 1990 to around $70 billion (3.6 per cent of GDP) two decades later. Inward remittances from overseas Indians also increased strongly: in 2013, this inflow was quantitatively as important as exports of IT services. Merchandise exports have advanced along a broad front. However, while overall export performance is creditable, it is much less spectacular than China's. In 1990, India's share of world merchandise exports was 0.5 per cent; in 2010, it had risen but only to 1.4 per cent. Over the same period, China's share grew

Table 12.4 INDIA: STRUCTURE OF THE BALANCE OF PAYMENTS ON CAPITAL ACCOUNT (% GDP UNLESS OTHERWISE INDICATED)

	1960	1990	2007	2012	2014	2014 $ billion
Capital Account	2.1	2.2	9.2	4.9	4.3	88.2
Loans	1.5	1.7	3.5	1.7	0.2	3.2
Ext. Assistance	1.5	0.8	0.2	0.1	0.1	1.7
Comm. Borrowing	Neg.	0.8	2.0	0.5	0.1	1.6
Short-Term Credit	Neg.	1.1	1.4	1.2	−0.0	−0.1
FDI (net)	Neg.	0.6	1.4	1.1	1.6	32.6
Inflows	Neg.	0.6	3.0	1.5	1.7	34.4
Outflows	Neg.	Neg.	−1.6	−0.4	−0.1	−1.8
Portfolio Investment	Neg.	Neg.	2.3	1.5	2.1	42.2
Other Items	0.6	−0.1	2.0	0.6	0.5	10.2
Forex Reserves (Increase)	−0.3	−0.9	7.9	0.1	3.0	61.4
Memo Items						
Forex Reserves (Total)	1.8	2.0	24.3	15.6	15.6	–
Forex Reserves ($ billion)	0.6	5.8	299.1	260.0	317.0	317.0
Forex Reserves (months)	3.0	2.5	14.4	6.2	8.3	–
Exchange Rate (Rs./$)	4.76	17.9	40.2	54.4	61.1	–

Source: Reserve Bank of India (2015, and various earlier years).

from 1.8 per cent to 10.4 per cent (see Table 12.5). A related point is that China, unlike India, has conquered the world market for labour-intensive manufactured goods. Another major difference between the export performances of the two countries is that China, unlike India, has been closely integrated into global manufacturing networks. In other words, India has been a successful recipient of cross-border outsourcing in services, but not in manufacturing (see Chapter 5).[5]

On the capital account, official aid flows, which were critical for India's balance of payments in the 1960s, have dwindled to negligible levels. Inward foreign direct investment (FDI) was no more than a trickle prior to the 1991 economic reforms because of the restrictive policies of previous governments and the lingering suspicion of multi-national corporations (MNCs). Thereafter, the Indian government slowly opened up to foreign investment. The FDI policy regime switched from a positive list to a negative list, thereby expanding the range of industries which could attract foreign money. Inward FDI steadily increased throughout the 1990s, and moved into a higher gear in the next decade (see Table 12.6).[6] Now foreign investors can, in principle, invest in most sectors with minimal government policy barriers (though transactions costs on the ground still remain

Table 12.5 INDIA, CHINA, SOUTH KOREA: SHARES
OF WORLD MERCHANDISE EXPORTS (PER CENT)

	India	China	South Korea
1950	2.0	1.3[a]	0.5[a]
1980	0.4	0.9	0.9
1990	0.5	1.8	2.0
2000	0.7	3.9	2.7
2007	1.1	8.9	2.7
2010	1.4	10.4	3.1

[a] Chinese and South Korean data refer to 1953.
Source: International Monetary Fund (various years).

Table 12.6 INDIA, CHINA: FDI INFLOWS
AND OUTFLOWS ($ BILLION)

	1990	2007	2013
Inflows			
India	0.1	35	31
China	3.5	85	106
Outflows			
India	Neg.	18	9
China	Neg.	25	101

Sources: Indian data from Reserve Bank of India (2015, and earlier
years); Chinese data from UNCTAD (2015, and earlier years).

high). Portfolio equity investments by foreign institutional investors into
Indian stock markets were liberalized early on in the reform programme.
These inflows have been strong but volatile. Investment in government and
corporate bonds has also been deregulated gradually in the last few years.

An interesting development is the growth of outbound FDI from India.[7]
MNCs used to be viewed as the devil's apprentice in Indian intellectual
thinking; now there is pride in attracting and nurturing Indian MNCs. In
the last 10 years, Indian outward FDI has moved more or less in step with
inward FDI, albeit at a lower level. In 2010, inward FDI was around $29 bil-
lion and outward FDI around $17 billion. In the last few years, large foreign
acquisitions by Indian companies have attracted considerable attention.
Examples include Tata's acquisition of Corus ($12.1 billion)[8] and Jaguar
Land Rover ($2.3 billion), Bharti Airtel's acquisition of the African assets
of Zain telecom ($10.7 billion), and Fortis' expansion in Southeast Asia,
emerging in the process as the largest private tertiary health provider in

developing countries. These investments are significant not only because of their large size but also because of the reputational advantages that they give Indian MNCs at home and abroad. Moreover, as Indian MNCs start becoming more visibly active abroad, the ideological justifications for rejecting foreign MNCs' activities and investment in India have become less vociferous (although the political outcry over allowing FDI in retail in 2011 shows that in some sectors political resistance continues to be high).[9]

Despite the liberalization of foreign investment, it is striking that India, like China, has refrained from full-scale capital account liberalisation. While direct and portfolio equity inflows were unrestricted in large measure, debt inflows, especially if short-term, were tightly controlled, using multiple instruments—quantitative limits, and price-based and administrative measures. The aim has been to avoid the build-up of excessive foreign debt of a volatile nature, and to restrain foreign currency-denominated borrowing by domestic entities, including banks, which could turn into large balance sheet losses in the event of a devaluation of the exchange rate. Capital-outflow restrictions have been lifted but only partially and gradually. These measures, which were departures from mindless laissez faire, have made a major contribution to India's economic stability.[10]

Another element of India's growing engagement with the world economy, in addition to trade and capital movements, has been international migration. Outward migration from independent India was initially driven by the large demand for unskilled and semi-skilled workers in the United Kingdom, following the end of the Second World War. From the late 1960s onwards, two major streams of migration emerged. The first, to the Middle East, was dominated by unskilled or semi-skilled temporary workers and nearly four-fifths of these labour flows were to just three Middle Eastern countries (Saudi Arabia, UAE, and Oman). The second stream, comprising skilled professionals, migrated to OECD countries, and especially to the United States. The Indian-born population in the United States grew from around 12,000 in 1960 to 51,000 in 1970. It then climbed to 206,000 in 1980, 450,000 in 1990, 1 million in 2000 and 3.2 million in 2010.

INDIA'S GLOBAL ENGAGEMENT: IMPACT ON INDIA

The development discourse in post-independent India was dominated by fears of the ruinous effects of foreign exposure, such as deindustrialization, destabilization, and general impoverishment. Opening up of the economy has dispelled these apprehensions: the outcomes of India's globalisation have been substantially positive. Foreign industry has not destroyed Indian industry and foreign companies have not devoured Indian companies. Instead, gradual but firm liberalization of trade and foreign investment (along with other reform measures) has contributed to a sharp increase in the rate of productivity growth.[11] Entrepreneurial response has also been vigorous. India now has world class companies in many sectors such as iron and steel, cement, automobiles, pharmaceuticals, and information technology. And as we saw above, several Indian companies, not content with domestic expansion, have been making large foreign acquisitions.

Opening up did not destabilize the Indian economy. It escaped relatively unscathed the East Asian crisis of 1997 and the global credit crisis of 2008. An important reason for this benign outcome is that India rejected full capital account convertibility (even when it was being actively promoted by the IMF and the US Treasury before the East Asian crisis), while being permissive towards equity inflows. The controls on 'hot money' gave the authorities policy space, by enabling them to target the exchange rate at a competitive level and accumulate (sterilized) reserves, without losing control of monetary policy.[12] To be sure, there was macroeconomic turmoil after 2010, including an alarming rise in the current account deficit in 2011 and 2012. But this was the result of macro-mismanagement, not closer integration with global economy (see Chapter 8).

Trade liberalization has clearly not led to general impoverishment, indeed quite the contrary. Of course, poverty reduction has been slower than desired. Could it be that external liberalisation led to growth that is rapid but not sufficiently 'inclusive' (despite the theoretical presumption that a move towards freer trade would increase the demand for unskilled labour in a labour-abundant country)? This line of criticism is not persuasive. Inclusivity depends on employment creation, social empowerment, and income redistribution. It is indeed true that India's industrialisation, unlike that in East Asia, has not been employment-creating for unskilled labour. But the reason for this outcome can be traced to domestic policies. In practice, a host of domestic policy impediments—small-scale industry reservations, rigid labour laws, infrastructure deficiencies, lack of access to credit, weak human capital policies, and discouragement of FDI in labour-intensive industries—has suppressed the demand for low-skilled labour.[13] (In contrast, the demand for skilled labour has risen, and with it the wage premium for skills, which is one reason why income inequality increased over this period.) Income redistribution policies, such as cheap food via the PDS, and social empowerment policies, such as provision of education and health care, have not worked satisfactorily due to design problems and weak state capacity to deliver public services. Thus, India's inclusion deficit has domestic roots and cannot be blamed on globalisation.[14]

A subtle but important outcome of India's increasing global integration is its political impact. India's trade with the United States increased to $100 billion in 2012 (a quadrupling from 2000), and trade with China reached the same level in 2015 (from barely $3 billion in 2000). Naturally, commercial interests now loom much larger in India's bilateral relations with these major powers. Similar considerations have affected the relationship with other trading partners. The emergence of Indian firms as large investors in Britain's ailing manufacturing sector cannot but have an effect in shaping the bilateral relationship between the two countries. Indian MNCs as well as state-owned corporations, particularly in the energy and natural resources sectors, have started investing abroad in a big way in countries ranging from Australia to Indonesia to Bolivia, and of course Africa, and these capital flows are opening new avenues in India's bilateral relationships with the countries in question. Unlike China, whose overseas investments are dominated by state-owned enterprises, private firms dominate in the Indian case (with the exception of the oil and gas sector). While the aims of these firms may not be as aligned with the national interest as is the case with China, they do appear less threatening to the host countries.

International migration from India has also had multiple economic and political effects.[15] The economic effects of migration work through three mechanisms: financial flows, global networks, and the diaspora's role as reputational intermediaries. The Chinese diaspora has been a critical source of FDI into China. The Indian diaspora's role in this regard has been modest; instead, it has been an important source of financial flows into India in the form of remittances. Remittances emerged as an important component of the country's balance of payments in the mid-1970s and increased dramatically after the onset of economic liberalization in 1991. They have grown from $2.1 billion (0.7 per cent of GDP) in 1990 to $66 billion (3.5 per cent of GDP) in 2013. These figures reflect both the rise in the stock of Indian citizens residing abroad (especially in North America) and the degree to which their earning power has multiplied. Policy changes over the last two decades including the devaluation of the rupee, liberalization of gold imports, and rupee convertibility for current account transactions, have also made a difference, especially in bringing remittances from the Middle East through official markets rather than underground (*hawala*) channels.[16]

The Indian diaspora has created a web of cross-national networks, thereby encouraging the inflow of tacit information, business ideas, and technologies. It has also enabled 'home sourcing,' as illustrated by the rapid growth of India's diamond cutting and polishing industry on the one hand

and of India's IT sector on the other. The selectivity of recent Indian emigration and the success of migrants abroad have transformed the 'brain drain' into a 'brain bank.' This has resulted in positive spillover effects for India, with diasporic networks acting as reputational intermediaries and as credibility-enhancing mechanisms. The Indian diaspora's success in Silicon Valley has had a big impact on global perceptions of India, particularly as regards India's technology businesses. There is little doubt that by the 1990s, India's human-capital-rich diaspora, especially in the United States, became an international business asset for India.

One issue that has acquired some salience, as this book goes to press, is the implication for India of a possible long-term growth slowdown in both the advanced countries and in China. (China is slowing down as it rebalances its economy towards consumption. The West may slow down since the expected sharp fall in labour force growth is unlikely to be compensated by a faster pace of technical progress.) If this came to pass, India would face less favourable terms of trade and less advantageous demand conditions for its exports. Other things equal, its growth rate may fall somewhat. But this is not an argument for reversing liberalization of trade and foreign investment. Such policies would make matters worse and reduce growth even further.

INDIA'S GLOBAL ENGAGEMENT: IMPACT ON THE WORLD

India's impact on the world economy has been small so far. However, if the country continues to grow at 6 per cent a year or more, its global presence will become much more significant. While India's overall consumption and production levels are still too low to shape world prices, in certain areas such as oil (where it is a major importer) or cotton, sugar, and rice (where it is a major exporter), its impact is already being felt. Moreover, the more India integrates with the global economy, the more its emerging demographic bulge will affect global labour markets. And if trends such as 'frugal engineering'—the development of low-cost innovative processes and products, such as cheap cars and cheap generic pharmaceuticals— continue to deepen in India, they could disturb the existing market strategies of other countries and major international companies. Of course, these outcomes are by no means certain: while India has significant strengths it also has major weaknesses. If, however, India's advance continues, it would raise the question: What kind of power will India want to be? Will it seek to uphold the international order established by the Western powers, and especially the United States, in the aftermath of the

Second World War? Or will it seek to change this order, and if so, in which ways? The predicament that India will face is that as a major global economic power, the world will expect it to shoulder the burden of providing global public goods, such as climate change mitigation, even while it will continue to be a relatively poor country in terms of per capita income, with severe internal challenges.

A major change that is already occurring is India's transformation from foreign aid recipient (indeed the largest aid recipient, in absolute terms, in the second half of the 20th century) to foreign aid donor.[17] A key inflexion point in Indian foreign aid was the decision in 2003 to repay its bilateral debt to all but four countries, not to accept tied aid in the future, and accept bilateral aid from only five countries and the EU. Since it is no longer a low-income country, India is also poised to graduate from International Development Association (IDA) soft loans, which are one of the cornerstones of the global multilateral aid system. India's activity as aid donor, through both bilateral and multilateral channels, is acquiring quantitative weight.[18]

On international trade policy, India's changing stance is reflected in somewhat greater willingness to agree to binding international commitments. Although it was seen as a spoiler in the Doha round, other major powers have been at least as responsible. With global trade talks at an impasse, India has become more (at least by its own past record) aggressive in pursuing bilateral and regional trade agreements (see below). But it has so far stood outside 'mega-regional' deals, which may shape the future of world trade.

At the macro level, India's impact on the world has to be seen in the context of China's simultaneous rise. There will be not one but two emerging giants in the world economy, with India the smaller of the two. China and India will provide rapidly growing markets for advanced as well as developing countries. Indeed, they are already acting as global engines of growth. Even so, the long-run effects of their rise on the rest of the world are likely to be complex, some favourable, others unfavourable. Three types of effect could usefully be distinguished: on global stability, on overall living standards, and on the distribution of income.

The effects on global stability will depend, *inter alia*, on exchange rate policy in China and India. In the last decade, China's policy raised hackles because it was seen as impeding international adjustment (see below). The point to note is that in future years India's exchange rate policy too will begin to matter globally. So, any scheme for global exchange rate and monetary coordination will have to involve India because it is likely to be a 'systemically important' country. The long-run effect of the rise of China and India on overall living standards in the rest of the world may turn out to be substantial but is hard to predict. The effect will operate principally through the terms of trade, which could move favourably or unfavourably. For example, China's and India's large weight in commodities will influence commodity prices up or down in a major way, with major effects on commodity producers, e.g. in Africa and the Middle East, and in the opposite direction, on commodity importers. China's and India's success in producing goods and services cheaply will make consumers in many countries better off. By the same token, countries which compete with China and India in third-country markets may be adversely affected due to a worsening of their terms of trade. The distribution of income within countries will also be influenced by the integration of China and India into the world economy, and the consequent 'doubling of the world's labour force'. The eventual impact is likely to be favourable. But in the short run, unskilled wages in the West may be adversely affected. Equally important, as skills in China and India improve, there will be downward pressure on skilled wages in electronically-offshoreable jobs in Western countries.

No serious discussion of the impact of China and India can exclude consideration of the climate change issue. Though the responsibility for putting the accumulated stock of carbon in the atmosphere rests mainly with the advanced countries, China and India will be increasingly important in future carbon emissions production. While it is right that all countries should make efforts to counter global warming, it is also fair and reasonable that the associated financial burden should be borne by the advanced countries for a couple of decades.[19] Since this is a deeply contested matter, international agreement will be far from easy. Even so, in the recent Paris accord India has made quite an ambitious 'intended nationally determined contribution' (see Chapter 7).

It thus seems likely that on all the major global economic issues such as exchange rates, trade, and climate change, global action will have to involve the participation of China and India. The optimistic vision for the future is of a world in which the great powers, old and new, cooperate to supply global public goods. The pessimistic vision is one of disharmony and conflict between the major powers, similar to that which has accompanied some power transitions in the past. For good or ill, China and India will matter in the 21st century for each other and for the world.

INDIA'S STANCE ON GLOBAL ECONOMIC ISSUES

India's economic resurgence in recent years has led to its gaining greater prominence in the councils of the world economy. India is a member of the G20, which has succeeded the old G7 as the 'premier forum for global economic governance'. Its share of the vote in the IMF has gone up modestly. It is now represented on the Financial Stability Board (FSB), as well as the Basel Committee on Bank Regulation (BCBR) and other bodies that set financial standards. It has become a highly influential member of the World Trade Organization. The question that naturally arises is, how should it position itself on the major issues confronting the world economy? For reasons of space, I restrict myself here to two main areas: international money and finance, and international trade.

International Money and Finance

The global financial crisis (GFC) of 2008 exposed many long-standing flaws in international monetary and financial arrangements, of which the most striking was the lax regulatory supervision of financial institutions. In response, tightening and harmonization of bank regulation was accelerated under the aegis of the BCBR, and the G20 gave the go-ahead for implementation and phasing-in of the so-called Basel III standards by 2018. These require that banks keep more capital, and better-quality capital, in relation to risk-weighted assets than hitherto, as well as introduce an overall minimum leverage ratio.[20] On cross-border banks, Basel III has recommended that foreign branches of banks should be converted into subsidiaries in the host countries in order to separate their assets and liabilities more clearly from those of their parent banks. In addition, the Basel Committee has announced its intention to lay down minimum levels of liquidity and 'stable funding' for banks, to ensure that they can withstand short-term funding stress and longer-term liquidity mismatches. Regulations are also being contemplated in several other areas such as 'shadow banks', derivatives, bank resolution, and banks that are 'too big to fail'.

India has adopted the Basel III capital adequacy and leverage standards, indeed slightly tougher ones, to err on the side of safety.[21] The RBI has also issued guidelines on liquidity management, and the expectation is that it will go along with the Basel Committee's liquidity ratios, and its regulations on shadow banking, derivatives trading etc., as and when they arrive. In addition, the more welcoming policy towards the entry of foreign banks, recently announced by the RBI, is predicated on their coming in as subsidiaries, exactly as Basel III has proposed. All this makes good sense as an accompaniment of further liberalization of the financial sector. If India is to have more inward and outward foreign investment in banking, it cannot afford to ignore harmonized global standards, which promote financial soundness, and level the playing field for competition among banks.[22]

Though inadequate regulation of the financial sector was one of the main villains of the piece, there is little doubt that various other flaws in the international monetary system (IMS) also played a part in causing and amplifying the GFC. The crisis has underlined forcefully the importance of correcting them if the world is to be made safer and less crisis-prone. Firstly, the IMS is not conducive to adjustment of balance of payments disequilibria, especially of countries that run surpluses, and those that issue international reserves. Secondly, the IMS does not have a satisfactory mechanism for providing countries with international liquidity, in a crisis situation, and also over the longer run. Thirdly, it has no mechanism to prevent destabilizing capital flows or to counteract their effects. Consider each in turn.

Lack of adjustment of global current account imbalances played a major role in the build-up to the GFC. (It can be argued, plausibly, that the trend of widening global imbalances from 2000 to 2007 would have eventually produced a severe global crisis if the US housing bubble had not imploded first.) A necessary condition of avoiding excessive imbalances is an exchange rate system that is conducive to adjustment. But the current exchange rate system, which was adopted after the second amendment of the IMF Articles in 1978, permits each country to choose any exchange rate regime that it pleases. This 'non-system' has a radical flaw from a systemic perspective. While an individual country's choice of exchange rate regime does not generally matter much to other countries, this is not true of 'key countries' (i.e. systemically important countries) that have a significant weight in the world economy. A glaring example of this was provided by the US-China relationship in the middle years of the last decade. China resisted exchange rate appreciation against the US dollar in the pursuit of export-led growth and reserve accumulation, and ran large and growing current account and balance payments surpluses.[23] These surpluses transmitted a deflationary impulse to the US economy. Since the US could not devalue against China, it had to rely on highly expansionary monetary policies to maintain full employment, which fuelled a rise in liquidity and added to the downward pressure on interest rates that came from the placement of the mounting Chinese reserves in US treasuries. The result of ultra-low interest rates was a 'search for yield' and a colossal credit bubble, whose eventual implosion triggered the GFC. The episode confirmed the point that large and growing imbalances are a recipe for disaster.

In the aftermath of the GFC, there was extensive discussion of global imbalances and the adjustment problem in the G20 and elsewhere but in the end it went nowhere. G-20 countries agreed they would carry out a continuous 'mutual assessment process' (MAP) of imbalances and macroeconomic policies, overseen by the IMF. But when push came to shove, countries like China and Germany blocked any agreement on measures to curb surpluses. The impetus to reform the system has now waned because imbalances have reduced. But the problem has not gone away for good. Large imbalances could easily return when world growth resumes. Many remedial alternatives have been proposed. One way forward, which I commend, harks back to Maynard Keynes. This would consist of an agreement that countries which run 'excessive' and 'persistent' current account surpluses (say more than 3 per cent of GDP for three years on the run) should pay a tax to the IMF (say an amount equal to half the surplus), which it could use for other desirable purposes such as lending to deficit countries. Right now, while current account imbalances are not a burning issue, would be a good time to negotiate such a move. India is in a special position. Not only does it have an interest in global stability but it has the advantage of being a major country with no axe to grind on this issue. It has aimed at modest deficits, not large surpluses; and its growth strategy has been much more balanced between domestic and foreign markets than China's. It should be loudly demanding international rules that promote adjustment. The need for such rules has been underlined in the recent past by fears that shortage of global demand may lead key countries down the path of competitive depreciation of currencies.

The second area of concern about the IMS is the provision of international liquidity. Current arrangements for liquidity-provision in a crisis rely to a large extent on countries insuring themselves by accumulating foreign exchange reserves. But this route has major problems. It is inefficient because it ties up scarce resources in low-yielding assets. It is also collectively dangerous because it encourages growing current account imbalances: countries are tempted to undervalue their exchange rates in order to run current account surpluses to build up owned (rather than borrowed) reserves, whose counterpart is current account deficits of reserve issuers such as the United States.[24] The world needs a better way of meeting the increase in demand for reserves in emergencies. During the GFC, the demand for reserves (from countries which had not self-insured) was met principally by swap arrangements hurriedly organized by the US Fed and the European Central Bank (ECB). But this may not be possible, or enough, next time there is a crisis; and in any case these arrangements largely excluded the developing countries.[25] The IMF has tried to step in by creating some new low-conditionality and quick-disbursing lending facilities. But there have been very few takers because countries fear being stigmatized in financial markets. The IMF's regular quota resources are too small to provide enough unconditional liquidity in a global crisis, even though the doubling of quotas that had been agreed by the G20 and the IMF is finally about to happen.[26] There would be understandable objections to a quota expansion big enough to cope with all emergencies since it would involve a huge and permanent expansion of unconditional liquidity. The neatest way to meet the need for liquidity would surely be to make it possible to have a quick and temporary increase in the supply of Special Drawing Rights (SDRs) in an emergency. (The increase could be temporary because SDRs can be cancelled after the emergency is over.) But this would require amendment of the IMF articles. India should work towards mobilizing support for this, though it would of course be resisted by the IMF's largest shareholders. As things stand, there is a large gap in the ability of the IMS to expand international liquidity rapidly to manage a global crisis.[27]

The global reserve system is also deeply problematic from a long-run perspective due to the potential instability involved in national currencies serving as international reserves (in other words, a modern version of the old 'Triffin problem').[28] If a reserve issuer (such as the United States) runs persistent surpluses, the world is starved of liquidity; if it runs persistent deficits, its external debt rises too fast and confidence in the reserve currency is sapped. The number of reserve currencies is set to rise in future. The euro has joined the dollar as a major reserve currency though its future is still rather clouded due to the troubles of the eurozone. The Chinese renminbi is the obvious next candidate in line, if and when it becomes freely convertible.[29] Optimists hope that competition between reserve currencies will discipline reserve issuers and resolve the 'new Triffin problem'. But this is too sanguine. Currently, instability is kept in check by the fact that those who wish to flee from the dollar have few good alternatives. In a world in which there were, say, three reserve currencies, there could be large destabilizing movements of money, if confidence in one of them were to weaken. China's recent moves to 'internationalize' the renminbi suggest that it is committed to making it an international reserve currency. So, in the long run, the drive to a multi-currency reserve system is probably unstoppable. In principle, an SDR-based reserve system would be much more stable. But despite the agreement in 2009 to increase the supply of SDRs by $200 billion, they constitute only 4 per cent of global reserves. Of course, it is natural that reserve issuers are not interested in promoting the SDR since they would forego various 'exorbitant privileges' thereby. India can afford to take a more objective view and become an advocate for the SDR. In practice, this would mean keeping it alive as a reserve asset, and removing its various disadvantages, so that if the multi-currency system ran into trouble, the SDR would be available to step in. The main disadvantage of the SDR is that its supply cannot be increased without the approval of governments with at least 85 per cent of votes in the IMF. This means that an increase can be blocked by the United States or the European countries as a bloc. India should work towards mobilizing the emerging and developing countries in the IMF to amending the Articles so that all decisions that require 85 per cent super-majorities can be taken with, say, 67 per cent super-majorities instead. As things stand, the United States and the EU have a stranglehold on IMF decision-making.[30]

The third problem with the IMS is volatility of capital flows, which has the potential to cause financial havoc. Capital controls are a measure that attacks this problem directly. They used to be regarded by the IMF as beyond the pale but India has maintained them, even after overall liberalization, to good effect. This is a case where the IMF's position has moved closer to India's over the years. The IMF now recognizes that capital controls may be necessary to defend national financial stability. The East Asian crisis of 1997 was partly responsible for the change of view. More recently, in the aftermath of the GFC, this was reinforced by the experience of the highly expansionary monetary policies (including so-called 'quantitative easing' [QE]) that were undertaken by central banks in the advanced countries. When the US Fed introduced the second round of QE in 2010, many emerging counties were threatened with huge and disruptive capital inflows. Several of them (e.g. Brazil, South Korea, Thailand, Indonesia) introduced capital inflow controls to prevent their currencies from rising to uncompetitive levels. (On this occasion, India did not do so, and paid for it dearly, as seen in Chapter 8.) In the summer of 2013, the reverse happened. The Fed hinted that it would begin tapering down QE; this time there were large capital outflows from emerging markets; some responded by reversing inflow controls (e.g. Brazil) or introducing outflow controls (e.g. India).

The IMF has acknowledged that liberalization of the capital account 'may not be the right goal for all countries at all times' but it wants to establish multilateral 'rules of the game' for capital controls since they may have harmful spill-over effects on other countries. For example capital inflow controls may act as a 'beggar-my-neighbour' policy by keeping the imposing country's exchange rate more depreciated than it would otherwise be. In practice, it would be impossible to lay down operationally useful criteria to distinguish benign from harmful capital controls. There is a danger that the 'rules of the game' may degenerate into rigidly applied tick-boxes, which harass small countries that do not have clout with the IMF. Moreover, fair symmetry surely requires that capital flow problems should be tackled 'at both ends', i.e. in source countries as well as recipient countries. But there is little hope of that since central banks such as the US Fed will not agree to be constrained in their use of monetary policy. So, India has quite rightly been lukewarm about establishing multilateral rules for capital controls.

International Trade

India's trade policy, which had been highly protectionist for three decades from the mid-1950s, became much more open after the advent of economic reform. But the country's position in the conduct of international trade negotiations was broadly unchanged. India continued to be highly circumspect, even negative, about accepting binding agreements for trade liberalization. While it unilaterally cut its 'applied' tariffs after 1991, it reduced its 'bound' tariffs much less; and in services too, its liberalization was far greater *de facto* than *de jure*. Behind the caution was an intense desire to guard the country's sovereignty and to maximize policy space (including preserving the freedom to reverse liberalization selectively). Another aspect of continuity was India's role as spokesperson for developing countries. In the 1970s, it had been one of the key actors in the GATT, helping to secure 'special and differential treatment' for the third world. Again, after the WTO came into being in 1994, it played a major role in preventing a broadening of the trade agenda to cover 'behind the border issues' such as government procurement, competition, and investment.

Going forward, should India maintain its defensive stance? I think not. There cannot any longer be any doubt that India's national interest lies in promoting an open global economy. India needs expanding markets for its exports, free entry for outward investment by its multinationals, and easier restrictions on temporary emigrants from its shores. In order to secure these conditions, it will have to be willing to offer reciprocal concessions to other countries. In textbook economics, a strong case is made that it is in a country's interest to liberalize unilaterally. However, the national interest is even better served if other countries liberalize as well. So, countries tend to use their own trade liberalization as a bargaining chip to persuade other countries to liberalize. Indeed, that is the very basis of the WTO. As it happens, for several decades in the second half of the last century, this logic was in abeyance for the developing countries. They had a free ride because the advanced countries were willing to liberalize without expecting a *quid pro quo*. That era is now winding down and India's strategy of 'unilateral liberalization without binding commitment' has probably run its course.[31] In the new climate, India's traditional strategy would end up depriving it of a lever for opening up foreign markets.[32]

It follows that India should be more active than hitherto in securing reciprocal trade agreements. In doing so, it will have to take account of an important change in the trade landscape. This is the waning importance of multilateral negotiations in the WTO and the corresponding spread of preferential trade agreements (PTAs). Orthodox free traders rightly regard this as a retrograde development. The standard argument is that while trading blocs create trade between participants, they also divert trade from non-participants, which may be cheaper sources of supply; as a result, the net benefits from PTAs may be negative not only for non-participants but for participants as well. Even so, PTAs have proliferated. The number of PTAs in the world economy has shot up from 70 in 1990 to around 350 in 2013. (According to the WTO, every country, except Mongolia, is part of at least one PTA!)

This suggests that PTAs are undertaken for motives such as the desire to bind partner countries to lower and more stable levels of 'behind the border' barriers to trade. The desire follows quite naturally from the growth of 'offshoring', 'global supply chains', and 'international fragmentation of production'. It is now quite usual to find manufactured products whose parts and components are made in several different countries and assembled in yet another country, with only design and coordination functions performed in the home-country headquarters. Though India is as yet largely uninvolved, 'network trade' is estimated to account for around 50 per cent of the world trade in manufactured goods. As such trade has increased, so has the need for disciplines on 'behind the border' items such as competition, investment, and intellectual property; and these are much easier to negotiate successfully in PTAs than in multilateral settings. At the same time, multilateral negotiations have proved to be extremely slow and unproductive. The WTO is an unwieldy body with 160 countries. It has so far worked mostly on the basis of consensus approval of 'single undertaking' agendas, a procedure whereby nothing is agreed until everything is agreed by all members. This worked better when advanced countries were overwhelmingly dominant in world trade. They could make deals among themselves, and developing countries either acquiesced or were bought off by 'special and differential treatment'. Now, developing countries account for more than half of world trade and some of them, India included, have the clout to block agreements. Moreover, the advanced countries are no longer interested in offering differential treatment. As a result, the WTO has moved at the pace of a tortoise and has been able to agree only on relatively minor issues. The recent accord in Bali (December 2013) is a good example. It was the first agreement in the WTO's 18-year history but all it produced was a 'trade facilitation agreement' (TFA) to reduce customs red tape: all the more substantive issues relevant to reducing protection in agriculture and industry had already been taken off the agenda. (In the event, even the TFA was nearly scuppered, by none other than India. Fortunately, it went ahead in 2014 when India agreed to sign after extracting an indefinite pass for its agricultural support programmes.)

India was a latecomer to PTAs and signed up to only one before 2000. Since then, it has frenetically signed 15 (see Table 12.7). Many of these are bilateral agreements with single countries, the major exceptions being the PTAs with ASEAN and with MERCOSUR.[33] According to the Ministry of Commerce, 17 more are being negotiated. Some of these are brand-new; others are expansions of existing ones to turn them into so-called Comprehensive Economic Cooperation/Partnership Agreements, which have a broader compass than trade. It is very doubtful if this blitz of trade agreements, mostly bilateral and with unimportant countries, has been worth the trouble, especially as most of them have long lists of 'exceptions' to the products covered, as well as complicated 'rules of origin'. Far more fruitful, if they were successful, would be the India-EU Trade and Investment Agreement that is being negotiated (but the negotiations are currently stalled), and the Regional Comprehensive Economic Partnership (RCEP) in East Asia, which is supposed to include ASEAN plus six other countries (Australia, China, India, Japan, South Korea, and New Zealand). If these agreements came to pass, they would be major extensions of India's global engagement, since the countries involved account for a significant share of global trade. Eight of the 16 countries in the RCEP are also participants, along with others, in negotiating with the United States to form the Trans-Pacific Partnership (TPP). In October 2015, the TPP negotiations were successfully concluded though the agreement is still awaiting ratification by national legislatures, including the US Congress.[34] TPP excludes both China and India. On the other side of the world, the United States is also negotiating a Transatlantic Trade and Investment Partnership (TTIP) with the EU. One of the aims of the United States was said to be to present the negotiated TPP and TTIP, which would cover well over half of

Table 12.7 INDIA'S TRADE AGREEMENTS

Before 1990	1
1990–1999	0
2000–2005	3
2006–2013	12
Under Negotiation	17

Source: Government of India, Ministry of Commerce.

world trade, as *faits accomplis*, which the rest of the world, including China and India, would then have to accept, along with the disciplines negotiated therein. However, things have moved on because China is itself angling to be involved in the US-led mega-regionals. One development that is being mooted is an extension of the TPP to include all the 21 members of the Asia Pacific Economic Cooperation (APEC) forum that are not already part of it. (China is part of APEC.) An even more comprehensive entity that is being envisaged is the Free Trade Area of the Asia Pacific (FTAAP). China has indicated that it would like to negotiate its own entry into the TPP, and is also canvassing the formation of the FTAAP, into which both the TPP and the RCEP could be incorporated.

The advent of the mega-regionals confronts India with a major challenge.[35] When completed, these agreements would potentially cover more than two-thirds of world trade and set its rules for years to come. If India missed the bus, it could suffer trade diversion, especially in services trade, as well as having to put up with trade disciplines in whose shape and content it had played no part. (The losses would be greater if China joined the US-led mega-regionals.) Correspondingly, India could gain substantially if it engaged fully with the new entities.[36] It could acquire markets for exports of services and manufactured goods (including, crucially, labour-intensive manufactures such as textiles) and a much-needed entry into global value chains. Exposure to cheaper imports and higher standards could well spur productivity growth, directly, as well as indirectly by catalysing domestic reform efforts. Thus, India urgently needs to devise a strategy to deal with the PTA jig-saw. In my judgement, the safest course, because it would hedge all bets, would be try and energize the slow-moving RCEP talks but simultaneously open negotiations to join APEC, with a view to a possible entry into the TPP, and eventually into the FTAAP, if the latter became a reality.[37] At the same time, India should shift away from negotiating shallow bilateral agreements with all and sundry. A revival of India-EU negotiations would also be very desirable. None of this would be possible without a change in India's aversion to making meaningful trade concessions (to secure meaningful concessions in return).

That said, mega-regionals led by the major advanced countries have various downsides that must be guarded against. Their emphasis on 'deep', behind-the-borders integration has the potential to smuggle in rules and regulations that reflect the interests of powerful lobby groups in the United States and the EU. For example, the TPP goes well beyond existing bilateral and multilateral agreements on protection of intellectual property. This could have damaging implications for India's generic pharmaceutical industry, and more generally for the availability of affordable medicines in

developing countries. The same goes for the labour and environmental s'
dards in the TPP, and the requirements it imposes with regard to freedo
capital movements, which do not necessarily conform to India's preferences
and needs. There are also systemic issues. A world in which the WTO is mar-
ginalized would have costs for all countries. The trading system would lack
a common forum in which trade issues could be discussed and trade-offs
negotiated. Moreover, the excellent and well-functioning dispute settlement mechanism for trade issues, which is administered by the WTO, could
be thrown into confusion and disarray when mega-regionals introduce their
own competing mechanisms, with the attendant danger that world trade
governance would become more power-based and less rules-based.

India has to tread a careful path. On the one hand, it has to face the
fact that mega-regionals are here to stay. It cannot afford to shun them
altogether on grounds of high-minded principle: the danger of isolation
is very real, especially if China joins the TPP. On the other hand, it must
not be a pushover in negotiations on matters where it has cogent reasons
for taking a different view from the advanced countries. This would not be
unduly difficult. It is a large country, with a large market that major countries would want to access, so it holds strong cards in its hand that it must
put to good use. At the same time, it would not be sensible to abandon the
WTO route altogether since there is no certainty that the current trend
towards PTAs will not end up in a morass of exclusionary trade blocs, which
will have to be 'multilateralized' in due course. Moreover, the WTO is not
completely fossilized. It has now adapted itself to encompass 'plurilateral'
agreements in which a group of countries can come to a trade agreement
on a specific issue, provided it remains open for other countries to join. The
conclusion, untidy though it is, has to be that India has to advance on all
fronts, unilateral, multilateral, plurilateral, and preferential. In the following paragraphs, I leave it open which of these routes is the most desirable.
The choice of route may vary with the issue in question.[38]

Consider first the core trade issues in industry, agriculture, and services. In *industry*, India's interest in reciprocal tariff reduction needs no
further elaboration. In *agriculture*, India has so far been extremely cautious
because of concerns about food security for India's large poor population.
It has accordingly maintained a huge wedge between bound and applied
tariffs, and made frequent use of changes in tariffs and export controls to
keep domestic prices low. But this policy needs rethinking. As explained
in Chapter 6, India now has a comparative advantage in a wide variety of
agricultural products. This advantage could be realized by allowing producer
prices to be aligned with international prices. Of course this will have implications for consumers but their interests could and should be protected by

a) income transfers to poor consumers and b) negotiated 'safeguards' that allow changes in tariffs and export duties, if world price changes exceed pre-determined thresholds. In *services* too, a more flexible posture would help. WTO terminology divides services into four 'modes'. India has an obvious interest in Mode 1 ('cross-border supply') because of its dynamic software services sector, which needs assured market access in the face of fears in the advanced countries about employment disappearing offshore. It has a similar obvious interest in Mode 4 ('movement of natural persons') to capitalise on exports of professional and construction services. Mode 2 ('consumption abroad') and Mode 3 ('commercial presence') were thought to be less important but this is changing. In Mode 2, health and educational services, as well as tourism, are areas of interest for foreign exchange earnings. In Mode 3, India's outward FDI would benefit from low and stable restrictions. None of these advantages could be secured without bargaining (which could be both within and across 'modes') for reciprocal concessions. India will get what it needs only if it stands ready to open its markets in return.

Discussions in the WTO have also covered several 'trade-related' items such as intellectual property, government procurement, competition policy, investment regulation, environment, and labour; and, as already noted, these issues have acquired even more prominence in PTA negotiations. India has been very reluctant so far to enter into agreements on these matters. In some cases, this has been sensible. For example, India has quite rightly fought attempts to bring labour issues into the WTO since 'harmonization of labour rights' is often a cloak for naked protectionism by labour unions in the West. Domestic environmental issues too are best left outside the WTO because countries differ greatly in their preferences in this area.[39] A global environmental issue like climate change is a different matter. It will need, among other measures, an international agreement to reduce carbon emissions, and trade restrictions may have to play a part in enforcing it. It would obviously be important to agree on the appropriate rules. India should, in its own interest, participate in such rule-making. On other trade-related issues too, a blanket negative response is no longer in India's interest. In intellectual property, many of the country's dynamic firms, even in the pharmaceuticals industry, now want patent protection in foreign markets. In government procurement, Indian firms want to be able to compete on an equal footing for government contracts in foreign countries. As regards competition, India's exporters want competitive markets in foreign countries, and on the import side India would be helped by action against foreign export cartels. On investment, India has an interest because outward FDI has become an important feature of the investment plans of its companies.

In the above list of items, there are two, services and government procurement, which are of special interest because there are existing plurilateral agreements pertaining to them, viz. the Trade in Services Agreement (TISA) and the Agreement on Government Procurement (GPA). In my judgement, India would be wise to seek admission. India is a major exporter of services and surely needs to be in TISA to secure foreign market access. The GPA too would create opportunities because, as a low-cost supplier, India is in a good position to bid for government contracts in its 50 or so member countries. Of course, India could secure its interests only by offering concessions in return.[40] India should not be a sucker in these negotiations. It should negotiate hard but it must also bear in mind that sovereignty is not an absolute value, and it may be beneficial in the national interest to cede it partially to make advantageous bargains.

NOTES

1. The first three sections of this chapter rely heavily on Joshi and Kapur (2014).
2. 'Applied tariff' means the actual tariff rate. This may be lower than the 'bound tariff', which is the tariff rate that the country has made a binding WTO commitment not to exceed.
3. 'Bound' tariffs in agriculture remain much higher than applied tariffs (see below).
4. 2011 and 2012 were exceptions to this general statement. In these years the current account deficit widened sharply to around 4.5 per cent of GDP. This episode has been analysed in some detail in Chapter 8.
5. See Athukorala (2014).
6. However, China's FDI inflows are much more impressive than India's. This can be explained, though only partially, by the fact that reform in India began 10 years later than China.
7. See Athukorala (2009).
8. However, as this book goes to press, Tata is about to wind up its steel business in the UK, a casualty of the glut of Chinese steel in world markets.
9. In 2011, the central government announced its decision to permit up to 51 per cent FDI in multi-brand retail and then backtracked in the face of opposition. In September 2012, it re-introduced the measure and enacted it, with an option for each state to go along with it or not. It remains a politically sensitive issue for the Modi government, given the fears of displacement of retail traders (who are among its strong supporters).
10. However, since 2012 there has been significant liberalization of debt inflows. In my judgement, this is a hostage to fortune (see Chapter 8).
11. See Bhagwati and Panagariya (2013), Panagariya (2004), Goldberg, Khandelwal, Pavenik. and Topalova (2009), Nataraj (2011), and Topalova and Khandelwal (2011).
12. This point has been discussed at some length in Chapter 8. See also Joshi (2003a, 2003b), Joshi and Sanyal (2004), and Joshi (2008).

13. See Chapter 5.
14. There is somewhat greater ambiguity about the distributional impact of globalization across Indian states, socio-economic groups, and the rural-urban divide. Some studies have claimed that in rural districts whose industries were relatively more exposed to liberalization, poverty reduction was adversely affected, principally due to very limited factor mobility across sectors and states (see Topalova 2007). But this is a strongly disputed matter and other studies do not find such effects (see Hasan, Mitra, and Ural 2007). Moreover, with time, factor mobility has improved and growth-divergence across Indian states has fallen.
15. This paragraph, and the one that follows, rely heavily on Kapur (2010a).
16. The large remittances into India that have resulted from international migration have also mitigated the effects of external shocks through a range of mechanisms, from increased consumption to provision of social insurance, at both the household and national level. (For instance, remittances enhanced India's ability to withstand sanctions imposed in the aftermath of its nuclear tests.) Remittances have also had significant distributional consequences, affecting income inequalities across states, social groups, and households. In the state of Kerala, remittances account for nearly a quarter of state net domestic product and appear also to have had considerable effects on policy incentives. (These effects were not always beneficial. The income uplift provided by remittances may have reduced public pressure for desirable policy change.) However, while labour flows from Kerala were dominant in the 1970s and 1980s, by 2010 Uttar Pradesh had emerged as the largest state for low-skilled international labour outflows.
17. See Kapur (2012).
18. Between 2003 and 2010, India provided $5.1 billion in lines of credit, of which $3.3 billion went to Africa and $1.8 billion to South Asia. In May 2011, India announced $5 billion of low-interest loans over the next three years for Africa and an additional $1 billion to pay for education, railways, and peacekeeping, a massive increase from the $25 million that India provided as aid to Africa a year ago. India also provided $2.1 billion to its South Asian neighbors in grants and loans and $346 million to other developing countries. In addition, it has emerged as a significant contributor to multilateral assistance, through financial contributions to the UN system and multilateral organizations. It remains to be seen whether India will try to marshal its limited foreign aid resources through bilateral channels, and those small multilateral institutions where it has a leadership role, or operate through large global institutions where its voice is relatively limited.
19. See Joshi (2009), Joshi and Patel (2009), and Kapur, Khosla, and Mehta (2009).
20. The main ratios mandated by Basel III for banks are as follows: i) the minimum ratio of capital to risk-weighted assets (CRWA) goes up from 8 per cent to 10.5 per cent, of which the extra 2.5 per cent is a 'capital conservation buffer'; ii) the common equity component of CRWA goes up from 2.0 to 4.5 percentage points (7 per cent inclusive of the capital conservation buffer); iii) on top of the CRWA there is to be a 'counter-cyclical buffer' of up to 2.5 percentage points, to be imposed by policymakers, if necessary, for 'macro-prudential purposes' (to moderate a boom); iv) separately from all of the above, banks will have to maintain a minimum leverage ratio (i.e. ratio of equity capital to assets not weighted by risk). The imposition of (iv) is designed to act as a back-stop

against the possibility of banks gaming the calculation of risk-weights. The Basel Committee has said that it is minded, after a trial run, to impose a leverage ratio of 3.0. The Committee also proposes to impose in due course an additional capital surcharge on 'systemically important' banks.

21. The RBI has decided to impose a minimum common equity requirement that is one percentage point higher than the Basel standard. So, Indian banks will have to attain a minimum equity requirement of 5.5 per cent of CRWA, and a CRWA of 11.5 per cent by 2018. The RBI has also indicated that it plans to introduce a leverage ratio of 4.5. Indian banks will have to raise a substantial amount of capital (up to 3.5 per cent of 2013 GDP) in the next few years to meet these standards. This will be extremely challenging, given the present ownership and governance structure of public sector banks (see Chapter 7).

22. It may be feared that adhering to Basel standards would raise the cost of credit, which would hurt growth. But the alternative of a risky banking system would surely be extremely undesirable. Moreover, the cost of Basel III would not have to be borne by depositors and borrowers if bank efficiency improved and the cost of intermediation came down. In India, there is plenty of scope for this, as indicated by the net interest margin of 3 per cent in Indian banks, which is very high by international standards. Note also Gupta (2015), which shows, using Indian bank data for 1997–2007, that banks with higher CRWAs have higher profitability and do *not* exhibit higher interest rates on loans.

23. China also sterilized the monetary effects of these surpluses to prevent an erosion of export competitiveness via inflation, thus blocking an alternative route to current account adjustment. On the global exchange rate regime see Joshi (2006).

24. Countries prefer owned to borrowed reserves because the latter can evaporate in a crisis (because it may not be possible to roll over the borrowing).

25. The Fed's swaps expired in 2010. It then reauthorized them (and later converted them into standing arrangements) for only six countries, none of which were emerging or developing countries.

26. In 2010, the IMF approved a package that included a doubling of quotas (to around $750 billion) and a realignment of quotas (and thus of voting power) to reduce the share of Europe and increase the share of the BRICS countries (Brazil, China, India, Russia, and South Africa). But the package could not come into effect without ratification by the legislatures of member countries with at least 85 per cent of the votes, and the United States has more than 15 per cent of votes (see Woods 2014). After a delay of five years, the US Congress has finally agreed to ratify the reform. The 2010 agreement called for another IMF quota review by the end of 2014 but that has been stalled and is unlikely to happen any time soon.

27. In 2014, India joined the other BRICS countries to set up a development bank and a 'contingency reserve fund' to share currency reserves. But the latter is miniscule in size. See Steil (2014).

28. Triffin (1960).

29. The IMF decided at the end of 2015 to include the renminbi in the SDR basket. This is an important staging post on the way to the renminbi becoming a reserve currency.

30. If BRICS and other emerging countries had presented a united front, they could have secured substantial changes in IMF governance after the 2008 crisis, when they became major lenders to the IMF, and European countries became major borrowers.

31. This is certainly true for emerging countries such as India. However, a consensus still remains that the 'least developed countries' should continue to enjoy 'special and differential treatment'.

32. A greater willingness to get into reciprocal binding agreements may also bring some internal political-economy advantages, since it would harness the interests of exporters and outward investors in building support for trade liberalization.

33. The members of ASEAN are: Brunei, Cambodia, Indonesia, Laos, Malaysia, Myanmar, Philippines, Singapore, Thailand, and Vietnam. MERCOSUR has the following members: Argentina, Brazil, Paraguay, Uruguay, and Venezuela.

34. All the major Republican and Democratic candidates for the US presidency in 2016 are making noises against the TPP. These electioneering postures are likely to be reversed in office by an incoming president.

35. See Kelkar and Singh (2015).

36. On one estimate, which may be over-optimistic, India's national income would be permanently 25 per cent higher if it joined the TPP as well as the FTAAP, and its exports would be permanently 60 per cent higher, with the gains phased in over 10 years (see Bergsten 2015). Bergsten's forceful paper is marred by an overly aggressive stance in favour of US-led mega-regionals.

37. The United States, Japan, and Australia have signalled that they would welcome India's entry into APEC but so far without a response from India.

38. India should also be put its weight behind moves to improve WTO governance. The 'consensus procedures' of the WTO have probably had their day.

39. However, India cannot avoid engaging with these issues in the mega-regionals. The right course is to negotiate hard and influence the rules, not stand out altogether and suffer having rules imposed by *force majeure*.

40. Binding agreements may further domestic reform. For example, allowing foreign firms to compete for government procurement contracts may help to reduce costs and corruption. And a competition agreement may strengthen the hand of the Competition Commission in enforcing India's competition laws.

PART V

The Future

Long Is the Way, and Hard . . .

CHAPTER 13

What Is to Be Done? What Lies Ahead?

It is now common ground among all informed observers that the highly protectionist, highly controlled 'Old India Model' that guided economic policy in the first three decades after independence was, in large part, a failure. Its convoluted regulations on economic activity stifled enterprise and resulted in slow growth of national income which was also not shared by the mass of the people. Fortunately, the model was abandoned, at first gingerly in the 1980s, and then more definitively in the 1990s. The response was indisputably dramatic. India's national income has grown at more than 6 per cent a year (around 4 per cent a year per capita) during the past three decades, a major achievement that puts it in the select club of the world's fastest-growing countries. Even so, in the recent past, the momentum of advance has shown distinct and disturbing signs of running out of steam. If India is to make a rapid ascent to prosperity, it needs to undertake more sweeping reform of a deeper variety.

This chapter concludes the book and is organized as follows. The first section explains the need and rationale for radical reform. The second section sets out the main features of the radical reform agenda that, in my judgement, should govern future economic policy. In so doing, I bring together the threads of the argument advanced in previous chapters (though, inevitably, without the accompanying detail and nuance). The same section also appraises the performance of the Modi government two years into its term of office in the light of the said reform agenda. In the third and final section, I end with some reflections about the likely shape of India's future.

RADICAL REFORM: RATIONALE AND SETTING

Economic policy after 1980, and especially after 1991, followed what I have called a 'Partial Reform Model'. Its focus was mainly on deregulating goods markets and, to a lesser extent, financial markets. To this end, restrictions on foreign trade and investment were liberalized. Investment licensing was abolished and the reservation of hundreds of items for production by small-scale firms was progressively scrapped. A beginning was made in liberalizing interest rates and reducing government capture of bank credit. Even so, the process of change did not go nearly far enough. In many crucial respects, the reforms remained incoherent and incomplete; and as a result, some of the tangled undergrowth of institutions, policies, and laws bequeathed by the Old India Model has continued to impede the country's progress.

To become a prosperous nation, India needs super-fast and high-quality growth for the next two or three decades. If per capita income in India grew at 7 per cent a year from 2016 onwards, it would reach in 24 years a level of $28,000 a year at today's prices, measured at purchasing power parity. This would put India in 2040 at about the same per capita level of income that countries at the top of the lowest quartile of high-income countries (such as Greece or Portugal) enjoy today. This would surely be a very satisfactory outcome. However, such a feat, which would require rapid and continuous productivity improvements over a long period, is of a magnitude that the vast majority of countries in the world have found to be beyond their capacity (see Chapter 1). There can be little doubt that the Partial Reform Model has left India unprepared for undertaking such a massive endeavour.

The basic flaw of the Partial Reform Model is a failure to put the role of the state, and the relation between the state, the market, and the private sector, on the right footing—a failure that continues to this day. There is, in India, an overall lack of clarity about the economic borders of the state, in other words about what the government should own, finance, regulate, produce (these various aspects do not have to go together), or leave well alone. The Indian state is still too much of a jack of all trades. It now needs to master those that lie in its proper province. Deeper liberalization is necessary to release business energy and allow the market to perform its dynamic and allocative role, combined with 'smart regulation' to correct market failures. Smart regulation would recognize that 'government failure' can be as harmful as market failure. It would be accurate, transparent, and independent of vested interests from outside and from within the state itself. This kind of regulation is an art that India has yet to learn. A key function of the state is to enable individuals and society to flourish by ensuring the provision of pure public goods and 'public services' for all citizens, and a robust safety-net to protect them from extreme poverty. Pure public goods must certainly be *paid for* by the state because the market is incapable of doing so, and this is often also true of public services that the poor cannot afford to buy. But it does not follow that the state must necessarily *produce and deliver* public services or even pure public goods. This may sometimes be done more efficiently by private markets, although some contracting or regulation would almost always be necessary. Nonetheless, there remain plenty of things that the state and only the state can do. Unfortunately, the Indian state has shown itself unequal to the challenge of discharging core tasks. This is partly because it has taken on too much that is outside its proper domain. But it is also in part because its implementation capacity is deficient and has atrophied over time; and it is, in addition, subject to corruption and crony capitalism on an extensive scale. These shortcomings are serious enough to hamper, perhaps even to wreck, India's prospects for rapid and inclusive growth. The implication is that the state urgently needs to reform itself. A radical reform agenda would have to address all these deficiencies.

Economic reform has to take account of the setting and context in which it is undertaken. Three points are relevant though I do not have the space to discuss them in detail. The first concerns India's ambition to be a 'global power'. It would surely be unwise to elevate this desire to the status of a national objective (see Chapter 1). India has size in its favour. It will become a global power quite naturally if it achieves its economic goals. The country's most important foreign policy goals should be a) to maintain a balance of power, especially in the Asian theatre, that would prevent the country's economic ascent being scuppered by hostile states and b) to play a full part in the institutions of global economic governance so that it can take advantage of world trade and finance to support economic development. More ambitious foreign policy goals would be a distraction from the development agenda.

The second point is about the global economic environment that confronts India. This promises to be unfavourable. Though the United States may perhaps be recovering from the global credit crisis, Europe and Japan are not. China is slowing down sharply, which does not bode well for growth in Europe and in various emerging countries, especially those that rely on commodity exports. Perhaps even more important is another problem: the advanced countries may well be suffering from so-called 'secular stagnation' that will slow their medium- and long-term growth in the coming decades.[1] Deflationary winds are blowing hard in the global economy.

The implication for India is that it cannot, very probably, count on any tail-wind from the world economy to support its growth, let alone to boost it. This only reinforces the case for radical reform.

The third point is more speculative and concerns domestic political economy. Economic strategies that put a heavy reliance on a strong and capable state have to contend with the facts of Indian history, culture, and political development. Historically, India has been a weak state, unlike some other countries, such as China, which have a long tradition of central-ized rule.[2] Post-independence development in India stressed intrusive and centralized state intervention but the outcomes were far from encourag-ing. I think there is a germ of truth in the idea that statist solutions do not go with the grain of Indian history. This creates a presumption in favour of India adopting decentralized and market solutions to problems, not statist command and control.[3]

The main responsibility for economic reform rests with the national government though state governments are also increasingly important. In May 2014, on the crest of a 'Modi wave', the BJP won a small absolute majority in the Lok Sabha (LS), and the NDA (i.e. BJP plus its allied parties) won a sizeable majority. The NDA was, however, in a minority in the Rajya Sabha (RS), where it controlled only around a third of the seats. Its prime ministerial candidate, Narendra Modi, campaigned on the theme of *vikaas* (economic development) and delivery of *achche din* (good days) to come. He was widely regarded as a strong, decisive leader who would reverse the paralysis that in popular perception had overtaken policy-making. Though the government does not have a majority in the RS, the latter cannot hold up money bills. Moreover, quite a lot can be done without new legislation, simply on the basis of 'executive action'. Lack of a majority in the RS was also not a completely new problem: other governments in the past have faced it quite successfully by using their negotiating skills. It was therefore widely expected that the new government would undertake a programme of sweeping economic reform. As this book goes to press, the Modi govern-ment has been in power for nearly two years. Enough time has passed to enable a preliminary assessment of its economic performance.

An important caveat is necessary at this point. Any criticism that I make of the Modi government should not be interpreted as commenda-tion of the previous Congress-led government. The present condition of the Indian state and the Indian economy is the result of actions for which both the present and previous governments are responsible. I focus on the Modi government because I am interested in how the country should move forward from its present position, not in dispensing praise or blame for the past.[4]

There would surely be wide agreement that the objective of economic reform in India should be to achieve 'rapid, inclusive, stable, and sustainable growth within a political framework of liberal democracy'. (I sometimes refer to this briefly as 'high-quality growth'.) I have argued in this book that to achieve this objective, radical reform is essential. In my view, the main requirements of a radical reform model can be grouped under the following seven headings: a) Macroeconomic Stability; b) Investment Climate; c) 'Deep Fiscal Adjustment' and a Universal Basic Income; d) Markets, Ownership, and Regulation; e) External Economic Engagement; f) Social Protection and Enablement; and g) Reform of the State. These areas are not wholly exclusive categories. They have plenty of overlap as well as strong interdependencies but it is nevertheless useful to examine them separately. The temptation to rank-order them in importance should be resisted. They are all indispensable components of the reform package and it would be foolish to ignore any of them. The main policy shifts that are called for in each area, and the Modi government's performance in undertaking them, are discussed below. So what follows can also act as a structured summary of large parts of the book. Some recent policy changes (between December 2015 and March 2016) are briefly discussed in various end-notes.

MACROECONOMIC STABILITY

Macroeconomic stability, comprising internal balance, external balance, and fiscal sustainability, is a pure public good that only the state or its subsidiary organs such as the central bank can deliver.[5] It is also a necessary requirement for rapid growth, as underlined in India by the painful consequences of instability in the first half of the 2010s (see Chapter 8).

On *internal balance*, India must surely accept the truth that inflation above a threshold level (in India around 4 to 5 per cent a year) has no long-run growth pay-off. While the fight against inflation requires various supporting policies such as fiscal prudence and improved supply management, a credible monetary anchor is a critical condition of success. (The bout of high inflation after 2008 had several causes but its persistence owed much to the fact that there was no such anchor, and the RBI chose to pursue a soft monetary policy in an environment of growing indexation and rampant inflationary expectations.) To keep inflation in check, India should adopt 'flexible inflation targeting', along with its usual supporting institutions. In such an arrangement, the government chooses the inflation target but the central bank has full operational independence to achieve it.[6]

The objective of *external balance* boils down to aiming for a current account deficit that can be financed safely and sustainably, say an average of 2 per cent of GDP, and more generally, to make the economy less vulnerable to crises caused by volatile capital flows. For this purpose, inflation control is obviously important but so is the exchange rate regime. India should continue with the tried and tested regime of 'managed floating' of the exchange rate. Contrary to some purist views, inflation targeting and a managed float of the exchange rate are not incompatible, if they are supported by some focused capital controls and occasional foreign exchange intervention, sterilized or unsterilized as necessary. (This could be called a regime of 'managed floating plus'.)

Fiscal sustainability is the third leg of the tripod that supports a stable macro-economy. India suffers from excessive fiscal deficits and government debt. They need to be reduced gradually in order to maintain confidence in national solvency, prevent crowding out of private investment, and preserve fiscal space for countercyclical policy. However, India also faces another fiscal problem, separate from fiscal consolidation. To promote inclusive growth, it needs to make a root-and-branch change in the pattern and composition of government expenditure and taxation (see the section on 'deep fiscal adjustment' below).

The Modi Government and Macroeconomic Stability

Before coming to the Modi government's performance on longer-term reform in this area, something needs to be said about its short-term macroeconomic management of the economy. The government has performed creditably though much credit also goes to good luck. Soon after the government came into office in May 2014, global oil prices crashed and ended up at around $50 a barrel, roughly half the level in the previous year. (They have fallen even further since then.) This had an enormously favourable impact on all the three major macroeconomic concerns: inflation, current account deficit, and fiscal deficit.[7] The oil-price fall put significant downward pressure on inflation, directly and indirectly. But the Reserve Bank also played a key role in bringing down inflation by tightening the monetary stance (though a start had been made a few months before the Modi government came in). Inflation is now running at about 5 per cent a year, a welcome relief from several years at twice that rate, and it has enabled the Reserve Bank to begin reducing nominal interest rates.[8]

The oil price decline also made a direct contribution to reducing the current account deficit since India is a huge net importer of oil. In 2015, the deficit was down to a very safe level of around 1 per cent of GDP. Satisfaction has to be qualified, however, since exports have collapsed (though imports have fallen even more due to the growth slowdown). Slow growth of world activity and trade partly accounts for the miserable export performance. But it is notable that the real effective exchange rate has been allowed to appreciate quite substantially in 2014 and 2015. This implies some departure from the policy of 'managed floating' to preserve trade competitiveness. In my opinion, this is unwise. As and when there is a strong recovery, the trade deficit could widen dangerously if exports continue to languish.

Fiscal policy has been sensible. The Modi government stepped up public investment in 2015 to combat the economic slowdown that it had inherited; it also increased slightly the net transfer to the states, following its acceptance of the recommendations of the 14th Finance Commission. And it was able to do these things while deviating only slightly from the pre-agreed path of fiscal consolidation in 2015/16 (see Chapter 8) because the oil price windfall made possible both a reduction in fuel subsidies and a hike in excise taxes on fuel products, without raising consumer prices. Though no hard political decisions were necessary, the technocratic decisions were good, for which the government deserves credit.[9]

In sum, since the Modi government took office, there has been a definite improvement in macroeconomic stability. But macro-policy is also about revival of private investment and reversal of economic slowdown. These hoped-for outcomes have been conspicuous by their absence (see the section on 'investment climate' below). So the record on macroeconomic policy is by no means unblemished.[10]

What about reform of the long-term policy framework for macro-stability? On internal balance, one of the Modi government's good decisions was to adopt a regime of 'inflation targeting'. Of course, the ground had been prepared by the publication of the landmark Urjit Patel committee report in early 2014. The Modi government took the idea seriously even though it involved a surrender of its power to intervene in monetary policy. In February 2015, there was an agreement between the Finance Ministry and the RBI, which gave the latter the operational authority to achieve an agreed inflation target (see Chapter 8). Discussions on setting up a 'monetary policy committee' are ongoing, and some items such as the composition of the committee are as yet undecided.[11] While inflation targeting is definitely a step forward in macro-management, its efficacy could be considerably improved by reforms in the transmission mechanism of monetary policy. As of now, transmission is rather poor. (For example, only half of the interest reductions that the RBI undertook in 2015 were passed on by the banks to their customers.) Poor transmission arises from the constraints imposed on commercial banks by various structural characteristics of the system, including interest rates fixed by the government on small savings (together with associated tax concessions), a high statutory liquidity ratio, and interest rate subventions for specified activities that the banks are forced to provide. These are all features of 'financial repression' that should be removed over the medium term. There needs to be a programme, agreed between the RBI and the government, to phase out the distortions along with fiscal consolidation.[12]

In the policy framework for external balance, the main component is the exchange rate regime. As seen above, the Reserve Bank seems to have abandoned the policy of using the exchange rate to maintain export competitiveness. This is surely a mistake. It should return to a regime of 'managed floating plus' to prevent excessive real appreciation. This would be the right exchange rate regime for India until growth of employment and exports is on a firmer footing, and fiscal consolidation and financial sector reform are further advanced. In my view, the RBI should lean less towards liberalization of capital flows and more towards a competitive exchange rate than it has been doing of late.

As regards the fiscal policy framework, the frequent chopping, changing, and amending of fiscal rules and targets, as seen in the past decade or more, is surely bad for the government's credibility. India needs a new and revamped fiscal responsibility act that establishes a time-path for deficit reduction that consists of declining annual bands within which various deficit magnitudes (such as overall, revenue, and primary deficits) each year should lie, depending on both the cyclical condition of the economy and the need to bring down the government debt ratio to safe levels. There would then be less excuse for the government to depart from a timetable for fiscal consolidation. An independent fiscal council should be set up, as in many other countries, to assess the government's annual and medium-term fiscal performance. One of the challenges of fiscal consolidation in the future is that targeting low inflation, and unwinding financial repression, will tend to keep real interest rates on government borrowing at a higher average level than in the past.

INVESTMENT CLIMATE

Growth of national income requires physical capital accumulation, via saving and investment.[13] A high savings rate is of course essential but if the savings are not to go to waste, they have to be matched by a *desire to invest*. Private investment, in particular, will not be forthcoming unless the expected return from investment is high. It follows that business sentiment and confidence are crucial in maintaining a high rate of investment. For this, a stable macroeconomic environment is necessary but not sufficient. The investment climate also needs to be 'friendly' in other ways.

India is notorious for putting unnecessary bureaucratic obstacles in the way of investors, as confirmed time and again by its very low rank in the World Bank's 'ease of doing business' surveys. These obstacles are a major constraint on the growth of firms, not least small firms, whose expansion is critical for producing 'good jobs' in the organized sector. One of the reasons for the corporate investment famine in the closing years of the UPA government was a paralysis in decision-making in such matters as land acquisition and environment permits. Of course, there have to be some regulations for various perfectly good reasons. But they must be administered speedily and fairly, and they should not be so restrictive as to stifle the incentive to invest. Similarly, the tax regime for business should be moderate, stable, and non-arbitrary; retrospective tax changes are a thoroughly bad idea. India continues to have major difficulties in all these areas. The country has yet to learn that putting superfluous and unreasonable restrictions on business amounts to strangling the goose that lays the golden eggs.

While a business-friendly climate is essential, it is equally important to encourage the right kind of business that is productive, innovative, dynamic, and entrepreneurial, not business that makes money by unproductive rent-seeking, and expends energy and resources in subverting the government to secure valuable permits and licenses to exploit scarce resources. That means auctioning licenses rather than handing them out arbitrarily, encouraging competition (an active Competition Commission is essential), and, more generally, taking steps to tackle corruption and crony capitalism. Thus, reform of the state (see below) has a close bearing on stimulating *productive* entrepreneurship and investment.

The Modi Government and the Climate for Investment

Reviving the climate for investment by simplifying, streamlining, and relaxing business regulations was one of the declared aims of the Modi government. As a signal of its intent, it announced a target of raising India's rank from 134 to 50 in the World Bank's Ease of Doing Business index by 2020. The rank has inched up to 130 so far. There has certainly been an effort to cut red tape by opening 'single windows' to streamline the large number of permissions needed to start a business. Indeed the government's 'e-biz portal' claims that 'from this simple website you will be able to apply and manage all your licenses, clearances, registrations and regulatory filings. You will no longer need to go from department to department or wait in line or hop multiple websites for information and services.' Another initiative, as yet only in the planning stage, is to have a single 'unique enterprise number' (probably the permanent account number used for taxation purposes) to take the place of the 30-odd identification numbers that businesses have to maintain to meet various requirements. How much improvement has occurred on the ground is not clear. There have been both positive and negative opinions expressed by observers but movement is certainly pointed in the right direction.[14]

The Department of Industrial Policy is working closely with state governments to help identify constraints on business freedom. A 'commercial courts bill' is said to be in the works to set up judicial mechanisms for quicker resolution of commercial disputes. But no improvement has been reported on a major spoiler of the business climate, viz. the arbitrary and high-handed behaviour of the tax authorities. The government has announced a phased reduction in the corporation tax from 30 per cent to 25 per cent over the next few years, along with rationalization/removal of unnecessary exemptions. This will be a step forward if and when it comes to pass.[15] There has been significant liberalization in the limits and procedures for foreign direct investment (see below). This is all to the good but the government's emphasis on 'ease of doing business' should not obscure an obvious point: improving the business climate will also depend on making a success of other aspects of the reform process, such as rectifying infrastructure deficits and making factor markets function more smoothly.

A more immediate problem is that an investment revival is being hampered by the debt overhang in large parts of the corporate sector and the impaired financial position of the public sector banks (PSBs). The former blunts the desire to invest and the demand for credit; the latter restricts the supply of credit. What is to be done? In a normally functioning economy, the banks would call the shots by forcing companies to repay loans or restructure/liquidate assets. In India, this is held up in several ways. There is a culture of banks letting big borrowers off the hook; and company exit is difficult because of the deficiencies in bankruptcy arrangements. The position is much worse than it needs to be because these basic problems have not been addressed in the past. I think the government underestimated the size of the problem when it took office; and it is probably still underestimating what needs to be done. The stressed assets of the PSBs are currently around 15 per cent of total loans, a manifestly unsatisfactory base for an increase in lending.

The steps that the government and the RBI are taking (see Chapters 7 and 8) may not be bold enough and seem to rely too much on waiting for a recovery. What may be needed is a government-backed asset reconstruction company (a 'bad bank') that removes contaminated assets from PSBs quickly by buying them at a discount, and concentrates on recovering value from the acquired loans. With cleaned balance sheets, and recapitalization by the government, the PSBs could approach the market to increase their equity. To succeed, there would simultaneously have to be radical governance reforms (if not privatization, at least a firm distancing of the government from the banks, along the lines suggested by the Nayak Committee: see below). The danger with the present slow strategy is that the problems may continue to fester, thereby impeding an investment revival. As things stand, nearly all indicators of economic activity, other than the CSO's national accounts, show continuing absence of any robust recovery from the 'growth recession' that began in 2012. The economy is very probably growing at less than 6 per cent a year (see Chapter 8). Crucially, corporate investment is very subdued, investment proposals are a fraction of pre-recession levels, and stalled projects are not showing enough forward movement.

DEEP FISCAL ADJUSTMENT AND A UNIVERSAL BASIC INCOME

The pattern of government expenditure in India is dysfunctional.[16] Far too much is spent on subsidies, explicit and hidden. The main explanation for their presence is that, despite overall goods-market liberalization, there remain price controls and subsidies on various key commodities, in the name of helping the poor. Examples include food (especially cereals), some oil-related products such as kerosene, cooking gas and aviation fuel, coal, natural gas, fertilizers, electricity, water, and rail services. These commodities (and many others), which are not pure public goods, are sold at prices that are well below their costs of production (sometimes the sale prices are not revised for years on end). Explicit subsidies are of course a direct charge on the budget. But there are also hidden subsidies outside the budget that take the form of losses or lower profits for companies that are owned by the government. (Electricity is a prime example.) Apart from burdening the fisc, the subsidies also misallocate resources, with damaging effects on economic efficiency. Since price controls reduce profitability, investment is discouraged, so supplies of the controlled commodities are excessively curtailed, while demand is excessively stimulated. What is more, the incidence of the subsidies is highly regressive. They are very badly targeted: the benefits go mostly to the well-off, not to the poor. This is not surprising: a fixed price subsidy per unit consumed gives a larger benefit to those who consume more.

It is high time the dysfunctional explicit and implicit subsidies were wound up. This follows from the basic economic principle that prices should reflect costs unless there are demonstrable 'external effects'. The fear that removal of subsidies would harm the poor is misplaced. The fiscal savings from subsidy elimination would easily enable any adverse effects on the poorer sections of society to be more than generously compensated by direct income transfers in cash. The medium-run aim should be to abolish price subsidies (other than those that pertain to pure public goods) and move to a system of universal cash transfers to provide a 'basic income' for all, set at a level that would eliminate extreme poverty. The point of making the transfers universal is to a) cut through the vexed problem of identifying the poor and b) forestall resistance from people who would otherwise be excluded from receiving the benefits.

As I show in Chapter 10, a 'basic income' scheme that disbursed an unconditional cash grant of Rs. 17,500 a year in 2014/15 prices to every household in the country, i.e. about Rs. 3500 per head per year, would abolish extreme poverty (estimated to affect 270 million people in 2011). I also show that the scheme would be fiscally viable, if the superabundance of counterproductive subsidies was scaled back: the requisite universal transfers would cost at most 3.5 per cent of GDP, a sum which is well below the fiscal resources that would be released by subsidy elimination. (Moreover, though I do not favour this, the cost of the scheme could be reduced substantially by introducing an element of self-selection, for example by making people go in person to identify themselves biometrically and collect their monthly cash transfer.) In fact, since the basic income would be paid to all households, the scheme would do a lot more. It would also compensate a large number of households above the poverty line fully against the rise in the cost of living from subsidy elimination, and, in addition, give many of them an income supplement to their earnings. This is important since there are hundreds of millions of people who are poor though not 'extremely poor' (in part because there is a significant bunching of households around the poverty line). In addition, the universal subsidy would have the merit of blunting resistance to income transfers from well-off individuals, since they too would receive some compensation for cost of living increases, though not full compensation.

The key to the financial feasibility of the scheme is to undertake 'deep fiscal adjustment', of which removal of subsidies is a part. The resources that could be raised by 'deep fiscal adjustment' would be very large, around at least 10 per cent of GDP, if the following sources were tapped: a) winding up dysfunctional 'non-merit subsidies'; b) abolishing some 'tax expenditures', e.g. unnecessary tax exemptions for companies, and tax breaks for 'small savings' that are regressive and serve no useful purpose;[17] c) more vigorous privatization of public sector enterprises; d) widening the tax base, in part by taxing agricultural incomes; and e) shaving off some badly targeted social expenditures.

India would gain four times over by introducing such a package. Firstly, growth would be stimulated because the closer correspondence of prices and costs would raise efficiency and private investment. Secondly, growth would be further stimulated because more money would be available for raising public investment in physical and human capital. Thirdly, growth would be far more inclusive because poor people could be given an income supplement that would eliminate extreme poverty. Finally, some of the fiscal savings could be deployed to reduce the fiscal deficit, which would make more growth more stable and possibly faster (by crowding in private investment).

Needless to say, achieving 'deep fiscal adjustment' is not a simple task that can be done overnight. It is best thought of as a complex multi-year programme. There are three technical requirements. The first is to extend Aadhar-linked bank accounts to cover all households. Thankfully, this is on the way to completion. Secondly, sound monetary policy would be needed to prevent inflation taking off as a result of the change in relative prices that would be caused by subsidy removal. A regime of 'inflation targeting' obviously helps. Thirdly, the sequencing of the wind-up of subsidies would have to be worked out carefully and coordinated across central and state governments and line ministries. There would be political obstacles of course. As argued above, an unconditional and universal basic income scheme would avoid some of the usual sources of resistance. Even so, the requisite 'deep fiscal adjustment' would confront many challenges. Subsidy removal, privatization, removal of tax exemptions, widening the tax base, and taxing agricultural incomes are issues that would certainly arouse resistance from many interested parties. But the social payoff of success would be enormous.

The Modi Government and 'Deep Fiscal Adjustment'

The Modi government has made some changes that are helpful for 'deep fiscal adjustment' but it has not articulated any clear overall vision along these lines. The encouraging steps, already alluded to, have taken the form of using the oil-price windfall to deregulate diesel prices and thus abolish the subsidy on diesel (gasoline had already been deregulated in 2010), and, going further, to raise excise taxes on both these fuels. While the subsidy on cooking gas remains, its volume has been reduced. Consumers have been limited in the number of subsidized gas cylinders they can buy. And they have to buy them at market prices, while the subsidy is paid directly into their bank accounts, thereby eliminating ghost beneficiaries and reducing the diversion of gas to commercial uses. But the kerosene subsidy (around 50 per cent of which goes to the well-off) continues unaltered.[18] The overall result of these changes is that the fuel subsidy has fallen sharply to 0.2 per cent of GDP (from 1.7 per cent in 2012), while improving income distribution and reducing carbon emissions at the same time. These moves have been highly desirable but they were easy to implement, given the fall in oil prices. As argued above, for 'deep fiscal adjustment', the government would have go much further, and take steps that are politically more challenging. The subsidies on cooking gas and kerosene should go, along with fertilizer and food subsidies. So should a multitude of other subsidies, explicit and hidden.

It is high time the government began a programme to reduce (and ultimately abolish) the whole range of dysfunctional subsidies, say by a small predetermined amount every month (as was done with diesel subsidy from 2013 onwards), accompanied by a gradual rise in cash transfers of 'basic income'. So far, the Modi government's approach to this kind of radical programme can only be described as very timid, despite various hints in both the Economic Surveys that it has produced since it took office.[19]

MARKETS, OWNERSHIP, AND REGULATION

Improvements in productivity are a critical determinant of growth of output per worker.[20] Though productivity advance was rapid in the three decades from 1980 there are signs that it is faltering. It is clearly essential to speed up productivity growth for the next two or three decades to exploit the huge potential for catching up with rich countries. Catch-up is partly about adopting available best-practice technologies. But it is also about producing more output out of available resources by ironing out the manifold distortions and inefficiencies that pervade the Indian economy. This will involve market and ownership reforms.

Several areas provide an opportunity for major productivity gains. The first major distortion is the huge differential in labour productivity between the organized and unorganized sectors. This, in essence, is what the 'employment problem' in the country is all about. There is little open unemployment in India in the Western sense since the absence of a generous social security system means that most people have to scratch a living somehow. The problem is rather the shortage of 'good jobs' that have high labour productivity and therefore provide decent incomes. These are largely to be found in the organized sector, while most workers are bottled up in the unorganized sector. The high-labour-productivity organized sector is part of the 'employment problem' in the sense that it manifests *inordinately low demand for labour*. The unorganized sector has an 'employment problem' in the quite different sense that the *quality of employment* is poor as a result of very low labour productivity. The latter is not usefully called an employment problem. It is better thought of as a general development problem to be attacked by measures that boost agricultural productivity (see Chapter 6), and improve human capital via education and health care, to enable people to respond to the demand for their services from the organized sector and from within the unorganized sector, and to equip them with the skills for jobs in the organized sector.

In the organized sector, it is critically important to stimulate the demand for labour. This is because labour transfers from low-productivity unorganized sector jobs to higher-productivity organized sector jobs would result in higher overall productivity and faster growth.[21] In this context, the demographic bulge in India is a major opportunity as well as a major threat. It could be an opportunity if the rapidly rising labour force were productively employed. It would become a social, political, and economic disaster if the growing numbers of workers simply added to the huge stock of labour that is crowded into low-productivity jobs. Many East Asian countries achieved labour reallocation towards the organized sector by a focus on labour-intensive manufactured exports. At the present juncture, the export route seems somewhat less promising for India though it would also be very foolish to ignore it.[22]

How should the organized sector's demand for labour be stimulated? The demand for labour will depend partly on how fast the sector grows and partly on how labour-intensive the growth is. The growth of the sector is held back by obstacles to the expansion of firms.[23] Other than labour laws, the major constraints on the growth of firms (and hence indirectly on growth of employment) are infrastructure deficiencies (especially electricity but also transport); corruption and payoffs to government functionaries such as tax inspectors; problems in land acquisition; scarcity of skilled labour; difficulties in enforcing contracts and resolving insolvencies; and excessively numerous, onerous, and bureaucratic procedures for various permissions and licenses (e.g. business start-up procedures, property registrations, construction permits, environmental clearances, electricity access, and so on). The presence of these impediments, worse than in the majority of countries, has been confirmed repeatedly by independent surveys. So, part of the answer to the employment problem must surely be to remove these obstacles and improve the 'ease of doing business', and enhance thereby the inducement to invest.[24]

Despite the above constraints, organized sector growth does take place. Why is it not more labour-using? This is in significant measure the result of India's labour laws and regulations, which are job-destructive, even anti-labour. Their rigidity strongly encourages employers to economize on labour use, and inhibits investment in labour-intensive products and labour-using techniques of production. Labour market reform is essential. The laws with regard to labour retrenchment and dismissal, labour re-deployment within companies, and employment of contract labour need drastic revision. The requirement to obtain prior government approval for labour retrenchment needs should be abolished.[25] However, greater flexibility in labour laws has to be combined with more generous severance benefits and more effective schemes for job-search and training, if it is to be acceptable to workers. In other words, labour market reform will be possible only if it is negotiated with trade unions as a package that strengthens income security though it weakens job security. (Incidentally, the universal 'basic income' scheme, advocated above and in Chapter 10, would obviously be very helpful in this regard.) There are strong disagreements about which is the more important obstacle to the growth of jobs: on the one hand infrastructure, ease of doing business, and credit constraints, and on the other hand labour laws. In truth, they all matter and India cannot afford to ignore any of them. The demographic challenge demands nothing less: the labour force is growing by around 10 million potential jobseekers each year. (Incidentally, one recent sign of the shortage of jobs is the strident demand for extension of job reservations to non-backward castes.)

The second set of distortions that impedes productivity growth pertains to the markets for goods and services. One issue has already been discussed above under 'deep fiscal adjustment'. Several key goods, including major inputs such as fertilizers, electricity, and water are sold at controlled prices, well below what it costs to produce them and/or their scarcity value. This leads to serious misallocation of resources, which could be corrected by winding up the subsidies, open or hidden (while the real incomes of poor people are protected by direct cash transfers). Some other issues also deserve attention. Competition, domestic and international, needs to be boosted. It would be desirable to further the process of trade liberalization (see below), and to promote domestic competition by encouraging the Competition Commission to be pro-active in initiating inquiries on its own motion. Another major issue concerns indirect taxation of goods and services, which is unavoidably necessary to raise revenue. Despite some improvement, India's indirect tax system continues to be a haphazard mixture of sundry taxes, duties, and cesses that produce massive inefficiency. (The inefficiency goes beyond standard economic considerations and includes huge losses due to waste of time. It is estimated that 60 per cent of the travel time for India's freight transport by road consists of waiting at border checkpoints to pay various levies.) The move to a nation-wide uniform goods and services tax (GST) is therefore urgently needed to make the country a common market. The only items outside the GST system should be those on which extra corrective taxes are necessary on 'demerit' grounds, e.g. carbon taxes and taxes on alcohol and tobacco.

Thirdly, factor markets and financial markets need to be liberalized, with appropriate regulation. Only then will reforms in the markets for goods and services yield their full benefits in terms of productivity growth. The market for labour has already been considered. Land and capital markets also need reform. Land markets in India are thin and highly imperfect; the government should put much more energy into improving land records to make the land market more 'liquid'. The land acquisition law of 2013 needs changes to make it less cumbersome, with better methods of price-discovery, while being fair to displaced communities. In the capital market, the arrangements for resolving company distress and bankruptcy need to be drastically overhauled so that capital moves smoothly to alternative uses. Productivity growth depends as much on exit of inefficient companies as on entry of potentially efficient ones. Present arrangements that keep moribund companies alive for years on end involve a huge waste of resources. In finance, major reforms are required to improve the access of poor people to the financial system by implementing new models of financial inclusion.

The fourth major area for productivity improvement is public sector enterprises (PSEs). The sensational losses of Air India are well-known but inefficiency in PSEs is a much wider problem. The losses of all the state-owned loss-making enterprises add up to a staggering 1 per cent of GDP each year, a large liability that the country can ill-afford. An essential part of the solution is to make public enterprises compete with private companies, domestic and foreign, on a level playing field. There has been some movement in this direction, and to good effect. But the logic of this solution also implies a willingness to see PSEs die a speedy death if they cannot stand up to competition. Since this is politically very hard, competition will not suffice as a solution, and privatization is necessary to raise the efficiency of resources that are currently tied up in PSEs that make losses or produce meagre profit surpluses.[26] The benefits of privatization would be especially powerful in sectors that can be exposed to competition (so that public monopolies are not simply replaced by private monopolies). Candidates for privatization obviously include PSEs in sectors that produce internationally tradable goods, such as the manufacturing sector, but also those in sectors producing non-tradable infrastructure goods and services, such as electricity generation and distribution, which can be made subject to competition. Different considerations arise with non-tradable natural monopolies such as electricity transmission and rail tracks. Whether these should be privatized is ambiguous since private monopolies may be no better for efficiency than state monopolies. Be that as it may, what is certain is that all infrastructure industries that have network characteristics, whether or not they are natural monopolies, need regulation and coordination that is competent, transparent, and independent of political interference. This is certainly not the case at present and will remain problematic until regulatory capacity is massively improved, and domination of regulators by politicians is reined in.

The fifth area that is crying out for improvement is infrastructure, a related topic to that just discussed. The quantity and quality of the physical infrastructure continues to be a serious constraint on overall productivity growth, though the problem has been known for years. Progress has been substantial in telecommunications, and fairly good in air transport and ports, but less than satisfactory in road and rail transport, while electricity and urban infrastructure are outstanding black spots. Opening up infrastructure industries to the private sector has helped to boost the efficiency and volume of investment. In recent years, the government has also made extensive use of public-private partnerships (PPPs). Experience with these has been mixed at best, and indicates clearly that the government needs to become much more adept at contract design, monitoring of private parties, dispute resolution, and fulfilling its side of the PPP bargain. In electricity, private and public investments have added greatly to generation capacity. Electricity shortages continue nevertheless, due to a long-standing dysfunction in the predominantly state-owned and state-managed distribution segment of the system, which faces a crippling burden of accumulated debt and cannot afford to buy power from the generating companies. The underlying cause is that it does not charge economic prices and is also not sufficiently motivated to deal with operational problems, such as theft of electricity. Root and branch reform is thus necessary in electricity distribution companies ('discoms'). The solution would certainly have to include a write-off of their debts but only in combination with other fundamental changes (see below).

The sixth area where reform is urgently called for is agriculture, which still harbours half the country's workforce. In this sector, the need is for liberalization of state controls in activities where the private sector has a comparative advantage, such as moving, storing, and marketing of produce, combined with targeted state action where markets would by their nature fail to do what is necessary. The latter includes improving the supply chain in agriculture by enforcing competition in agricultural marketing, and opening up to retail multinationals that could modernize transportation of produce. An absolutely essential step is to turn the mix of subsidies and public investment in agriculture on its head. Existing subsidies for agriculture are inefficient as well as regressive, and need to be eliminated (compensation for poor farmers should be guaranteed by the provision of a 'basic income', and insurance against crop failures). More public investment and public promotion are sorely needed in areas where markets can fail to provide, such as rural roads and electrification, irrigation, extension services, crop insurance, environmental protection including water management, and agricultural research. Greater exposure of agriculture to international trade would also pay dividends in the long run.

The seventh area for market and regulatory reform is environmental protection, which is valuable in its own right but also for growth and inclusion, the former because growth would eventually self-destruct if the environment was not attended to, and the latter because pollution and environmental decay impinge on poor people with particular severity. Environmental problems are often connected with absence of ownership and property rights. The state has a responsibility to step in when private or community property rights to environmental resources (such as air, water, and forests) are absent or unenforced, assume the property rights itself, and regulate the use of the resources in the national interest (in economic jargon, by internalizing the environmental externalities) to prevent pollution and degradation of natural capital. On this front, the Indian state's record so far has been dismal: the steep decline in air quality, the alarming extent of depletion and toxicity of water supplies, and the large loss of forest cover speak for themselves. Price and non-price remedial measures would be feasible and are necessary to pursue environmental goals within the country, and to contribute towards international efforts to combat global warming (of which India would be a major victim). One essential measure is a gradually rising tax on fossil fuels (until it reaches a level much higher than exists now). This would advance domestic as well as global environmental objectives.

The Modi Government: Markets, Ownership, and Regulation

The Modi government was expected to do a great deal in this area. Expectations have been belied, and overall vision has been lacking. In the markets for goods and services, the main challenges were getting rid of dysfunctional subsidies and introducing the GST. On subsidies, not much has happened apart from the partial withdrawal of some fuel subsidies (see above). As for the GST, the required constitutional amendment was passed by the Lok Sabha in December 2014 but it has been stuck in the Rajya Sabha where debates on the bill scheduled to be held in the Monsoon and Winter sessions of 2015 were totally washed out by the disruption of proceedings by the opposition. The distance between the government and the opposition on this issue is quite small but the will to compromise has been lacking.[27] There has also been little action on furthering the scope of competition.[28]

On factor markets, it was thought that the Modi government would amend land and labour laws. It issued three successive time-bound ordinances to weaken the 'consent' and 'social impact' clauses in the Land Acquisition Act of 2013 but then gave up in the face of opposition in the RS. The matter has now been left to individual states, with the implication that if they amend the law as the government wishes, presidential assent will be forthcoming. So far only a couple of states have shown some interest in doing so. As things stand, the laws governing land acquisition remain in a very unsatisfactory state both as regards the price of acquired land and the length of time taken to complete transactions. This is clearly undesirable for a country that wishes to industrialize rapidly (see Chapter 6). On labour laws, despite various nods and winks early on, it has become clear that the government does not have the stomach for a fight with trade unions. Again, the states have been left to do their own thing. Three states (Rajasthan, Madhya Pradesh, Gujarat) have tweaked labour laws to make them a bit more flexible. None of this adds up to a step-change for the country as a whole. On capital market reform, there has been some progress. The committee set up to propose a new bankruptcy act has produced its report, along with a draft 'insolvency and bankruptcy code'. It still has to run the gauntlet of being passed by both houses of parliament. Moreover, the administration of the code will be no easy matter. It will require a whole supporting system to be developed, including 'insolvency professionals', 'insolvency information utilities', and an 'insolvency regulator'. It will thus be some years before India has effective bankruptcy procedures. But when the Act is passed, at least a start will have been made.[29]

There is better news on some aspects of financial sector reform. The Reserve Bank has energetically pursued measures for increasing financial inclusion and bank competition. Following a strong impetus from the Modi government, it has led a successful campaign to increase rapidly the number of people with bank accounts (though as yet only two-thirds of the accounts are even minimally active), and licensed two new universal banks, 11 'payments banks', and 12 'small finance banks'. These are highly desirable reforms that will contribute to inclusive growth in the long run by improving access to the financial system, enabling direct benefit transfers, increasing bank competition, and reducing the cost of credit for small firms and self-employed people. But the RBI has been much less bold in dealing with the problem of poor governance in public sector banks; admittedly, it could only have done so with the active joint participation of the government (see below).

Reform of public sector enterprises and public sector banks has been timid in the extreme.[30] Unlike the BJP government of 1999–2004, the present government seems to be wedded to the fetish of 51 per cent state ownership, so its 'privatization' efforts are just a continuation of the Congress government's policy of 'disinvestment', i.e. selling small slices of state-owned companies. Full privatization has not been tried, either in Air India, which continues to bleed money, or in any of the other 65 loss-making PSEs. Disinvestment can raise some revenue but without any of the efficiency advantages of a change of ownership and management.[31] In any case, even the volume of disinvestment has been meagre.[32] For example, in 2015/16, disinvestment is clearly going to be only a quarter of a small budgeted figure. And the excuse of poor market conditions for sale does not explain why the figure was just as low in the previous year when the stock market was booming. The need to have continuous sales throughout the year has been talked about but nothing has been done.[33]

On public sector banks, the government has preferred largely to bury its head in the sand. Its so-called 'Indradhanush' initiative does not get to grips with the severe governance problems that underlie their unsatisfactory performance. Implementation of the Nayak Committee report (see Chapter 7) is the minimum that is called for, even if privatization were regarded as beyond the pale. 'Indradhanush' does not attempt to set up a Bank Investment Company, as recommended by Nayak, to distance the government from the banks.[34] There is no new mechanism (such as a 'bad bank') to enable them to clean their balance sheets quickly and start afresh. And it seems highly likely that the amount the government has budgeted to recapitalize them is well short of what will be required.

On infrastructure, there has been a considerable amount of energy and forward movement from the Modi government, for example in accelerating the highway building programme and starting work on two major freight corridors, as well as the Delhi-Mumbai industrial corridor (though the latter is as yet only in the land-acquisition stage). But two outstanding problems are still unresolved: the parlous condition of the state electricity discoms, and the difficulties experienced with managing public-private partnerships (PPPs). On the former, the government has initiated a scheme called UDAY, which purports to provide a 'permanent solution' to the discoms problem but is in truth just another bailout, similar to other partial bailouts in the past. There is nothing in the scheme to make or enable discoms to address the underlying causes of their problems, viz. electricity prices that do not reflect costs, and operational issues such as electricity theft. So the UDAY 'solution' amounts to little more than kicking the can down the road.[35] An enduring solution of the discoms mess would surely require not just a write-off of their liabilities but also cost-reflective prices, privatization, competition, and improved regulatory supervision. The second major issue in the infrastructure space is how to make PPPs function better. As explained in detail in Chapter 7, PPPs have suffered from many problems. A committee set up by the Modi government produced an excellent report towards the end of 2015, with many useful recommendations on improving risk-allocation between public and private partners, setting up better dispute resolution mechanisms, and building capacity and expertise within government. It remains to be seen whether the government will implement it in earnest.[36]

There have been no radical initiatives in the agricultural sector. The dysfunctional mix of large subsidies and low public investment has not been attacked. If the subsidies were wound up and substituted by cash transfers, money would be saved, which could be deployed for irrigation and other investments to enhance productivity. Agrarian distress has been mounting lately due to bad weather conditions and poor profitability. Crop insurance schemes are clearly urgently necessary but no action has been forthcoming thus far.[37]

On the environment too, there is nothing much to write home about. The environment minister has used his discretionary powers to speed up clearances for some investments but that is on an ad hoc basis. Nothing has been done to put in place an expeditious and fair system of environmental licensing, despite an excellent report from the T. S. R. Subramanian committee (see Chapter 7). No major new initiatives have been undertaken to control environmental pollution and degradation of natural capital. (The exception is the trial of a scheme to ban cars with odd numbers on even dates and vice versa in Delhi but that was undertaken by the Delhi state government.) The much-touted cleaning of the Ganga has gone nowhere so far. There is, however, one positive fact to report. The government has encouraged an ambitious programme for solar energy (though it is running well behind schedule) that will help to fulfil India's contribution to global climate mitigation targets.

Fearful of external competition, India remained a highly closed economy until the 1980s and paid a large price in terms of dynamic efficiency.[38] Since then, it has opened up substantially (with the important and wise exception of retaining some restrictions on short-term capital movements). Quantitative controls on imports have largely gone and tariffs have been slashed, particularly in manufactured goods. Restrictions on foreign direct and portfolio equity investment have been progressively liberalized. As a result, trade has risen three-fold as a proportion of GDP, and inward and outward foreign investment have increased substantially. Overall, the effects of India's globalization have been very favourable. External liberalization has made a major contribution to productivity growth.

Even so, in the recent past, trade policy has suffered from neglect and complacency. In the 2010s, exports have been sluggish, and in the last couple of years have shown negative growth. There seems to be little realization that trade expansion and exposure to global competition are essential components of a strategy to sustain rapid growth and to address India's employment problem. (It is noteworthy that no country has achieved durable super-fast growth, especially of its manufacturing sector, that has not had super-fast growth in its exports.) Indian policymakers have also failed to recognize the changing character of international trade, especially the importance of global value chains and the associated movements in the direction of tighter 'behind the border' disciplines. All of India's major trading partners are now contemplating, negotiating, or concluding mega-regional agreements that take these new developments on board. When completed, these agreements are potentially likely to cover more than two-thirds of world trade and to set its rules and framework for years to come. The danger is that if India stood aside, it would suffer trade diversion and discrimination. (If China's entry into US-led mega-regionals came to pass, that would make matters even worse.) Correspondingly, India may reap potentially large gains if it changed its defensive stance and took active steps to turn the tide to its advantage.

India has various trade agreements but they are largely inconsequential, some bilateral, with small and unimportant countries, and others that are shallow and timid, with many exemptions. The only mega-regional agreement that it is negotiating is the RCEP, and that too falls in the 'shallow' category, at least so far. Ironically, China, which is a prime member of the RCEP, is making overtures towards membership of TPP, of which the United States is the leader, and is even joining the United States in promoting the much wider FTAAP.

India needs to pursue a much more energetic trade policy along four fronts. Firstly, it should continue with unilateral trade liberalization, which has virtually halted in recent years. Secondly, it should seek to join existing 'plurilateral' agreements between WTO members, especially the TISA, the Information Technology Agreement (ITA), and the GPA. (Note that China has applied for membership of TISA.) As a large exporter of services, India surely needs to be in TISA and ITA to engage in negotiations for market access. The GPA too holds promise because India, as a low-cost supplier, is in a good position to bid for government contracts in its 50 member countries. Thirdly, India should, as soon as possible, work out a strategy with regard to the mega-regionals. Non-engagement runs the risk of leaving India isolated. Probably the safest course, because it hedges all bets, would be to try and energize the RCEP negotiations, but also apply to join APEC, some of whose major countries have indicated that they would welcome India as a member. (This would leave open the possibility of future negotiation to join the TPP if that became expedient, and even the FTAAP if it became a reality.) Of course, India must not cave in on issues on which it takes a very different view from the advanced countries, especially the United States, on matters such as intellectual property and labour standards. And it need not do so because as a large country with a rapidly expanding internal market, it can play a strong hand. But engagement is vital so that India can negotiate from a position of strength and avoid having rules imposed on it willy-nilly. If India makes an entry into these mega-regionals without compromising on its main demands, large advantages are likely to accrue. India would gain easier access to foreign markets for exports of services and manufactures (including, crucially, labour-intensive manufactures such as apparel and clothing). Exposure to lower-cost imports and higher foreign standards could raise productivity in Indian manufacturing and services, and prepare these sectors to participate in global value chains. At the same time, as in many countries (e.g. in China, after it joined the WTO), trade policy commitments may serve to catalyse domestic reform efforts. Fourthly, India should also fight to keep the WTO process going because multilateralism continues to have some solid advantages (see Chapter 12). It will not be easy to strike the right balance between these four different tracks. It will need clear thinking and competent execution. Despite the complexities, however, the bottom-line is simple enough. It is that as an emerging economic power India has a huge stake in open markets for trade and an open door for foreign investment. Since trade negotiations are a two-way street, if India wants other countries to offer meaningful concessions, it will have to offer meaningful concessions in return.

In the international monetary arena, India has no axe to grind, unlike several key countries that run large current account surpluses and/or have currencies that are in demand as international reserves. It should try to use its non-partisan status to nudge countries towards adopting more satisfactory mechanisms for international balance of payments adjustment and provision of international liquidity. Progress on these issues would benefit India as well as the world economy more generally.

The Modi Government and External Economic Engagement

The Modi government moved significantly on liberalization of foreign direct investment (FDI) early on in its tenure, and again towards the end of 2015 across a wide range of sectors. Ownership limits have been made more generous. 'Automatic' approval of investment proposals is rapidly becoming the norm, and domestic-sourcing benchmarks have become much more flexible. (The big exception is multi-brand retail. In this sector, though 51 per cent ownership is formally allowed, states retain the freedom to set tighter limits or even to ban entry. The government has made it clear informally that it would not look favourably on the entry of supermarkets.) In addition, Prime Minister Modi has, on his numerous foreign tours, made a very effective sales pitch for India as an investment destination. As a result, there have been many expressions of investment intent. While such intentions do not always materialize, inflows of FDI in 2014/15 and 2015/16 have certainly been very strong. One of the determining factors in the future growth of FDI will be India's success in improving the investment climate on the ground by tackling the usual suspects, such as ease of doing business, land and labour laws, intellectual property protection, and trade facilitation. Retrospective taxation is another important issue. The Modi government came in with a promise to end it but did not quite live up to its word. Though it has forsworn any such actions in the future, past cases such as the tax disputes with Vodafone and Cairn still remain in play, and irritations continue. For example, at one stage recently, India's tax authorities made a large demand on foreign institutional investors for payment of the 'minimum alternate tax' for the previous six years, going back on an understanding that they were exempt from this tax. Though the government relented in due course, the episode left a sour taste. It would be wise to bury the practice of retrospective taxation once and for all. A stable tax regime is one of the cardinal features of a welcoming environment for foreign investment.

On the whole, the Modi government's unilateral actions on foreign investment have been very constructive. The same cannot be said about its policy performance with regard to foreign trade, and trade and investment agreements.[39] The WTO's Nairobi conference at the end of 2015 in effect sounded the death-knell for the Doha Development Agenda, emphasizing the need to come to grips with the challenge of moving simultaneously on four fronts: unilateral, plurilateral, mega-regional, and multilateral. Unfortunately, the Modi government has done next to nothing towards this end. (All it can show for itself is the negative achievement of petulantly breaking off negotiations on the India-EU trade and investment agreement.) A strategic vision is conspicuous by its absence, and the old-India mentality of wanting something for nothing in trade talks is still much in evidence.

SOCIAL PROTECTION AND ENABLEMENT

Rapid growth is pointless unless it is inclusive and widely shared.[40] Social protection schemes that provide a minimum income to citizens, regardless of earning capacity, are institutions that all social democracies should aspire to have. At present, India relies mainly on price subsidies to provide social protection. As argued above in the section on 'deep fiscal adjustment', they should be substituted by an unconditional and universal cash transfer set at a level that would abolish extreme poverty. The resulting pay-off for growth and inclusion would be very large. The fiscal implications would be quite easily manageable if the dysfunctional explicit and implicit subsidies were wound up, which would in any case be desirable for several other reasons.

Social protection is an essential feature of a good society. However, in the medium and long run, rising living standards for poor people depend much more on expansion of employment (discussed above), and provision of education and health care, than on redistributive transfers. Education and health care contribute to raising the growth rate by augmenting human capital. They are also of crucial importance in spreading the fruits of growth widely and enabling individuals to achieve their full potential and lead fulfilling lives. In both these sectors, there is a strong case for state intervention on equity and market-failure grounds. The critical question is: what should be the form and extent of state intervention?

India has taken large strides in spreading literacy and enrolling children in primary schools (although it still lags well behind China, and even some low-income countries, in female literacy). Enrolment in secondary schools has also improved (though it remains well behind China). What is shocking is the abysmal quality of primary and secondary education. The performance of the average Indian schoolchild in the basic skills of reading, writing, and arithmetic is massively short of satisfactory. The consequences for future employment and growth are too terrible to contemplate, especially given the demographic bulge.

Low learning outcomes are to be explained partly by current pedagogic practices (such as the emphasis on 'finishing the curriculum' even if most students are falling behind) but mainly by lack of teacher effort. A large body of rigorous empirical research indicates that in government schools, teacher absenteeism and lack of teaching commitment are pervasive, resulting from a near-total lack of accountability. Teacher unions are politically very powerful and it is impossible to suspend teachers even for gross misbehaviour. Incentives are more appropriately aligned in private schools, which, in consequence, show much greater teacher effort and somewhat better learning outcomes than government schools. Moreover, these outcomes are delivered far more cheaply (since teachers in private schools are paid a third or less of the salaries in government schools).

Reform of the Indian education system depends critically on improving teacher accountability in government schools. What is ideally needed is a drastic cull of delinquent teachers! But change from within the government sector is very unlikely to happen, given entrenched union power and the inertia in the system. There is thus a strong pragmatic case in India for an education voucher system in which all schools, including government schools, would charge fees to cover their costs, and poor people would be given education vouchers to enable them to send their children to government or private schools, whichever they prefer, with the presumption that schools that fail to attract applicants would have to contract or close down. (Of course, government schools would have to continue to be the sole source of instruction in remote areas where private schools do not exist or do not come up.) Such a scheme should have been piloted in many parts of the country where both government and private schools are present in abundance. Instead, the Congress government brought in the Right to Education Act (RTEA) in 2010.

The RTEA mandates that private schools must reserve 25 per cent of entry for students from the economically backward sections of society, with the cost to be covered by the government. But the Act does nothing to address the core problems of the quality of education, especially teacher accountability in government schools. Without an attack on this basic flaw, expanding the number of regular teachers to achieve a large increase in the teacher-pupil ratio, as targeted by the Act, would be an exercise in futility. In government schools, the said target would be better achieved by expanding the number of contract teachers (who could and should be put on a career progression to become regular teachers, subject to good per-formance). The evidence shows that contract teachers with modest train-ing are cheaper and much more effective in improving learning levels. The Act has many other shortcomings detailed in Chapter 9. It is pedagogically faulty because it institutionalizes automatic progression of students to higher grades without any formal hurdle to check that they have achieved a minimum standard of competence. It also mandates excessively rigid norms for 'recognition' of private schools that may lead to many of them closing down.

In sum, India's elementary education system has run into the sand. Without drastic reforms to improve teacher accountability and teaching methods, it will not provide millions of young people with the means to invest in the single asset they possess, namely themselves. And it will not generate the human capital to support a rapid growth rate. India's higher education system is also in poor shape. Universities suffer from intrusive micro-management by regulators. Standards will not improve without much more autonomy. As for vocational education, the needs are huge but the country still lacks a workable model of public-private participation. There is also a dearth of on-the-job training. To encourage apprenticeship programmes, there is a strong case to subsidize firms that undertake them, financed by a small tax on all firms.

In health care, despite some progress, India's performance as a 'lower middle income' country is no better than the average low-income coun-try, and on some indicators, particularly child nutrition and sanitation, it is worse. Total spending on health, around 4 per cent of GDP, is about average for lower middle income countries but government spending on health (about 1 per cent of GDP) is very low by international standards. An expansion of government spending would certainly be desirable but only if it departed from existing grooves.

The strength of the market-failure case for state intervention in health care varies with the type of care. It is absolutely decisive in 'traditional pub-lic health' (TPH), strong in in-patient secondary care, and relatively weak in out-patient primary care. TPH, which covers items such as mosquito eradication, immunization, child nutrition, and safe water and sanitation, is critically important but woefully neglected. The market is incapable of financing TPH, and it would also be very difficult, if not impossible, to devolve its provision to the private sector via contractual arrangements. Thus, the government's role in both finance and delivery is absolutely essential. Since the social returns to TPH are very high, public expenditure on TPH needs to be increased sharply, and its delivery needs to be under-taken 'in mission mode'.

In secondary in-patient (i.e. hospital) care, there is a powerful market-failure case for state intervention to make health insurance compulsory for everyone in order to avoid 'adverse selection', which leads to many people being uncovered by insurance (as in the United States, until the Obama reform). There is also a powerful equity case for the state to pay the insurance premiums of poor people. But in the interests of efficiency, actual delivery of care should be carried out competitively by both government and private hospitals. (In India, 58 per cent of inpatient care in rural areas and 68 per cent in urban areas were already delivered by private providers in 2014.) India's RSBY scheme, which has followed roughly the Northern European track of state insurance plus a mixture of public and private delivery, seems a very sensible way to address finance and provision of secondary care in India though coverage and benefits could do with being greatly increased. Of course, regulation would be necessary to control costs and raise quality standards over time. Subject to the proviso about competition, there certainly needs to be a large increase in the provision of government hospitals.

In primary care, market failures are not of decisive importance. The case for risk-sharing via insurance is much weaker. In any case, state insurance for primary care would be a bad idea because it is likely to be systematically abused by doctor-patient collusion. There is of course an overwhelming equity argument for state assistance to help poor people defray health care costs. But the best way to do that would be to add a fixed sum to the cash-transfer 'basic income' paid to all households. Financial assistance by the state does not necessarily imply that the state should deliver care. Whether the state should deliver depends on its performance on the ground, relative to the private sector. There has been plenty of detailed empirical research on this. The results show clearly that while government doctors are better qualified than private doctors, they provide worse care. Absenteeism of government doctors and nurses is high and effort is low. As with government teachers, there appears to be an insuperable accountability problem. Not surprisingly, most primary care is already delivered by private providers. (In 2014, they provided 72 per cent of primary care in rural areas and 79 per cent in urban areas.) It would be unrealistic as well as contrary to the consumer interest, for the government to take over primary care. There are two ways forward. The government could get out of primary care altogether, except of course in remote locations that lack private providers. (The money saved could be used for improving regulation, see below.) Or there could be a 'money follows the patient' scheme in which primary care would be provided competitively by public and private providers, with patients free to spend their (augmented) 'basic income' to buy care. The understanding would have to be that providers, public or private, that do not attract patients would have to contract or close down. I see no realistic hope of improving the abysmal quality of care in the public sector without competition.

Of course, the system I envisage would need state regulation. Though market failures are not pervasive in primary care, they are certainly not absent. Supplier-induced demand undoubtedly exists. For example, patients may be cajoled or even deceived by private doctors into taking antibiotics they do not need. (There are some similar horror stories in secondary care as well, for example of women being 'persuaded' to have unnecessary hysterectomies.) So, regulation is inescapable, combined with programmes to train unqualified private doctors, and measures to curb the open availability of prescription drugs and medicines across the counter. The big question is: should India carry on with the present system in the hope that state delivery of primary care can somehow be reformed from within or should there be a move towards a system in which the emphasis shifts to putting public and private providers on a level competitive playing field, with the state playing a financing and regulatory role? In my view, experience strongly points to the superiority of the latter alternative.

That the state should deliver universal free education and health care at the point of service has been one of the central tenets of government policy. But the scale of 'government failure' in India is such that this conventional position has to be substantially modified. Transfers of 'basic income' or vouchers by the state, combined with compulsory health insurance for secondary care (with insurance premiums paid by the state for poor people), and a mix of public and private providers competing to deliver education and health services, with the whole system subject to regulation by the state, constitutes a more appropriate vision to guide India in the future.

The Modi Government, Social Protection, and Social Enablement

The Modi government has not decisively abandoned the principle of providing social protection via a complex network of inefficient, hit-and-miss price subsidies. The ideal that the government should be aiming at is to make a decisive shift to providing a 'basic income' in cash, which could be easily financed by the savings from subsidy withdrawal (see above). The government has put real energy behind the extension of the Aadhar card and Aadhar-linked bank accounts but it seems in no hurry to take the next, politically more difficult, steps.

In education and health care, it is evident that the old model of providing these basic public services is broken. With business-as-usual policies on education and health, the country is virtually certain to run into a human capital constraint that will block its economic ambitions. Unfortunately, business-as-usual is all that has been on offer from the Modi government so far at all levels of education, primary, secondary, and tertiary. There is no sign that it is facing up to the profound problems of high cost and low quality in state-provided primary and secondary education, resulting from pedagogic infirmities and a near-complete lack of accountability of teachers. The government is currently conducting a public consultation to formulate a New Education Policy. I would not bet on it addressing the core issues but I hope I am proved wrong. In the higher education sector, little has happened to change the prevailing license raj mentality and actuality.[41] In vocational training, there is a target of training for 500 million workers by 2022 but no credible plan to attain it.

The Modi government came out with a Draft National Health Policy at the end of 2014.[42] The document advocated the enactment of a justiciable 'right to health', and an increase in government expenditure on health from 1 per cent to 2.5 per cent of GDP.[43] I have nothing against such an increase if policies can be put in place to improve the quality of the spending. What is lacking in the draft policy document is any understanding of why past policies have failed to improve the atrocious quality of health care. It does not make the important distinction between public financing and public delivery, and has next to nothing to say about the problems of incentives and accountability in government provision of primary care and how they should be tackled. Neither does it set out a coherent scheme for harnessing the large presence of the private health care sector and for regulating it. Perhaps the final version of the national health policy will improve on the draft. (I would be pleasantly surprised if it did).

In secondary care, the Modi government appears to have set its face against the RSBY, which had stabilized after some teething troubles. The RSBY involves the state paying the insurance premiums of poor people and setting fee-for-service rates for providers. But it uses insurance companies to manage the insurance policies, e.g. organizing hospitals into provider networks, buying services from them, and settling their claims. The new philosophy, if the draft policy document is any indication, seems to be that the government will take over the management of insurance. This seems unwise because it implies that the state would run the mechanics of the scheme, which it surely lacks the expertise to do. Another inefficient inspector raj could be the end-result. For the moment, the RSBY appears still to be running but with a cloudy future. Rationalization of the patchwork of various existing schemes has not even begun. Overall, confusion reigns.[44]

Nonetheless, on one health-related initiative, the Modi government can be commended unequivocally. This is the emphasis it has put on building latrines, and curbing open defecation, as part of its Swachh Bharat (Clean India) programme (though the attendant problems of ensuring water supply and refuse clearance, and changing public attitudes, remain formidable).

REFORM OF THE STATE

The two fixed points in the socio-political setting of the Indian state's development policies are that the country is a democracy, and an extremely diverse society.[45] But state intervention to secure inclusive growth has become increasingly difficult over time because the impact of these 'givens' has been exacerbated by the twin forces of 'social and political awakening' and 'institutional decay'. 'Awakening' refers to the increasing self-assertion of hitherto disadvantaged castes and downtrodden groups. This has resulted in an increasingly fragmented polity that puts an overload of economic demands on the treasury. At the same time, institutional decay has reduced the capacity of the state to fulfil its core functions, orchestrate compromise between interest groups, break collective-action deadlocks, and control corruption and crony capitalism. 'Awakening' is an inevitable, indeed desirable, accompaniment of greater democratization. But 'institutional decay' will certainly have to be reversed if India is to achieve its development aims.

The deterioration in the quality of the state's performance in its functions, core and non-core, has gone so far that its correction will require a combination of different lines of attack. Firstly, the state should withdraw from activities in which it does not have a comparative advantage relative to the private sector; and in those activities where the advantage is ambiguous, it should compete with the private sector on a level playing field. In other words, part of the answer will have to come from limiting the state's ambition to match its current capacity. I have already dwelt on this at length, so no further elaboration is necessary. Secondly, decentralization may help. For example, local governments may be in a better position to control absenteeism of teachers and doctors at the ground level than state governments which may be hundreds of miles away. However, actual and potential devolution to state and local levels underlines sharply the need for improvement in administrative capacity, which is manifestly deficient at provincial and local levels (see below). Thirdly, there needs to be a series of internal reforms in the civil service, the police force, and the judiciary to repair severe shortages of personnel, increase expertise and competence, align incentives and penalties to the quality of performance, and reduce corruption and rank politicization.[46] Especially important is the need to increase regulatory capacity. Shortfalls in this area are quite evident in the regulation of infrastructure services and PPPs. But the point is more general. Markets have many virtues but they can only rarely regulate themselves. Regulation is a function that the state cannot abdicate or devolve; and it has become a very complex and technical subject. India is lagging badly in this area. At the moment, regulation is India is mostly amateurish, simultaneously heavy-handed and ineffectual. Fourthly, and most difficult of all, a way has to be found somehow to get government functionaries to internalize the mission of serving the public interest.

The previous point about public interest brings me to corruption, which is another manifestation of institutional decay. Corruption is rife in India despite the demise of the old license raj. It is not a harmless phenomenon that can be treated with benign neglect. It can impose severe efficiency costs by subverting the discipline of the market. Even worse, it can delegitimize the state. The prime locations of big ticket' corruption, and its close cousin, crony capitalism, are no longer import licenses (as in the *ancien regime*) but government procurement, state allocation of rights to exploit scarce resources, and election finance. To combat the first two, it would help to reduce as far as possible the scope for discretionary decisions by politicians and bureaucrats and substitute these by transparent methods such as open auctions, and transfer of decision-making to independent bodies. However, it would clearly be neither feasible nor desirable to do away with discretion completely. Hounding officials for honest mistakes would be wrong as well as counterproductive since it would smother initiative and drive. Finding the middle course between being tough on corruption and being over-zealous in attacking it is a difficult act to get right but it has to be carried out as best as possible. To attack electoral corruption, it would be essential to grant the Election Commission powers to monitor closely the activities and finances of political parties, and to tighten laws on election finance that are shot through with holes. (At present, 75 per cent or more of the income of the major political parties comes from undocumented sources.)[47]

The Modi Government and Reform of the State

The UPA government, in its dying days, was perceived to be afflicted by administrative paralysis. The Modi government has shaken off this perception, at least so far. This is partly because lines of authority are clearer. The government has an absolute majority in the Lok Sabha, and is not beholden to coalition partners. The writ of the prime minister is unquestioned and his office is in full control in making appointments of top civil servants, and in deciding strategic policy issues. Indeed the danger is one of over-centralization, not one of too many centres of power. On corruption, there has been a pleasing absence of visible mega-scams at the national level. (This may be related in part to the collapse in the prices of minerals, whose extraction and use were a prime locus of corruption during the UPA regime.) It is said that ministers and civil servants are scared of the prime minister. Perhaps that helps to keep them mostly on the straight and narrow. The question is whether all of this is anything more than a temporary phenomenon and that too only at the top level of government.

There are some grounds for hope more generally. Auctioning as a method of allocating resources seems to gaining traction. Banks, with the support of the Reserve Bank, are getting tougher on promoters who default strategically and milk the system. At the 'small-ticket' level, corruption is being deterred by technological devices such as transfers of benefits directly into bank accounts. At the same time, large-scale institutional change is lacking. Firstly, there have been no legislative moves on internal reform of political parties or of election funding, which provides the fuel for running the wheels of corruption. Secondly, a lot of corruption takes place at the level of the states and municipalities, where deals have less visibility but the aggregate sums involved in contracts and licenses are enormous. It is doubtful if there has been any material change in the prevalence of corrupt practices in these locations. To make a real difference to corruption, the government would have to attack election funding at both national and state levels.

The lack of action is even more glaring on improving state capacity. There have been no measures of administrative reform at the higher levels of government on matters such as quality of personnel to perform complex tasks. There is no evidence of any thought being given to radical measures for improving the delivery of public services on the ground. The same largely goes for reform of the state, apart from the welcome attempts to simplify procedures for 'ease of doing business'. The large deficits in administrative, regulatory, and judicial capacity, both quantitative and qualitative, that plague the country continue to be neglected. Note, in this context, that the move towards decentralization of governmental responsibilities, recently boosted by boosted the award of the 14th Finance Commission, is decidedly double-edged. On the one hand, moving decision-making closer to the people has much to be said for it for obvious reasons. On the other hand, it exposes even more the weakness of state capacity at the level of state and local governments.

THE MODI GOVERNMENT: OVERALL ASSESSMENT, TWO YEARS ON

Overall, the Modi government's economic performance has been mixed at best. It has successfully stabilized the economy and moved firmly in the direction of inflation targeting. But it has not been able so far to re-ignite private investment in the face of the inherited debt overhang, and thereby return the economy to rapid growth. The economy is not showing signs of robust recovery, whatever the national accounts say.

Of course, recovery will come sooner or later. This leads naturally to the question: is the Modi government doing enough to promote rapid, sustainable, and inclusive growth *in the long term*? It has certainly made a creditable effort to make it easier to do business. It has energetically pursued the project of enabling individuals to obtain biometric identification cards and the scheme for extending the coverage of bank accounts across the population. However, apart from the reduction in fuel subsidies, made possible by the fall in global oil prices, it has made no concerted effort to exploit the huge potential that lies dormant in changing the pattern of government expenditure by undertaking 'deep fiscal adjustment'. (The prize would be the release of enough resources to end extreme poverty, and enable higher public investment and social sector spending, without compromising fiscal consolidation.) Reform of land and labour laws has gone approximately nowhere. The much awaited GST is not yet in the bag but a new bankruptcy code seems finally to be in the offing. There has been very little action on privatization, even of public sector enterprises that make huge losses each year. There have been encouraging steps in creating new banks that will advance financial inclusion but none in materially changing the appalling governance structures of public sector banks. The government has increased public investment in infrastructure and tried to get stalled projects moving, with some success. However, there has been no fundamental reform of the crucial electricity sector, only another bailout of SEBs. The modalities of managing public-private partnerships remain unchanged. In the agricultural sector, there has been no reform in agricultural marketing or in altering the present perverse mix of high subsidies combined with low public investment. But there has been an encouraging recent acceptance of the principle of introducing a crop insurance scheme, though the details still have to be worked out and the machinery is not in place. Very little has been done to reduce environmental pollution of air and water. There has been significant liberalization of restrictions on inward foreign investment but no real advance in external economic engagement in trade, and no coherent policy towards mega-regional agreements. In the social sectors, there is no sign that the government is facing up to the profound incentive and accountability problems in the delivery of education and health care by the state, and the challenge of harnessing private sector delivery (combined with state regulation). There is no movement on institutional change to increase the state's administrative capacity or to curb corruption and crony capitalism via reform of election funding.

I would therefore sum up the government's performance so far as good on macro-stability; in parts passable, in parts decent, but generally underwhelming on investment revival, investment climate, and reform of markets, ownership, and regulation; and quite poor in addressing the fundamental problems involved in 'deep fiscal adjustment', international trade, education and health care, and reform of state institutions.

The Modi government has announced many targets and time-lines, set up many 'missions', and started many projects. (Some of these were started by the previous government but have been repackaged and reintroduced with new names and more fanfare.) A list of 30 official targets announced in the first year of the government was compiled by *The Economist* magazine. Several of them are manifestly unattainable in the stipulated time horizon (which is not to say they are not worth attempting).[48] Others such as the excellent programme of latrine building under the Clean India initiative are being effected rather poorly because they are far more complex than they appear on the surface, and are dogged by severe implementation problems. One of the flagship missions is 'Make in India', which has a target of creating 100 million new jobs and raising the share of manufacturing from 16 per cent to 25 per cent of GDP by 2022.[49] But achieving this target would require deep reforms in land and labour markets and infrastructure sectors (especially power and transport), and in creation of skills, thus involving almost the entire reform agenda; and the back-up policies are lacking. Another government target, relevant to 'Make in India' is to raise India's share of world exports from 2 per cent to 5 per cent by 2020. But this would require a major thrust with regard to unilateral trade liberalization, and suitable regional trade agreements, which is not happening. All this points to a general difficulty with the Modi government's approach: it is focussed too much on specific projects and too little on broad policy reform, without which the projects are likely to be under-achieved or to fail. The problem is that the government lacks a well thought out vision for economic reform to guide its efforts. Incremental change is all very well but it will not deliver the economic transformation that India needs for faster productivity growth and greater inclusion. Surprisingly, the government has also not shown much political skill in securing cooperation for its policies from opposition parties, unlike some governments in the past, which had less secure parliamentary positions. However, all is not lost by any means. The government still has two years before serious electioneering begins at the national level. The losses in the Delhi and Bihar state elections appear to have instilled a new humility in the government, in contrast to the hubris that characterized its earlier stance. There is still time for it to take the major steps that are required to put the country on the road to economic transformation.

No assessment of the Modi government would be complete without reference to an issue that many people regard as its most worrying aspect: an ambiguous adherence to the values of *liberal* democracy. As is well understood, there is no necessary connection between democracy, defined simply as rule by an elected majority, and respect for personal freedoms. Democratic rule, without protection of individual and minority rights, has the potential to degenerate into majoritarian tyranny. Will India's democracy retain its liberal character? The question arises because the Modi government is a government of the BJP, which is the political wing of the Rashtriya Swayamsevak Sangh (RSS), a Hindu nationalist organization whose core principle is that India is a Hindu nation.

Modi himself has not made any active attempt to advance a Hindu revivalist project. But his victory seems to have emboldened others, including some ministers, members of his party in parliament, and RSS leaders, to pursue, encourage, or condone a polarizing 'cultural' agenda. One early example was *'ghar wapsi'* ('homecoming'), a campaign to re-convert Muslims and Christians back to Hinduism. Another example was the campaign against so-called 'love jihad', the supposed attempt by Muslim men to seduce Hindu women into marrying them and converting to Islam. It is also the case that many people have been made to feel afraid that actions that are not in accord with the extremist version of Hinduism will be met with violent reprisals. A particularly ghastly example occurred recently (September 2015) in a village near Delhi where a Muslim man was lynched by a Hindu mob, apparently instigated by BJP cadres, acting on a rumour that he and his family had eaten and stored beef. Unfortunately the government's response to this tragedy was initial silence, followed by anodyne homilies. There have also been many recent incidents which have led to a widespread perception that freedom of expression is under threat.

Ideally, the BJP would sever its links with the RSS but that is not going to happen any time soon. At the very least, the present government should be resolute in keeping Hindu revivalist elements in check. I believe strongly that this would be the right thing to do. It would also be expedient. If India became an illiberal democracy, it would suffer a huge loss of reputation that would harm its international relations, including the outlook for inward foreign investment. It is also obvious that economic reform would not thrive in an atmosphere of conflict and discord. India has more Muslims (175 million) than all countries bar Indonesia, and is on course to become the 'largest Muslim country' within the coming three decades. If Indian Muslims felt insecure and became radicalized, the effects on all aspects of the country's development could be devastating. It is of course not easy for Modi to embrace secularism. He was an RSS *pracharak* (i.e. proselytiser) in his early career and the RSS electoral machine has made a major contribution to his electoral success. He will surely be tempted to keep the communal pot simmering so that it can be brought to the boil, as and when electorally necessary. Whatever the merits of such a political strategy for the BJP, it would be contrary to the country's long-run interest. Modi still has huge pan-Indian electoral support. He needs to become a true statesman, rise above the concerns of the RSS, and maintain India's liberal and secular traditions. As of now, it is uncertain whether he will.

WHAT DOES THE FUTURE HOLD FOR INDIA'S ECONOMIC AMBITIONS?

What does the future hold for India in its search for prosperity? The country has significant assets but also has major liabilities. On the asset side, it has a high propensity to save and invest, so there is no hard barrier to capital accumulation so long as the climate for investment remains friendly. It has an entrepreneurial class that is manifestly dynamic. It has a favourable demographic profile in that the ratio of dependents to workers is set to fall until the middle of this century. It has a 'latecomer advantage' for at least a couple of decades yet, so the potential for productivity growth from economic reform and technology assimilation is huge. Its internal market is large and expanding fast, so there is plenty of scope for economies of scale. It has a democratic system that is securely established, so a political implosion looks highly improbable.

At the same time, the handicaps are also formidable. The country has a rotten physical infrastructure and an underdeveloped financial system. There are large distortions in the functioning of goods and factor markets. Inefficient public sector enterprises and banks impose a large fiscal and efficiency burden. The skill base of the population is meagre in relation to what is needed for a dynamic modern economy. The quality of education is appalling at all levels. Standards in health care and sanitation are miserably low. There is severe environmental degradation. The state's capacity is weak and its major institutions are sorely in need of regeneration. Corruption and crony capitalism have not subverted the state altogether but are nevertheless deeply embedded in the system. India's democratic functioning leaves a lot to be desired, as exemplified by the repeated gridlocks that afflict parliament due to the obstructive behaviour of legislators, whichever party is in power. The list could go on.

Observers have variously identified two factors that may tilt the balance towards the asset side of the ledger. The first is the growing weight of the middle class. The second is the change in the political centre of gravity away from the central government and towards the states. Estimates of the size of the middle class vary because there is no agreed way of defining the concept. If the middle class is defined as those people above a uniform threshold level of income that is comparable across countries, its size in India is quite small, at most 100 million people. If it is defined more generously to include the so-called 'neo middle class' perhaps another 200 million could be added to that number.[50] (Interestingly, the number of people who identify themselves as middle class is much higher.)[51] On either definition, the size of the middle class is due to expand rapidly in the coming decades (how rapid depends on the assumed growth rate of national income).

The key feature of the middle class is that its members do not live from hand to mouth, and have the income and the energy to do other things besides worrying about survival. This has been associated in parts of the West with 'middle class values' that are favourable to economic development such as demand for excellence in education and health care, insistence on quality in consumption and infrastructure services, penchant for entrepreneurship, backing for competition, meritocracy, the rule of law, clean and accountable government, democratic norms, respect for property rights, and stable economic policies. It is certainly possible that the Indian middle class will be similarly progressive in outlook but I doubt that one could count on that with certainty. After all, the middle classes in Latin America and Southern Europe have acted at various times in the past as fodder for reactionary and authoritarian regimes. It is also not clear to me that the Indian middle class will necessarily be favourably disposed towards 'inclusive' policies or better public services (rather than just exiting the system). And in any case, the force of the middle-class demand for various good things will not be felt all that strongly in the immediate future until its numerical strength has built up. India has to lay the foundations for the future right now.

Another idea that is very much in fashion is that the ongoing shift of economic and political power away from the centre will release the constraints on Indian development. The 14th Finance Commission has helped the cause of devolution by an award (accepted by the Modi government) that has increased significantly the untied, discretionary funding that is available to state governments.[52] The presumed benefits include more democratic participation, and more responsive and accountable government, which would result in better delivery of public services. Governments would come closer to the people, so they could design programmes better suited to people's needs. Another argument in favour is that more discretion in the hands of the states will lead to more competition between them, and the demonstration effect will work its magic.

Whether this faith in greater devolution is justified remains to be seen.[53] There are many imponderables. Much depends on whether the states increase development spending and social sector programmes to compensate for the roll-back of centrally sponsored schemes. Ironically, in recent years, decentralization of power from the central government has been accompanied by greater *de facto* centralization of power in many states in the hands of chief ministers. (Half of India's states show complete or near-complete dominance of chief ministers.)[54] More untied revenue may simply increase their capacity to indulge in populist giveaways. There are large variations in the quality of governance in different states. It is possible that differences in state performance will be exacerbated by the movement of resources to the better-performing states. A competitive 'race to the bottom' in giving concessions to attract investment is another danger. It seems obvious, therefore, that 'competitive federalism' needs to be balanced by 'cooperative federalism' to coordinate the policies of the states, and see to it that they do not act at cross-purposes. (Radical programmes, such as the 'deep fiscal adjustment' that I have advocated, would require centre-states cooperation of a high order.) While this is recognized in principle, the institutions do not exist to make it a reality. The inter-state council, which is supposed to perform this function, has been moribund for years. The least that should be done is to re-activate it. Making cooperative federalism work is hugely important but easier said than done.

It could also be argued, quite plausibly, that the full benefits of devolution would be obtained only by empowering local governments. Unfortunately, putting this idea into practice would be far from easy. Local governments do not have any independent sources of revenue, and the Constitution assigns the state governments huge powers in deciding the functions to be devolved to local bodies and the funding they receive. Even the union finance commissions can only recommend, not mandate, what state governments should do. The 14th Finance Commission has made available a sizeable increase in funds to the states (three times the previous award) for the purpose of funding local bodies. The distribution within states has to be done in line with the recommendations of state finance commissions. But some states have not even constituted such bodies on a regular basis. There are also cases of states blatantly violating the Constitution by not establishing local bodies and not holding local elections. To make a success of decentralization, there will have to be much more clarity about the assignment of functions to local bodies, as well as more oversight to ensure that the states fulfil the intentions behind the provisions in the Constitution. The position at local levels does not help. Local elites are just as greedy as national and state elites. In addition, due to past neglect, administrative competence is seriously lacking for making good use of disbursed funds. If devolution is to be effective, there will have to be a major strengthening of local structures in various areas such as planning, investment appraisal, accounting and auditing, and public procurement. Thus, greater decentralization is not a panacea by any means. It may work to promote economic development or it may not. Only time will tell.

There is fundamentally nothing mysterious about the basic political economy problem facing India. The country has huge economic potential. But it needs a consistent and coherent economic package of policies that would enable it to achieve rapid and high-quality growth for an extended period. In essence, the package would involve re-imagining the state–market–private sector relationship so that the state on the one hand, and the market and the private sector on the other, perform the tasks that they are best suited for, and perform them well. The root problem of Indian development is that the Indian state may not have the capacity, drive, will, and stamina to deliver such a package. (By the 'state' I mean not just the central government but also state and local governments, and the executive, legislative, and judicial apparatus at all three tiers.) India clearly needs both less of the state and more of the state. The difficulty is that a large part of necessary reform involves the state reforming itself.

Crucially, the Indian state has to carry out the reform project in the context of India's democracy. It is sometimes tempting to look to an authoritarian regime as a solution to India's problems but it is wise to look away. Democracy has intrinsic value, even for the poorest people, so long as it includes not only periodic elections but protection of basic rights and civil liberties. Moreover, it is difficult to imagine a country as complex and heterogeneous as India being run on authoritarian lines. Democracies have a pronounced informational advantage over authoritarian regimes and their popular legitimacy gives them an edge in managing social conflicts. As a result, long-established democracies, among which India now belongs, tend to acquire a socially beneficial immunity to endogenous systemic upheavals. And finally, all authoritarian regimes raise the ancient question: who or what is there to ensure they will remain benevolent? It is just as well that, in India, democracy is now the only game in town.

Nonetheless, it is wishful thinking to believe that the present condition of Indian democracy is compatible with radical economic transformation. Recent history supports the observation that the only reforms that are possible in India, except in the aftermath of a major crisis, are of the slow, stealthy, and incremental variety. Democracy in India suffers from many of the faults associated with this form of government in other parts of the world in times past and present. It is obstinately short-termist, with populist tendencies, and shows an inclination to drift without facing hard truths. It has certainly shown great resilience in the face of various shocks such as droughts, external wars, revolutionary movements, macroeconomic turmoil, and social and religious strife. Unfortunately this same feature has reinforced a complacency that is perhaps its principal shortcoming. India's democracy exhibits in exaggerated form what David Runciman has called democracy's 'confidence trap'[55]. The feeling that Indian democracy can survive anything that is thrown at it has as its dark side a propensity to let things slide, and an inability to pursue long-term, purposive strategies.

Finally, what are India's likely economic prospects over the next two or three decades? Though making predictions about the future is a mug's game, the reader may like to know (and accept or discard) the opinion that I have formed on the basis of the considerations advanced in this book. I return here to a point made in the introductory chapter. It would be odd to call India 'prosperous' if it did not enjoy the per capita income level of a 'high-income country' by today's standards. At any rate, that sets a relevant benchmark. To reach that benchmark in the next quarter century, India would need to have average per capita growth of at least 6 per cent a year, and preferably 8 per cent a year. This kind of performance requires rapid and continuing productivity improvements over a long period, and it has been exceedingly rare. Strictly speaking, only three countries (China, South Korea, and Taiwan) have succeeded.[56] India's target is even tougher since it is aiming at *high-quality* growth that is inclusive and environmentally sustainable (to be fair, China, South Korea, and Taiwan have all had inclusive growth. But its environmental quality has not been up to scratch, at least in the case of China). It is also noteworthy that China is not a democracy, and neither were South Korea and Taiwan during their fast-growth phases.

Is India's democracy motivated and tenacious enough in its collective will to defy regression to the mean, and achieve high-quality per capita growth of 7 or 8 per cent a year (i.e. aggregate growth of 8 or 9 per cent a year) for an extended period of two or three decades? My patriotic heart leaps up to say 'yes'. But my objective and analytical head says 'doubtful' because no democracy has ever done so, the international economic environment is now much harsher than what the few successful countries had to face, and India will quite rightly have to take environmental objectives much more seriously than they did. I think there is a fair chance of high-quality per capita growth of 6 per cent a year (i.e. aggregate growth of 7 per cent a year) over a prolonged stretch of time if Indian democracy could pull itself together and embark on a truly radical programme of economic and governance reforms. That would be a challenging, highly rewarding, and not unreasonably ambitious project. More modest per capita growth of 4 or 5 per cent a year (aggregate growth of 5 or 6 per cent a year) is more likely, which would nevertheless put India among the upper middle income countries (by today's standards) at the end of the next quarter century. Even that would be no mean accomplishment and would require substantial economic reform to combat the ever-present threat of a slowdown in the rise of productivity. Unfortunately, given India's political economy, regression to a lower-than-modest growth rate cannot be ruled out. It is as well to remember that rapid, high-quality growth can never be taken for granted.

At least two-thirds of India's people have incomes and opportunities that are meagre enough to limit sharply their capacity to lead a fulfilling life. To remedy this state of affairs thoroughly and completely must surely be the country's supreme policy objective. A radical reform agenda can be designed to achieve this ambition within the next two and a half decades. In implementing it, India's biggest challenge will be to become less of a fractious and lackadaisical democracy, and more of a resolute and purposeful one, while retaining its liberal and secular personality. There is no blueprint, template, or formula that contains the secret of how this is to be done.

NOTES

1. Some explanations for secular stagnation focus on stagnant demand, i.e. households and firms are not spending enough even at zero interest rates. Others focus on the supply side, especially ageing of the population, and slowdown in the rate of technical progress.
2. See Fukuyama (2011). I am of course well aware that history may not determine destiny. North and South Korea have the same history and culture but have had vastly different recent trajectories.
3. For an interesting take on this argument, see Das (2012).
4. Readers who are interested in a comparison of the Congress-led government of 2004–2014 and the BJP-led government of 1999–2004 may like to see Ghatak, Ghosh, and Kotwal (2014) and Nayar (2015).
5. For background to this section, see Chapter 8.
6. Inflation targeting should be 'flexible', giving the central bank leeway in the length of time it takes to hit the target, depending on the state of the real economy.

7. To be fair to the previous government, it had initiated stabilization policies in 2013/14, which were already showing some success. But the oil price decline helped to solidify the success.

8. An important related issue is discussed in n. 34, Chapter 8.

9. he Modi government actively considered departing from the FRBM and 14th FC fiscal road map yet again in 2016/17. In the event, the budget for 2016/17 wisely stuck to a target fiscal deficit of 3.5 per cent of GDP. However, it has to be said that this projected deficit is based on an over-optimistic forecast for non-tax revenue from disinvestment (if past performance is anything to go by). Note also that the states are unlikely to meet their fiscal targets in 2016/17 since they have taken on some of the debt of discoms; and their wage and salary bills will go up in response to the award of the seventh pay commission. The outlook for reducing the consolidated fiscal deficit is thus quite challenging.

10. Note also that though the macro aspects of fiscal policy have been well handled, there has been little progress in reforming the pattern of taxes and government expenditures, a hugely important requirement of inclusive growth (see below under 'deep fiscal adjustment').

11. The Finance Minister announced in the budget for 2016/17 that the government would proceed to amend the RBI Act to give a statutory basis to the inflation targeting regime, including the appointment of a monetary policy committee. It is obviously important that the independence of the monetary policy committee should be closely guarded. In my view, the committee should have equal representation of members chosen by government and RBI, with a casting vote for the RBI governor.

12. In March 2016 the government started to change the arrangements with regard to small savings. It announced that it would in the future change the interest rates on most small savings products quarterly rather than annually. It has also brought various small savings rates closer to bank deposit rates though a gap still remains.

13. This section is based on the material in parts of Chapters 4, 5, 6, and 8.

14. The Finance Minister announced in his 2016/17 budget speech the government's intention to amend the Companies Act to remove impediments to start-ups, and the ease of doing business more generally.

15. Movement towards this goal in the budget for 2016/17 can only be described as trivial.

16. The material in this section is covered in greater detail in Chapters 6 and 10.

17. The government's Economic Survey for 2015/16 has an excellent chapter that quantifies 'bounties to the rich', including the subsidies for various small savings products that go mostly to the well-off. Subsidies for gold, rail fares, LPG, electricity, aviation fuel, and even kerosene also go quite substantially to the well-off. See Government of India (2016).

18. See Chapter 6 of Government of India (2016).

19. In the budget of 2016/17, the Finance Minister announced the intention of the government to introduce a bill to give Aadhar a statutory status so that it can be made the basis for direct transfers. Shortly thereafter, the said bill was introduced as a 'money bill' in the Lok Sabha and passed. This constitutes an important preparatory move for direct benefit transfers. But the budget contained practically nothing on eliminating subsidies, other than a proposed pilot in a few districts to carry out direct transfer of fertilizer subsidies. As for the Aadhar bill itself, substantial privacy concerns remain, and regulatory and judicial safeguards need to be put in place (see Mehta 2016).

20. For more explanation and detail on the material covered in this section, see Chapters 5, 6, and 7.
21. The added growth would also pack an inclusiveness punch because it would create extra incomes *directly* in the hands of poor people rather than *indirectly* by mechanisms of redistribution.
22. India should certainly try to increase its share of world markets in labour-intensive goods. But it is not in a position to rely *predominantly* on such a strategy because China is an established competitive force, and several other countries with lower unit labour costs are now in a strong position to compete as Chinese costs rise. Moreover, the prospects for rapid global growth are far from rosy. So India will also have to obtain the rapid productivity growth that arises from labour reallocation by greater reliance on the domestic market than was the case in East Asia. Of course, this does not mean that India should become protectionist. That would only make matters worse. Engagement with mega-regionals in East Asia may be part of the answer (see below).
23. This is why India has a striking dearth of mid-sized firms compared with East Asia. Indian industry has instead a huge number of tiny firms that stay tiny and do not enjoy economies of scale (see Chapter 5).
24. Another major constraint, especially for small firms in both the organized and unorganized sectors, is access to credit. There is clearly a market failure in this area but correcting it is a difficult design problem that financial sector reform has to address. The solutions lie in improving the availability of credit via better financial and credit infrastructure, not in blanket interest rate subsidies that inevitably fail to discriminate between good and bad borrowers.
25. Employers have partially circumvented the rigidity of the employment laws by hiring contract workers but this is an unsatisfactory solution not only from the workers' standpoint but also from the national standpoint since employers do not have any incentive to train them.
26. Another rationale for privatization is provided by its fiscal impact. Public sector inefficiency means that many PSEs could be sold at prices that are considerably higher than the present value of future dividends under state ownership, so there would be a net fiscal gain. More generally, a privatization programme should be seen as a way for the state to rearrange its asset portfolio, thereby allowing it to focus on socially beneficial investments that the private sector would be reluctant to undertake.
27. The opposition's main demands are: a) to drop the 1 per cent central sales tax on inter-state transactions that is part of the bill; b) to enshrine in the Constitution a maximum GST rate of 18 per cent; and c) to set up a judicial appellate body to resolve disputes, instead of the inter-state council. As regards (a), the government is quite rightly willing to concede on the inter-state sales tax, which makes no economic sense; on (b), it is willing to agree on the maximum GST rate, provided, very sensibly, that it is not made into a rigid constitutional provision; on (c) the disagreement could be resolved quite easily, if there were the will to do so.
28. The budget speech of 2016/17 announced the government's intention to amend the Motor Vehicles Act to end the government monopoly in state bus transport. This would be a good pro-competition move. Regrettably, the budget also contained some anti-competitive trade protection measures (see below).
29. In the budget for 2016/17, the Finance Minister announced his intention to bring forward a bill containing a 'code for resolution of financial firms' in addition to the 'insolvency and bankruptcy code' referred to above.

30. One encouraging development that deserves mention is the decision to allow private companies to mine coal for commercial sale. This is not privatization but it does end the state monopoly in this area, a very desirable change.
31. Even the revenue gain is modest since buyers are not likely to pay a high price if the enterprises remain under government control.
32. Moreover, disinvestment sometimes involves just a transfer of an asset from one arm of the government to another. For example, the government recently sold 10 per cent of Indian Oil Corporation but 90 per cent of the shares were bought by the state-owned Life Insurance Corporation of India.
33. The central budget for 2016/17 puts considerable reliance on disinvestment to balance the books but no convincing reason is given to expect a more successful outcome than in the previous year.
34. 'Indradhanush' does set up a Bank Boards Bureau to handle appointments in PSBs. However, since both the government and the RBI will be represented on it, the change may turn out to be of form only.
35. According to the UDAY scheme, willing state governments are to take over 75 per cent of the debt of the discoms and give the lending banks state government bonds instead. The rest of the debt is to be converted in the market by the lending banks into state-guaranteed bonds. The interest rate on the government bonds would be lower than the banks obtained previously, so they would take a 'haircut'. The rise in the fiscal deficits of the state governments would not be counted in assessing their performance in meeting fiscal targets. The state governments are also supposed to take over up to 50 per cent of the future losses of discoms on a graded basis. Will state governments put pressure on discoms to improve their future performance? And would such pressure be effective in the absence of pricing and other reforms? I am not optimistic. For a critique of the scheme, see Govinda Rao (2015b).
36. See Ministry of Finance (2015b). The committee was chaired by Vijay Kelkar. A major innovation suggested by the committee was to reverse the usual order of business in PPPs. The government could build infrastructure and sell it to the private sector to run. This may raise efficiency since risks would be better distributed. Moreover, since the sale of built assets could finance the building of new ones, the process could be self-financing.
37. One of the few innovative measures in the central budget for 2016/17 was an allocation of funds for a crop insurance scheme. With modern technologies to assess crop damage and move money directly into farmers' bank accounts, the scheme could be very beneficial. But it will probably take at least a couple of years to set up the supporting structures. In other respects, the budget did little beyond the ordinary for agriculture.
38. See Chapter 12 for elaboration of the material covered in this section.
39. In its budget for 2016/17, the Modi government has unfortunately shown signs of wavering even on the unilateral trade liberalization that has already occurred. Tariffs were raised on quite a wide range of inputs on the specious ground of 'incentivising domestic value addition to help Make in India'. This economic illiteracy will not help to create a competitive manufacturing sector.
40. This section is based on the material in Chapters 9 and 10.
41. In the budget for 2016/17, it is mooted that some 'special universities' will be set up that are free of the usual micro-regulation. Time will tell.
42. See Ministry of Health and Family Welfare (2014).

43. The expenditure increase is supposed to go largely into expansion of free, publicly provided, primary care. As seen above, this seems very unwise, given the dysfunctions in public delivery in this area.
44. In the budget of 2016/17, the Finance Minister announced an intention to launch yet another health insurance scheme aimed at the poor, which will offer health cover up to Rs. 100,000 per family. How this will relate to the RSBY is left unexplained.
45. Analytical and empirical support for this section can be found in Chapter 11.
46. For some detail, see Chapter 11. Administrative reform has been exhaustively examined by many government committees, including most recently the Second Administrative Reforms Commission, which reported in 2009. Many sensible recommendations were made but nothing has been done.
47. 'Petty' corruption involves small sums of money per transaction but its total impact is as large as that of big ticket corruption. It is especially prevalent in the issue of permits at the retail level, the diversion of funds from the government's transfer programmes, and 'theft of time' by government functionaries who are absent when they should be working. Reducing petty corruption will require various methods, including the use of technologies of e-governance.
48. See The Economist (2015). Examples of completely unrealistic targets are: Clean the river Ganges by 2019; eradicate tuberculosis and measles by 2020; build a hundred 'smart cities' by 2020; train 500 million people by 2022; roll out broadband in over 600,000 villages by 2017.
49. For a useful commentary on 'Make in India', see Sharma (2015).
50. These are very approximate numbers. See Birdsall (2015), Ninan (2015), and Pew Research Centre (2015).
51. See Kapur and Vaishnav (2014b).
52. The effect of the award of the 14th Finance Commission was to increase untied tax devolution from the centre to the states in 2015/16 by approximately 1 per cent of GDP, and untied transfers by 0.1 per cent of GDP, but to reduce tied transfers (centrally sponsored schemes) by 0.6 per cent of GDP. Thus net transfer went up by only 0.5 per cent of GDP but the proportion of the total transfer that is untied went up substantially. In addition, the Commission tripled the transfer to the states for distribution to local governments.
53. See Govinda Rao (2015a).
54. See Manor (2015).
55. See Runciman (2013).
56. See Chapter 1. A few other countries have also done impressively well over several decades, including in particular Japan and Singapore.

REFERENCES

Abreu, D., P. Bardhan, M. Ghatak, A. Kotwal, D. Mookherjee, and D. Ray (2014a), '(Mis)leading Attack on NREGA', *Ideas for India*, 12 November.

Abreu, D., P. Bardhan, M. Ghatak, A. Kotwal, D. Mookherjee, and D. Ray (2014b), 'Response to the Bhagwati-Panagariya Rejoinder on MNREGA', *Ideas for India*, 14 December.

Acharya, S. (2006), *Essays in Macroeconomic Policy in India*, Oxford University Press, New Delhi.

Acharya, S. (2012), 'India and the Global Crisis', in C. Bergsten and C. Henning (eds.), *Global Economics in Extraordinary Times*, 157–176, Peterson Institute of International Economics, Washington, DC.

Acharya, S., and R. Mohan (eds.) (2010), *India's Economy – Performance and Challenges: Essays in Honour of Montek Ahluwalia*, Oxford University Press, New Delhi.

Ahluwalia, I., R. Kanbur, and P. Mohanty (eds.) (2014), *Urbanization in India: Challenges, Opportunities and the Way Forward*, Sage Publications, New Delhi.

Ahluwalia, M. (2011), 'Prospects and Policy Challenges in the Twelfth Plan', *Economic and Political Weekly*, Vol. 46(21), 88–105.

Ahluwalia, M. (2013), 'Policies for Strong Inclusive Growth', in S. Kochhar (ed.), *An Agenda for India's Growth: Essays in Honour of P. Chidambaram*, 55–93, Academic Foundation, New Delhi.

Ahsan, A., and C. Pages (2009), 'Are All Labour Regulations Equal? Evidence from Indian Manufacturing', *Journal of Comparative Economics*, Vol. 37(1), 62–75.

Aiyar, S. (2016), 'Dodgy Statistics and Global Tempests Can Sink Budget Calculations', *Economic Times*, 2 March.

Aiyar, Y., and M. Walton (2014), 'Rights, Accountability and Citizenship: Examining India's Emerging Welfare State', Accountability Initiative, Working Paper, Centre for Policy Research, New Delhi.

Akerlof, G. (1970), 'The Market for Lemons: Quality Uncertainty and the Market Mechanism', *Quarterly Journal of Economics*, Vol. 84(3), 488–500.

Alfaro, L., and A. Chari (2010), 'India Transformed? Insights from the Firm Level 1988–2005', *India Policy Forum 2009/10*, Vol. 6, 153–224.

Amin, A. (2009), 'Labour Regulation and Employment in India's Retail Stores', *Journal of Comparative Economics*, Vol. 37(1), 47–61.

Anand, R., D. Coady, A. Mohommad, V. Thakoor, and J. Walsh (2013), 'The Fiscal and Welfare Impacts of Reforming Fuel Subsidies in India', Working Paper No. WP/13/28, International Monetary Fund, Washington, DC.

Anand, S., and V. Joshi (1979), 'Domestic Distortions, Income Distribution and the Theory of Optimum Subsidy', *Economic Journal*, Vol. 89(354), 336–352.

Asian Development Bank (2009), *Enterprises in Asia: Fostering Dynamism in SMEs*, Asian Development Bank, Manila.

Athukorala, P. (2009), 'Outward Direct Investment from India', *Asian Development Review*, Vol. 26(2), 125–153.

Athukorala, P. (2014), 'How India Fits into Global Production Sharing: Experience, Prospects, and Policy Options', *India Policy Forum 2013/14*, Vol. 10, 57–116.

Balakrishnan (2010), *Economic Growth in India: History and Prospects*, Oxford University Press, New Delhi.

Banerjee, A. (2012), 'Comment' (on the Mahal-Fan paper), *India Policy Forum 2011/12*, Vol. 8, 83–87.

Banerjee, A. (2015), 'Policies for a Better-Fed World', Working Paper No. 15-09, Department of Economics, MIT.

Banerjee, A., R. Banerji, E. Duflo, R. Glennerster, and S. Khemani (2010), 'Pitfalls of Participatory Programs: Evidence from a Randomized Evaluation in Education in India', *American Economic Journal: Economic Policy*, Vol. 2(1), 1–30.

Banerjee, A., S. Cole, and E. Duflo (2004), 'Banking Reform in India', *India Policy Forum 2004*, Vol. 1, 277–323.

Banerjee, A., A. Deaton, and E. Duflo (2004), 'Health Care Delivery in Rural Rajasthan', *Economic and Political Weekly*, Vol. 39(9), 944–949.

Banerjee, A., and E. Duflo (2011), *Poor Economics*, MIT Press, Cambridge, MA.

Banerjee, A., E. Duflo, and R. Glennerster (2008), 'Putting a Band-Aid on a Corpse: Incentives for Nurses in the India Public Health Care System', *Journal of the European Economic Association*, Vol. 6(2–3), 487–500.

Banerjee, A., and T. Piketty (2005), 'Top Indian Incomes 1922–2000', *World Bank Economic Review*, Vol. 19(1), 1–20.

Bardhan, P. (1984), *The Political Economy of Development in India*, Oxford University Press, New York.

Bardhan, P. (2010), *Awakening Giants, Feet of Clay: Assessing the Economic Rise of China and India*, Princeton University Press, Princeton, NJ.

Bardhan, P. (2011), 'Challenges for a Minimum Social Democracy in India', *Economic and Political Weekly*, Vol. 46(10), 39–43.

Bardhan, P. (2015a), 'The State and Development: The Need for a Reappraisal of the Current Literature', Available as BREAD Working Paper No. 451. Forthcoming in *Journal of Economic Literature*.

Bardhan, P. (2015b), 'Reflections on Indian Political Economy', *Economic and Political Weekly*, Vol. 50(18), 14–17.

Baumol, W. J. (1990), 'Entrepreneurship: Productive, Unproductive and Destructive', *Journal of Political Economy*, 98(5), 893–921.

Bergsten, C. (2015), 'India's Rise: A Strategy for Trade-Led Growth', Briefing Paper No. 15-4, Peterson Institute of International Finance.

Bertrand, M., R. Hanna, S. Djankov, and S. Mullainathan (2007), 'Obtaining a Driving License in India: An Experimental Approach to Studying Corruption', *Quarterly Journal of Economics*, 122(4), 1639–1676.

Besley, T., and R. Burgess (2004), 'Can Labour Regulation Hinder Economic Performance: Evidence from India', *Quarterly Journal of Economics*, Vol. 119(1), 91–134.

Bhagwati, J. (1993), *India in Transition*, Oxford University Press, New York.

Bhagwati, J., and P. Desai (1970), *India: Planning for Industrialization*, Oxford University Press, New York.

Bhagwati, J., and A. Panagariya (2013), *Why Growth Matters*, Public Affairs, New York.

Bhagwati, J., and A. Panagariya (2014a), 'Rural Inefficiency Act', *Times of India*, 23 October.

Bhagwati, J., and A. Panagariya (2014b), 'Rejoinder on NREGA', *Times of India*, 19 November.

Bhagwati, J., and V. Ramaswami (1963), 'Domestic Distortions, Tariffs, and the Theory of Optimum Subsidy', *Journal of Political Economy*, Vol. 71(1), 44–50.

Bhalla, S. (2011), 'Indian Inflation: Populism, Politics and Procurement Prices', Developing Trends, *Oxus Research Report*, Vol. 1(2).

Bhattacharjea, A. (2006), 'Labour Market Regulation and Industrial Performance in India: A Critical Review of the Empirical Evidence', *Indian Journal of Labour Economics*, Vol. 49(2), 211–231.

Bhattacharjea, A. (2012), 'India's New Anti-Trust Regime: The First Two Years of Enforcement', *Anti-Trust Bulletin*, Vol. 57(3), 449–484.

Birdsall, N. (2015), 'Does the Rise of the Middle Class Lock in Good Government in the Developing World?', Centre for Global Development, Washington, DC.

Blom, A., and H. Saeki (2011), 'Employment and Skill Set of Newly Employed Graduate Engineers in India', Policy Research Working Paper No. 5640, World Bank.

Bosworth, B., and S. Collins (2015), 'India's Growth Slowdown: End of an Era?', *India Review*, Vol. 14(1), 8–25.

Bosworth, B., S. Collins, and A. Virmani (2007), 'Sources of Growth in the Indian Economy', *India Policy Forum 2006/7*, Vol. 3, 1–50.

Buchanan, J., and G. Tullock (1962), *The Calculus of Consent: The Logical Foundations of Constitutional Democracy*, University of Michigan Press, Ann Arbor.

Chakravorty, S. (2013), 'A New Price Regime: Land Markets in Urban and Rural India', *Economic and Political Weekly*, 48(17), 45–54.

Chatterjee, E. (2015), 'Power-Hungry: The Indian State and the Troubled Transition in Indian Electricity', in B. Harriss-White and J. Heyer (eds.), *Indian Capitalism in Development*, 208–225, Routledge, New York.

Chaudhary, N., J. Hammer, M. Kremer, K. Muralidharan, and H. Rogers (2006), 'Missing in Action: Teacher and Worker Absence in Developing Countries', *Journal of Economic Perspectives*, Vol. 20(1), 91–116.

CII/KPMG (2014), *Ease of Doing Business in India*.

Coase, R. (1960), 'The Problem of Social Cost', *Journal of Law and Economics*, Vol. 3, 1–44.

Corbridge, S., J. Harriss, and C. Jeffrey (2013), *India Today*, Polity Press, Cambridge.

Das, G. (2012), *India Grows at Night*, Penguin Allen Lane, New Delhi.

Das, J., and J. Hammer (2005), 'Which Doctor? Combining Vignettes and Item Response to Measure Doctor Quality', *Journal of Development Economics*, Vol. 78(2), 348–383.

Das, J., and J. Hammer (2007), 'Money for Nothing: The Dire Straits of Medical Practice in Delhi, India', *Journal of Development Economics*, Vol. 83(1), 1–36.

Das J., and J. Hammer (2012), 'Health and Health Care Policy in India: The Case for Quality of Care', in C. Ghate (ed.), *The Oxford Handbook on the Indian Economy*, Oxford University Press, New York.

Das, J., A. Holla, V. Das, M. Mohanan, D. Tabak, and B. Chan (2012), 'In Urban and Rural India, a Standardized Patient Study Showed Low Levels of Provider Training and Huge Quality Gaps', *Health Affairs*, Vol. 31(12), 2774–2784.

Das, J., and T. Zajonc (2010), 'India Shining and Bharat Drowning: Comparing Two Indian States to the Worldwide Distribution in Mathematics Achievement', *Journal of Development Economics*, Vol. 92(2), 175–187.

Das Gupta, M. (2012), 'Public Health', in K. Basu and A. Maertens (eds.), *The New Oxford Companion to Economics*, 573–578, Oxford University Press, Delhi.

Dasgupta, P. (2010), 'The Place of Nature in Economic Development', in D. Rodrik and M. Rosenzweig (eds.), *Handbook of Development Economics*, Vol. 5, 4977–5046, Elsevier, Amsterdam.

Datt, G. (1997), *Poverty in India 1951–1994: Trends and Decompositions*, World Bank, Washington, DC.

Datt, G., and M. Ravallion (2010), 'Shining for the Poor Too', *Economic and Political Weekly*, 45(7), 55–60.

Davala, S., R. Jhabvala, G. Standing, and S. Mehta (2015), *Basic Income: A Transformative Policy for India*, Bloomsbury Academic, London.

Deaton, A. (2013), *The Great Escape: Health, Wealth, and Inequality*, Princeton University Press, Princeton, NJ.

Deaton, A., and J. Dreze (2009), 'Food and Nutrition in India: Facts and Interpretations', *Economic and Political Weekly*, Vol. 44(7), 42–65.

Debroy, B. (2014), 'Correcting the Administrative Deficit', in B. Debroy, A. Tellis, and R. Trevor (eds.), *Getting India Back on Track*, 265–280, Carnegie Endowment for International Peace, Washington, DC.

Desai, M. (2011), *The Rediscovery of India*, Bloomsbury Academic, London.

Desai, N. (2010), 'Sustaining High Growth', in S. Kochhar (ed.), *India on the Growth Turnpike: Essays in Honour of Vijay Kelkar*, 59–90, Academic Foundation, New Delhi.

Desai, S. B., A. Dubey, L. Joshi, M. Sen, A. Sharif, and R. Vanneman (2010), *Human Development in India: Challenges for a Society in Transition*, Oxford University Press, New Delhi.

Desai, S., A. Dubey, R. Vanneman, and R. Banerji (2009), 'Private Schooling in India: A New Educational Landscape', *India Policy Forum 2008/9*, Vol. 5, 1–38.

Dobbs, R., A. Madgavkar, D. Barton, E. Labaye, J. Manyika, C. Roxburgh, S. Lund, and S. Madhav (2012), *The World at Work: Jobs, Pay, and Skills for 3.5 Billion People*, McKinsey Global Institute.

Dougherty, S., V. Frisancho, and K. Krishna (2014), 'State-Level Reforms and Firm-Level Productivity in India', *India Policy Forum 2013/14*, Vol. 10, 1–56.

Dreze, J. (2010), 'Employment Guarantee and the Right to Work', in N. Jayal and P. Mehta (eds.) *The Oxford Companion to Politics in India*, 510–517, Oxford University Press, New York.

Dreze, J., and A. Sen (1995), *India: Economic Development and Social Opportunity*, Oxford University Press, New York.

Dreze, J., and A. Sen (2013), *An Uncertain Glory: India and Its Contradictions*, Penguin Allen Lane, London.

Economist, The (2011), 'Business in India—Adventures in Capitalism', 22 October .

Economist, The (2015), 'Modi's Many Tasks', 23–29 May.

Eichengreen, B., and P. Gupta (2011), 'Service Sector: India's Road to Economic Growth', *India Policy Forum 2010/11*, Vol. 7, 1–42.

Fourteenth Finance Commission (Chairman: Y. V. Reddy) (2015), *Report of the Fourteenth Finance Commission*, New Delhi.

French, R., and G. Kingdon (2010), 'The Relative Effectiveness of Private and Government Schools in Rural India: Evidence from ASER Data', DoQSS Working Paper No. 10-03, Institute of Education.

Fukuyama, F. (2011), *The Origins of Political Order*, Profile Books, London.

Gandhi, A., and M. Walton (2012), 'Where Do India's Billionaires Get Their Wealth?', *Economic and Political Weekly*, Vol. 47(40), 10–14.

Ghani, E. (ed.) (2010), *The Service Revolution in South Asia*, Oxford University Press, New York.

Ghatak, M., and P. Ghosh (2011), 'The Land Acquisition Bill: A Critique and a Proposal', *Economic and Political Weekly*, Vol. 46(41), 66–72.

Ghatak, M., and P. Ghosh (2015), 'Land Acquisition Debate: The Price Is Not Right', *Ideas for India*, 29 July.

Ghatak, M., P. Ghosh, and A. Kotwal (2014), 'Growth in the Time of UPA: Myths and Reality', *Economic and Political Weekly*, Vol. 49(16), 35–43.

Gill, K. (2009), 'A Primary Evaluation of Delivery under the National Rural Health Mission', Working Paper No. 1/2009, Programme Evaluation Division, Planning Commission.

Goldberg, P., A. Khandelwal, N. Pavenik, and P. Topalova (2009), 'Trade Liberalization and New Imported Inputs', *American Economic Review: Papers and Proceedings*, Vol. 99(2), 494–500.

Goswami, O. (1996), *Corporate Bankruptcy in India*, OECD, Paris.

Government of India (2013), *Green National Accounts in India: A Framework*, A Report by an Expert Group Convened by the National Statistical Organization.

Government of India (2014), *Millennium Development Goals: India Country Report 2014*, Ministry of Statistics and Programme Implementation, New Delhi.

Government of India (2015a), *Economic Survey, 2014–15*, Ministry of Finance, New Delhi.

Government of India (2015b), *Report of the High Level Committee on Re-orienting the Role and Restructuring of Food Corporation of India* (Chairman: Shanta Kumar), New Delhi.

Government of India (2016), *Economic Survey 2015–16*, Ministry of Finance, New Delhi.

Government of India, Central Statistics Office (2011), *National Accounts Statistics, Back Series, 1950–51 to 2004–05*, New Delhi.

Government of India, Central Statistics Office (2012, 2013, 2014, 2015, 2016), *Press Notes on Estimates of National Income, Expenditure, Saving and Capital Formation*, New Delhi.

Govinda Rao, M. (2011), 'Curing the Cancer of Concessions', *Financial Express*, 5 December.

Govinda Rao, M. (2015a), 'For a Truer Decentralization', *Financial Express*, 2 November.

Govinda Rao, M. (2015b), 'UDAY Lacks Brightness', *Financial Express*, 20 November.

Govinda Rao, M. (2016), 'The Tyranny of the Status Quo: The Challenge of Reforming the Indian Tax System', *India Policy Forum 2015/16*, Vol. 12 (forthcoming).

Gowda, M., and E. Sridharan (2012), 'Reforming India's Party Financing and Election Expenditure Laws', *Election Law Journal*, Vol. 11(2), 226–240.

Goyal, S., and P. Pandey (2013), 'Contract Teachers in India', *Education Economics*, Vol. 21(5), 464–484.

Greenstone, M., and R. Hanna (2014), 'Environmental Regulations, Air and Water Pollution, and Infant Mortality', *American Economic Review*, Vol. 104(10), 3032–3072.

Greenstone, M., and B. Jack (2015), 'Envirodevonomics: A Research Agenda for an Emerging Field', *Journal of Economic Literature*, Vol. 53(1), 5–42.

Grout, P., and M. Stevens (2003), 'The Assessment: Financing and Managing Public Services', *Oxford Review of Economic Policy*, 19(2), 215–234.

Guha, R. (2007), *India after Gandhi: The History of the World's Largest Democracy*, Macmillan, New York.

Gulati, A. (2010), 'Accelerating Agriculture Growth', in S. Acharya and R. Mohan (eds.), *India's Economy: Performance and Challenges. Essays in Honour of Montek Singh Ahluwalia*, 213–244, Oxford University Press, New Delhi.

Gulati, A. (2015), 'Drones and Doves', *Indian Express*, 4 July.

Gupta, N. (2013), 'Selling the Family Silver to Pay the Grocer's Bill? The Case of Privatization in India', in J. Bhagwati and A. Panagariya (eds.), *Reforms and Economic Transformation in India*, 141–167, Oxford University Press, New York.

Gupta, P. (2014), 'What Do Voters Reward?', in B. Jalan and P. Balakrishnan (eds.), *Politics Trumps Economics: The Interface of Economics and Politics in Contemporary India*, 43–61, Rupa Publishers, New Delhi.

Gupta, P. (2015), 'Financial Sector Reforms under G20 and the Indian Banks', in P. Shome (ed.), *The G20 Macroeconomic Agenda: India and the Emerging Economies*, 57–92, Cambridge University Press, Cambridge.

Gupta, P., R. Hasan, and U. Kumar (2009), 'Big Reforms but Small Payoffs: Explaining the Weak Record of Growth in Indian Manufacturing', *India Policy Forum 2008/9*, Vol. 5, 59–124.

Gupta, P., and A. Panagariya (2014), 'Growth and Election Outcomes in a Developing Country', *Economics and Politics*, 26(2), 332–354.

Hardin, G. (1968), 'The Tragedy of the Commons', *Science*, Vol. 162(3859), 1243–1248.

Hart, O. (2003), 'Incomplete Contracts and Public Ownership', *Economic Journal*, Vol. 113(486), C69–76.

Hasan R., and K. Jandoc (2013), 'Labour Regulations and Firm Size Distribution in Indian Manufacturing', in J. Bhagwati and A. Panagariya (eds.), *Reforms and Economic Transformation in India*, 15–48. Oxford University Press, New York.

Hasan, R., S. Lamba, and A. Sen Gupta (2013), 'Growth, Structural Change, and Poverty Reduction: Evidence from India', ADB Working Paper Series No. 22.

Hasan, R., D. Mitra, and B. Ural (2007), 'Trade Liberalization, Labour Market Institutions, and Poverty Reduction: Evidence from Indian States', *India Policy Forum 2006/7*, Vol. 3, 71–110.

Hausmann, R., and D. Rodrik (2003), 'Economic Development as Self-Discovery', *Journal of Development Economics*, Vol. 72(2), 603–633.

Hayek, F. (1940), 'Socialist Calculation: The Competitive Solution', *Economica*, Vol. 7(26), 125–149.

Hayek, F. (1945), 'The Use of Knowledge in Society', *American Economic Review*, Vol. 35(4), 519–530.

Himanshu (2015), 'Inequality in India', *Seminar* 672, August.

Hirschman, A. O. (1970), *Exit, Voice and Loyalty*, Harvard University Press, Cambridge, MA.

International Monetary Fund (2014), *World Economic Outlook*, Washington, DC.

International Monetary Fund (various years), *International Financial Statistics*. Washington, DC.

Jha, S., and B. Ramaswami (2012), 'The Percolation of Public Expenditure: Food Subsidies and the Poor in India and the Philippines', *India Policy Forum 2011/12*, Vol. 8, 95–127.

Joshi, V. (2003a), 'India and the Impossible Trinity', *World Economy*, Vol. 26(4), 555–583.

Joshi, V. (2003b), 'Exchange Rate Regimes—Is There a Third Way?', *World Economics*, Vol. 4(4), 15–36.

Joshi, V. (2006), 'Why We Need to Rethink the Exchange Rate System', *Financial Times*, 15 December.

Joshi, V. (2008), 'Convertibility Now? No, Thanks', in R. Kumar and A. Sen Gupta (eds.), *India and the Global Economy*, 285–303, Academic Foundation and ICRIER, New Delhi.

Joshi, V. (2009), 'How to Share the Burden of Combating Climate Change', *Vox*, http://www.voxeu.org/.

Joshi, V. (2014), 'Comment' (on Kapur and Mohan 2014), *India Policy Forum 2013/14*, Vol. 10, 288–292.

Joshi, V., and D. Kapur (2014), 'India and the World Economy', in D. Davin and B. Harriss-White (eds.), *China—India: Pathways of Economic and Social Development*, 77–92, British Academy and Oxford University Press, Oxford.

Joshi, V., and I. Little (1994), *India: Macroeconomics and Political Economy, 1964–1991*, World Bank and Oxford University Press, Washington, DC and Delhi.

Joshi, V., and I. Little (1996), *India's Economic Reforms 1991–2001*, Oxford University Press, Oxford and Delhi.

Joshi, V. and U. Patel (2009a), 'India and Climate Change Mitigation', in D. Helm and C. Hepburn (eds.), *The Economics and Politics of Climate Change*, 167–196, Oxford University Press, New York.

Joshi, V., and U. Patel (2009b), 'India and a Carbon Deal', *Economic and Political Weekly*, Vol. 44(31), 71–77.

Joshi, V., and S. Sanyal (2004), 'Foreign Inflows and Macroeconomic Policy in India', *India Policy Forum 2004*, Vol. 1, 135–187.

Kapur, D. (2010a), *Diaspora, Development, and Democracy: The Domestic Impact of International Migration from India*, Princeton University Press, Princeton, NJ.

Kapur, D. (2010b), 'The Political Economy of the State', in N. Jayal and P. Mehta (eds.), *The Oxford Companion to Politics in India*, 443–458, Oxford University Press, Delhi.

Kapur, D. (2010c), 'Indian Higher Education', in C. Clotfelter (ed.), *American Universities in the Global Market*, 305–334, University of Chicago Press, Chicago.

Kapur, D. (2011), 'Addressing the Trilemma of Indian Higher Education', *Seminar* 617, January.

Kapur, D. (2012), 'Graduation Day at Bretton woods', *Business Standard*, 12 March.

Kapur, D. (2014), 'Can India's Higher Education Be Saved from the Rule of *Babus*?', *Business Standard*, 22 June.

Kapur, D., R. Khosla, and P. Mehta (2009), 'Climate Change: India's Options', *Economic and Political Weekly*, Vol. 44(31), 34–42.

Kapur, D., and P. Mehta (2007), 'Mortgaging the Future? Indian Higher Education', *India Policy Forum 2007/08*, Vol. 4, 101–143.

Kapur, D., and P. Nangia (2015), 'Social Protection in India: A Welfare State sans Public Goods', *India Review*, Vol. 14(1), 73–90.

Kapur, D., N. Sircar, and M. Vaishnav (2014), 'All in a Surname', *Times of India*, 16 March.

Kapur, D., and M. Vaishnav (2011), 'Quid Pro Quo: Builders, Politicians and Election Finance', Working Paper No. 276, Centre for Global Development.

Kapur, D., and M. Vaishnav (2014a), 'Strengthening the Rule of Law', in B. Debroy, A. Tellis, and R. Trevor, *Getting India Back on Track*, 247–263, Carnegie Endowment for International Peace, Washington, DC.

Kapur, D., and M. Vaishnav (2014b), 'Being Middle Class in India', *Hindu*, 9 December.

Kapur, M., and R. Mohan (2014), 'India's Recent Macroeconomic Performance: An Assessment and the Way Forward', *India Policy Forum 2013/14*, Vol. 10, 205–296.

Kavita Rao, R. (2013), 'Revenue Foregone Estimates: Some Analytical Issues', *Economic and Political Weekly*, Vol. 48(13), 21–24.

Kelkar, V. (2010), 'On Strategies for Disinvestment and Privatization', Sir Purushottamdas Thakurdas Memorial Lecture, Press Information Bureau, Government of India, Ministry of Finance, New Delhi. Reprinted in U. Kapila, *Indian Economy since Independence* (21st ed.), 499–511, Academic Foundation, New Delhi.

Kelkar, V., and A. Shah (2011), 'Indian Social Democracy: The Resource Perspective', Working Paper No. 2011-82, National Institute of Public Finance and Policy, New Delhi.

Kelkar, V., and H. Singh (2015), 'India Can Become a Global Trading Power If It Takes Mega-Trade Negotiations Seriously', *Economic Times*, 13 April.

Khera, R. (ed.), (2011), *The Battle for Employment Guarantee*, Oxford University Press, New Delhi.

Kingdon, G. (2010), 'The Implications of the Sixth Pay Commission on Teachers' Salaries in India', RECOUP Working Paper No. 29, Faculty of Cambridge.

Kingdon, G., and M. Muzammil (2010), 'The School Governance Environment in Uttar Pradesh, India', RECOUP Working Paper No. 31, Faculty of Cambridge.

Klein, M., and J. Shambaugh (2013), 'Is There a Dilemma with the Trilemma', *Vox*, http://www.voxeu.org/.

Kohli, R., and J. Bhagwati (2011), 'Organized Retailing in India: Issues and Outlook', Working Paper No. 2011-1, Columbia Program on Indian Economic Policies.

Kumar, U., and A. Subramanian (2011), 'India's Growth in the 2000s: Four Facts', Working Paper No. WP 11-17, Peterson Institute for International Economics.

Lahiri, A., and U. Patel (2016), 'Challenges of Effective Monetary Policy in Emerging Economies', RBI Working Paper No. WPS(DEPR) 01/2016, Reserve Bank of India, Mumbai.

Lall, R., and R. Anand (2014), 'Modernizing Transport Infrastructure', in B. Debroy, A. Tellis, and R. Trevor (eds.), *Getting India Back on Track*, 135–150, Carnegie Endowment for International Peace, Washington, DC.

Lall, S., and T. Vishwanath (2014), 'Managing Urbanization', in B. Debroy, A. Tellis, and R. Trevor (eds.), *Getting India Back on Track*, 151–170, Carnegie Endowment for International Peace, Washington, DC.

Lange, O. (1936), 'On the Economic Theory of Socialism', *Review of Economic Studies*, Vol. 4, 53–71.

Lewis, J. (1962) *Quiet Crisis in India*, Brookings Institution, Washington, DC.

Little, I. (1999), 'Trade and Industrialization Revisited', in I. M. D. Little, *Collection and Recollections: Economic Papers and Their Provenance*, 191–212, Clarendon Press, Oxford.

Mahal, A., and V. Fan (2012), 'Expanding Health Coverage for Indians: An Assessment of the Policy Challenge', *India Policy Forum 2011/12*, Vol. 8, 37–80.

Mani, M. (2014), *Greening India's Growth: Costs, Valuations and Trade-offs*, Routledge, New York.

Manor, J. (1983), 'The Electoral Process amid Awakening and Decay', in P. Lyon and J. Manor (eds.), *Transfer and Transformation: Political Institutions in the New Commonwealth*, 87–116, University of Leicester Press, Leicester.

Manor, J. (2010), 'Local Governance', in N. Jayal and P. Mehta, *The Oxford Companion to Politics in India*, 61–79, Oxford University Press, New York.

Manor, J. (2015), *Politics and State-Society Relations in India*, C. Hurst & Co., London.

Mazumdar, D., and S. Sarkar (2008), *Globalization, Labour Markets and Inequality in India*, Routledge, New York.

McCartney, M. (2009), *India: The Political Economy of Growth, Stagnation and the State*, Routledge, New York.

Mehrotra, S. (ed.) (2014), *India's Skills Challenge*, Oxford University Press, New Delhi.

Mehrotra, S., and D. Ghosh (2014), 'International Experience with National Training Funds for India', *Economic and Political Weekly*, Vol. 44(26–27), 77–85.

Mehta, P. (2016), 'Privacy after Aadhar', *Indian Express*, 26 March.

Ministry of Environment, Forests and Climate Change, Government of India (2014), *Report of the High Level Committee on Forest and Environment Related Laws* (Chairman: T. S. R. Subramanian), New Delhi.

Ministry of Finance (2015a), *Indian Public Finance Statistics 2014/15*, New Delhi.

Ministry of Finance (2015b), *Report of the Committee on Revisiting and Revitalizing Public Private Partnership Model of Infrastructure* (Chair: Vijay Kelkar), New Delhi.

Ministry of Health and Family Welfare (2014), *Draft National Health Policy 2015*, New Delhi.

Mody, A., A. Nath, and M. Walton (2011), 'Sources of Corporate Profits in India: Business Dynamism or Advantages of Entrenchment?', *India Policy Forum 2010/11*, Vol. 7, 43–96.

Mohan, R., and M. Kapur (2015), 'Pressing India's Growth Accelerator: Policy Imperatives', Working Paper WP-15-53, International Monetary Fund, Washington, DC.

Mohanty, D. (2012), 'India's Post-crisis Macroeconomic Challenges', *RBI Monthly Bulletin*, September.

Mookherjee, D. (2014), 'MNREGA: Populist Leaking Bucket or Successful Anti-poverty Programme?', *Ideas for India*, 28 May.

Mukerji, S., and M. Walton (2013), 'Learning the Right Lessons: Measurement, Experimentation and the Need to Turn India's Right to Education Act Upside Down', in *India Infrastructure Report 2012*, 109–126, IDFC Foundation, Routledge, New Delhi.

Mundle, S., and M. Govinda Rao (1991), 'The Volume and Composition of Government Subsidies in India, 1987–88', *Economic and Political Weekly*, Vol. 26(18), 1157–1172.

Muralidharan, K. (2013), 'Priorities for Primary Education Policy in India's 12th Five Year Plan', *India Policy Forum 2012/13*, Vol. 9, 1–46.

Muralidharan, K. (2016), 'A New Approach to Public Sector Hiring in India for Improved Service Delivery', *India Policy Forum 2015/16*, Vol. 12 (forthcoming).

Muralidharan, K., J. Das, A. Holla, and A. Mohpal (2014), 'The Fiscal Cost of Weak Governance: Evidence from Teacher Absence in India'. NBER Working Paper No. 20299, National Bureau of Economic Research, Cambridge, MA.

Muralidharan, K., P. Niehaus, and S. Sukhtankar (2014), 'Payments Infrastructure and the Performance of Public Programs: Evidence from Bio-metric Smartcards in India', NBER Working Paper No. 19999, National Bureau of Economic Research, Cambridge, MA.

Muralidharan, K., and V. Sunderaraman (2013), 'Contract Teachers: Experimental Evidence from India', NBER Working Paper No. 19440, National Bureau of Economic Research, Cambridge, MA.

Muralidharan, K., and V. Sunderaraman (2014), 'The Aggregate Effect of School Choice: Evidence from a Two-Stage Experiment in India', NBER Working Paper No. 19441, National Bureau of Economic Research, Cambridge, MA.

Nagaraj, R. (2013), 'India's Dream Run: Understanding the Boom and Its Aftermath', *Economic and Political Weekly*, Vol. 48(20), 39–51.

Nataraj, S. (2011), 'The Impact of Trade Liberalization on Productivity: Evidence from India's Formal and Informal Sectors', *Journal of International Economics*, Vol. 85(2), 292–301.

National Sample Survey Office (2014), *Key Indicators of Employment and Unemployment in India, NSS 68th Round, July 2011–June 2012*, NSSO, New Delhi.

Nayak, P. (2012), 'Privatization', in K. Basu and A. Maertens (eds.), *The New Oxford Companion to Economics in India*, 564–657, Oxford University Press, New Delhi.

Nayak, P. J. (2015), 'In This Kafkaesque World Where Does Integrity Lie?', *Financial Times*, 12 October.

Nayar, B. (2015), 'The Political Economy of Reform under UPA, 2004–2014: The Tension between Accumulation and Legitimacy', *India Review*, Vol. 14(2), 175–202.

NCEUS (National Commission for Enterprises in the Unorganized Sector) (2009), *The Challenge of Employment in India*, Academic Foundation, New Delhi.

Niehaus P., and S. Sukhtankar (2013a), 'Corruption Dynamics: The Golden Goose Effect', *American Economic Journal: Economic Policy*, 5(1), 206–238.

Niehaus, P., and S. Sukhtankar (2013b), 'The Marginal Rate of Corruption in Public Programs: Evidence from India', *Journal of Public Economics*, 104, 52–64.

Ninan, T. (2015), *The Turn of the Tortoise: The Challenge and Promise of India's Future*, Penguin Random House, New Delhi.

Noland, M., and H. Pack (2003), *Industrial Policy in an Era of Globalization: Lessons from Asia*, Institute for International Economics, Washington, DC.

Nordhaus, W. (2015), *The Climate Casino*, Yale University Press, New Haven.

OECD (2007, 2011), *OECD Economic Surveys: India*, OECD Publishing, Paris.

Ostrom, E. (1990), *Governing the Commons: The Evolution of Institutions for Collective Action*, Cambridge University Press, Cambridge.

Pack, H., and K. Saggi (2006), 'Is There a Case for Industrial Policy?', *World Bank Research Observer*, Vol. 21(2), 267–297.

Panagariya, A. (2004), 'India's Trade Reform', *India Policy Forum 2004*, Vol. 1, 1–57.

Panagariya, A. (2008), *India: The Emerging Giant*, Oxford University Press, New York.

Pew Research Centre (2015), 'A Global Middle Class Is More Promise Than Reality', Washington, DC.

Pigou, A. C. (1920), *Economics of Welfare*, Macmillan, London.

Planning Commission (2005), 'Performance Evaluation of Targeted Public Distribution System', Technical Report of the Programme Evaluation Organization, New Delhi.

Planning Commission, Government of India (2009), *A Hundred Small Steps: Report of the Committee on Financial Sector Reforms* (Chairman: Raghuram Rajan), New Delhi.

Planning Commission, Government of India (2013a), *Twelfth Five Year Plan 2012–2017*, Sage Publications, New Delhi.

Planning Commission, Government of India (2013b), *Press Note on Poverty Estimates, 2011–12*, Government of India, Press Information Bureau.

Planning Commission, Government of India (2014a), *Report of the Expert Group to Review the Methodology for the Measurement of Poverty* (Chairman: C. Rangarajan), New Delhi.

Planning Commission, Government of India (2014b), *The Final Report of the Expert Group on Low-Carbon Strategies for Inclusive Growth* (Chairman: Kirit Parikh), New Delhi.

Planning Commission, Government of India (2014c), Data and Statistics. http://planningcommission.nic.in/data/datatable/index.php?data=datatab.

Pratap, K. (2014), 'Floundering Public-Private Partnerships', *Economic and Political Weekly*, Vol. 49(15), 21–23.

Pratham Educational Foundation (2015), *Annual Status of Education Report (Rural) 2014, Provisional Report*, Mumbai.

Pritchett, L., and A. Beatty (2012), 'The Negative Consequences of Overambitious Curricula in Developing Countries', Harvard Kennedy School Research Working Paper No. RWP 12-035.

Pritchett, L., and R. Murgai (2007), 'Teacher Compensation: Can Decentralization to Local Bodies Take India from Perfect Storm through Troubled Waters to Clear Sailing', *India Policy Forum 2006/07*, Vol. 3, 123–177.

Pritchett, L., and L. Summers (2014), 'Asiaphoria Meets Regression to the Mean', Working Paper No. 20573, National Bureau of Economic Research, Cambridge, MA.

Purfield, C. (2006), 'Mind the Gap: Is Economic Growth in India Leaving Some States Behind?', IMF Working Paper No. WP/06/103, International Monetary Fund, Washington, DC.

Rajan, R. (2014), 'Fighting Inflation', *RBI Monthly Bulletin*, March.

Rajaraman, I. (2006), 'Fiscal Perspective on Irrigation Water Pricing: A Case-Study of Karnataka, India', *Water Policy*, Vol. 8(2), 171–181.

Rajaraman. I. (2012), 'Stallflation', *Business Standard*, 25 December.

Rajaraman, I. (2014), 'Spatial Distribution of Public Services within States in India', *Economic and Political Weekly*, Vol. 49(12), 47–51.

Ram Mohan, T. (2014), 'Corporate Governance: Issues and Challenges', in B. Jalan and P. Balakrishnan (eds.), *Politics Trumps Economics: The Interface of Economics and Politics in Contemporary India*, 111–119. Rupa Publications, New Delhi.

Rangarajan, C., and P. Mishra (2013), 'India's External Sector: Do we Need to Worry?', *Economic and Political Weekly*, 48(7), 52–59.

Rangarajan, C., Seema, and E. Vibesh (2014), 'Developments in the Workforce between 2009–10 and 2011–12', *Economic and Political Weekly*, Vol. 49(23), 117–121.

Reserve Bank of India (2009), *Annual Report*, Mumbai.

Reserve Bank of India (2014a), *Report of the Expert Committee to Revise and Strengthen the Monetary Policy Framework* (Chairman: Urjit Patel), Mumbai.

Reserve Bank of India (2014b), *Report of the Committee to Review Governance of Boards of Banks in India* (Chairman: P. J. Nayak), Mumbai.

Reserve Bank of India (2015), *Handbook of Statistics on the Indian Economy 2014/15*, Mumbai.

Rey, H. (2015), 'Dilemma Not Trilemma: The Global Financial Cycle and Monetary Policy Independence', NBER Working Paper No. 21162, National Bureau of Economic Research, Cambridge, MA.

Rodrik, D. (2013), 'Unconditional Convergence in Manufacturing', *Quarterly Journal of Economics*, Vol. 128(1), 165–204.

Roy, R. (2015), 'Put India First, Not Air India', *Business Standard*, 2 April.

Runciman, D. (2013), *The Confidence Trap*, Princeton University Press, Princeton, NJ.

Sen, A. (1999), *Development as Freedom*, Oxford University Press, New York.

Sen, A., and T. Jamasb (2012), 'Diversity in Unity: An Empirical Analysis of Electricity Deregulation in Indian States', *Energy Journal*, Vol. 33(1), 83–130.

Sen, K., and S. Kar (2014), 'Boom and Bust? A Political Economy Reading of India's Growth Experience, 1993–2013', *Economic and Political Weekly*, Vol. 29(50), 40–51.

Shah, A. (2015), 'Has the Recession Which Began in 2012 Ended?', *Ideas for India*, 4 September.

Shah, A. (2016), 'A Call to Arms for Reforms', *Business Standard*, 26 February.

Sharma, M. (2015), 'Make in India, as yet Unmade', *Seminar* 675, November.

Shankar, S., and R. Gaiha (2013), *Battling Corruption: Has NREGA Reached India's Poor?*, Oxford University Press, New Delhi.

Singh, A. (2015), 'Private School Effects in Urban and Rural India', *Journal of Development Economics*, Vol. 113, 16–32.

Singh, N. (2010), 'The Dynamics and Status of India's Reforms', MPRA Paper No. 24479, Munich.

Singh, P. (2012), 'CBI Needs Real Autonomy', *Indian Express*, 22 December.

Sivasubramonian, S. (2000), *The National Income of India in the Twentieth Century*, Oxford University Press, New York.

Spears, D. (2013), 'Policy Lessons from the Implementation of India's Total Sanitation Campaign', *India Policy Forum 2012/13*, Vol. 9, 63–105.

Sridharan, E., and M. Vaishnav (2015), 'The Resilience of Briefcase Politics', *Indian Express*, 4 February.

Srinivasan, T. N. (2010), 'Employment and India's Development and Reforms', *Journal of Comparative Economics*, Vol. 38(1), 82–106.

Srinivasan, T. N. (2011), *Growth, Sustainability and India's Economic Reforms*, Oxford University Press, New York.

Srivastava, D., C. Bhujanga Rao, P. Chakraborty, and T. Rangamannar (2003), *Budgetary Subsidies in India*, National Institute of Public Finance and Policy, New Delhi.

Srivastava, S. (2013), 'Congress Bureau of Investigation', *Open Magazine*, 6 April.

Steil, B. 'Brics Bank Is a Feeble Strike against the Dollar', *Financial Times*, 2 October.

Stern, N. (2015), *Why Are We Waiting?*, MIT Press, Cambridge, MA

Subramanian, A. (2009), 'Preventing and Responding to the Crisis of 2018', *Economic and Political Weekly*, Vol. 44(2), 32–36.

Subramanian, A. (2012a) 'Not All Capital Flows Are Alike', *Business Standard*, 27 June.

Subramanian, A. (2012b), 'Growth and Social Outcomes, I and II', *Business Standard*, 25 and 26 July.

Sukhtankar, S. (2012), 'Sweetening the Deal? Political Connections and Sugar Mills in India', *American Economic Journal: Applied Economics*, 4(3), 43–63.

Sukhtankar, S. (2015), 'The Impact of Corruption on Consumer Markets: Evidence from the Allocation of 2G Wireless Spectrum in India', *Journal of Law and Economics*, Vol. 58(1), 75–108.

Sukhtankar, S., and M. Vaishnav (2015), 'Corruption in India: Bridging Research Evidence and Policy Options', *India Policy Forum 2014/15*, Vol. 10, 193–276.

Topalova, P. (2007), 'Trade Liberalization, Poverty and Inequality: Evidence from Indian Districts', in A. Harrison (ed.), 291–336, *Globalization and Poverty*, University of Chicago Press, Chicago.

Topalova, P., and A. Khandelwal (2011), 'Trade Liberalization and Firm Productivity: The Case of India', *Review of Economics and Statistics*, Vol. 93(3), 995–1009.

Triffin, R. (1960), *Gold and Dollar Crisis: The Future of Convertibility*, Yale University Press, New Haven.

UNCTAD (2015), *World Investment Report*.

UNDP (United Nations Development Programme) (2015), *Human Development Report 2015*.

Vaishnav, M. (2014), 'Crime but No Punishment in Indian Elections', Carnegie Endowment for International Peace, 24 January, Washington, DC.

Vaishnav, M., and R. Swanson (2013), 'Does Good Economics Mean Good Politics in India?', Carnegie Endowment for International Peace, 19 December, Washington, DC.

Van Zwieten, K. (2015), 'Corporate Recue in India: The Influence of the Courts', *Journal of Corporate Law Studies*, Vol. 15(1), 1–31.

Walker, M. (2011), *PISA 2009 Plus Results*, Australian Council for Educational Research.

Weisskopf, T. (2011), 'Why Worry about Inequality in India's Booming Economy?', *Economic and Political Weekly*, Vol. 46(47), 41–51.

Woods, N. (2014), 'Global Economic Governance after the 2008 Crisis', GEG Working Paper No. 2014/89, Global Economic Governance Programme, University of Oxford.

World Bank (1982, 1983, 2003), *World Development Review*, Washington, DC.

World Bank (2008), 'Skill Development in India: The Vocational Education and Training System', Discussion Paper Series Report No. 22.

World Bank (2010), *India's Employment Challenge: Creating Jobs, Helping Workers*. Oxford University Press, New Delhi.

World Bank (2011), *More and Better Jobs in South Asia*, World Bank Publications, Washington, DC.

World Bank (2014), *Doing Business 2014: Understanding Regulations for Small and Medium Enterprises*.

World Bank (2015), *World Development Indicators Online*, Washington, DC.

World Health Organization (2014), *Ambient Air Pollution Database*.

World Trade Organization (2014), *Tariff Profiles*.

Yale Centre for Environmental Law and Policy (2014), *2014 Environmental Protection Index: Full Report and Analysis*, Yale University.

INDEX

land market 94
  price-discovery in, 96, 291
land law:
  reform, 95–7, 294
liberal democracy, 35–6, 279,
  311–12, 315–16
liberalization, 7, 18, 22–4, 26, 54, 61–2,
  104, 159, 215, 252–5, 262
  of foreign direct investment
  (FDI), 299
license raj, 27, 184, 307
licenses, 19, 40, 100, 122, 230, 235,
  237–9, 283
life expectancy, 20, 186
literacy, 28
  adult, 20
  female, 29
local government, 314–15
low-income countries, 28, 186, 256,
  300, 302

macroeconomic stability, 7, 35, 37, 43,
  53, 59, 139–65, 279–82
  and external balance, 155–9
  and fiscal balance, 159–65
  and internal balance, 141–55, 281–2
  Modi Government and, 280–2
Mahatma Gandhi National Rural
  Employment Guarantee Scheme
  (NREGS) 203–5, 210, 213,
  215, 239
  arguments for and against, 204–5
  description of, 203–4
'Make in India', 105, 310
managed floating, 155–6, 280–1; see also
  exchange rate policy
Mandal commission, 22, 226–7; see also
  reservations
manufacturing, 68, 71–2, 250, 310
  share of employment in, 68
market/markets, 7, 19–20, 35–41,
  43–4, 102–4, 123–4, 154, 187–8,
  276–7, 288–93
  failures of, 37–9, 40–1, 44, 75, 94,
  187–8, 190, 191–2, 276, 303–4
  for factors of production, 65–72,
  77–82, 94–102, 289, 291, 294
  for goods and services, 87–94,
  290–1, 293–4
  liberalization of, 36, 229

prices, 37, 41, 90–1, 95, 143, 164,
  202, 288
  reform of, 77–82, 87–105, 290–6
  virtues of, 37
  see also competition; natural
    monopoly
Mayawati, 227
mega-regional agreements, 297, 309
merit goods, 38, 213
Mid-Day Meals scheme, 177, 206
middle class, 313
mobile banking, 207
Modi, Narendra, 25
  foreign tours, 299
  pan-Indian electoral support
    for, 312
  as RSS pracharak, 312
Modi government, 82, 96, 100, 105,
  278, 280–1, 299–300, 304–6,
  307–8, 310–12
Monetary Framework Committee,
  151, 281
monetary policy, 142, 144–5, 151–2,
  166–8, 281–2
  transmission of, 152, 281–2
  reform of policy framework, 151–2,
  166–8, 281–2
monopolistic exploitation, 39, 117
multi-currency system, 261–2
multilateral negotiations, 264

Narasimha Rao, P.V., 23, 26
National Rural Employment Guarantee,
  Act, 232; see also Mahatma Gandhi
  National Rural Employment
  Guarantee Scheme
nationalization, 40, 41
natural capital, 123–8
natural monopoly, 38–9, 117
Nayak, P.J., 118, 285, 295
Nehru, Jawaharlal, 4, 17–18
non-tradable goods, 117
nuclear agreement with US, 24
nutrition, 186, 189

oil prices, 18, 22, 89, 144, 152,
  159, 288
oil-related products, 88, 285
'Old India Model', 275–5
organized industry, 69–70

public sector, 7, 19–20, 42–3, 58, 66, 115, 119–21, 180, 193, 196
public sector banks (PSBs), 118, 154–5, 284, 295, 309
   reform of, 118, 154, 295
public sector enterprises (PSEs), 19–20, 24, 41, 93, 113–18, 164–5, 180, 213, 287, 291, 295, 309
   and the Modi government, 294
   reform of, 115–18, 291, 295
public telecom companies, 114
Punjab, 30, 102, 127, 226, 227
   separatist movement in, 22
purchasing power parity (PPP), 5, 276
pure public goods, 37–8, 43, 102, 140, 164, 188, 191, 210, 212, 277, 285–6

quantitative easing, 158, 262

Radical Reform Model, 276 - 308
Ram, K., 227
rail services, 90, 285
Rajan, R., 99, 152, 159
Rangarajan, C., 28, 210
Rashtriya Swasthya Bima Yojana (RSBY), 191, 195–6, 205, 303, 305
Rashtriya Swayamsevak Sangh (RSS), 311–12
real effective exchange rate (RER), 158, 281
recapitalization, 118, 154, 162, 285
recession, 18, 23, 36, 160; *see also* slowdown
Reddy, Y.V., 157
reform/reforms, *see* economic reform/ reforms
Regional Comprehensive Economic Partnership (RCEP), 265, 266, 297
regulation, 7, 43–4, 77–8, 117–18, 125, 240–2, 258–9, 276–7, 288–93, 303–4, 307
remittances, 249, 254
reservations, 22, 72, 234, 276
Reserve Bank of India (RBI), 100, 145, 151–2, 154, 156–9, 162, 258, 279, 281–2, 284, 295
resource/resources
   allocation, 7, 36, 44, 87, 91–3
   degradation of, 124, 127
   scarcity of, 38, 40, 236–7, 260

Right to Education Act (RTEA), 181–3, 231, 301; *see also* education
Right to Information Act (RTIA), 240
rights, 18, 36, 38, 40, 43, 76, 95, 96, 98, 123–4, 231–2, 236–7, 268, 293, 307, 311, 313, 315

sanitation, 28, 76, 126, 188–9, 196, 201, 203, 302, 312
Sarva Shiksha Abhiyan, 177
savings, 19, 26–7, 52–3, 58–9, 70, 73, 92, 152, 213, 282, 286–7
   domestic, 56, 156
   household, 27, 58–9
   public, 58–9, 148
scandals and scams, 25, 27, 62, 151, 191, 203, 237
security, 9–10
services, 41–3, 55, 67–8, 70, 71, 72, 93–4, 100, 104–5, 247–50, 266–8, 290–2, 298
shadow banks, 258
Shanta Kumar committee, 203
Shastri, Lal Bahadur, 17
Sick Industrial companies Act (SICA), 97–8
Singh, Manmohan, 23–5, 206
Singh, V.P. 22–3; *see also* Mandal Commission; reservations
skill/skills, 77, 252, 310; *see also* human capital; vocational and technical education and training
skill-intensive sectors, 69–70, 104–5
small firms, 71, 72, 73–7, 283, 295
small-scale industry reservations, 72
social:
   awakening, 226, 306
   democracy, 36, 201–2, 300
   security benefits, 66–7
social enablement 163, 165, 201, 202, 300-6
   Modi government and, 304–6
social protection, 163, 201–22, 279, 300, 304
   framework for, 202, 203, 210, 300–4
   Modi government and, 304
   reform, 208-15
   schemes, 202, 206, 210, 300
social safety net, 201–22, 239, 277

South Korea, 5, 6, 20, 68, 70, 157, 262, 265, 316
Special Drawing Rights (SDRs), 261–2
state:
    accountability, 230–5
    capacity, 231–5, 254
    intervention, 7, 19, 36, 37–44, 142, 187–90, 192, 226, 228, 300, 302
    and market relationship, 8, 36–44
    ownership, 18, 36, 40, 41, 113-18, 163
    political economy of, 225–30
    reform of, 233–5, 241–3, 247
state electricity boards (SEBs), 89–90, 122, 309; *see also* UDAY
state public sector enterprises (SPSEs), 114, 115, 116
states:
    deprivation in, 28
    growth in, 27
    inequality between, 29–30
    poverty in, 28
    see also Centre and States
sterilized intervention, 156
stressed assets, 122, 154, 284
subsidies, 30, 38, 43–4, 87–92, 101–4, 163–4, 205–8, 212–13, 230, 285–8, 293–4
    elimination of, 214–15, 230
    explicit, 163–4
    hidden, 87, 92, 123, 164, 212, 285
    problems in unwinding, 214
Subbarao, D., 158–9
Subramanian, T.S.R., 127
Swachh Bharat, 306, 310

Targeted Public Distribution System (TPDS), *see* Public Distribution System
tax/taxes/tax system, 35, 38, 40, 44, 89, 92–3, 124–5, 128, 131, 163, 286–7, 290–1
    exemptions, 93, 163, 213, 284
    indirect tax, 92–3, 163, 290–1
    on international trade, 93, 247; *see also* trade liberalization
    minimum alternate tax, 299
    reform, 92-3, 162–3, 291, 293
    retrospective, 151, 299
    and revenue, 35, 37, 51, 163

see also government expenditure; subsidies
teachers, 179–83
telecom spectrum, 38, 236
Tendulkar, S., 28, 210–11, 216
total factor productivity (TFP), 52, 53–7, 72, 80, 87, 104; *see also* productivity
tradable goods, 88, 117, 291
trade, *see* international trade
Trade Facilitation Agreement (TFA), 264–5
Trade in Services Agreement (TISA), 269, 298
trade unions, 66, 79, 82
    and political parties, 82
    teachers' unions, 179, 183, 229
'traditional public health' (TPH), 188–9, 196, 303
tragedy of the commons, 38
Transatlantic Trade and Investment Partnership (TTIP), 265
Trans-Pacific Partnership (TPP), 265–6, 298
transparency, 44, 240

UDAY, 296
unemployment, 65
United Progressive Alliance (UPA), 24–5, 95, 97, 117, 143, 164, 202, 283, 307–8
United States, 8, 252, 255
    and China rivalry, 10
    gilded age, 240, 243
    as 'hyper-power', 9
    and India, civil nuclear agreement, 9
University Grants Commission (UGC), 184–5
unorganized sector, 66–7, 69–70, 76–7, 78, 99, 288–9
    definition of, 66
    low-labour-productivity in, 66
    low-quality jobs in, 73
    output of, 67, 69
    as 'own account enterprises', 76
    workers in, 65
urban:
    infrastructure, 97, 120, 123, 292
    land, 96, 131
urbanization, 96

Vajpayee, Atal Behari, 24
value-added tax (VAT), 92–3
vocational and technical education and
    training (VTET), 185

water, 75, 90–1, 101–3, 125–7,
    206, 212, 285, 290, 293,
    309
  over-extraction of, 126
  pricing, 126–7
women, 29, 72, 73, 204, 205, 210,
    233, 304, 311; *see also* female
    labour force participation rate;
    literacy, female
workforce, 66–7, 77, 80, 94, 292
  income of organized, 145
  informal, 67, 69

mal-distributed, 66
non-farm, 67
poor, 100
in unorganized sector, 66–7
  see also labour/labour force
World Bank, 28, 186
  'Ease of Doing Business' reports of,
    74, 283
  and foreign aid, 18
  survey of Indian firms, 74
World Trade Organization (WTO),
    263–4, 267–8

Yadav, Lalu Prasad, 227
Yadav, Mulayam Singh, 227

zamindari, abolition of, 226